Technology & Design

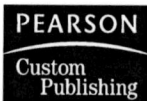

A Pearson Custom Publication

Technology & Design

Compiled from:

Structural Mechanics
Seventh Edition
by H Al Nageim, F Durka, W Morgan and D T Williams

Construction Technology
Fourth Edition
by Roy Chudley and Roger Greeno

PEARSON
Custom
Publishing

Pearson Education Limited
Edinburgh Gate
Harlow
Essex CM20 2JE

And associated companies throughout the world

Visit us on the World Wide Web at:
www.pearsoned.co.uk

First published 2011

This Custom Book Edition © 2011 Published by Pearson Education Limited

Compiled from:

Structural Mechanics
Seventh Edition
by H Al Nageim, F Durka, W Morgan and D T Williams
ISBN 978 0 132 23964 6
Copyright © H Al Nageim, F Durka, W Morgan and D T Williams 1980, 2010

Construction Technology
Fourth Edition
by Roy Chudley and Roger Greeno
ISBN 978 0 131 28642 9
Copyright © Pearson Education Limited 1973, 2005

ISBN 978 1 84959 934 4

Printed and bound in Great Britain by Henry Ling Limited at the Dorset Press,
Dorchester, DT1 1HD

Contents

2.2

FOUNDATIONS

A foundation is the base on which a building rests, and its purpose is to safely transfer the load of a building to a suitable subsoil.

The Building Regulations require all foundations of buildings to:

- safely sustain and transmit to the ground the combined dead and imposed loads so as not to cause any settlement or other movement in any part of the building or of any adjoining building or works;
- be of such a depth, or be so constructed, as to avoid damage by swelling, shrinkage or freezing of the subsoil;
- be capable of resisting attack by deleterious material, such as sulphates, in the subsoil.

Subsoils are the soils below the topsoil, the topsoil being about 300 mm deep. Typical bearing capacities of subsoils are given in Table 2.2.1.

Table 2.2.1 Typical subsoil bearing capacities

Type	Bearing capacity (kN/m^2)
Rocks, granites and chalks	600–10 000
Non-cohesive soils; compact sands; loose uniform sands	100–600
Cohesive soils; hard clays; soft clays and silts	< 600
Peats and made ground	To be determined by investigation

Terminology
- **Backfill**   Materials excavated from site and if suitable used to fill in around the walls and foundations.
- **Bearing capacity**   Safe load per unit area that the ground can carry.

- **Bearing pressure**   The pressure produced on the ground by the loads.
- **Made ground**   Refuse, excavated rock or soil deposited for the purpose of filling in a depression or for raising the site above its natural level.
- **Settlement**   Ground movement, which may be caused by:
  - deformation of the soil due to imposed loads;
  - volume changes of the soil as a result of seasonal conditions;
  - mass movement of the ground in unstable areas.

▢ ◼ ◼ CHOICE OF FOUNDATION TYPE

The choice and design of foundations for domestic and small types of buildings depends mainly on two factors:

- the total loads of the building;
- the nature and bearing capacity of the subsoil.

The total loads of a building are taken per metre run and calculated for the worst case. The data required is:

1. Roof material dead load on the wall plus imposed load from snow, i.e. 1.5 kN/m^2 < 30° pitch or 0.75 kN/m^2 > 30° pitch (1 m wide strip from ridge to eaves).
2. Floor material dead load on the wall, plus an imposed loading allowance of < 1.5 kN/m^2 for people and furniture (1 m wide strip from centre of the floor to the wall).
3. Wall load on the foundations (1 m wide strip of wall from top to foundation).
4. Total load on the foundations (summation of 1, 2 and 3, plus any additional allowances for wind loading that may be necessary in exposed situations).

[*Note*: Material loading due to the materials can be found in BS 648: *Schedule of weights of building materials*.]

The average total loading for a two-storey domestic dwelling of traditional construction is 30–50 kN/m.

The nature and bearing capacity of the subsoil can be determined by:

- trial holes and subsequent investigation;
- boreholes and core analysis;
- local knowledge.

Clay is the most difficult of all subsoils with which to deal. Down to a depth of about 1 m clays are subject to seasonal movement, which occurs when the clay dries and shrinks in the summer and conversely swells in the winter with heavier rainfall. This movement occurs whenever a clay soil is exposed to the atmosphere, and special foundations may be necessary.

Subsoils that readily absorb and hold water are subject, in cold weather, to **frost heave**. This is a swelling of the subsoil due to the expansion of freezing water held in the soil; like the movement of clay soils, it is unlikely to be even, and special foundations may be needed to overcome the problem.

▨▩■ TYPES OF FOUNDATION

Having ascertained the nature and bearing capacity of the subsoil, the width of the foundation can be determined by one of the following methods:

1. Calculating the total (dead + imposed) load per metre run of foundation and relating this to the analysed safe bearing capacity of the subsoil, i.e.

$$\frac{\text{total load of building per metre}}{\text{safe bearing capacity of subsoil}} = \text{minimum foundation width}$$

For example, if the total load is 40 kN/m and the subsoil safe bearing capacity is 80 kN/m^2, then the foundation width is:

$$\frac{40}{80} = 0.5 \text{ m} \quad \text{or} \quad 500 \text{ mm}$$

[*Note*: Safe bearing capacity is determined by obtaining the actual bearing capacity by laboratory analysis and applying a factor of safety.]

2. The minimum guidance as given in design tables, such as Table 2.2.2, where size of foundations are related to subsoil type, wall loading and field tests on the soil.

Foundations are usually made of either mass or reinforced concrete and can be considered under two headings:

- **Shallow foundations**   Those that transfer the loads to subsoil at a point near to the ground floor of the building such as strips and rafts.
- **Deep foundations**   Those that transfer the loads to a subsoil some distance below the ground floor of the building such as a pile.

Raft foundations are often used on poor soils for lightly loaded buildings, and are considered capable of accommodating small settlements of the soil. In poor soils the upper crust of soil (450–600 mm) is often stiffer than the lower subsoil, and to build a light raft on this crust is usually better than penetrating it with a strip foundation.

Typical details of the types of foundation suitable for domestic and similar buildings are shown in Figs 2.2.1–2.2.3.

Table 2.2.2   Guide to strip foundation width relative to subsoil type

Subsoil type	Subsoil condition	Field test	Bearing capacity (kN/m^2)	Minimum width of strip (mm) for a total load (kN/m) of:					
				20	30	40	50	60	70
Rock	Stronger than sandstone limestone or chalk	Requires mechanical device to break up	> 600	Wall thickness at least					
Chalk	Solid	Requires a pick to remove	600	Wall thickness at least					
Gravel	Medium density	Requires a pick to excavate	> 600	250	300	400	500	600	650
Sand	Compact	Breaks down when dry	> 300	250	300	400	500	600	650
Clay Sandy clay	Stiff	Pick or mechanical device required to remove	150 to 300	250	300	400	500	600	650
Clay Sandy clay	Firm	Manually excavated and can be moulded by hand	75 to 150	300	350	450	600	750	850
Sand or Gravel Silty sand Clayey Sand	Loose	Manually excavated with a spade, 50 mm square peg easily driven in	> 200 Lab. test needed	400	600	Traditional strip foundation not suitable for loading > 30 kN/m, consider reinforced strip, deep strip or short bored piling			
Silt Clay Sandy or silty clay	Soft	Easily excavated manually, can be moulded by hand	Lab. test needed	450	650	As above			
Silt, clay, sandy or silty clay	Very soft	Samples exude water when squeezed	Lab. test needed	Subsoil of this condition is not suitable to receive unreinforced strip foundations. Consider reinforced strip, deep strip and end bearing piled foundations to solid strata					

Ground level

Solid or
cavity wall

Depth below ground
level generally 750 to
overcome seasonal
movement and
frost heave in clay
a minimum of
1.000 will comply

P

P

P

Not less than
P and in no
case less
than 150

Width determined
by total building
load and bearing
capacity of subsoil

Mass concrete foundation
not less than 1:3:6/40 mm agg.
(15–20 N/mm²)

Strip foundations

Solid or cavity wall

D

Mass concrete
foundation of
monolithic construction

Minimum of *D*,
twice the step
height or 300 mm,
take the greater
value

Change in level

Solid or
cavity wall

P

P

P

P

P

P

**Projections
and Piers**

Mass concrete
foundation

Figure 2.2.1   Strip foundations and building regulations.

Insulation

External cavity wall

50 thick floor screed

DPC

50 insulation

DPM

150 thick concrete ground floor slab

Ground level

150 thick compacted hardcore

Not less than 1.000

Mass concrete 1:3:6 mix (15–20 N/mm²)

$$\text{Width} = \frac{\text{load per m run}}{\text{bearing capacity}}$$

(min. width = 380)

Deep strip foundation

Insulated external cavity wall

50 thick floor screed

DPC

50 insulation

DPM

150 thick concrete floor slab

Ground level

150 thick compacted hardcore

Mass concrete short bored piles

300 × 200 RC ground beam – reinforcement to design

40 thick sand or lean concrete blinding

Per pile
Diameter 250–300
Length 2.000–3.500
Spacing 1.800–2.500
Loading 40–125 kN

Short bored pile foundation

Figure 2.2.2   Alternative foundations for clay soils.

Insulation

External cavity wall

DPC

50 thick floor screed and insulation

DPM

75 min. permanent concrete perimeter paving to protect edges of raft from frost and weathering

150 RC raft forming ground floor slab

225

75 mm gravel or coarse sand

Ground level

450

Steel fabric reinforcement to BS 4483

1.000 min.

Edge thickening

Building paper or similar joint

Insulated external cavity wall

50 thick floor screed and insulation

DPC

DPM

150 thick RC raft forming ground floor slab

Ground level

Compacted hardcore

50 sand or lean concrete blinding

Steel fabric reinforcement to BS 4483

750 min.

300 min.

Mass concrete edge beam

Figure 2.2.3   Typical raft foundations.

REINFORCED CONCRETE FOUNDATIONS

The function of any foundation is to transmit to the subsoil the loads of the structure. Where a structure has only light loadings, such as a domestic dwelling house, it is sufficient to use a mass concrete strip foundation or a simple raft. Where buildings are either heavy, or transmit the loadings at a series of points, such as in a framed building, it is uneconomic to use mass concrete. The plan size of a foundation is a constant feature, being derived from:

$$\frac{\text{point or column load}}{\text{safe bearing capacity of subsoil}}$$

For example, if the column shown in Fig. 2.3.1 transmits a 50 kN load to subsoil of safe bearing capacity 80 kN/m^2, then the square column foundation dimensions are:

$$\sqrt{\frac{50}{80}} = 0.79 \text{ m} \quad \text{or} \quad 790 \text{ mm (800 mm square)}$$

The thickness of a mass concrete foundation for a heavy point load would result in a foundation that is costly and adds unnecessary load to the subsoil. Reinforced concrete foundations are generally cheaper and easier to construct than equivalent mass concrete foundations but will generally require the services of a structural engineer to formulate an economic design. The engineer must define the areas in which tension occurs and specify the reinforcement required, as concrete is a material which is weak in tension. Further studies of reinforced concrete principles can be found in Chapter 10.2.

▪▪▪ TYPES OF FOUNDATION

The principal types of reinforced concrete foundation for buildings are:

1. strip foundations;
2. isolated or pad foundations;

Heavy wall

Reinforced concrete
(1:2:4/20 mm agg.
– 25 N/mm^2)
strip foundation

Weak
concrete
blinding

Distribution bars

Main bars

RC strip foundation

75 mm kicker

Starter bars
for column

Ground floor
position

Reinforced concrete
(1:2:4/20 mm agg.
– 25 N/mm^2)
column foundation

Reinforced
concrete column

Weak concrete
blinding

Main bars in
both directions

RC isolated or pad foundation

Figure 2.3.1   Reinforced concrete strip and pad foundations.

3. raft foundations;
4. combinations of 1, 2 and 3;
5. piled foundations.

The foundations listed in 4 and 5 above are included in *Advanced Construction Technology* and are therefore not considered in this volume.

STRIP FOUNDATIONS

Reinforced concrete strip foundations are used to support and transmit the loads from heavy walls. The effect of the wall on the relatively thin foundation is to act as a point load, and the resultant ground pressure will induce tension on the underside across the width of the strip. Tensile reinforcement is therefore required in the lower face of the strip, with distribution bars in the second layer running longitudinally (see Fig. 2.3.1). The reinforcement will also assist the strip in spanning any weak pockets of soil encountered in the excavations.

ISOLATED OR PAD FOUNDATIONS

This type of foundation is used to support and transmit the loads from piers and columns. The most economic plan shape is a square, but if the columns are close to the site boundary it may be necessary to use a rectangular plan shape of equivalent area. The reaction of the foundation to the load and ground pressures is to cup, similar to a saucer, and therefore main steel is required in both directions. The depth of the base will be governed by the anticipated moments and shear forces, the calculations involved being beyond the scope of this volume. Incorporated in the base will also be the starter bars for a reinforced concrete column or the holding-down bolts for a structural steel column (see Fig. 2.3.1).

RAFT FOUNDATIONS

The principle of any raft foundation is to spread the load over the entire area of the site. This method is particularly useful where the column loads are heavy and thus require large bases, or where the bearing capacity is low, again resulting in the need for large bases. Raft foundations can be considered under three headings:

- solid slab rafts;
- beam and slab rafts;
- cellular rafts.

Solid slab rafts are constructed of uniform thickness over the whole raft area, which can be wasteful because the design must be based on the situation existing where the heaviest load occurs. The effect of the load from columns and the ground pressure is to create areas of tension under the columns and areas of tension in the upper part of the raft between the columns. Very often a nominal mesh of reinforcement is provided in the faces where tension does not occur to control shrinkage cracking of the concrete (see Fig. 2.3.2).

Column starter bars

Reinforced concrete (1:2:4/20 mm agg. – 25 N/mm²) solid slab raft

75 mm high kicker

Weak concrete blinding

RC solid slab raft foundation

Column starter bars

RC suspended slab of *in-situ* or precast concrete

Columns positioned on beam intersection

RC upstand beams in 2 directions

75 mm high kicker

Weak concrete blinding

Reinforced concrete raft (1:2:4/20 mm agg. – 25 N/mm²)

RC beam and slab raft foundation

Figure 2.3.2   Reinforced concrete raft foundations.

Figure 2.3.3 Typical cellular raft details.

Beam and slab rafts are an alternative to the solid slab raft and are used where poor soils are encountered. The beams are used to distribute the column loads over the area of the raft, which usually results in a reduction of the slab thickness. The beams can be upstand or downstand depending upon the bearing capacity of the soil near the surface. Downstand beams will give a saving on excavation costs, whereas upstand beams create a usable void below the ground floor if a suspended slab is used (see Fig. 2.3.2).

CELLULAR RAFTS

This form of foundation can be used where a reasonable bearing capacity subsoil can be found only at depths where beam and slab techniques become uneconomic. The construction is similar to reinforced concrete basements except that internal walls are used to spread the load over the raft and divide the void into cells. Openings can be formed in the cell walls, allowing the voids to be utilised for the housing of services, store rooms or general accommodation (see Fig. 2.3.3).

▨▥■ BLINDING

A blinding layer 50 to 75 mm thick of weak concrete or coarse sand should be placed under all reinforced concrete foundations. The functions of the blinding are to fill in any weak pockets encountered during excavations and to provide a true level surface from which the reinforcement can be positioned. If formwork is required for the foundation some contractors prefer to lay the blinding before assembling the formwork; the alternative is to place the blinding within the formwork and allow this to set before positioning the reinforcement and placing the concrete.

TREES: EFFECT ON FOUNDATIONS

Close proximity of trees to buildings can result in direct physical damage to foundations, drains, paths, drives, etc., by growth and expansion of root systems. With conventional strip foundations and those provided for pre-1950s dwellings, where the concrete was rarely placed deeper than 0.5 m, it is advisable to maintain a distance at least equal to the mature tree's height between building and tree. Some relaxation may be applied where tree species can be identified as having less water demand. Guidance is given in Table 2.7.1 with approximate heights of mature trees.

In the UK, shrinkable clays occur in specific areas found roughly below an imaginary line linking the Humber estuary with a point intersecting the mouth of the River Severn, as shown in Fig. 2.7.1.

Clay subsoils are particularly prone to changes in moisture content, with a high degree of shrinkage apparent during periods of drought. When added to the effect of moisture abstraction by vegetation (trees), voids and swallow holes are to be expected. Clay heave is the opposite phenomenon, attributed partly to saturation from inclement weather. It is more likely to be caused by removal of trees within the immediate 'footprint' of new buildings or the immediate surrounds. Figure 2.7.2 shows cracking patterns in buildings due to these indirect sources of damage.

The accepted depth for foundations in clay subsoils is at least 900 mm in the absence of trees. However, where trees are apparent or have been within the preceding three years, the minimum depth of foundation must be calculated. Where insurers issue structural guarantees, this depth can be determined from tables provided in procedure manuals issued by the National House Building Council or Zurich Municipal. Figure 2.7.3 provides some guidance, as an indication only, of the likely depths of foundation excavation necessary where tree distance (d) to height (h) ratios are less than unity. Beyond 1.5 m depth, conventional strip foundations will not be economical or practically viable, but trench-filled concrete will be appropriate. For foundations over 2 m, short-bored piles with ground beams are preferred.

Species	Approximate mature height (m)	Water demand: H = high, M = medium, L = low
Elm	30	H
Oak	30	H
Poplar	30	H
Ash	30	M
Cedar	30	M
Chestnut	30	M
Hemlock	30	M
Lime	30	M
Larch	30	L
Scots pine	30	L
Cypress	25	H
Willow	25	H
Maple	25	M
Sycamore	25	M
Walnut	25	M
Beech	25	L
Birch	25	L
Holly	20	L
Cherry	15	M
Hawthorn	15	M
Rowan	15	M

Note: Where groups of trees occur and the subsoil is known to be moisture responsive (i.e. shrinkable clay), the suggested building distance is 1.5 × mature height.

Figure 2.7.1   Area of UK with zones of shrinkable clay subsoils.

Subsoil dehydration and shrinkage

Ground heave

Figure 2.7.2 Indirect damage to buildings.

Figure 2.7.3   Tree proximity and foundation depth.

Species of tree	Depth of foundation trench (m)						
	d/h = 0.1	0.25	0.33	0.5	0.66	0.75	1.0
Poplar, elm willow and oak	Not acceptable	2.8	2.6	2.3	2.1	1.9	1.5
Others	Not acceptable	2.4	2.1	1.8	1.5	1.2	1.0

▨ ■ ■ HEAVE PRECAUTIONS

In addition to foundation depths exceeding soil movement zones, the areas closer to the surface must be provided with additional treatment. Here, prior to concreting, the trench is prepared with a lining of low-density expanded polystyrene (or other acceptable compressible material) along with an outer polythene sheet sleeving. The polystyrene is designed to absorb seasonal clay movement, and the polythene acts as a slip membrane preventing soil adhesion to the foundation. Figure 2.7.4 shows application to trench fill and piled foundations.

Precast concrete
suspended floor
(see Ch. 4.2)

External
cavity wall

DPC

150 mm
min. void

Compressible
material on
inside face of
foundation

Polythene sheet
prevents soil
adhesion to concrete

Mass concrete (reinforced
if required) foundation

Note: Compressible material may be required to both sides of foundation

Deep strip or trench fill

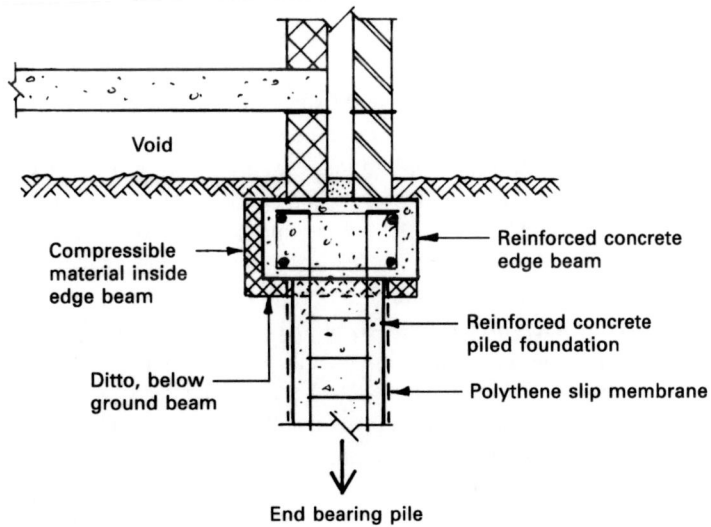

Void

Compressible
material inside
edge beam

Reinforced concrete
edge beam

Reinforced concrete
piled foundation

Ditto, below
ground beam

Polythene slip membrane

End bearing pile

Alternative piled foundation

Figure 2.7.4   Precautionary treatment to foundations in shrinkable clay.

CONCRETE

Concrete is a mixture of cement, fine aggregate, coarse aggregate and water. The proportions of each material control the strength and quality of the resultant concrete.

■■■ PORTLAND CEMENT

Cement is the setting agent of concrete, and the bulk of cement used in this country is Portland cement. This is made from chalk or limestone and clay, and is generally produced by the **wet process**.

In this process the two raw materials are washed, broken up and mixed with water to form a slurry. This slurry is then pumped into a steel rotary kiln, which is from 3 to 4 m in diameter and up to 150 m long and lined with refractory bricks. While the slurry is fed into the top end of the kiln a pulverised coal is blown in at the bottom end and fired. This raises the temperature at the lower end of the kiln to about 1400 °C. First the slurry passing down the kiln gives up its moisture; then the chalk or limestone is broken down into carbon dioxide and lime, and finally it forms a white-hot clinker, which is transferred to a cooler before being ground. The grinding is carried out in a ball mill, which is a cylinder some 15 m long and up to 4.5 m in diameter containing a large number of steel balls of various sizes, which grind the clinker into a fine powder. As the clinker is being fed into the ball mill, gypsum (about 5%) is added to prevent a flash setting off the cement.

The alternative method for the preparation of Portland cement is the **dry process**. The main difference between this and the wet process is the reduction in the amount of water that has to be driven off in the kiln. A mixture of limestone and shale is used, which is proportioned, ground and blended to form a raw meal of low moisture content. The meal is granulated in rotating pans with a small amount of water before being passed to a grate for preheating prior to entering the kiln. The kiln is smaller than that used in the wet process but its function is the same – that is, to form a clinker, which is then cooled, ground and mixed with a little gypsum as described for the previous process.

Rapid-hardening Portland cement is more finely ground than ordinary Portland cement. Its main advantage is that it gains its working strength earlier than ordinary cement. The requirements for both ordinary Portland and rapid-hardening Portland cement are given in BS EN 197-1.

▨▨■ HIGH-ALUMINA CEMENT – BS 915-2

This is made by firing limestone and bauxite (aluminium ore) to a molten state, casting it into pigs, and finally grinding it into a fine powder. Its rate of hardening is very rapid, and produces a concrete that is resistant to the natural sulphates found in some subsoils. It can, however, cost up to two and a half times as much as ordinary Portland cement. However, high-alumina cement has its limitations. When hydrated, the cement converts or undergoes a chemical change that can reduce the concrete's strength and resistance to aggressive chemicals. The manner and extent of conversion vary with the amount of free water/cement ratio, the temperature in which the concrete is located, and the amount of moisture or humidity in the surrounding environment. All these factors are applicable during the cement's manufacture, subsequent curing and design life. Because of a number of structural failures, notably in the humid atmospheres of swimming pools, high-alumina cement is not now normally permitted in exposed concrete structures.

Other forms of cement available are as follows:

- Portland blastfurnace – BS 146;
- low-heat Portland – BS 1370;
- low-alkali sulphate-resisting – BS 4027;
- high-slag blastfurnace – BS 146;
- supersulphated – BS 4248;
- masonry – BS EN 413-1;
- Portland pulverised fuel ash – BS 6588;
- pozzolanic pulverised fuel ash – BS 6610;
- Portland limestone – BS 7583.

Cement should be stored on a damp-proof floor in the dry and kept for short periods only, because eventually it will harden as a result of the action of moisture in the air. This is known as **air hardening**, and any hardened cement should be discarded.

▨▨■ AGGREGATES

These are the materials that are mixed with the cement to form concrete, and are classed as a fine or coarse aggregate. Fine aggregates are those that will pass a standard 5 mm sieve, and coarse aggregates are those that are retained on a standard 5 mm sieve. All-in aggregate is a material composed of both fine and coarse aggregates.

A wide variety of materials (for example, gravel, crushed stone, brick, furnace slag and lightweight substances, such as foamed slag, expanded clay and vermiculite) are available as aggregates for the making of concrete.

In making concrete, aggregates must be graded so that the smaller particles of the fine aggregate fill the voids created by the coarse aggregate. The cement paste fills the voids in the fine aggregate thus forming a dense mix.

Aggregates from natural sources and synthetic aggregates are defined in BS EN 12620: *Aggregates for concrete*.

WATER

The water used in the making of concrete must be clean and free from impurities that could affect the concrete. It is usually specified as being of a quality fit for drinking. A proportion of the water will set up a chemical reaction, which will harden the cement. The remainder is required to give the mix workability, and will evaporate from the mix while it is curing, leaving minute voids. An excess of water will give a porous concrete of reduced durability and strength.

The quantity of water to be used in the mix is usually expressed in terms of the **water/cement ratio**, which is:

$$\frac{\text{total weight of water in the concrete}}{\text{weight of cement}}$$

For most mixes the ratio is between 0.4 and 0.7.

Concrete mixes can be expressed as volume ratios thus:

- 1:2:4 = 1 part cement, 2 parts fine aggregate and 4 parts coarse aggregate;
- 1:5 = 1 part cement and 5 parts all-in aggregate.

SOME COMMON MIXES

- 1:10 – not a strong mix but suitable for filling weak pockets in excavations and for blinding layers.
- 1:8 – slightly better than the last, suitable for paths and pavings.
- 1:6 – a strong mix suitable for mass concrete foundations, paths and pavings.
- 1:3:6 – the weakest mix equivalent to that quoted in Approved Document A as deemed to satisfy the requirements of Building Regulation A1.
- 1:2:4 – a strong mix that is practically impervious to water; in common use especially for reinforced concrete.

MIXING CONCRETE

Concrete can be mixed or batched by two methods:

- by volume;
- by mass.

A 25 kg bag of cement has a volume of approximately 0.02 m^3.

Batching by volume

This method is usually carried out using an open bottom box (of such dimensions as to make manual handling possible) called a **gauge box**. For a 1:2:4 mix a gauge box is filled once with cement, twice with fine aggregate and four times with coarse aggregate, the top of the gauge box being struck off level each time.

If the fine aggregate is damp or wet its volume will increase by up to 25%, and therefore the amount of fine aggregate should be increased by this amount. This increase in volume is called **bulking**.

Batching by mass

This method involves the use of a balance that is linked to a dial giving the exact mass of the materials as they are placed in the scales. This is the best method, because it has a greater accuracy, and the balance can be attached to the mixing machine.

Hand mixing

This should be carried out on a clean, hard surface. The materials should be thoroughly mixed in the dry state before the water is added. The water should be added slowly, preferably using a rose head, until a uniform colour is obtained.

Machine mixing

The mix should be turned over in the mixer for at least 2 minutes after adding the water. The first batch from the mixer tends to be harsh, because some of the mix will adhere to the sides of the drum. This batch should be used for some less important work such as filling in weak pockets in the bottom of the excavation.

Ready mixed

This is used for large batches with lorry transporters up to 6 m^3 capacity. It has the advantage of eliminating site storage of materials and mixing plant, with the guarantee of concrete manufactured to quality-controlled standards. Placement is usually direct from the lorry: therefore site-handling facilities must be coordinated with deliveries.

Handling

If concrete is to be transported for some distance over rough ground the runs should be kept as short as possible, because vibrations of this nature can cause segregation of the materials in the mix. For the same reason concrete should not be dropped from a height of more than 1 m. If this is unavoidable a chute should be used.

Placing

If the concrete is to be placed in a foundation trench it will be levelled from peg to peg (see Fig. 1.4.2), or if it is to be used as an oversite bed the external walls could act as a levelling guide. The levelling is carried out by tamping with a straight-edge board; this tamping serves the dual purpose of both compacting the concrete and bringing the excess water to the surface so that it can evaporate. Concrete must not be over-tamped, as this will bring not only the water to the surface but also the cement paste that is required to act as the matrix. Concrete should be placed as soon as possible after mixing to ensure that the setting action has not commenced. Concrete that dries out too quickly will not develop its full strength: therefore new concrete should be protected from the drying winds and sun by being covered with canvas, straw, polythene sheeting or damp sawdust. This protection should be continued for at least 3 days, because concrete takes about 28 days to obtain its working strength.

Specifying concrete

Any of four methods may be used to specify concrete:

- designed mix;
- prescribed mix;
- standard mix;
- designated mix.

Designed mix

The mix is specified by a grade corresponding to the required characteristic compressive strength at 28 days. There are 12 grades, from C7.5 to C60, the C indicating compressive and the number the strength in N/mm^2 or MPa. Flexural (F) strength grades may also be specified as F3, F4 or F5, e.g. 3, 4 or 5 N/mm^2. In addition to stating the strength grades the purchaser must also specify any particular requirements for cement and aggregate content and maximum free water/cement ratio.

Prescribed mix

This is a recipe of constituents with their properties and quantities used to manufacture the concrete. The specifier must state:

- the type of cement;
- type of aggregates and their maximum size;
- mix proportions by weight;
- degree of workability (slump and/or water/cement ratio) and the application.

Prescribed mixes are based on established data indicating conformity to strength, durability and other characteristics. Basic examples could include 1:3:6/40 mm aggregate and 1:2:4/20 mm aggregate.

Standard mix

Mixes are produced from one of five grades, ranging from ST1 to ST5, with corresponding 28-day strength characteristics of 7.5 to a limit of only 25 N/mm^2. Mix composition and details are specified by:

- cement to aggregate by weight;
- type of cement;
- aggregate type and maximum size;
- workability;
- use or omission of reinforcement.

These mixes are most suited to site production, where the scale of operations is relatively small. Alternatively, they may be used where mix design procedures would be too time consuming, inappropriate or uneconomic.

Designated mix

These mixes are selected relative to particular applications and site conditions, in place of generalisations or use of alternative design criteria that may not be entirely appropriate. Grading and strength characteristics are extensive, and vary with application as indicated:

- General (GEN), graded 0–4, ranging from 7.5 to 25 N/mm^2 characteristic strength. For foundations, floors and external works.
- Foundations (FND), graded 2, 3, 4A and 4B with characteristic strength of 35 N/mm^2. These are particularly appropriate for resisting the effects of sulphates in the ground.
- Paving (PAV), graded 1 or 2 in 35 or 45 N/mm^2 strengths respectively. A strong concrete for use in driveways and heavy-duty pavings.
- Reinforced (RC) and prestressed concrete graded 30, 35, 40, 45 and 50 corresponding with characteristic strength and exposures ranging from mild to most severe.

    In addition to application, the purchaser needs to specify:

- reinforced or unreinforced;
- prestressed;
- heated or ambient temperature;
- maximum aggregate size (if not 20 mm);
- exposure to chemicals (chlorides and sulphates);
- exposure to subzero temperatures (placing and curing).

Because of the precise nature of these designated mix concretes, quality control is of paramount importance: therefore producers are required to have quality assurance product conformity accreditation to BS EN ISO 9001.

[*Note*: Further details of concrete grades and analysis are found in BS EN 206-1: *Concrete. Specification, performance, production and conformity.*]

▧▨■ TESTING OF CONCRETE

There are many different test procedures for determining the properties of concrete. These are detailed in BS 1881: *Testing concrete*, BS EN 12350: *Testing fresh concrete* and BS EN 12390: *Testing hardened concrete*. The two most common tests are the slump test, applied to wet or fresh concrete, and the compression test, applied to hardened concrete.

SLUMP TEST – BS EN 12350-2

The slump test is suitable for establishing uniformity of mixes in subsequent batches or deliveries. It is not strictly a test for workability, but it can be used as a guide when constituents are known to be constant. Mixes of the same slump can vary with regard to their cement content and grade of aggregates.

Equipment

Shown in Fig. 2.4.1 comprises an open-ended steel frustum of a cone, a tamping rod and a rule.

Procedure – the cone is one-quarter filled with concrete and tamped 25 times. A further three layers are applied, each layer tamped as described. Surplus concrete is struck from the surface, and the cone is raised immediately.

Typical slump

Mass concrete/thick sections of reinforced concrete,   50 mm.
Roads, hand tamped and general use,   100 mm.
Thin sections of reinforced concrete,   150 mm.
Maximum aggregate size, 40 mm.

Figure 2.4.1   Slump test.

COMPRESSION TEST – BS EN 12390-1

Concrete test cubes are made from samples taken from site. Specimens are taken before and during the placing of concrete.

Equipment

Shown in Fig. 2.4.2. Standard machined steel mould, 150 mm × 150 mm × 150 mm for aggregate size up to 40 mm. 100 mm cube moulds may be used for aggregates up to 20 mm. Internal faces of the mould are lightly oiled prior to receiving concrete. A 25 mm square steel tamping rod, 380 mm long.

Procedure

Concrete is placed in the mould in 50 mm layers; each layer is tamped 35 times for 150 mm cubes or 25 times for 100 mm cubes. Alternatively, the concrete may be compacted by vibration. Surplus concrete is struck off. Samples remain in the mould for 24 hours ± 30 minutes, covered with a damp sack or similar. After this time specimens are marked, removed from the mould and submersed in water at a temperature between 10 and 21 °C until required for testing.

The cube strength is the stress failure after 7 days. If the strength specification is not achieved at 7 days, a further test is undertaken at 28 days. If the specification is not achieved at 28 days, specimen cores may be taken from the placed concrete for laboratory analysis.

Typical 28-day characteristic crushing strengths (that below which not more than 5 per cent of the test results are allowed to fall) are graded 7.5, 10, 15, 20, 25, 30, 35 and 40 N/mm^2.

As a guide, shear stress of the concrete is taken at approximately one-tenth of the stress under compression.

Figure 2.4.2   Compression test.

3.2

BRICKWORK

The history of the art of brickmaking and the craft of bricklaying can be traced back to before 6000 BC. It started in western Asia, spread eastwards, and was introduced into this country by the Romans. The use of brickwork flourished during the third and fourth centuries, after which the craft suffered a rapid decline until its reintroduction from Flanders towards the end of the fourteenth century. Since then it has been firmly established, and remains as one of the major building materials.

BS 3921 specifically relates to bricks manufactured from clay for use in walling. Other standards exist for units produced from calcium silicate (BS 187) and concrete (BS 6073). A brick is defined in BS 3921 as a walling unit with coordinating or format size of 225 mm length, 112.5 mm width and 75 mm height. Bricks are known by their format size – that is, the actual or work size plus a 10 mm mortar joint allowance to three faces. Therefore the standard brick of 225 mm $\times$ 112.5 mm $\times$ 75 mm has actual dimensions of 215 mm $\times$ 102.5 mm $\times$ 65 mm. The terms used for bricks and brickwork are shown in Figs 3.2.1, 3.2.2 and 3.2.3.

Brickwork is used primarily in the construction of walls by the bedding and jointing of bricks into established bonding arrangements. The term also covers the building-in of hollow and other lightweight blocks. The majority of the bricks used today are made from clay or shale conforming to the requirements of BS 3921.

■■■ MANUFACTURE OF CLAY BRICKS

The basic raw material is clay, shale or brickearth, all of which are in plentiful supply in this country. The raw material is dug, and then prepared either by weathering or by grinding before being mixed with water to the right plastic condition. It is then formed into the required brick shape before being dried and fired in a kiln.

Figure 3.2.1   Brickwork terminology.

Figure 3.2.2   Standard brick.

Figure 3.2.3   Keyed brick.

Different clays have different characteristics, such as moisture content and chemical composition: therefore distinct variations of the broad manufacturing processes have been developed, and these are easily recognised by the finished product.

PRESSED BRICKS

This is the type of brick most commonly used, accounting for nearly two-thirds of the 5000 million produced on average in this country each year. There are two processes of pressed brick manufacture: the semi-dry method and the stiff plastic method.

By far the greatest number of bricks are made by the **semi-dry pressed process** and are called **flettons**; these form over 40% of the total brick production in Britain. The name originates from the village of Fletton outside Peterborough, where the bricks were first made. This process is used for the manufacture of bricks from the Oxford clays, which have a low natural plasticity. The clay is ground, screened and pressed directly into the moulds.

The **stiff plastic process** is used mainly in Scotland, the north of England and south Wales. The clays in these areas require more grinding than the Oxford clays, and the clay dust needs tempering (mixing with water) before being pressed into the mould.

All pressed bricks contain **frogs**, which are sometimes pressed on both bed faces. In general, pressed bricks are more accurate in shape than other clay bricks, with sharp arrises and plain faces.

WIRE-CUT BRICKS

Approximately 28% of bricks produced in Britain are made by this process. The clay, which is usually fairly soft and of a fine texture, is extruded as a continuous ribbon and is cut into brick units by tightly stretched wires spaced at the height or depth for the required brick. Allowance is made during the extrusion and cutting for the shrinkage that will occur during firing. Wire-cut bricks do not have frogs, and on many the wire-cutting marks can be clearly seen.

SOFT MUD PROCESS BRICKS

This process is confined mainly to the south-eastern counties of England, where suitable soft clays are found. The manufacture can be carried out by machine or by hand, either with the natural clay or with a mixture of clay and lime or chalk. In both methods the brick is usually frogged, and is less accurate in shape than other forms of bricks. Sand is usually used in the moulds to enable the bricks to be easily removed, and this causes an uneven patterning or creasing on the face.

▨▧■ BRICK CLASSIFICATION

Bricks are a diverse product: therefore they are difficult to standardise for classification. They may be known by the terms used in BS 3921 – that is, compressive strength

(N/mm^2) and percentage by mass water absorption. Alternatively, the manufacturer's name or catalogue descriptions may be used, possibly in combination with the BS characteristics. The minimum compressive strength acceptable to the Building Regulations is 5 N/mm^2 over gross sectional area (2.8 N/mm^2 for blocks).

Some common terminology:

VARIETIES

- **Common**   Suitable for general building work but having no special claim to give an attractive appearance.
- **Facing**   Specially made or selected to have an attractive appearance when used without rendering or plaster.
- **Engineering**   Having a dense and strong semi-vitreous body conforming to defined limits for absorption and strength.

QUALITIES

- **Internal**   Suitable for internal use only; may need protection on site during bad weather or during the winter.
- **Ordinary**   Less durable than special quality but normally durable in the external face of a building. Some types are unsuitable for exposed situations.
- **Special**   For use in conditions of extreme exposure where the structure may become saturated and frozen, such as retaining walls and pavings.

TYPES

- **Solid**   Those in which small holes passing through or nearly through the brick do not exceed 25% of its volume, or in which frogs do not exceed 20% of its volume. A small hole is defined as a hole less than 20 mm wide or less than 500 mm^2 in area.
- **Perforated**   Those in which holes passing through the brick exceed 25% of its volume and the holes are small as defined above.
- **Hollow**   Those in which the holes passing through the brick exceed 25% of its volume and the holes are larger than those defined as small holes.
- **Cellular**   Those in which the holes are closed at one end and exceed 20% of the volume of the brick.

OTHER CLASSIFICATIONS

Bricks may also be classified by one or more of the following:

- place of origin, for example London;
- raw material, for example clay;
- manufacture, for example wire-cut;
- use, for example foundation;
- colour, for example blue;
- surface texture, for example sand-faced.

▨▥■ CALCIUM SILICATE BRICKS

These bricks are also called sandlime and sometimes flintlime bricks and are covered by BS 187, which gives several classes of brick: the higher the numbered class, the stronger is the brick. The format size of a calcium silicate brick is the same as that given for a standard clay brick.

These bricks are made from carefully selected clean sand and/or crushed flint mixed with controlled quantities of lime and water. At this stage colouring pigments can be added if required; the relatively dry mix is then fed into presses to be formed into the required shape. The moulded bricks are then hardened in sealed and steam-pressurised autoclaves. This process, which takes from 7–10 hours, causes a reaction between the sand and the lime, resulting in a strong homogeneous brick that is ready for immediate delivery and laying. The bricks are very accurate in size and shape but do not have the individual characteristics of clay bricks.

▨▥■ CONCRETE BRICKS

These are made from a mixture of inert aggregate and cement in a similar fashion to calcium silicate bricks, and are cured either by natural weathering or in an autoclave. Details of the types and properties available as standard concrete bricks are given in BS 6073.

▨▥■ MORTARS FOR BRICKWORK

The mortar used in brickwork transfers the tensile, compressive and shear stresses uniformly between adjacent bricks. To do this it must satisfy certain requirements:

- It must have adequate strength, but not greater than that required for the design strength.
- It must have good workability.
- It must retain plasticity long enough for the bricks to be laid.
- It must be durable over a long period.
- It must bond well to the bricks.
- It must be able to be produced at an economic cost.

If the mortar is weaker than the bricks, shrinkage cracks will tend to follow the joints of the brickwork, and these are reasonably easy to make good. If the mortar is stronger than the bricks, shrinkage cracks will tend to be vertical through the joints and the bricks, thus weakening the fabric of the structure.

MORTAR MIXES

Mortar is a mixture of sand and lime or a mixture of sand and cement with or without lime. Proportioning of the materials can be carried by volume, but this method is inaccurate, and it is much better to proportion by weight. The effect of the lime is to make the mix more workable, but as the lime content increases the mortar's resistance to damage by frost action decreases.

Plasticisers, by having the effect of entraining small bubbles of air in the mix and breaking down surface tension, will also increase the workability of a mortar.

Mortars should never be re-tempered, and should be used within 2 hours of mixing or be discarded.

Typical mixes (by volume)

- **Cement mortar (cement:sand):**
  - 1:3 – suitable for brickwork in exposed conditions such as parapets and for brickwork in foundations;
- **Lime mortar (lime:sand):**
  - 1:3 – for internal use only;
- **Gauged mortars (cement:lime:sand):**
  - 1:1:6 – suitable for most conditions of severe exposure;
  - 1:2:9 – suitable for most conditions except those of severe exposure;
  - 1:3:12 – internal use only.

DAMPNESS PENETRATION

It is possible for dampness to penetrate into a building through the brick walls by one or more of three ways:

1. by the rain penetrating the head of the wall and soaking down into the building below the roof level;
2. by the rain beating against the external wall and soaking through the fabric into the building;
3. by ground moisture entering the wall at or near the base and creeping up the wall by capillary action and entering the building above the ground floor level.

Numbers 1 and 3 can be overcome by the insertion of a suitable damp-proof course in the thickness of the wall. Number 2 can be overcome by one of two methods:

- applying to the exposed face of the wall a barrier such as cement rendering or some suitable cladding such as vertical tile hanging;
- constructing a cavity wall, whereby only the external skin becomes damp, the cavity providing a suitable barrier to the passage of moisture through the wall.

DAMP-PROOF COURSES

The purpose of a damp-proof course in a building is to provide a barrier to the passage of moisture from an external source into the fabric of the building, or from one part of the structure to another. Damp-proof courses may be either horizontal or vertical, and can generally be divided into three types:

- those below ground level to prevent the entry of moisture from the soil;
- those placed just above ground level to prevent moisture creeping up the wall by capillary action; this is sometimes called **rising damp**;
- those placed at openings, parapets and similar locations to exclude the entry of the rainwater that falls directly onto the fabric of the structure.

Materials for damp-proof courses

BS 743: *Specification for materials for damp-proof courses* gives seven suitable
materials for the construction of damp-proof courses, all of which should have the
following properties:

- be completely impervious;
- be durable, having a longer life than the other components in the building and
  therefore not needing replacing during its lifetime;
- be in comparatively thin sheets so as to prevent disfigurement of the building;
- be strong enough to support the loads placed upon it without exuding from
  the wall;
- be flexible enough to give with any settlement of the building without fracturing.

The following also apply:

- BS 6398: *Specification for bitumen damp-proof courses for masonry*;
- BS 6515: *Specification for polyethylene damp-proof courses for masonry*;
- BS 8215: *Code of practice for design and installation of damp-proof courses in
  masonry construction*.

Lead
This should be at least to BS EN 12588: *Lead and lead alloys. Rolled lead sheet for
building purposes*; it is a flexible material supplied in thin sheets, and therefore large
irregular shapes with few joints can be formed, but it has the disadvantage of being
expensive.

Copper
This should have a minimum thickness of 0.25 mm; like lead it is supplied in thin
sheets and is expensive.

Bitumen
This is supplied in the form of a felt, usually to brick widths, and is therefore laid
quickly with the minimum number of joints. Hessian and other fibrous-based
bitumens may be found in older construction, but they are now largely superseded
by dpc's of plastic materials.

Mastic asphalt
Applied in two layers giving a total thickness of 25 mm; it is applied *in-situ* and is
therefore jointless, but is expensive in small quantities.

Polythene
Black low-density polythene sheet of single thickness not less than 0.5 mm thick
should be used; it is easily laid but can be torn and punctured easily.

Slates
These should not be less than 230 mm long nor less than 4 mm thick and laid in
two courses set breaking the joint in cement mortar 1:3. Slates have limited

flexibility but are impervious and very durable. Cost depends upon the area in which the building is being erected.

Bricks

These should comply with the requirements of BS 3921 'engineering' classification. They are laid in two courses in cement mortar, and may contrast with the general appearance of other brickwork in the same wall.

▨▨■ BRICKWORK BONDING

When building with bricks it is necessary to lay the bricks to some recognised pattern or bond in order to ensure stability of the structure and to produce a pleasing appearance. All the various bonds are designed so that no vertical joint in any one course is directly above or below a vertical joint in the adjoining course. To simplify this requirement special bricks are produced to BS 4729: *Specification for dimensions of bricks of special shapes and sizes*. Alternatively, the bricklayer can cut from whole bricks on site. Application of some of these specials is shown in Fig. 3.2.4, with some additions in Fig. 3.2.5. The various bonds are also planned to give the greatest practical amount of lap to all the bricks, and this should not be less than a quarter of a brick length. Properly bonded brickwork distributes the load over as large an area of brickwork as possible, so that the angle of spread of the load through the bonded brickwork is 60°.

COMMON BONDS

- **Stretcher bond**   Consists of all stretchers in every course and is used for half-brick walls and the half-brick skins of hollow or cavity walls (see Fig. 3.2.6).
- **English bond**   A very strong bond consisting of alternate courses of headers and stretchers (see Fig. 3.2.7).
- **Flemish bond**   Each course consists of alternate headers and stretchers; its appearance is considered to be better than English bond, but it is not quite so strong. This bond requires fewer facing bricks than English bond, needing only 79 bricks per square metre as opposed to 89 facing bricks per square metre for English bond. This bond is sometimes referred to as **double Flemish bond** (see Fig. 3.2.8).
- **Single Flemish bond**   A combination of English and Flemish bonds, having Flemish bond on the front face with a backing of English bond. It is considered to be slightly stronger than Flemish bond. The thinnest wall that can be built using this bond is a one-and-a-half brick wall.
- **English garden wall bond**   Consists of three courses of stretchers to one course of headers.
- **Flemish garden wall bond**   Consists of one header to every three stretchers in every course; this bond is fairly economical in facing bricks and has a pleasing appearance.

Figure 3.2.4   Special bricks.

Plinth header

Plinth stretcher

Plinth external return

Squint angle

Angle

Dogleg

Birdsmouth

Cant

Double cant

Bullnose on end
(cow nose)

Single bullnose

Double bullnose

Bullnose mitre

Single bullnose header

Double-headed bullnose

Figure 3.2.5   Purpose-made bricks.

Figure 3.2.6 Typical stretcher bond details.

Figure 3.2.7 Typical English bond details.

Queen closer

Return wall

Queen closer

$\frac{3}{4}$ bats

Queen closer

Raking back

Attached pier or pilaster

Square corner or quoin

Alternate courses similar

Queen closer

$\frac{3}{4}$ bats

Stopped end

Queen closer

Cross wall

Attached pier – for alternate bonding see Fig. 3.2.8

Figure 3.2.8 Typical Flemish bond details.

Note: The above example shows reverse bond, i.e. the end bricks in each course do not correspond – this technique can be used with all other bonds

Attached pier – for alternative bonding see Fig. 3.2.7

Queen closer

Queen closer

Stopped end

Attached pier or pilaster

Cross wall

Attached pier or pilaster

Queen closer

Return wall

Queen closer

Raking back

½ bat

¾ bats

¾ bats

Quoin

Alternate courses similar

Figure 3.2.9   Special bonds.

Figure 3.2.10   Reinforced stack bond.

SPECIAL BONDS

- **Rat-trap bond**   This is a brick on edge bond and gives a saving on materials and loadings, suitable as a backing wall to a cladding such as tile hanging (see Fig. 3.2.9).
- **Quetta bond**   Used on one-and-a-half brick walls for added strength; suitable for retaining walls (see Fig. 3.2.9).
- **Stack bond**   A brickwork feature used for partitions and infill panels. Bricks may be laid on bed or end with continuous vertical joints. Figure 3.2.10 shows steel-mesh-reinforced horizontal bed joints to compensate for the lack of conventional bond.

METRIC MODULAR BRICKWORK

The standard imperial format brick does not fit reasonably well into the system of dimensional coordination, with its preferred dimension of 300 mm. Metric modular bricks have been designed and produced with four different formats (see Fig. 3.2.11), but BS 6649: *Specification for clay and calcium silicate modular bricks* provides only for a single format of 200 mm × 100 mm × 75 mm.

The bond arrangements are similar to the well-known bonds but are based on third bonding: that is, the overlap is one-third of a brick and not one-quarter as with the standard format brick. Examples of metric modular brick bonding are shown in Fig. 3.2.11.

Metric modular bricks

Format size 300 × 100 × 100
or 300 × 100 × 75

Format size 200 × 100 × 100
or 200 × 100 × 75

Header and stretcher bond

Header stretcher bond

Figure 3.2.11 Metric modular brickwork.

Figure 3.2.12 Typical footings.

FOOTINGS

These are wide courses of bricks placed at the base of a wall to spread the load over a greater area of the foundations. This method is seldom used today; instead the concrete foundation would be reinforced to act as a beam or reinforced strip. The courses in footings are always laid as headers as far as possible; stretchers, if needed, are laid in the centre of the wall (see Fig. 3.2.12).

BOUNDARY WALLS

These are subjected to severe weather conditions and therefore should be correctly designed and constructed. If these walls are also acting as a retaining wall the conditions will be even more extreme, but the main design principle of the exclusion of water remains the same. The presence of water in brickwork can lead to frost damage, mortar failure and efflorescence. The incorporation of adequate damp-proof courses and overhanging throated copings is of the utmost importance in this form of structure (see Fig. 3.2.13).

Efflorescence

This is a white stain appearing on the face of brickwork caused by deposits of soluble salts formed on or near the surface of the brickwork as a result of evaporation of the water in which they have been dissolved. It is usually harmless, and disappears within a short period of time; dry brushing or with clean water

Figure 3.2.13   Typical boundary wall.

Figure 3.2.14   Lacing course (see also Fig. 3.1.7).

may be used to remove the salt deposit, but the use of acids should be left to the expert.

▨▨■ FEATURE BRICKWORK

Repetitive brickwork can be visually very monotonous. Some relief can be provided with coloured mortars and method of pointing. Greater opportunity for artistic expression is achieved by varying the colours and textures of the bricks to produce patterns and images on a wall. A further dimension is obtained by using cut and purpose-made bricks as projecting features. Some possible applications are shown in Figs 3.2.14–3.2.18.

215   60.5   102.5   102.5
65   23
102.5   158   215   158
Stretcher   **Wide-bed stretcher**   **Header**   **Wide-bed**

102.5
Wide-bed stretcher course
Stretcher course
102.5   56   102.5   42
Wide bed   Stretcher
215   158.5   144.5

Typical wall base   **Alternatives**

Figure 3.2.15 Plinth brickwork.

Brick on edge
215   Floor joist
Projecting cut brick courses
Wall plate
102.5   T/3 max.
T
Window feature or bracketing   **Traditional joist support**

Figure 3.2.16 Corbelling.

Figure 3.2.17   Dentil coursing.

Figure 3.2.18   Dogtooth coursing.

BLOCKWORK

A block can be defined as a walling unit exceeding the BS dimensions specified for bricks, and its height should not exceed either its length or six times its thickness. This avoids confusion with slabs or panels. Blocks are produced in clay and various cement/aggregate mixes, including wood chippings.

■■■ CLAY BLOCKS

These have format size of $300 \times 225 \times 62.5$, 75, 100 or 150 mm width. They are manufactured hollow by an extrusion process and are fired as for clay bricks. The standard six (150 mm) cavity block has been used for the inner skin of cavity walls, but has now been superseded by developments in lightweight concrete blocks. The three (75 mm) cavity block is intended primarily for partitions. 150 mm blocks are also used in the warmer climates of the world as a single-leaf external walling with rendered and emulsioned finish. Chapter 4.6 shows another application to structural concrete floors. Typical details are shown in Fig. 3.3.1.

■■■ PRECAST CONCRETE BLOCKS

The specification and manufacture of precast concrete blocks or masonry units is covered in BS 6073. Classification is by compressive strength categories: 2.8, 3.5, 5, 7, 10, 15, 20 and 35 N/mm^2.

The density of a precast concrete block gives an indication of its compressive strength – the greater the density the stronger the block. Density will also give an indication as to the thermal conductivity and acoustic properties of a block. The lower the density the lower is the thermal conductivity factor, whereas the higher the density the greater is the reduction of airborne sound through the block.

The actual properties of different types of precast concrete block can be obtained from manufacturers' literature together with their appearance classification such as plain, facing or special facing.

Figure 3.3.1 Hollow clay blocks and blockwork.

Aerated concrete for blocks is produced by introducing air or gas into the mix so that, when set, a uniform cellular block is formed. The usual method employed is to introduce a controlled amount of fine aluminium powder into the mix; this reacts with the free lime in the cement to give off hydrogen, which is quickly replaced by air and so provides the aeration.

Precast concrete blocks are manufactured to a wide range of standard sizes, the most common face format sizes being 400 mm × 200 mm and 450 mm × 225 mm, with thicknesses of 75, 90, 100, 140, 190 and 215 mm. Typical details are shown in Fig. 3.3.2.

Figure 3.3.2   Precast concrete blocks and brickwork.

Concrete blocks are laid in what is essentially stretcher bond and joined to other walls by block bonding or by leaving metal ties or strips projecting from suitable bed courses. As with brickwork the mortar used in blockwork should be weaker than the material of the walling unit; generally a 1:2:9 gauged mortar mix will be suitable for work above ground level.

Concrete blocks shrink on drying out: therefore they should not be laid until the initial drying shrinkage has taken place (usually this is about 14 days under normal drying conditions), and should be protected on site to prevent them from becoming wet, expanding and causing subsequent shrinkage, possibly resulting in cracking of the blocks and any applied finishes such as plaster. Where length of wall exceed 6 m or thereabouts, it is necessary to incorporate vertical movement joints. These comprise a stainless steel or galvanised steel former incorporating horizontal bed joint ties at 450 mm spacing. Figure 3.3.3 shows the installation with

Figure 3.3.3 Blockwork movement joint (BS 5628: Part 3: *Use of masonry*).

bonded profiled or perforated ties to one side and plastic-sleeved ties to the other to maintain continuity and facilitate movement.

The main advantages of blockwork over brickwork are:

- labour saving – easy to cut, larger units;
- easier fixings – most take direct fixing of screws and nails;
- higher thermal insulation properties;
- lower density;
- provides a suitable key for plaster and cement rendering.

The main disadvantages are:

- lower strength;
- less resistance to rain penetration;
- loadbearing properties less (one- or two-storey application);
- lower sound insulation properties.

STONEWORK

The natural formation of stones or rocks is a very long process, which commenced when the earth was composed only of gases. These gases eventually began to liquefy, forming the land and the sea, the land being only a thin crust or mantle to the still molten core.

Igneous rocks originated from the molten state, plutonic rocks are those in the lower part of the earth's mantle, and hypabyssal rocks solidified rapidly near the upper surface of the crust.

Stonework terminology

- **Arris**   Meeting edge of two worked surfaces.
- **Ashlar**   A square hewn stone; stonework consisting of blocks of stone finely squared and dressed to given dimensions and laid to courses of not less than 300 mm in height.
- **Bed joint**   Horizontal joint between two consecutive courses.
- **Bonders**   Through stones or stones penetrating two-thirds of the thickness of a wall.
- **Cramp**   Non-ferrous metal or slate tie across a joint.
- **Dowel**   Non-ferrous or slate peg mortised into adjacent joints.
- **Joggle**   Recessed key filled with a suitable material, used between adjacent vertical joints.
- **Lacing**   Course of different material to add strength.
- **Natural bed**   Plane of stratification in sedimentary stones.
- **Quarry sap**   Moisture contained in newly quarried stones.
- **Quoin**   Corner stone.
- **Stool**   Flat seating on a weathered sill for jamb or mullion.
- **String course**   Distinctive course or band used mainly for decoration.
- **Weathering**   Sloping surface to part of the structure to help shed the rain.

■■■ BUILDING STONES

Stones used in building can be divided into three classes:

- igneous;
- sedimentary;
- metamorphic.

IGNEOUS STONES

These stones originate from volcanic action, being formed by the crystallisation of molten rock matter derived from deep in the earth's crust. It is the proportions of these crystals that give the stones their colour and characteristics. Granites are typical of this class of stone, being hard, durable, and capable of a fine, polished finish. Granites are composed mainly of quartz, feldspar and mica.

SEDIMENTARY STONES

These stones are composed largely of material derived from the breakdown and erosion of existing rocks deposited in layers under the waters that, at that time, covered much of the earth's surface. Being deposited in this manner, their section is stratified, and shows to a lesser or greater degree the layers as deposited. Some of these layers are visible only if viewed under a microscope. Under the microscope it will be seen that all the particles lie in one direction, indicating the flow of the current in the water. Sandstones and limestones are typical examples of sedimentary stones.

Sandstones are stratified sedimentary rocks produced by eroded and disintegrated rocks such as granite, being carried away and deposited by water in layers. The brown and yellow tints in sandstones are due to the presence of oxides of iron.

Limestones may be organically formed by the deposit of tiny shells and calcareous (containing limestone) skeletons in the seas and rivers, or they may be formed chemically by deposits of lime in ringed layers. Limestones vary considerably, from a heavy crystalline form to a friable material such as chalk.

METAMORPHIC STONES

These are stones that have altered and may have been originally igneous or sedimentary rocks, but have since been changed by geological processes such as pressure, movement, heat and chemical reaction due to the infiltration of fluids. Typical examples of this type of stone are marbles and slates.

Marbles are metamorphic limestones, their original structure having been changed by pressure. Marbles, being capable of taking a high polish, are used mainly for decorative work.

Slate is a metamorphic clay, having been subjected to great pressure and heat; being derived from a sedimentary layer it can be easily split into thin members.

Stones are obtained from quarries by blasting and wedging the blocks away from the solid mass. They are partly worked in the quarry and then sent to store yards, where they can be sawn, cut, moulded, dressed and polished to the customer's requirements.

Today, natural stones are sometimes used for facing prestige buildings, constructing boundary or similar walls and, in those areas where natural stones occur, to preserve the character of the district. The distribution of natural stones in the British Isles is shown in Fig. 3.1.1.

CAST STONES

Substitutes for natural stones are available in the form of cast stones, either as reconstructed or as artificial stones. BS 1217 defines these as a building material manufactured from cement and natural aggregate, for use in a manner similar to and for the same purpose as natural stone.

RECONSTRUCTED STONE

These types of cast stone are homogeneous throughout and therefore have the same texture and colour as the natural stones they are intended to substitute for. They are free from flaws and stratification and can be worked in the same manner as natural stone; alternatively, they can be cast into shaped moulds giving the required section.

ARTIFICIAL STONE

These stones consist partly of a facing material and partly of a structural concrete. The facing is a mixture of fine aggregate of natural stone and cement or sand and pigmented cement to resemble the natural stone colouring. This facing should be cast as an integral part of the stone and have a minimum thickness of 20 mm. They are cheaper than reconstructed stones but have the disadvantage that, if damaged, the concrete core may be exposed.

ASHLAR WALLING

This form of stone walling is composed of carefully worked stones, regularly coursed, bonded and set with thin or rusticated joints, and is used for the majority of high-class facing work in stone. The quoins are sometimes given a surface treatment to emphasise the opening or corner of the building. The majority of ashlar work is carried out in limestone varying in thickness from 100 to 300 mm and set in mason's putty, which is a mixture of stone dust, lime putty and Portland cement, a typical mix ratio being 7:5:2.

RULES FOR ASHLAR WORK

- Back faces of ashlar stones should be painted with a bituminous or similar waterproofing paint.

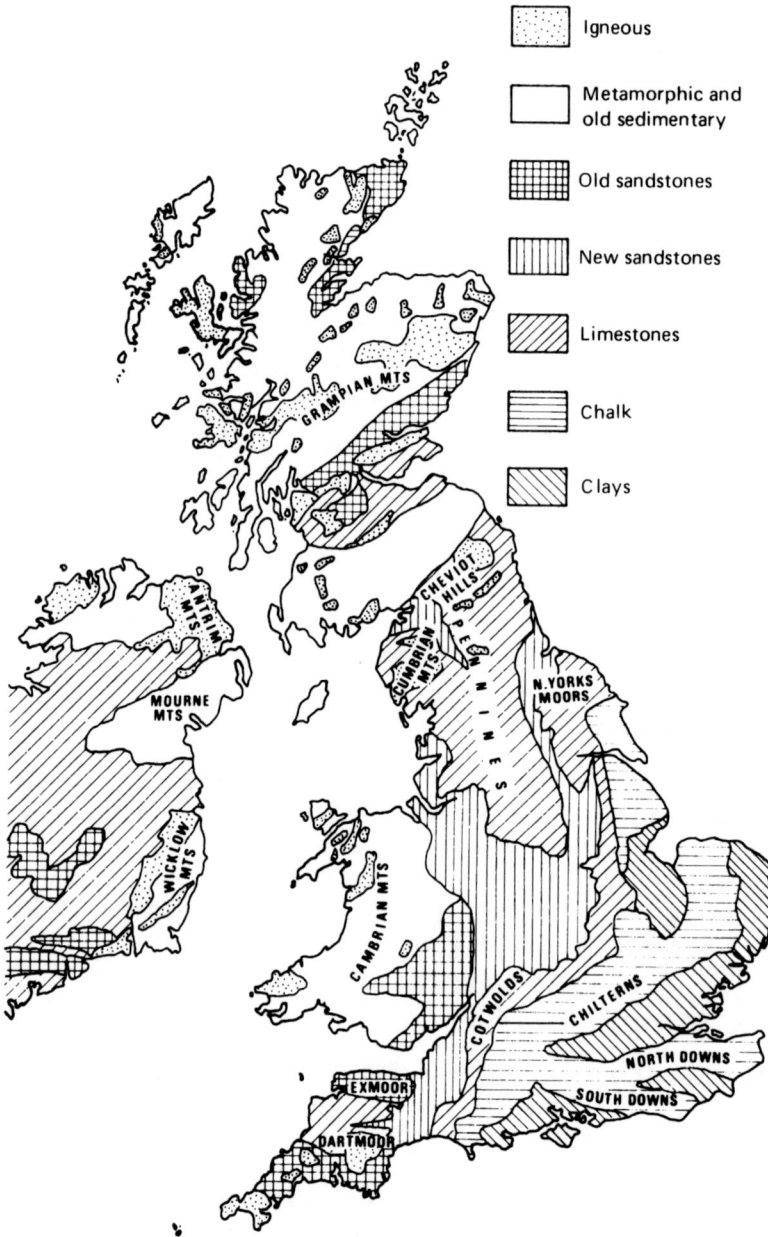

Figure 3.1.1   Distribution of natural stones.

Weathered stone coping

Lead dots at 750 c/c

Code 6 lead flashing

RC flat roof with asphalt finish

Code 6 lead weathering on layer of stout building paper

328

113   215

300

450

300

450

300

Brick backing

Ashlar facing

Internal finish

Skirting

DPC

Mass concrete foundation

Solid floor

Toggle joint

Asphalt

Slate dowel

Raglet

Code 6 lead flashing

Joggle joint

Moulded cornice

Alternative cornice detail showing joints

Run lead dot

30 dia.

12

20 sq.

25

Seam

Lead-welded cover dot

Brass screw and washer

Hardwood plug

Figure 3.1.2   Typical details of ashlar stonework.

Figure 3.1.3   Typical surface and joint treatments.

- External stonework must not be taken through the thickness of the wall, because this could create a passage for moisture.
- Ledges of cornices and external projections should be covered with lead, copper or asphalt to prevent damage by rain or birds.
- Moulded cornices should be raked back at 45° to counteract the cantilever action.
- Faces of stones should be given a protective coat of slurry during construction, the slurry being washed off immediately prior to completion.

Typical details of ashlar work are shown in Figs 3.1.2–3.1.5.

▨▦■ RUBBLE WALLING

These are walls consisting of stones that are left in a rough or uneven state, thus presenting a natural appearance to the face of the wall. These stones are usually laid with a wide joint, and are frequently used in various forms in many rural areas. They can be laid dry or bedded in earth in boundary walls, or bedded in lime mortar when used for the walls of farm outbuildings; if used in conjunction with ashlar stonework, a cement or gauged mortar is used. It is usual to build the quoins to corners, window and door openings in dressed or ashlar stones. As with ashlar work it is advisable to treat the face of any backing material with a suitable waterproofing coat to prevent the passage of moisture or the appearance of cement stains on the stone face.

Solid stone walls will behave in the same manner as solid brick walls with regard to the penetration of moisture and rain: it will therefore be necessary to take the same precautions in the form of damp-proof courses to comply with Part C of the Building Regulations.

Typical examples of stone and rubble walling are shown in Figs 3.1.4, 3.1.6 and 3.1.7.

Figure 3.1.4 Typical treatments to arch openings.

Figure 3.1.5 Typical treatments to square openings.

Rubble coping bedded
in cement mortar

Random rubble set
dry or bedded in
cement mortar

Gaps filled with
spalls or small
stones

Bonder or
through stone
1 per m²

Foundation of mass concrete
or large stones

Uncoursed random rubble wall

Weathered stone coping
bedded in cement mortar

Random rubble
bedded in cement
mortar and laid
in courses 225
to 450 high

Wide joints

Foundation of mass
concrete or large stones

Coursed random rubble wall

Figure 3.1.6 Typical rubble walls.

Segmental stone coping bedded in cement mortar

Roughly square rubble bedded in cement mortar and laid in courses 300 to 450 high

Thin joints

Foundation of mass concrete or large stones

Coursed square rubble wall

Saddleback stone coping bedded in cement mortar

Flints from the lower regions of the chalk strata bedded in cement mortar

Brick lacing courses for added strength

Foundation of mass concrete or large stones

Flint stone wall

Figure 3.1.7   Typical stone walls.

CAVITY WALLS

A wall constructed in two leaves or skins with a space or cavity between them is called a **cavity wall**, and it is the most common form of external wall used in domestic building today. The main purpose of constructing a cavity wall is to prevent the penetration of rain to the internal surface of the wall. It is essential that the cavity is not bridged in any way, as this would provide a passage for the moisture.

Air bricks have been used to ventilate the cavity, and these would be built in at the head and base of the cavity wall in order that a flow of air might pass through the cavity thus drying out any moisture that had penetrated the outer leaf. Unless the wall is exposed to very wet conditions the practice of inserting air bricks to ventilate the cavity is not now recommended, because it lowers the thermal and sound insulation values of the wall.

The main consideration in the construction of a cavity wall above ground-level damp-proof course is the choice of a brick or block that will give the required durability, strength and appearance and also conform to Building Regulation requirements. The main function of the wall below ground-level damp-proof course is to transmit the load safely to the foundations; in this context the two half-brick or block leaves forming the wall act as retaining walls. There is a tendency for the two leaves to move towards each other because of the pressure of the soil and the space provided by the cavity. To overcome this problem the cavity below ground level is filled with a weak mix of concrete, thus creating a solid wall in the ground (see Fig. 3.4.1). Alternatively, the substructural wall may be built solid. It is also advisable to leave out every fourth vertical joint in the external leaf at the base of the cavity and above the cavity fill, to allow any moisture trapped in the cavity a means of escape.

Parapets, whether solid or of cavity construction, are exposed to the elements on three sides and need careful design and construction. They must be provided with adequate barriers to moisture in the form of damp-proof courses, as dampness

Figure 3.4.1   Typical cavity wall details.

could penetrate the structure by soaking down the wall and bypassing the roof and entering the building below the uppermost ceiling level. A solid parapet wall should not be less than 150 mm thick and not less than the thickness of the wall on which it is carried, and its height should not exceed four times its thickness. The recommended maximum heights of cavity wall parapets are shown in Fig. 3.4.2.

▦▦■ BUILDING REGULATIONS

Regulation A1 requires that a building shall be so constructed that the combined dead, imposed and wind loads are sustained and transmitted to the ground safely

Figure 3.4.2 Parapets.

Sum of leaf thicknesses (mm)	Height (mm)
≤ 200	600 max.
200–250	860 max.

and without causing any movement that will impair the stability of any part of another building. Guidance to meet these requirements for cavity walls is given in Approved Document A.

Section 2C of this document considers full storey-height cavity walls for residential buildings of up to three storeys and requires that:

1. The compressive strengths of bricks and blocks should be not less than 5 N/mm^2 and 2.8 N/mm^2 respectively for buildings up to two storeys. Greater strength classifications are required for three-storey buildings (see Approved Document A, Section 2C, Diagram 7).
2. Cavities (gap between masonry faces) should be at least 50 mm, but may be up to 300 mm. Both leaves in cavity walls should have ties embedded at least 50 mm into adjacent masonry.
3. Wall ties should comply with BS EN 845-1: *Specification for ancillary components for masonry. Ties, tension straps, hangers and brackets.* Plastic and galvanised steel ties have been used, but now the preferred material is austenitic stainless steel. Maximum spacings are shown in Fig. 3.4.3. Cavities < 75 mm may be tied with butterfly pattern ties, but in excess of this they should be provided with twisted pattern ties.
4. Cavity walls normally have leaves at least 90 mm thick. An exception is with leaves of 65–90 mm thickness and cavity up to 75 mm with ties at 450 mm max. horizontal spacing.

Twisted pattern

150 to 425

50

Butterfly pattern

150 or 200

75 to 100

Double triangle pattern

150 or 200

64

Polypropylene tie

200

58

Unbonded jamb

Cavity wall with
50–300 mm cavity

Wall tie
positions

300
300
300
300
300
300

450
450
450
450

900   900

750 mm preferred spacing
if cavity > 75 mm

As near to opening as is practicable but within 225 mm

Figure 3.4.3   Wall ties.

5. The combined thickness of the two leaves of a cavity wall should be not less than 190 mm for a maximum wall height of 3.5 m and length not exceeding 12 m, and also for heights between 3.5 m and 9 m in wall lengths not exceeding 9 m. Wall lengths and heights up to 12 m require a minimum thickness of 290 mm. Variations:

Wall height	Wall length	Wall thickness
≤ 12 m	≤ 9 m	290 mm for one storey
		190 mm for remainder
≤ 12 m	≤ 12 m	290 mm for two storeys
		190 mm for remainder

6. Mortar should be as given for mortar designation (iii) in BS 5628-1: *Structural use of unreinforced masonry*, or a gauged mortar mix of 1:1:6 by volume, or its equivalent.
7. Cavity walls of any length need to be provided with roof lateral support. Walls over 3 m length will also require floor lateral support at every floor forming a junction with the supported wall. If roof lateral support is not provided by type of covering (tiles or slates), a pitch of 15° or more plus a minimum wall plate bearing of 75 mm, durable metal straps with a minimum cross-section of 30 mm × 5 mm will be needed at not more than 2 m centres (see Fig. 6.1.9). If the floor does not have at least a 90 mm bearing on the supported wall, lateral support should be provided by similar straps at not more than 2 m spacing, or the joists should be fixed using restraint-type joist hangers (see Fig. 4.7.1).

PREVENTION OF DAMP IN CAVITY WALLS

Approved Document C recommends a cavity to be carried down at least 150 mm below the lowest damp-proof course, and that any bridging of the cavity, other than a wall tie or closing course protected by the roof, is to have a suitable damp-proof course to prevent the passage of moisture across the cavity. Where the cavity is closed at the jambs of openings a vertical damp-proof course should be inserted unless some other suitable method is used to prevent the passage of moisture from the outer leaf to the inner leaf of the wall.

Approved Document C recommends a damp-proof course to be inserted in all external walls at least 150 mm above the highest adjoining ground or paving to prevent the passage of moisture rising up the wall and into the building, unless the design is such that the wall is protected or sheltered.

▧▦■ ADVANTAGES AND DISADVANTAGES

ADVANTAGES OF CAVITY WALL CONSTRUCTION

These can be listed as follows:

- able to withstand a driving rain in all situations from penetrating to the inner wall surface;
- gives good thermal insulation, keeping the building warm in winter and cool in the summer;

- no need for external rendering;
- enables the use of cheaper and alternative materials for the inner construction;
- a nominal 255 mm cavity wall has a higher sound insulation value than a standard one-brick-thick wall;
- can accommodate supplementary insulation material.

DISADVANTAGES OF CAVITY WALL CONSTRUCTION

These can be listed as follows:

- requires a high standard of design and workmanship to produce a soundly constructed wall – this will require good supervision during construction;
- the need to include a vertical damp-proof course to all openings;
- slightly dearer in cost than a standard one-brick-thick wall.

■ ■ ■ JOINTING AND POINTING

These terms are used for the finish given to both the vertical and the horizontal joints in brickwork irrespective of whether the wall is of brick, block, solid or cavity construction.

Jointing is the finish given to the joints when carried out as the work proceeds.

Pointing is the finish given to the joints by raking out to a depth of approximately 20 mm and filling in on the face with a hard-setting cement mortar, which could have a colour additive. This process can be applied to both new and old buildings. Typical examples of jointing and pointing are shown in Fig. 3.4.4.

Flush joint

Keyed joint

Recessed joint

Weathered pointing — Strong cm. mt. mix. — 20

Weathered joint

Raked-out joint — Applied finish — 20

Figure 3.4.4 Brick joints.

3.5

OPENINGS IN WALLS

An opening in an external wall consists of a head, jambs or reveals, and a sill or threshold.

▨▨■ HEAD

The function of a head is to carry the load of brickwork over the opening and transmit this load to the jambs at the sides. To fulfil this task it must have the capacity to support the load without unacceptable deflection. A variety of materials and methods is available in the form of a lintel or beam, such as:

- **Timber**   Suitable for light loads and small spans; the timber should be treated with a preservative to prevent attack by beetles or fungi.
- **Steel**
    - For small openings – a mild steel flat or angle section can be used to carry the outside leaf of a cavity wall, the inner leaf being supported by a concrete or steel lintel.
    - For medium spans – a channel or joist section is usually suitable.
    - For large spans – a universal beam section to design calculations will be needed.
    Steel lintels and beams that are exposed to the elements should be either galvanised or painted with several coats of bituminous paint to give them protection against corrosion.
- **Concrete**   These can be designed as *in-situ* or precast reinforced beams or lintels and can be used for all spans. Prestressed concrete lintels are available for the small and medium spans (see Chapter 10, *Advanced Construction Technology*).
- **Stone**   These can be natural, artificial or reconstructed stone but are generally used as a facing to a steel or concrete lintel (see Fig. 3.1.5).
- **Brick**   Unless reinforced with mild steel bars or mesh, brick lintels are suitable only for small spans up to 1 m but, like stone, bricks are also employed as a facing to a steel or concrete lintel.

Figure 3.5.1 Typical head treatments to openings (pre-1985 Building Regulations).

Figure 3.5.2   Typical head treatments to openings.

Lintels require a bearing at each end of the opening; the amount will vary with the span, but generally it will be 100 mm for the small spans and up to 225 mm for the medium and large spans. In cavity walling a damp-proof course will be required where the cavity is bridged by the lintel, and this should extend at least 150 mm beyond each end of the lintel. Open joints are sometimes used to act as weep holes; these are placed at 900 mm centres in the outer leaf immediately above the damp-proof course. Typical examples of head treatments to openings are shown in Figs 3.5.1 and 3.5.2.

ARCHES

These are arrangements of wedge-shaped bricks designed to support each other and carry the load over the opening round a curved profile to abutments on either side. Full details of arch construction are given in the next chapter.

JAMBS

In solid walls these are bonded to give the required profile and strength; examples of bonded jambs are shown in Fig. 3.2.4. In cavity walls the cavity can be closed at the opening by using a suitable frame, or by turning one of the leaves towards the other, forming a butt joint in which is incorporated a vertical damp-proof course as required by the Building Regulations. Typical examples of jamb treatments to openings are shown in Figs 3.5.3 and 3.5.4.

SILL

The function of a sill is to shed rainwater, which has run down the face of the window or door and collected at the base, away from the opening and the face of the wall. Many methods and materials are available; appearance and durability are the

Figure 3.5.3   Typical jamb treatments to openings (pre-1985 Building Regulations).

Figure 3.5.4 Typical jamb treatments to openings.

main requirements, as a sill is not a member that is needed to carry heavy loads. Sills, unlike lintels, do not require a bearing at each end. Typical examples of sill treatments to openings are shown in Figs 3.5.5 and 3.5.6.

■■■ CONSERVATION OF FUEL ENERGY

The details shown in Figs 3.5.1, 3.5.3 and 3.5.5 are no longer acceptable by UK building standards for new housing, because of inadequate thermal insulation and the opportunity for thermal bridging (see Chapter 8.3). However, much of our existing housing stock is constructed in this manner, and therefore these illustrations are retained as historic reference.

■■■ CHECKED OPENINGS

REVEAL

That part of an opening returning at right angles from the front face of a wall. The traditional construction for door and window reveals includes a check or recess to accommodate the frame. It also provides a barrier against draught and rain penetration. Examples of this dated, but nevertheless existing, construction are shown in Fig. 3.5.7.

Figure 3.5.5   Typical sill treatments to openings (pre-1985 Building Regulations).

Figure 3.5.6   Typical sill treatments to openings.

Figure 3.5.7   Traditional checked openings (sectional plans).

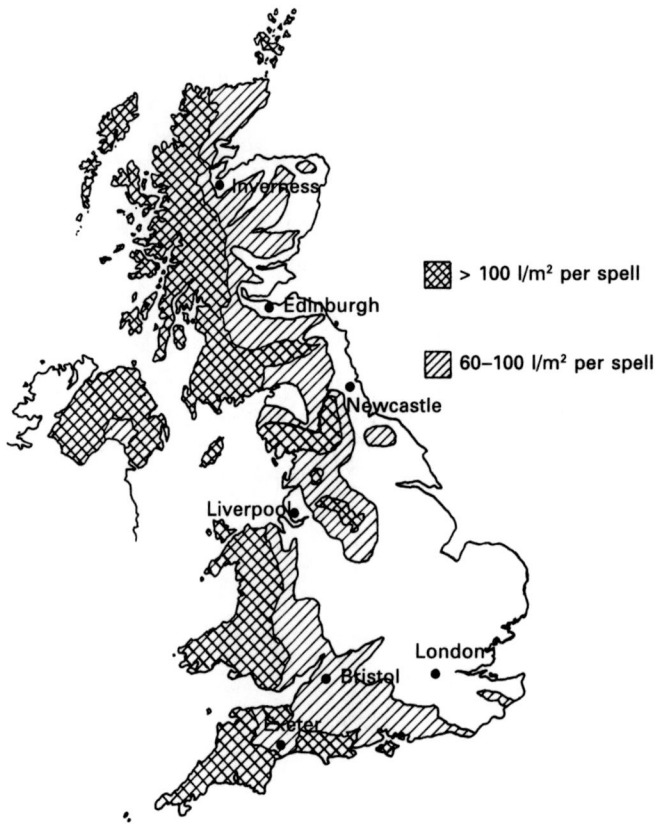

Figure 3.5.8 Principal areas exposed to driving rain.

BUILDING REGULATIONS

Approved Document C: *Site preparation and resistance to contaminants and moisture* identifies the need to incorporate checked rebates at openings exposed to driving rain. In the UK, driving rain exposure zones are mainly to the west and south-west coasts, as shown in Fig. 3.5.8. Isolated situations also occur, and location of these can be obtained from the local authority building control department. In keeping with the traditional construction shown, the frame is set behind the outer leaf of masonry. Contemporary practice also requires an insulated cavity, vertical dpc and cavity closer, as shown in Fig. 3.5.9.

Window head (vertical section)

Cavity tray

Weep holes

Galv. steel
box lintel

Sealant

25 mm check

**Window jamb/reveal
(sectional plan)**

25 mm check

Sealant

DPC

Window sill (vertical section)

Sealant

Sub-sill

DPC

50 mm cavity
(see notes)

Insulation

**Threshold (vertical section)
re. Disabled access**

Rubber weather seal
and aluminium
threshold plate

Drainage
channel

Brush
seal

Cavity
closer

Notes:
1. In areas most exposed to driving rain, a 50 mm air gap in the cavity between
   inner and outer leaf is necessary to prevent dampness bridging the insulation.
2. The detail shown has a 100 mm cavity part insulated and a 100 mm insulating
   block inner leaf. This will provide a *U* value of about 0.35. A 100 mm fully insulated
   cavity in a brick and insulating block wall has a *U* value of about 0.27.
3. To achieve the lesser *U* value and still retain a 50 mm air gap, the thickness of the
   inner leaf of insulating blockwork may be increased and/or additional insulation applied
   to the inside of the inner leaf behind a protective plasterboard lining.
4. See Part 8 – Insulation, for definition and calculation of *U* values.

Figure 3.5.9   Contemporary checked openings.

ARCHES

These are arrangements of wedge-shaped bricks called **voussoirs**, which are designed to support each other and carry the load over the opening, round a curved profile, to abutments on either side. An exception to this form is the flat or 'soldier' arch constructed of bricks laid on end or on edge.

When constructing an arch it must be given temporary support until the brick joints have set and the arch has gained sufficient strength to support itself and carry the load over the opening. These temporary supports are called **centres** and are usually made of timber; their design is governed by the span, load and thickness of the arch to be constructed.

■■■ SOLDIER ARCHES

This type of arch consists of a row of bricks showing on the face either the end or the edge of the bricks. Soldier arches have no real strength, and if the span is over 1000 mm they will require some form of permanent support such as a metal flat or angle (see Fig. 3.5.1). If permanent support is not given, the load will be transferred to the head of the frame in the opening instead of the jambs on either side. Small spans can have an arch of bonded brickwork by inserting into the horizontal joints immediately above the opening some form of reinforcement such as expanded metal or bricktor, which is a woven strip of high-tensile steel wires designed for the reinforcement of brick and stone walls. It is also possible to construct a soldier arch by inserting metal cramps in the vertical joints and casting these into an *in-situ* backing lintel of reinforced concrete.

■■■ ROUGH ARCHES

These arches are constructed of ordinary uncut bricks; being rectangular in shape, they give rise to wedge-shaped joints. To prevent the thick end of the joint from becoming too excessive, rough arches are usually constructed in header courses. The rough arch is used mainly as a backing or relieving arch to a gauged brick or stone arch, but they are sometime used in facework for the cheaper form of building or where appearance is of little importance.

▨▨■ GAUGED ARCHES

These are the true arches and are constructed of bricks cut to the required wedge shape, called **voussoirs**. The purpose of voussoirs is to produce a uniform thin joint that converges onto the centre point or points of the arch. There are two methods of cutting the bricks to the required wedge shape: **axed** and **rubbed**. If the brick is of a hard nature it is first marked with a tin saw, to produce a sharp arris, and then it is axed to the required profile. For rubbed brick arches a soft brick called a **rubber** is used; the bricks are first cut to the approximate shape with a saw, and are then finished off with an abrasive stone or file to produce the sharp arris. In both cases a template of plywood or hardboard to the required shape will be necessary for marking out the voussoirs. Typical examples of stone arches are shown in Fig. 3.1.4; the terminology and setting out of simple brick arches is shown in Fig. 3.6.1.

CENTRES

These are temporary structures, usually of light timber construction, which are strong enough to fulfil their function of supporting arches of brick or stone while they are being built and until they are sufficiently set to support themselves and the load over the opening. Centres can be an expensive item to a builder: therefore their design should be simple and adaptable so that as many uses as possible can be obtained from any one centre. A centre is always less in width than the soffit of an arch to allow for plumbing – that is, alignment and verticality of the face with a level or rule.

The type of centre to be used will depend upon:

■ the weight to be supported;
■ the span;
■ the width of the soffit.

Generally soffits not wider than 150 mm will require one rib at least 50 mm wide, and are usually called **turning pieces**. Soffits from 150 to 350 mm require two ribs, which are framed together using horizontal tie members called **laggings**. Soffits over 350 mm require three or more sets of ribs. The laggings are used to tie the framed ribs together and to provide a base upon which the arch can be built. Close laggings are those that are touching each other, forming a complete seating for a gauged arch; open laggings, spaced at twice the width of the laggings, centre to centre, are used for rough arches.

If the arch is composed of different materials – for example a stone arch with a relieving arch of brickwork – a separate centre for each material should be used. Typical examples of centres for brick arches are shown in Figs 3.6.2, 3.6.3 and 3.6.4.

Allow 40 mm for every 300 mm of span

Gauged brickwork

300

Allow 3 mm for
every 300 mm
of span

Camber to correct
illusion of sagging

Camber arch

Voussoirs

Key brick

Skewback

Abutment

Rise $\frac{1}{8}$ of
span

Span

Gauged segmental arch

Key brick

Voussoirs

Extrados

Intrados or
soffit

Springing

Springer

Abutment

Gauged semicircular arch

Figure 3.6.1   Typical examples of brick arches.

Figure 3.6.2   Centres for small-span arches.

Figure 3.6.3   Typical framed centre for spans up to 1500 mm.

Figure 3.6.4 Typical framed centre for spans up to 4000 mm.

Lightweight concrete
block inner leaf

Feature stone
or brick arch

Galv. or st./st.
cavity tray
and arch
support

Cavity wall
with closer

Arch opening

Brick
outer leaf

Gothic

**Elliptical or
three-centred**

Ogee

Triangular

Figure 3.6.5   Arch form and cavity tray.

CAVITY TRAYS

Arch construction can be simplified with structural support from a proprietary galvanised or stainless steel combined cavity tray and damp-proof course. Figure 3.6.5 shows the application and omission of conventional centring, saving considerable construction time as temporary supports are not required. The tray unifies the structural support with the damp-proof course and remains an integral part of the structure. Arch profiles are limited to tray manufacturers' designs and spans, but most will offer semicircular and segmental as standard, with gothic, elliptical, ogee and triangular styles available to order. Clear spans up to about 2 m are possible.

SOLID CONCRETE GROUND FLOOR CONSTRUCTION

The construction of a solid ground floor can be considered under three headings:

- hardcore;
- blinding;
- concrete bed or slab.

HARDCORE

The purpose of hardcore is to fill in any small pockets that have formed during oversite excavations, to provide a firm base on which to place a concrete bed and to help spread any point loads over a greater area. It also acts against capillary action of moisture within the soil. Hardcore is usually laid in 100–150 mm layers to the required depth, and it is important that each layer is well compacted, using a roller if necessary, to prevent any unacceptable settlement beneath the solid floor.

Approved Document C recommends that no hardcore laid under a solid ground floor should contain water-soluble sulphates or other harmful matter in such quantities as to be liable to cause damage to any part of the floor. This recommendation prevents the use of any material that may swell upon becoming moist, such as colliery shale, and furthermore it is necessary to ascertain that brick rubble from demolition works and clinker furnace waste intended for use as hardcore does not have any harmful water-soluble sulphate content.

BLINDING

This is used to even off the surface of hardcore if a damp-proof membrane is to be placed under the concrete bed or if a reinforced concrete bed is specified. First, it will prevent the damp-proof membrane from being punctured by the hardcore and, second, it will provide a true surface from which the reinforcement can be positioned. Blinding generally consists of a layer of sand 25–50 mm thick or a 50–75 mm layer of weak concrete (1:12 mix usually suitable) if a true surface for reinforced concrete is required.

▧▦■ CONCRETE BED

Thicknesses generally specified are:

- unreinforced or plain *in-situ* concrete, 100–150 mm thick;
- reinforced concrete, 150 mm minimum.

Suitable concrete mixes are produced to BS EN 206-1: *Concrete. Specification, performance, production and conformity*:

- plain *in-situ* concrete – 50 kg cement:0.11 m³ fine aggregate:0.16 m³ coarse aggregate or mix specification ST2;
- reinforced concrete – 50 kg cement:0.08 m³ fine aggregate:0.13 m³ coarse aggregate or mix specification ST4.

The reinforcement used in concrete beds for domestic work is usually in the form of a welded steel fabric to BS 4483. Sometimes a light square mesh fabric is placed 25 mm from the upper surface of the concrete bed to prevent surface crazing and limit the size of any cracking.

In domestic work the areas of concrete are defined by the room sizes, and it is not usually necessary to include expansion or contraction joints in the construction of the bed.

PROTECTION OF FLOORS NEXT TO THE GROUND

Building Regulation C2 requires that such part of a building as is next to the ground shall have a floor so constructed as to prevent the passage of moisture from the ground to the upper surface of the floor. The requirements of this regulation can be properly satisfied only by the provision of a suitable barrier in the form of a damp-proof membrane within the floor. The membrane should be turned up at the edges to meet and blend with the damp-proof course in the walls to prevent any penetration of moisture by capillary action at edges of the bed.

Suitable materials for damp-proof membranes are:

- polyethylene (LDPE) 1200 gauge (0.3 mm) sheet with sealed joints, which is acceptable and will also give protection against moisture vapour as well as moisture;
- hot-poured bitumen, which should be at least 3 mm thick;
- cold-applied bitumen/rubber emulsions, which should be applied in not less than three coats;
- asphalt/pitchmastic, which could be dual-purpose finish and damp-proof membrane.

Note: Prevention of the ingress of radon and/or methane gases from the ground will require a wire- or fibre-reinforced LDPE membrane of up to 1 mm thickness. Radon is a naturally occurring radioactive gas originating from uranium and radium deposits in certain rock subsoils found primarily in parts of the West Country, northern England and areas of Scotland. Methane is an explosive gas, which can build up in the ground as a result of deposited decaying organic materials. Where either of these gases is prevalent, it is now standard practice to construct suspended precast concrete floors with natural draught underfloor ventilation – see Chapter 4.5.

Figure 4.1.1 Typical solid floor details at external walls.

Thermal insulation

DPC

Reinforced cement/sand screed

Well-compacted hardcore

Heavily loaded internal wall

Damp-proof membrane

Plain *in-situ* concrete (1:3:6) bed

Mass concrete (1:3:6) strip foundation

Lightly loaded internal wall

Plain *in-situ* concrete (1:3:6) bed

DPC

Reinforced screed

Damp-proof membrane

Thermal insulation

Concrete bed thickened locally under wall

Well-compacted hardcore

Non-loadbearing internal wall

Plain *in-situ* concrete (1:3:6) bed

Well-compacted hardcore

DPC

Reinforced screed

Damp-proof membrane

Thermal insulation

Figure 4.1.2   Typical solid floor details at internal walls.

The position of a damp-proof membrane, whether above or below the concrete bed, is a matter of individual choice. A membrane placed above the bed is the easiest method from a practical aspect and is therefore generally used. A membrane placed below the bed has two advantages: first, it will keep the concrete bed dry and in so doing will make the bed a better thermal insulator and, second, during construction it will act as a separating layer preventing leakage of the cement matrix into the hardcore layer, which could result in a weak concrete mix. Typical details of solid floor construction are shown in Figs 4.1.1 and 4.1.2.

SUSPENDED CONCRETE GROUND FLOOR CONSTRUCTION

■■■ BEAM AND BLOCK FLOOR

This type of domestic floor system is derived from the principles of the precast hollow and composite floor systems used for commercial buildings and apartments, as detailed in Chapter 4.5. It has developed into a cost- and time-effective means of constructing domestic ground and upper floors, by incorporating precast concrete beams with lightweight concrete blocks as an infilling. The benefits of quality-controlled factory manufacture of components and simple site assembly with the aid of a mobile crane to hoist the beams add to the following advantages:

■ potential to span over unsound infilling, common to sloping sites.
■ application over movable subsoils such as shrinkable clay (see Chapter 2.7).
■ suitability where ventilation under the ground floor is required to dilute intrusive gases.

The Building Regulations, Approved Document C, requires a minimum clear void depth of 75 mm below these floors, but it is usual practice to leave at least 150 mm. Ventilation of the void is advisable to dilute and prevent concentration of gases from the ground (radon and/or methane) and possible leakage from piped services. Figure 4.2.1 shows typical construction of a domestic suspended beam and block floor, where the stripped topsoil leaves the underfloor surface lower than adjacent ground. This is acceptable only if the soil is free draining. Also, ground differentials should be minimal, otherwise the external wall becomes a retaining wall and will require specific design calculations. All organic material should be removed from the void, and the surface should be treated with weedkiller. Void depth may need to be as much as 225 mm in the presence of heavy clay subsoil and nearby trees (see Chapter 2.7).

Upper floors follow the same principles of assembly, with purpose-made trimmer shoes providing support to concrete beams around stair openings. Span potential is

Figure 4.2.1 Beam and block domestic ground floor.

only about 5 m: therefore intermediate support from a loadbearing partition or a steel beam is acceptable. Direct flange bearing is possible, but if a deep section is required the floor structure may be accommodated on ledger angles. Typical upper floor details are shown in Fig. 4.2.2.

▨ ▨ ■ BEAM AND EXPANDED POLYSTYRENE (EPS) BLOCK

Precast concrete beams with EPS block infill units have developed from the beam and block principles applied to domestic floor construction. As a construction technique it has the advantages of speed and simplicity with exceptional thermal performance. Thermal insulation U values for the floor as a whole are about 0.20 W/m^{2}K, depending on the thickness and amount of EPS relative to rib spacing. The system is in effect a structurally adequate floor, with integral insulation.

The construction principles are the same as described for suspended beam (rib) and block, with some variation on rib spacing to suit EPS block width. Figures 4.2.3 and 4.2.4 show different block forms and applications. Figure 4.2.3 shows EPS units functioning as both insulation and permanent shuttering to an in-situ reinforced concrete diaphragm suspended ground floor. Figure 4.2.4 shows typical dry construction, using a moisture-resistant chipboard surface finish.

Beams staggered

Loadbearing wall

Partition support

Partition

In-situ concrete filling

Double beam

Galv. steel trimmer shoe

Double beam support

PCC beam

In-situ concrete filling between staggered beams

RSJ or UB

75 mm nominal bearing (100 mm)

PCC beam notched to flange of UB

102 × 76 mm ledger angle welded to web of UB

100 mm bearing

Steelwork support – 2 methods

Figure 4.2.2   Beam and block – upper floor intermediate support.

Figure 4.2.3   Typical EPS block floor for structural screed topping.

Figure 4.2.4   Typical EPS block floor for a chipboard finish.

SUSPENDED TIMBER FLOORS

■■■ SUSPENDED TIMBER GROUND FLOORS

This type of floor consists of timber boards or other suitable sheet material fixed to joists spanning over sleeper walls, and was until 1939 the common method of forming ground floors in domestic buildings. The Second World War restricted the availability of suitable timber, and solid ground floors replaced suspended timber floors. Suspended precast concrete floors have gained popularity in recent times, not only as a precaution against radon and methane, but as a less expensive form of construction. These are considered in more detail in Chapter 4.2. Today the timber floor is still used on occasions because it has some flexibility and will easily accept nail fixings – properties that a solid ground floor lacks. It is a more expensive form of construction than a concrete floor and can only be justified to match existing construction where a building is extended. It could be used on sloping sites that require a great deal of filling to make up the ground to the specified floor level, although a precast concrete flooring system could also be used, and this is likely to be much cheaper.

Suspended timber ground floors are susceptible to dry rot and draughts, and are said to be colder than other forms of flooring. If the floor is correctly designed and constructed these faults can be eliminated.

The problem of dry rot, which is a fungus that attacks damp timber, can be overcome by adequate ventilation under the floor and the correct positioning of damp-proof courses to keep the under floor area and timber dry. Through-ventilation is essential to keep the moisture content of the timber below that which would allow fungal growth to take place: that is, 20% of its oven-dry weight. The usual method is to allow a free flow of air under the floor covering by providing air bricks in the external walls. These are sited near the corners and at approximately 2 m centres around the perimeter of the building. They must have an equivalent of 1500 mm^2/m run of wall; alternatively, 500 mm^2/m^2 of floor area will also be acceptable (take greater value). If a suspended timber floor is used with an adjacent solid ground floor, pipes of 100 mm diameter are used under the solid floor to convey air to and from the external walls to the suspended floor.

▨▩◼ BUILDING REGULATIONS

Building Regulation C2 applies as with solid floors and recommended provisions are given in Approved Document C. Figure 4.3.1 shows the minimum dimensions recommended in Approved Document C but in practice a greater space between the concrete bed and the timber is usual. The honeycomb sleeper walls are usually built two or three courses high to allow good through-ventilation. Sleeper walls spaced at 2000 mm centres will give an economic joist size. The width of joists is usually taken as 50 mm: this will give sufficient width for the nails securing the covering, and the depth can be obtained by reference to design tables recommended in Approved Document A or by design calculations. The usual joist depth for domestic work is 125 mm.

LAYOUT

The most economic layout is to span the joists across the shortest distance of the room: this means that joists could be either parallel or at right angles to a fireplace. The fireplace must be constructed of non-combustible materials and comply with Building Regulation J3. Typical examples are shown in Figs 4.3.2 and 4.3.3.

INSULATION IN GROUND FLOORS

Rigid polystyrene or high-density mineral wool can be incorporated within a solid floor structure to comply with the Building Regulations Approved Document L: *Conservation of fuel and power*. Location may be above the damp-proof membrane and below the concrete slab, or between the screed and concrete slab. If the latter, the screed should be at least 75 mm thickness and wire reinforced against cracking. Suspended timber floors can incorporate mineral fibre insulation draped on nylon netting between the joists, or have rigid insulation boards spanning the gap between joists. More detail of thermal insulation in floors is provided in Chapter 8.2.

▨▩◼ SUSPENDED TIMBER UPPER FLOORS

Timber, being a combustible material, is restricted by Part B of the Building Regulations to small domestic buildings as a structural flooring material. Its popularity in this context is due to its low cost in relationship to other structural flooring methods and materials. Structural softwood is readily available at a reasonable cost, is easily worked and has a good strength to weight ratio, and is therefore suitable for domestic loadings.

Figure 4.3.1   Building Regulations and suspended timber floors.

Cement particle board connecting piece

Air brick of galv. cast iron, plastic or terra cotta

Typical air brick detail

Underfloor space to be clear of debris and have through-ventilation

Concrete not less than 100 thick composed of 50 kg cement:0.13 m³ fine aggregate:0.18 m³ coarse aggregate laid entirely above highest adjoining ground unless laid to falls to drainage outlet at lowest level of adjoining ground

Thermal insulation between joists

t & g boards

150 min.

75 min.

Joists at 400 c/c fixed clear of external wall

Honeycomb built sleeper wall

DPC below level of wall plate

Well-compacted hardcore

Mass concrete strip foundation

Air bricks connected with slate trunking or similar

Cavity to extend 150 below lowest DPC

150

Cavity filling

Figure 4.3.2 Typical details of suspended floor – joists parallel to fireplace.

Note: Detail historic, therefore blockwork and insulation omitted

External wall

T & G flooring nailed to joists

125 × 50 joists at 400 c/c

100 × 75 wall plate

32 wide strap fixings at 750 c/c

DPC

Half-brick honeycomb sleeper walls at 2.000 c/c

Mass concrete bed

Well-compacted hardcore

Mass concrete strip foundation

Half brick fender wall

125 mm thick concrete constructional hearth

Rubble-filled void

DPC

150

500

328

T & G flooring nailed to joists

100×75 wall plate

32 wide strap fixings at 750 c/c

125×50 joists at 400 c/c

DPC

Half brick honeycomb sleeper walls at 2.000 c/c

Mass concrete bed

Well-compacted hardcore

Sleeper wall

External wall

Fender wall

Mass concrete strip foundation

150

500

328

125 mm thick concrete constructional hearth

Rubble filled void

DPC

Note: Detail historic, therefore blockwork and insulation omitted

Figure 4.3.3 Typical details of suspended timber floor – joists at right angles to fireplace.

Terminology
- **Common joist** A joist spanning from support to support.
- **Trimming joist** Span as for common joist, but it is usually 25 mm thicker and supports a trimmer joist.
- **Trimmer joist** A joist at right angles to the main span supporting the trimmed joists; is usually 25 mm thicker than a common joist.
- **Trimmed joist** A joist cut short to form an opening, and supported by a trimmer joist; it spans in the same direction as common joists and is of the same section size.

JOIST SIZING

There are three ways of selecting a suitable joist size for supporting a domestic type floor:

1. Rule of thumb for joists of 50 mm width, spaced at 400 mm centres:

$$\frac{\text{span in mm}}{24} + 50 \text{ mm} = \text{depth in mm}$$

For example, for a 3.6 m span:

$$\frac{3600}{24} + 50 = 170 \text{ mm}$$

Therefore commercial size of joist chosen is 175 mm × 50 mm @ 400 mm c/c.
   Some comparisons can be made with the methods shown in 2 and 3. However, the 'rule' is limited as a simple means of guidance for joist spacing at 400 mm only.

2. Calculation:

$$\text{BM} = \frac{fbd^2}{6} = \frac{WL}{8}$$

where   BM = bending moment
   f = maximum fibre stress in N/mm^2 (see Chapter 3.8)
   b = breadth in mm
   d = depth in mm
   W = total load on joist in newtons (N)
   L = clear length or span of joist in mm

For example, see Fig. 4.3.4.

   Loading on each joist:
      Imposed load = 4.5 m × 0.45 m × 1.5 kN = 3.04 kN
   Dead loads:
         Floorboards (4.5 m × 0.45 m × 10 kg)
      + Plasterboard (4.5 m × 0.45 m × 11 kg)
         = 42.53 kg × 9.81 × 10^{-3} = 0.42 kN

      Total loading on each joist = 3.04 kN + 0.42 kN = 3.46 kN (3460 N)

Figure 4.3.4   Joist calculations.

Note: The self-weight of the joist is usually omitted, as this is small compared with the load carried. Moreover, the commercial joist size selected is normally greater than the calculated size, and this will cover the self-weight.

$$\frac{fbd^2}{6} = \frac{WL}{8}$$

From Table 3.8.3, GS (general structural) grade timber of strength class C16 has a fibre stress (f) of 5.3 N/mm^2.

Transposing the bending moment formula to make d the subject and taking b, the breadth, as 50 mm:

$$d^2 = \frac{6WL}{8fb} = \frac{6 \times 3460 \times 4500}{8 \times 5.3 \times 50} = 44\ 066$$

$$d = \sqrt{44\ 066} = 210 \text{ mm}$$

225 mm is the nearest commercial timber size above 210 mm. Therefore 225 mm × 50 mm @ 450 mm spacing will be selected. 225 mm × 50 mm in Table 4.3.1 is comparable with a maximum clear span of 4.47 m for joists at 450 mm spacing.

3. Building Regulations. Approved Document A: *Timber intermediate floors for dwellings* and *Span tables for solid timber members*, both published by TRADA.

Table 4.3.1 provides some guidance where selection of timber is general structural (GS).

Table 4.3.1   Guide to span and loading potential for GS grade timber floor joists.

	Dead weight of floor and ceiling, excluding self-weight of joist (see notes)								
	< 25 kg/m^2 < 0.25 kN/m^2			25–50 0.25–0.50			50–125 0.50–1.25		
	Spacing of joists mm (c/c)								
Sawn size of joist (mm)	400	450	600	400	450	600	400	450	600
	Maximum clear span (m)								
38 × 100	1.83	1.69	1.30	1.72	1.56	1.21	1.42	1.30	1.04
38 × 125	2.48	2.39	1.93	2.37	2.22	1.76	1.95	1.79	1.45
38 × 150	2.98	2.87	2.51	2.85	2.71	2.33	2.45	2.29	1.87
38 × 175	3.44	3.31	2.87	3.28	3.10	2.69	2.81	2.65	2.27
38 × 200	3.94	3.75	3.26	3.72	3.52	3.06	3.19	3.01	2.61
38 × 225	4.43	4.19	3.65	4.16	3.93	3.42	3.57	3.37	2.92
50 × 100	2.08	1.97	1.67	1.98	1.87	1.54	1.74	1.60	1.29
50 × 125	2.72	2.62	2.37	2.60	2.50	2.19	2.33	2.17	1.77
50 × 150	3.27	3.14	2.86	3.13	3.01	2.69	2.81	2.65	2.27
50 × 175	3.77	3.62	3.29	3.61	3.47	3.08	3.21	3.03	2.63
50 × 200	4.31	4.15	3.73	4.13	3.97	3.50	3.65	3.44	2.99
50 × 225	4.79	4.66	4.17	4.64	4.47	3.91	4.07	3.85	3.35
63 × 100	2.32	2.20	1.92	2.19	2.08	1.82	1.93	1.84	1.53
63 × 125	2.93	2.82	2.57	2.81	2.70	2.45	2.53	2.43	2.09
63 × 150	3.52	3.39	3.08	3.37	3.24	2.95	3.04	2.92	2.58
63 × 175	4.06	3.91	3.56	3.89	3.74	3.40	3.50	3.37	2.95
63 × 200	4.63	4.47	4.07	4.44	4.28	3.90	4.01	3.85	3.35
63 × 225	5.06	4.92	4.58	4.91	4.77	4.37	4.51	4.30	3.75
75 × 125	3.10	2.99	2.72	2.97	2.86	2.60	2.68	2.58	2.33
75 × 150	3.72	3.58	3.27	3.56	3.43	3.13	3.22	3.09	2.81
75 × 175	4.28	4.13	3.77	4.11	3.96	3.61	3.71	3.57	3.21
75 × 200	4.83	4.70	4.31	4.68	4.52	4.13	4.24	4.08	3.65
75 × 225	5.27	5.13	4.79	5.11	4.97	4.64	4.74	4.60	4.07

Notes:
1. The table allows for up to 1.5 kN/m^2 of imposed loading due to furniture and people. For imposed loading greater than this, calculations must be used.
2. For dead loading in excess of 1.25 kN/m^2 calculations must also be used.
3. Softwood floor boards should be at least 16 mm finished thickness for joist spacing up to 450 mm. 19 mm min. thickness will be required for joist spacing of 600 mm.
4. Joists should be duplicated below a bath.
5. Dead loading is usually summated in kg. To convert to a force in newtons (N), multiply by the gravitational factor 9.81 (say 10). For example: 25 kg × 10 = 250 N, or 0.25 kN.
6. See BS 648: *Schedule of weights of building materials* for material dead loads.

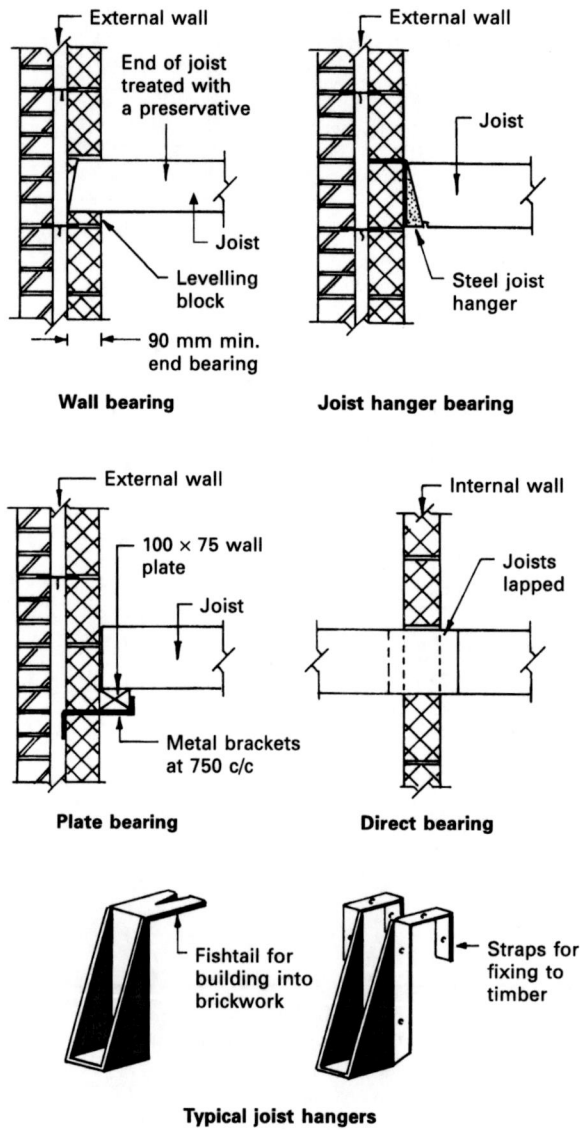

Wall bearing

- External wall
- End of joist treated with a preservative
- Joist
- Levelling block
- 90 mm min. end bearing

Joist hanger bearing

- External wall
- Joist
- Steel joist hanger

Plate bearing

- External wall
- 100 × 75 wall plate
- Joist
- Metal brackets at 750 c/c

Direct bearing

- Internal wall
- Joists lapped

Typical joist hangers

- Fishtail for building into brickwork
- Straps for fixing to timber

Note: Insulation in external wall cavity if required (see Ch. 8.2)

Figure 4.3.5   Typical joist support details.

JOISTS

If the floor is framed with structural softwood joists of a size not less than that required by the Approved Document, the usual width is taken as 50 mm. The joists are spaced at 400–600 mm centre to centre, depending on the width of the ceiling boards that are to be fixed on the underside. Maximum economy of joist size is obtained by spanning in the direction of the shortest distance to keep within the deflection limitations allowed. The maximum economic span for joists is between 3500 and 4500 mm; for spans over this a double floor could be used.

Support

The ends of the joists must be supported by loadbearing walls. The common methods are to build in the ends, or to use special metal fixings called **joist hangers**; other methods are possible but are seldom employed. Support on internal loadbearing walls can be by joist hangers or direct bearing when the joists are generally lapped (see Fig. 4.3.5).

Trimming

This is a term used to describe the framing of joists around an opening or projection. Various joints can be used to connect the members together, all of which can be substituted by joist hangers. Trimming around flues and upper floor fireplaces should comply with the recommendations of Approved Document J. It should be noted that, as central heating is becoming commonplace, the provision of upper-floor fireplaces is seldom included in modern designs, because they are considered to be superfluous. However, they are frequently encountered in renovation and maintenance work to older properties. Typical trimming joints and arrangements are shown in Figs 4.3.6 and 4.3.7.

Strutting

Shrinkage in timber joists will cause twisting to occur: this will result in movement of the ceiling below, and could cause the finishes to crack. To prevent this, strutting is used between the joists if the total span exceeds 2400 mm, the strutting being placed at mid-span (see Fig. 4.3.8).

DOUBLE FLOORS

These can be used on spans over 4500 mm to give a lower floor area free of internal walls. They consist of a steel beam or timber binder spanning the shortest distance, which supports common joists spanning at right angles. The beam reduces the span of the common joists to a distance that is less than the shortest span to allow an economic joist section to be used. The use of a timber binder was a popular method, but it is generally considered to be uneconomic when compared with a standard steel beam section. Typical details are shown in Fig. 4.3.9.

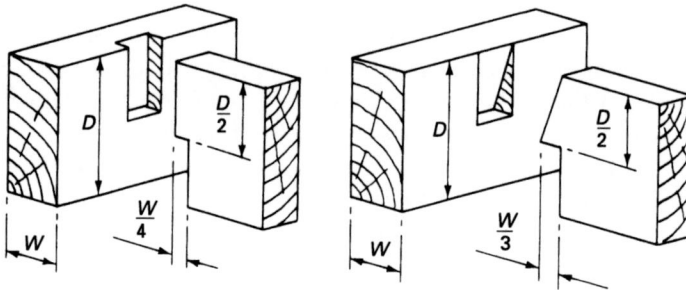

Housed joint

Bevelled housed joint

Tusked tenon joint

Typical stairwell trimming

Figure 4.3.6   Floor trimming joints and details.

200 min.

Flue from ground floor
fireplace

Common
joist

Trimmer

500
min.

Trimming
joist

Trimmed
joist

Trimming to upper floor fireplace

Stairwell

Common
joist

Trimming
joist

Joist/block
interface
mastic-sealed
against air leakage

Trimmer

Trimmed joist

Trimming to stairwell

200
min.

50
min.

Joist
hangers

Noggin

200 min.

50
min.

Trimming around flues

Note: Recess constructed of solid non-combustible material.

Figure 4.3.7   Typical trimming arrangements.

Figure 4.3.8 Strutting arrangements.

Typical double-floor layout

Cogged joint

Typical details using timber binder or steel beam

Figure 4.3.9   Double floor details.

If the span is such that a double floor is deemed necessary it would be a useful exercise to compare the cost with that of other flooring methods, such as *in-situ* reinforced concrete and precast concrete systems, which, overall, could be a cheaper and more practical solution to the problem.

COMPOSITE BEAMS/JOISTS FOR SUSPENDED FLOOR CONSTRUCTION

A double floor can be used for modest spans using a steel joist or large cross-section timber beam as intermediate floor joist support. For greater spans double flooring is uneconomic, as intermediate beams would need to be excessively large to carry the floor structure while still retaining minimal deflection (max. $0.003 \times$ span).

Spans up to about 8000 mm can be achieved cost-effectively by using composite beams at normal joist spacing of 400–600 mm. These are categorised as follows:

■ open-web or steel web system joists;
■ solid or boarded web joists.

Note: Where joists are built directly into blockwork, they must be mastic sealed against air leakage.

Figure 4.3.10   Open-web joist.

Open-web joists

These are a type of lattice frame, as shown in Fig. 4.3.10. They consist of a pair of parallel stress-graded timber flanges, spaced apart with V-shaped galvanised steel web members. Open-web joists are manufactured off-site to specific spans in a factory quality-controlled environment.

Solid or boarded web joists

These are an alternative high-strength, relatively lightweight factory-produced joist system. A typical manufactured boarded web joist is shown in Fig. 4.3.11. This comprises a pair of stress-graded timber flanges separated by a central solid web of plywood or oriented strand board (OSB). At comparable joist depths,

Figure 4.3.11   Solid or boarded web joist.

span potential is greater than with open web joists, with up to 10 000 mm possible. Solid web joists are less convenient for accommodating pipes and cables running at right angles to the joists. As for traditional timber-joisted floors, care and consideration must be exercised when cutting holes. The central area or neutral axis is the preferred location, away from the shear stress areas near supports. Flanges should never be notched.

Advantages of composite beams/joists
- Also suitable for other applications, e.g. roofing members.
- Factory produced to individual site/design dimensions; less site waste.
- High strength-to-weight ratio.
- Minimal shrinkage and movement, therefore limited use of strutting.
- Generally deeper than conventional joists, therefore less deflection.
- Wide section (typically ex. 75 mm flanges) provides large bearing area for floor deck and ceiling.

Open web joists have the additional benefit of providing virtually uninterrupted space for services, and they do not require end bearing; that is, joists can be top flange suspended.

4.4

RAISED ACCESS FLOORS

These are a system of elevated platforms suspended over the structural floor of *in-situ* or precast concrete. They are not new in concept, and form the basis of deck construction popular about the outside of North American homes. Used internally, they evolved primarily in response to the information technology revolution that occurred in the latter part of the twentieth century. Although the huge volume of power, telephone and data cabling in modern offices has been largely responsible for developments in raised platforms, location for service pipes and ventilation ducts has also been influential. The dominance of services issues has promoted a re-think for designers, with the need for greater floor-to-floor heights to incorporate these floor voids (and suspended ceilings).

▨▩■ PARTIAL ACCESS

This is where the floor finish is secured, and access is limited – possibly into simple ducts or trunking, as shown in Fig. 4.4.1. They are most suited for access to mains cabling for power and lighting, with void depths limited to about 100 mm. Accesses should be positioned to avoid furniture and be strategically located over junction boxes. This provides flexibility for changes in cable distribution where workstations and work functions may change.

▨▩■ FULL ACCESS

These comprise standard-size (600 mm × 600 mm) interchangeable floor panels elevated on adjustable pedestals to provide multi-directional void space. Heights usually vary between 100 and 600 mm, but extremes of as little as 50 mm and as much as 2 m are possible. Adjustable-height pedestals are manufactured from steel or polypropylene, with support plates containing four lugs or projections to locate loose-fit decking panels. Threaded flat support plates may be specified where panels are to be screw-fixed in place (see Fig. 4.4.2).

Carpet floor finish
if required

Detachable
panel

Screed

40, 50
or 65 mm

Structural
floor

Cable duct/trunking
of galv. steel or uPVC,
up to 200 mm wide

Figure 4.4.1 Floor duct.

Floor panel

Countersunk
screw

Threaded
support plate

Locating lug

Support plate

Adjustable
leg

Lock nut

Base
plate

Loose-fit
panel

**Alternative with
projecting lugs
(plan view)**

Resin bonding or
screw fixing to floor

Figure 4.4.2 Adjustable pedestal.

Figure 4.4.3   Raised access floor.

Floor panels or decking materials can vary considerably to suit application. Timber joists or battens may be used to support softwood boards or plywood/chipboard sheets, particularly if matching a traditional suspended floor. Office specification usually requires a fully interchangeable system with standard 600 mm × 600 mm panels. These are available in various gradings including light, medium and heavy, with corresponding maximum loadings of 10, 20 and 50 kN/m^2. Panel construction and application are shown in Fig. 4.4.3.

The combination of fully bonded chipboard within a steel casing provides structural soundness and integrity in the event of fire. The chipboard acts as a fire, acoustic and thermal insulator, and the steel resists tensile loading, also protecting the core against spread of flame. The presence of extraneous metal requires contact protection by electrical earth continuity through the complete floor system.

4.5

PRECAST CONCRETE FLOORS

The function of any floor is to provide a level surface that is capable of supporting all the live and dead loads imposed. Reinforced concrete, with its flexibility in design, good fire resistance and sound-insulating properties, is widely used for the construction of suspended floors for all types of building. The disadvantages of *in-situ* concrete are:

■ the need for formwork;
■ the time taken for the concrete to cure before the formwork can be released for reuse and the floor made available as a working area;
■ the very small contribution by a large proportion of the concrete to the strength of the floor.

Floors composed of reinforced precast concrete units have been developed over the years to overcome some or all of the disadvantages of *in-situ* reinforced concrete slab. To realise the full economy of any one particular precast flooring system the design of the floors should be within the span, width, loading and layout limitations of the units under consideration, coupled with the advantages of repetition.

■■■ CHOICE OF SYSTEM

Before any system of precast concrete flooring can be considered in detail the following factors must be taken into account:

■ maximum span;
■ nature of support;
■ weight of units;
■ thickness of units;
■ thermal insulation properties;

■ sound insulation properties;
■ fire resistance of units;
■ speed of construction;
■ amount of temporary support required.

The systems available can be considered as either precast hollow floors or composite floors; further subdivision is possible by taking into account the amount of temporary support required during the construction period.

PRECAST HOLLOW FLOORS

Precast hollow floor units are available in a variety of sections such as box planks or beams; tee sections, I beam sections and channel sections (see Fig. 4.5.1). The economies that can reasonably be expected over the *in-situ* floor are:

■ 50% reduction in the volume of concrete;
■ 25% reduction in the weight of reinforcement;
■ 10% reduction in size of foundations.

The units are cast in precision moulds, around inflatable formers or foamed plastic cores. The units are laid side by side, with the edge joints being grouted together; a structural topping is not required, but the upper surface of the units is usually screeded to provide the correct surface for the applied finishes (see Fig. 4.5.1). Little or no propping is required during the construction period, but usually some means of mechanical lifting is required to offload and position the units. Hollow units are normally the cheapest form of precast concrete suspended floor for simple straight spans with beam or wall supports up to a maximum span of 20.000 m. They are not considered suitable where heavy point loads are encountered unless a structural topping is used to spread the load over a suitable area.

The hollow beams or planks give a flat soffit, which can be left in its natural state or be given a skim coat of plaster; the voids in the units can be used to house the services that are normally incorporated in the depth of the floor. The ribbed soffit of the channel and tee units can be masked by a suspended ceiling; again, the voids created can be utilised to house the services. Special units are available with fixing inserts for suspended ceilings, service outlets and edges to openings.

COMPOSITE FLOORS

These floors are a combination of precast units and *in-situ* concrete. The precast units, which are usually prestressed or reinforced with high-yield steel bars, are used to provide the strength of the floor with the smallest depth practicable and at the same time act as permanent formwork to the *in-situ* topping, which provides the compressive strength required. It is essential that an adequate bond is achieved between the two components. In most cases this is provided by the upper surface texture of the precast units; alternatively a mild steel fabric can be fixed over the units before the *in-situ* topping is laid.

Floor finish

Anti-crack reinforcement

Cement/sand screed
to suit floor finish

125 to 200

400

Void

Grouted
joint

Edge shaped
to form key

Internal
support

Spans up to 13.000

Typical hollow floor unit details

Cement/sand screed
to suit floor finish

Floor finish

Grouted
joint

100 to 250

Edge shaped
to form key

400

Spans up to 6.750

Anti-crack reinforcement required if units
are continuous over internal supports

Typical channel section floor unit details

Figure 4.5.1   Precast concrete hollow floors.

Figure 4.5.2   Composite floors – prestressed plank.

Composite floors generally take one of two forms:

■ thin prestressed planks with a side key and covered with an *in-situ* topping (see Fig. 4.5.2).
■ reinforced or prestressed narrow beams, which are placed at 600 mm centres and are bridged by concrete filler blocks known as **pots**. The whole combination is covered with *in-situ* structural concrete topping. Most of the beams used in this method have a shear reinforcing cage projecting from the precast beam section (see Fig. 4.5.3).

In both forms temporary support should be given to the precast units by props at 1.800–2.400 m centres until the *in-situ* topping has cured.

▨▨■ COMPARISON OF SYSTEMS

Precast hollow floors are generally cheaper than composite; *in-situ* concrete is not required, and therefore the need for mixing plant and storage of materials is eliminated. The units are self-centring, therefore temporary support is not required; the construction period is considerably shorter; and generally the overall weight is less.

Composite floors will act in the same manner as an *in-situ* floor and can therefore be designed for more complex loadings. The formation of cantilevers is easier with this system, and support beams can be designed within the depth of the floor, giving a flat soffit. Services can be housed within the structural *in-situ* topping, or within the voids of the filler blocks. Like the precast hollow floor, composite floors are generally cheaper than a comparable *in-situ* floor, within the limitations of the system employed.

Mild steel
bar

In-situ
structural
concrete topping

Concrete
or clay
filler
blocks

50 to 250

Shear
cage

Void

High-
yield
bar

'Omnia'
precast concrete
planks at 600 c/c

440

225

40 mm
bearing

Mild steel bars

Max. span 12.000

Typical composite floor using PCC planks

In-situ structural
concrete topping

Max. span 6.000

150

Void

225

440

Precast
prestressed concrete
beams at 600 c/c

Concrete or clay filler blocks

Typical composite floor using PCC beams

Figure 4.5.3   Composite floors – beam or pot.

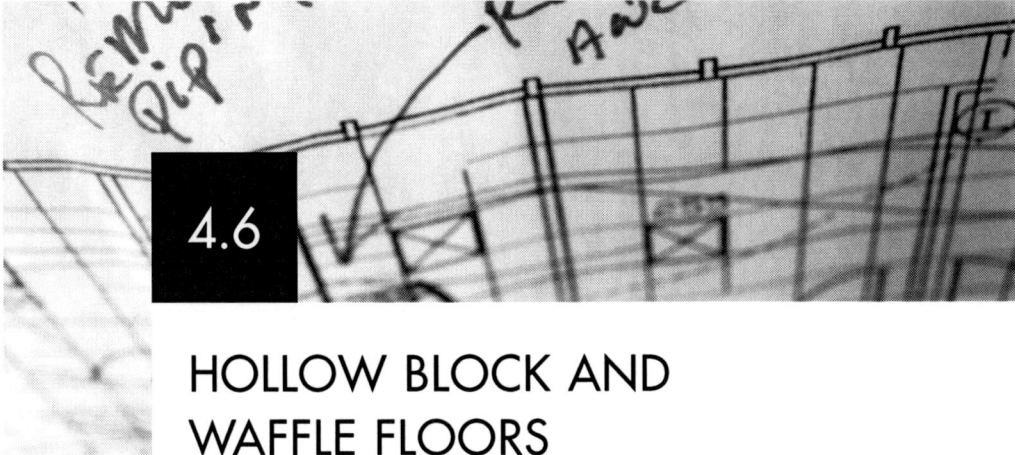

HOLLOW BLOCK AND
WAFFLE FLOORS

Precast concrete suspended floors are generally considered to be for light to medium loadings spanning in one direction. Hollow block, or hollow pot floors as they are sometimes called, and waffle or honeycomb floors can be used as an alternative to the single spanning precast floor, because they can be designed to carry heavier loadings. They are in fact ribbed floors consisting of closely spaced narrow and shallow beams giving an overall reduction in depth of the conventional reinforced concrete *in-situ* beam and slab floor.

■■■ HOLLOW BLOCK FLOORS

These are formed by laying over conventional floor soffit formwork a series of hollow lightweight clay blocks or pots in parallel rows, with a space between these rows to form the ribs. The blocks act as permanent formwork, giving a flat soffit suitable for plaster application, and impart good thermal insulation and fire resistance to the floor. The ribs formed between the blocks can be reinforced to suit the loading conditions of the floor, thus providing flexibility of design (see Fig. 4.6.1). The main advantages of this system are its light weight, which is generally less than comparable floors of concrete construction, and its relatively low cost.

■■■ WAFFLE OR HONEYCOMB FLOORS

These are used mainly as an alternative to an *in-situ* flat slab or a beam and slab suspended floor, because they require less concrete, less reinforcement, and can be used to reduce the number of beams and columns required, with resultant savings on foundations. The honeycomb pattern on the underside can add to the visual aspect of the ceiling by casting attractive shadow patterns.

The floor is cast over lightweight moulds or pans made of glass fibre, polypropylene or steel, forming a two-directional ribbed floor (see Fig. 4.6.2).

Figure 4.6.1   Hollow block floor.

Typical waffle
floor mould

Plan size 800 × 800
depths 225, 300 and 375

Rib reinforcement
to design

In-situ ribs at 800 c/c

In-situ ribs
at 800 c/c

50 mm thick *in-situ* topping
reinforced with welded fabric

RC edge beam

RC edge beam

Honeycomb
indents left
by moulds

Figure 4.6.2   Waffle or honeycomb floor.

The moulds are very strong, lightweight, and are capable of supporting all the normal loads encountered in building works. Support is reduced to the minimum because the moulds are arranged in parallel rows and span between the parallel lines of temporary supports.

The reinforcement in the ribs is laid in two directions to resist both longitudinal and transverse bending moments in the slab. Generally three mould depths are available, but the overall depth can be increased by adding to the depth of the topping.

With all floors using an *in-situ* topping it is possible to float the surface in preparation for the applied finishes, but this surface may suffer damage while being used by the following trades. It may therefore be better to allow for a floor

Figure 4.6.3   Inverted trough mould.

Figure 4.6.4   Inverted trough floor.

Figure 4.6.5   Temporary support to inverted trough floor.

screed to be applied to the *in-situ* topping at a later stage in the contract, prior to the fixing of the applied finish.

▓ ▓ ▓ INVERTED TROUGH FLOOR

The inverted trough moulds shown in Fig. 4.6.3 are used to produce an elongated reinforced concrete variation of the waffle trough type of floor. The moulds ensure that *in-situ* reinforced concrete is in specific locations only, saving considerably on concrete costs and the dead weight that the concrete would otherwise contribute. The one-way spanning floor is viewed from the underside in Fig. 4.6.4. Lateral beams may also be incorporated as interim support in large-span situations. The continuous longitudinal voids provide an unobtrusive location for service pipes and cables. Brackets or threaded inserts set in the underside of the concrete can provide support for services and for suspending a ceiling.

TEMPORARY SUPPORT

Support to troughs is from a framework of props, bearers and decking, as shown in Fig. 4.6.5. Prop spacing is determined by anticipated loading of operatives and wet concrete. After the concrete has gained strength and the temporary support is removed, the expanded polystyrene core and polypropylene mould are struck with a flat-bladed implement. With careful handling, cores and moulds have several reuses before being discarded.

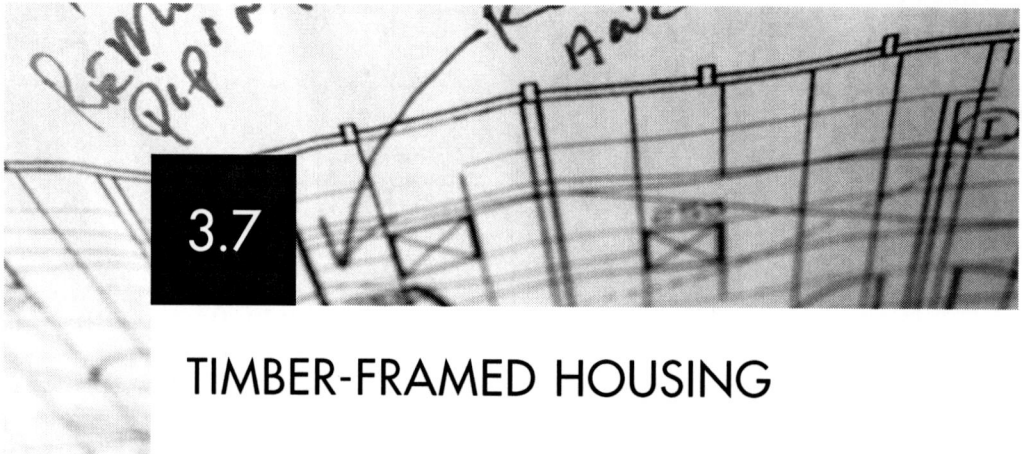

TIMBER-FRAMED HOUSING

Timber framing of softwood members and sheet facings has a long association with non-loadbearing partition walls (see timber stud partitions – Chapter 7.7). Loadbearing timber walls for small buildings such as dwelling houses may be constructed by creating a framework of relatively small timbers (up to ex. 150 mm × 50 mm (The 'ex' means 'out of'.)) spaced vertically at 400 or 600 mm. These are known as **studs** and have short struts of timber or noggins placed between them at 1 m maximum spacing to prevent distortion. Some panel prefabricators provide thin galvanised steel diagonal bracing as an alternative to struts. Head and sole plates complete the framing.

With the benefit of quality control procedures and efficient industrial manufacturing processes, the high cost of imported timber in the UK is offset by effective factory prefabrication of complete wall, floor and roof units. Furthermore, rationalised site assembly with mobile crane and semi-skilled operatives provides for considerable saving in construction time.

As a construction material, timber is comparatively light; it is therefore easy to handle and is less of a structural dead weight factor than traditional masonry. It has a high strength to weight ratio and is also very stiff when related to its strength. Prefabrication of structural units eliminates the need for skilled carpentry as all joints are simply nailed.

Apart from the cost of timber, the other disadvantages are poor resistance to fire in sizes under 150 mm × 100 mm, as there is insufficient substance to char-protect the inner structure, and its hygroscopic nature, which can support decay in damp situations. The effect of fire is limited by cladding with non-combustible material such as plasterboard internally and facing brick externally. Provided the timber is installed dry and assembled with correct protection (dpc, vapour control layers, etc.), dampness penetration will not be an issue.

Manufacture and construction techniques derive from the applications of **platform** or balloon framing. Figure 3.7.1 shows the principle of storey-height platform-framed walls made up of ex. 100 mm × 50 mm timber studding at 400 or 600 mm centres. These are supported at intermediate floor levels or platforms by

Roof truss

Storey height wall unit

Intermediate floor

Ground floor

Eaves

ex. 100 × 50 head binder

ex. 100 × 50 head plate

Cavity barrier

ex. 100 × 50 studs at 400 or 600 centres

Breather membrane

Outer brick wall

8 mm wood fibre or plywood sheathing

Stud

Sole plate

50 mm header

19 mm plywood flooring

Floor joists at 400 mm centres

Head binder

Head plate

Intermediate floor

Cavity barrier

Stud

ex. 100 × 50 sole plate

ex. 100 × 50 sill plate

DPC

12 mm anchor bolts at 2 m spacing

Ground floor

Figure 3.7.1 Timber frame construction – platform frame.

Note: Eaves and ground floor as Fig. 3.7.1

Figure 3.7.2 Timber frame construction – balloon frame.

nailing through the sole plates. Head plates are similarly fixed to a head binder, which links each prefabricated panel. Figure 3.7.2 shows the ground floor to eaves full-height balloon-framed wall. This is independent of the intermediate floor except for complementary bracing where the floor joists fix to studs and a **ribbon** or **ledger** let into the stud framing. Storey-height platform framing is simpler to handle and transport but less rapidly constructed on site than the one lift to roof level that balloon framing permits. The effects of timber movement are more easily contained and restrained in the smaller units of a platform frame.

An outer cladding of brickwork provides a traditional appearance, with galvanised steel angle wall ties spanning a cavity to secure the masonry outer leaf to the timber framing. The possibility of fire spread through the cavity is restrained with cavity barriers at strategic intervals. These normally occur at intersections of elements of construction, e.g. wall to roof and party wall to external wall. Fire resistance of cavity barriers in dwellings should be at least 30 minutes, i.e. 30 minutes' integrity and 15 minutes' insulation (see Building Regulations: Approved Document B3: Section 9, BS 476: *Fire tests on building materials and structures*, and Fig. 3.7.3).

12.5 mm plasterboard

Breather membrane

Alternative

500 gauge polyethylene vapour control membrane

80/100 mm mineral wool insulation between framing members

8 mm min. plywood sheathing

Brickwork outer leaf with wall ties every 5th course

Foil-faced glass fibre reinforced polyisocyanurate (Pi) foam board (10–67 mm) [Cellular plastic insulation board]

External wall construction

90 mm cavity

Mineral wool sound insulation quilt, flanged for stapling to framing (preferably in both stud frames)

19 mm plasterboard (horizontal)

12.5 mm plasterboard (vertical)

50 mm wire-meshed mineral wool fire/cavity barrier

Floor boarding

Floor joist

50 mm timber blocking between joists

Restraint ties at 1.2 m spacing

Party wall construction

Figure 3.7.3 Timber frame construction – further details.

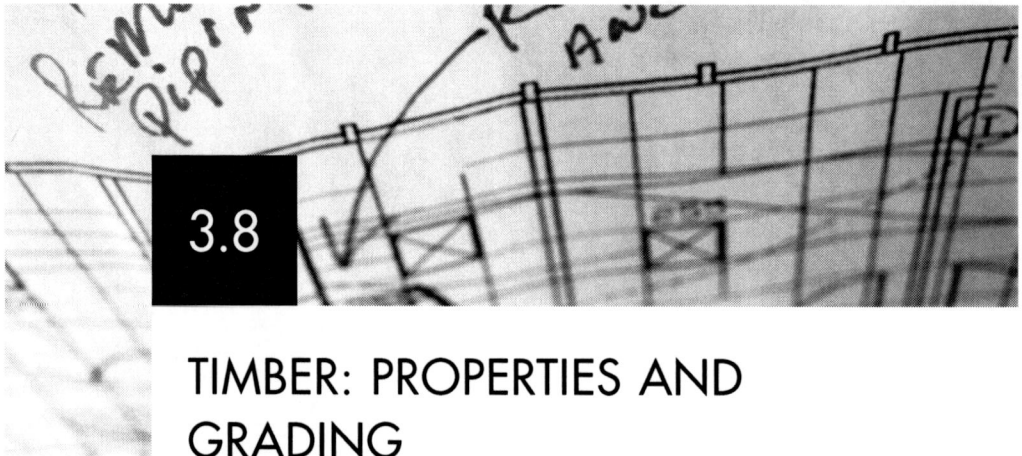

3.8

TIMBER: PROPERTIES AND GRADING

Timber derives from thousands of different tree species, but the botanical classification divides timber into **hardwood** and **softwood**. Hardwoods are from broad-leaved trees, most of which are deciduous, holly being an exception. Not all hardwoods are hard; balsa is an example of a *soft* hardwood. Softwoods are from coniferous trees, and not all of these are relatively soft: for example, yew is a very strong, dense and durable material. For structural purposes, strength characteristics and durability are more important means for classification. This is particularly important with softwood, which is used predominantly for structural timbers in the UK, because of the prohibitive cost of hardwood.

When specifying softwood structural timbers, the following should be stated:

- any preservative treatment;
- cross-sectional size and surface finish;
- the moisture content;
- the strength class.

■■■ PRESERVATIVE TREATMENT

The majority of softwood contains a high proportion of sapwood. This is less resilient than the denser heartwood found closer to the core of a timber trunk. Therefore, as a precaution against dampness and possible fungal decay (wet or dry rot), plus potential infestation from wood-boring insects, suitable preservatives may be required. The need will be determined by the position of timbers within a building and the geographical location. In parts of southern England there is a perceived risk of softwood timber infestation by the **house longhorn beetle**. The Building Regulations, Approved Document to support Regulation 7, define the particular boroughs where softwoods must be treated if applied in any aspect of roof construction. See also BS 8417: *Preservation of timber. Recommendations*, for clarification of acceptable chemical treatment.

▪▪▪ CROSS-SECTIONAL SIZE AND SURFACE FINISH

Softwood cross-sectional size has previously been specified under three classifications: sawn, planed (machined), and regularised. Sawn is the result of converting a timber log into commercially accepted sizes, e.g. 50 mm × 100 mm, 75 mm × 225 mm. Application of these sections is largely for unseen structural use, such as floor and roof members. Planed involves machining about 1.5 mm off each surface to provide a smooth finish: for example, 50 mm × 100 mm sawn becomes 47 mm × 97 mm, otherwise known as ex. 50 × 100. Regularising has been used to achieve a uniform width in timber to provide a more even final product. The timber may be sawn or planed to, say, 47 mm for uniformity in timber studding.

However, these terms are now redefined, with regularising no longer featured, in the requirements of BS EN 336: *Structural timber. Sizes, permitted deviations.* This standard specifies **target sizes** in order to simplify the previous confusion over the finished dimensions. Target size is in only two tolerance classes: T1, applicable to sawn surfaces; and T2, applicable to planed timber. For example, if a section of timber is required 50 mm wide sawn and 197 mm in depth planed, it will be specified as 50 mm (T1) × 197 mm (T2).

▪▪▪ MOISTURE CONTENT

When timber is felled it is saturated. In this state it is unworkable and, if allowed to remain so, will be prone to shrinkage, distortion and the effects of fungal growths. Natural drying or seasoning is possible in some climates, but most commercial organisations use kilns to reduce the moisture content of rough sawn softwood to between 12% and 20%. This is expressed as the weight of water in the timber as a percentage of the weight of the timber dry:

$$\text{moisture content } \% = \frac{(\text{wet weight}) - (\text{dry weight})}{\text{dry weight}} \times \frac{100}{1}$$

After seasoning it is essential that the product remains in a well-ventilated, atmospherically stable environment. Timber is hygroscopic, i.e. made up of cells that will absorb moisture readily. Therefore significant changes in temperature and humidity may cause it to react by expanding, contracting, deforming or twisting. Moisture content of stored timber can be checked regularly with a surveyor's moisture meter. These have two pointed probes, and respond to conductance due to the amount of electrical moisture in the material.

▪▪▪ STRENGTH CLASSES

Grading of timber may be visual or by the more efficient use of computerised grading machines. Individual pieces are assessed against permissible defects limits and marked accordingly. Some examples of grade markings are shown in Fig. 3.8.1.

Grading occurs in this country or the country of origin. BS EN 518 and 519 (European standards for visual and machine grading, respectively) effectively

Figure 3.8.1 Examples of grading stamps on softwood timber.

rationalise much of the timber graded in Europe and many surrounding countries, e.g. Scandinavia, but confusion may occur with timber graded elsewhere in the absence of an international standard. Visual grading in the UK may be in accordance with BS 4978. This provides two quality standards: GS (general structural) and SS (special structural). The letter M preceding GS or SS indicates grading by machine. GS and SS grades will meet the requirements of the aforementioned European standards.

Timber imported from North America is independently graded to rules applicable in Canada and the USA. The Canadian National Lumber Grades Authority (NLGA) and the American National Grading Rules for Dimension Lumber (NGRDL) grade in accordance with product application: see Table 3.8.1.

Comparisons can be drawn, and Table 3.8.2 provides an indication of the similarity of product grades and strength classes to BS EN 338: *Structural timber. Strength classes.*

As can be seen from Table 3.8.2, using GS or SS graded timber from different sources may not result in the same strength characteristics, as these can vary between species. The full listings of BS EN 338 strength classes are shown in

Table 3.8.1 North American timber grades and markings

Timber mark	Grade	Application	Range of nominal widths
Sel str No. 1 No. 2 No. 3	Select structural Number 1 Number 2 Number 3	Structural joists and planks	150 mm and over
Sel str No. 1 No. 2 No. 3	Select structural Number 1 Number 2 Number 3	Structural light framing	50 mm to 100 mm
Const Std Util Stud	Construction Standard Utility Stud	Light framing	50 mm to 100 mm

Table 3.8.2 Timber grading and strength class comparisons

Species	Standard	C14	C16	C18	C22	C24	C27/TR26	C30
	BS EN 338	C14	C16	C18	C22	C24	C27/TR26	C30
	Bldg Regs		SC3			SC4	SC5	
Whitewood or redwood	BS 4978		GS			SS		
British spruce	BS 4978	GS		SS				
British pine	BS 4978	GS			SS			
Canadian S-P-F or hem-fir	NLGA or NGRLD (J&P/SLF)		No. 1 No. 2			Sel		
	NLGA or NGRLD (LF)	Const						
	NLGA or NGRLD (Stud)	Stud						

Key: S-P-F = Spruce, pine, fir.
hem   = Hemlock.
Others, see Table 3.8.1.

Notes
1. North American machine stress rated (MSR) grades are also accepted in the UK and correspond across the BS EN 338 range given above.
2. For a full and more detailed comparison, refer to BS5268-2: *Structural use of timber. Code of practice for permissible stress design, materials and workmanship.*

Table 3.8.3   Grade stresses and moduli of elasticity for various strength classes: for service classes 1 and 2

Strength class	Bending parallel to grain (N/mm²)	Tension parallel to grain (N/mm²)	Compression parallel to grain (N/mm²)	Compression perpendicular to grain* (N/mm²)	Shear parallel to grain (N/mm²)	Modulus of elasticity		Characteristic density, ρ_k† (kg/m³)	Average density, ρ_{mean}† (kg/m³)
						Mean (N/mm²)	Minimum (N/mm²)		
C14	4.1	2.5	5.2	2.1	1.6	0.60	6 800	4 600	290	350
C16	5.3	3.2	6.8	2.2	1.7	0.67	8 800	5 800	310	370
C18	5.8	3.5	7.1	2.2	1.7	0.67	9 100	6 000	320	380
C22	6.8	4.1	7.5	2.3	1.7	0.71	9 700	6 500	340	410
C24	7.5	4.5	7.9	2.4	1.9	0.71	10 800	7 200	350	420
TR26‡	10.0	6.0	8.2	2.5	2.0	1.10	11 000	7 400	370	450
C27	10.0	6.0	8.2	2.5	2.0	1.10	12 300	8 200	370	450
C30	11.0	6.6	8.6	2.7	2.2	1.20	12 300	8 200	380	460
C35	12.0	7.2	8.7	2.9	2.4	1.30	13 400	9 000	400	480
C40	13.0	7.8	8.7	3.0	2.6	1.40	14 500	10 000	420	500
D30	9.0	5.4	8.1	2.8	2.2	1.40	9 500	6 000	530	640
D35	11.0	6.6	8.6	3.4	2.6	1.70	10 000	6 500	560	670
D40	12.5	7.5	12.6	3.9	3.0	2.00	10 800	7 500	590	700
D50	16.0	9.6	15.2	4.5	3.5	2.20	15 000	12 600	650	780
D60	18.0	10.8	18.0	5.2	4.0	2.40	18 500	15 600	700	840
D70	23.0	13.8	23.0	6.0	4.6	2.60	21 000	18 000	900	1080

Note: Strength classes C14 to C40 and TR 26 are for softwoods, D30 to D70 are for hardwoods.

*   When the specification specifically prohibits wane at bearing areas, the higher values of compression perpendicular to grain stress may be used, otherwise the lower values apply.

†   The values of characteristic density given above are for use when designing joints. For the calculation of dead load, the average density should be used.

‡   The strength class TR26 is essentially for the manufacture of trussed rafters but may be used for other applications with the grade stresses and moduli given above. For joints, the tabulated permissible loads for strength class C27 should be used. When used with the provisos given in BS 5268: Part 3 the grade stresses are similar to the former M75 redwood/whitewood so timber and trussed rafter designs to this M75 grade/species combination are interchangeable with timber and trussed rafter designs using the TR26 strength class.

Table 3.8.3, extracted from BS 5268-2, with kind permission of the British Standards Institution. It provides a comprehensive comparison of timber strength properties and characteristics, which may be used as a basis for structural design and timber selection.

Note: Service classes 1 and 2 in Table 3.8.3 refer to timber used in moderate climates where ambient temperature is about 20 °C and relative humidity does not exceed 65% and 85% respectively for more than a few weeks per year. Respective moisture contents will not exceed 12% and 20%. Service class 3 exists where climatic conditions impose higher moisture contents than service class 3.

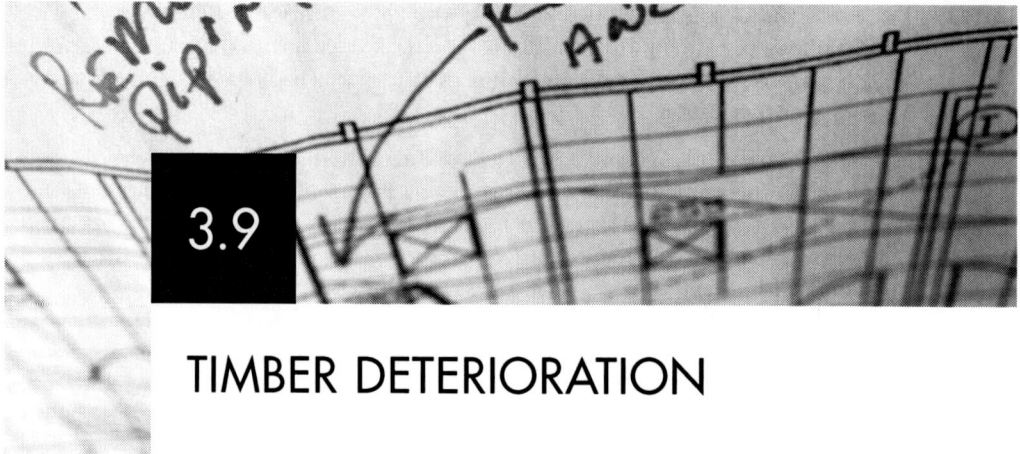

TIMBER DETERIORATION

Timber is a very resilient and robust material in normal atmospheric conditions. It can even retain its structure in a permanently wet environment, as evidenced by stanchions and wooden pier foundations that have remained intact for centuries. As well as being very durable, timber will outlast many other building materials succumbing to the effects of rain, frost and chemicals. However, the weakness of both hard and softwoods is its source as a food for plant growths in the form of fungi and to certain species of insect. With each, enzymes digest the cellulose fibres and lignin adhesive comprising the structure of wood.

■■■ FUNGAL ATTACK

Fungi, unlike other plant growths, have no leaves, and do not require chlorophyll or sunlight, but will readily consume organic material. For a fungal growth on timber to succeed, the timber will require a moisture content in excess of 20% (see Chapter 3.8). Generally, softwoods for internal structural use will be commercially seasoned to a moisture content of about 12–16%. Internal softwood for joinery and hardwoods will be seasoned to a lower figure of around 10%.

Certain species of fungus will attack trees during growth, but these are an issue for the timber producer. The principal concern for builders, building owners and users is the fungi known to develop on seasoned timber in service.

CATEGORIES OF ROT ATTRIBUTED TO FUNGI

Brown rot

So named because the wood becomes dark in colour. It is further characterised by the timber drying and cracking to produce small surface squares, manifesting as cubes within the depth of the wood. This shrinking is caused by destruction of the cellulose tissues.

White rot

This leaves the wood pale in colour, soft, and fibrous to touch. The timber structure decays as both cellulose tissues and lignin adhesive are destroyed.

DRY AND WET ROT

Generally, timber deterioration due to fungal attack is more conveniently categorised as dry or wet rot, depending on the extent of exposure to dampness. The initial indication of rot infestation is usually a stale or musty smell emanating from a damp source below floors, in cellars or within a roof space. Closer investigation often reveals whitish/grey fungal plant growths and possibly coloured fruiting bodies depending on how far the fungus has advanced.

Dry rot

Dry rot is known biologically by the Latin name *Serpula lacrymans* or *Merulius lacrymans*. It is a 'brown rot', leaving the timber dry and friable. Fungal growth is caused when red/rusty-coloured spores from an established fungus drift through the air to settle and germinate on damp timber. The spores develop into white strands (hyphae) appearing as cotton-wool-like patches (mycelium) growing flesh-textured fruiting bodies (sporophores), in turn producing more spores.

Early detection can eradicate the problem. The source of dampness must be removed or rectified. Undetected leaking plumbing is often the cause, or condensation due to inadequate underfloor or roof space ventilation. Eliminating the initial dampness may not always eradicate dry rot, as it can still thrive by developing small vein-like tubing of 2–3 mm diameter (rhizomorphs) to extract dampness from areas adjacent to the timber food source. This can include moisture in brickwork, render, plaster or concrete. Moisture from the air can be sufficient for dry rot to live, particularly in areas of high humidity.

Optimum growth conditions are a combination of dampness and warmth. Temperatures between 13 °C and 24 °C are ideal. At freezing temperatures the fungus becomes dormant, but it will die in temperatures above 40 °C.

Treatment of dry rot
- Eliminate the source of dampness.
- Dry out the building area affected.
- Cut out all affected timber at least 500 mm beyond the decay.
- Remove all affected plaster and other finishes within the vicinity of attack.
- Sterilise the affected area by applying heat from a blowtorch (carefully!) to all adjacent masonry, concrete and sound plaster.
- Where the attack is severe, drill close-spaced inclined holes of about 12 mm diameter into the adjacent masonry and liberally feed the holes with patent fungicide to saturate the structure.
- Make good jointing and pointing to masonry and plasterwork with a zinc oxychloride additive or similar fungicide in the mix. Specialist paints containing fungicide are also available.
- Replace all affected timber with well-seasoned, preservative-treated wood.

Following on from remedial work, regular monitoring is essential for several months to ensure successful eradication of dry rot. Even though the source of dampness may be removed, dry rot has an irritating habit of reappearing, somehow managing to thrive on only a nominal amount of moisture.

Wet rot

The most common types of wet rot fungus in the UK are known biologically by the Latin names of *Coniophora puteana* or *Coniophora cerebella* and *Phellinus contiguus* or *Poria contigua*. The growth and development of both fungi are similar to those of dry rot, but fruiting bodies are rare.

   Coniophora, otherwise known as cellar fungus, prefers very damp conditions. It is a 'brown rot', splitting the internal structure of the host timber longitudinally and laterally into small cube shapes, but leaving the surface largely intact. The timber crumbles when prodded, and it is dull dark brown or black in colour.

   Phellinus has become more associated with decay in external joinery. It is a 'white rot', attacking poor-quality sapwood where used in door and window frames, fascia boards, cladding, etc. Inadequate treatment of the timber, poor jointing techniques, inappropriate adhesives and lack of aftercare will all contribute to rainwater penetration. Wood in these situations is often painted, and the first sign of fungal decay is usually surface irregularities. Closer inspection will reveal splitting within the body of wood, breaking into soft strands.

   Optimum growth conditions are as for dry rot, but wet rots are more easily controlled as they require greater exposure to dampness to thrive. Hence, once the moisture source is removed, the decayed timber can be replaced. Adjacent timber, brickwork, plaster, etc. are unlikely to be affected, but as a precaution the whole area should be brush-treated with a fungicide.

▨▪■ INSECT ATTACK

SPECIES

There are several species of wood-boring insect that are capable of seriously damaging structural timber and joinery in buildings. During their relatively short time in adult form they are classified as beetles. Most of their life is in the larval stage, gnawing and burrowing through timber – hence the general descriptive term of wood borer or woodworm. Most species of larvae have a preference for the less dense sapwood growth areas as their source of food.

   The most common species in the UK are:

- common furniture beetle (*Anobium punctatum*);
- death watch beetle (*Xestobium rufovillosum*);
- powder post beetle (*Lyctus* family);
- house longhorn beetle (*Hylotrupes bajulus*).

Figure 3.9.1 compares the species proportionally. The largest is the adult house longhorn beetle at about 25 mm overall.

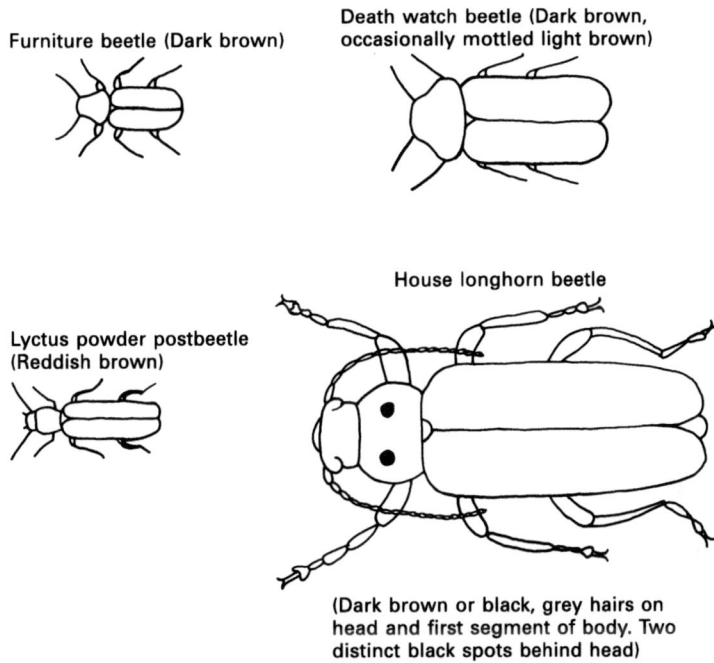

Figure 3.9.1   Common wood-boring beetles.

HABITAT

Most species prefer a slightly damp, draught-free environment. Unventilated roof spaces and recesses behind eaves cupboards are ideal areas in which to thrive. Other areas suitable to the lifestyle of the woodworm include understair cupboards and voids within enclosed baths and other sanitary fittings. Timber of intermediate floors in housing is also vulnerable to attack, but raised timber ground floors are less vulnerable if peripheral air vents remain clear for air circulation.

LIFE CYCLE

Wood-boring insects are most active during the warmer spring and summer months. The life cycle shown in Fig. 3.9.2 is similar for all species, progressing from egg, through larva (grub) and pupa (chrysalis), to adult (beetle). Adult female beetles seek rough crevices of sawn timber or former borehole exits to deposit their eggs. As the larvae hatch they bore into the wood, using it as food and shelter. The tunnelling effect of hundreds of larvae from each batch of eggs can be extremely damaging. The larval stage is the predominant part of an insect's life, extending for several years before maturing to a chrysalis. The chrysalis develops into an adult beetle just beneath the timber surface, from where it emerges to reproduce, lay eggs and generate more damage. Table 3.9.1 provides some comparison of the behavioural characteristics of species.

2–8 weeks   Eggs

Larvae   Adult beetle

1–5 years (10 years,   Pupae   2–8 weeks
longhorn beetle)

Figure 3.9.2   Wood borers – life cycle.

Table 3.9.1   Common wood borers

Name	Egg quantity	Egg maturity	Laval period	Pupal stage	Emergence as a beetle	Location	Exit holes
Furniture beetle	20–50	4–5 weeks	2–3 years	4–8 weeks	May–Sept	Sapwood of soft or hard wood	1–2 mm dia.
Death watch beetle	40–80	2–8 weeks	4–6 years	2–4 weeks	Mar–June	Hardwoods, preferably decayed oak	3 mm dia.
Powder post beetle	70–200	2–3 weeks	1–2 years	3–4 weeks	May–Sept	Sapwood of new hardwood	1–2 mm dia.
Longhorn beetle	< 200	2–3 weeks	3–10 years	About 3 weeks	July–Sept	Sapwood of softwood	5 mm × 10 mm oval

Note: Periods given will vary relative to ambient temperatures.

RECOGNITION AND TREATMENT

Woodworm is usually first recognised by the distinctive flight holes and powdery deposits (**frass**) on the surface of timber. By this stage the internal structure of the timber may have suffered considerable damage. The extent of damage may be established by chiselling away the timber surface to examine the borings or galleries produced by the larvae.

If the damage is slight and there are only a few exit holes, remedial spraying or brushing with liberal applications of a proprietary insecticide will control the problem. Structural timbers seriously damaged must be removed and burnt. All new timber must be pre-treated, preferably with a vacuum/pressure-impregnated insecticide sourced from a commercial timber supplier.

In new construction, prevention of woodworm infestation by using pre-treated timber is the only effective method of control. The Building Regulations, Approved Document A: *Structure* (Section 2B) provides specific reference and guidance for the use of treated timber for roof construction in parts of Surrey and adjacent areas. This requirement originated several decades ago following a very serious attack by the house longhorn beetle on roof timbers in Camberley.

Reference sources for acceptable methods of timber preservation include:

- The British Wood Preserving and Damp-Proofing Association's Manual;
- BS 5589: *Code of practice for preservation of timber*;
- BS 5268-5: *Structural use of timber. Code of practice for the preservative treatment of structural timber*;
- BS 5707: *Specification for preparations of wood preservatives in organic solvents.*

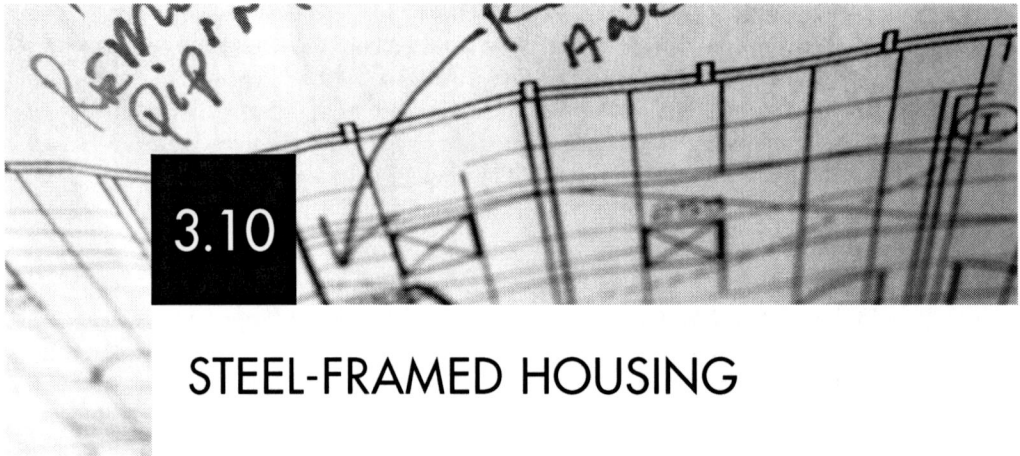

3.10

STEEL-FRAMED HOUSING

Steel-framed housing is similar to timber frame in that standard sections are used to make up a structural frame. The frame is lined with plasterboard and infilled with insulating material. An outer leaf of brick cladding retains a traditional image and protection from the elements.

Advantages
- dimensionally stable (timber warps);
- will not rot;
- will not burn;
- does not absorb moisture;
- unpalatable to insects and animals;
- predictable consistent expansion and movement characteristics;
- requires only semi-skilled labour to assemble;
- components factory-manufactured to quality-controlled standards;
- relatively large span to weight/size possible.

Disadvantages
- unpredictable behaviour in fire;
- risk of corrosion.

▪▪▪ BACKGROUND

Steel-framed dwellings were first built in the UK c.1920. They did not catch on, and were soon displaced as 'breeze' block and brick technology developed. During the post World War II building boom, when traditional building materials were scarce and demand for housing was high, there was a resurgence of interest. At this time a variety of structural steel frame systems for housing were produced, but they were labour intensive, and components were costly. Technically the concept was sound, and these buildings have performed well in the long term.

▨ ▨ ■ DEVELOPMENT

Apart from some ventures into the manufacture of prefabricated modular units, timber frame has been the only real alternative to traditional masonry construction. However, since about 1990 there have been many new initiatives based on the use of economical cold-formed steel sections (see Part 10) for fabrication of simple frames. This has provided a cost-competitive alternative to timber frame and traditional masonry construction.

▨ ▨ ■ COMPONENTS

WALLS

Basically a stud frame of cold-formed galvanised steel channels produced by rolling, notching, holing and folding. These can be delivered to site for cutting and bending to shape, and fixing with self-drilled, self-tapping screws. Generally, panels are made up in a factory to modular sizes (600 mm) and assembled on site to make up a structural frame.

ROOF TRUSSES

Channel sections can be used, but some manufacturers prefer sigma profile sections for roof members.

COMPONENT SIZES

Sizes differ marginally from various system producers, but are generally as indicated in Fig. 3.10.1. Figures 3.10.2 and 3.10.3 show typical construction details.

SUPPLEMENTARY EARTH BONDING

Otherwise known as cross-bonding. The steel frame must not be used for local earthing of electrical services. The frame is regarded as extraneous metalwork and could conduct electricity if contacted by an electrical fault. It must be earthed at one point and all electrical earth connections in the circuit wired back to this point.

Prefabricated galvanised steel channel section (typical dimensions)

Holes for wall tie fixing and bolted connections

Slots cut in channel sides to facilitate bending

41 mm

1 mm thickness

73, 92 or 149 mm

St/st wall tie

Hooked end through channel hole or attached bracket

Fishtail end for bedding in masonry

Intermediate infill stud

Stud frame

1200 mm

Storey height

Self-drilled, self-tapping screws

Fibre cement building board or plasterboard internal lining

Figure 3.10.1   Steel frame sections.

Queen post truss

Storey-height frame

Channel section intermediate floor joists

Concrete ground floor

Sigma or channel rafter

Channel tie

Eaves

Bolted connection

Wall plate (optional)

18 mm OSB

Cavity barrier

Channel studding at 600 or 1200 mm spacing

Insulation projecting into cavity

St/st wall tie

50 mm cavity

Breather membrane

Wall tie

Masonry external leaf

Cavity barrier

Breather membrane

Channel stud

Plywood decking

Intermediate floor

Channel section floor joists

<150 mm fire-retardant insulation within framing and projecting into cavity

12.5 mm vapour-check plaster board screwed to framing

Anchor bolt

Dpc

Reinforced concrete slab or beam and block floor

Ground floor

Figure 3.10.2   Typical steel frame construction.

12.5 mm plasterboard

Rigid insulation batt

50 mm cavity

Vapour control layer

Steel channel stud frame with rock-fibre insulation

Self-drilling retaining screw

Brickwork outer leaf

External wall construction

Plaster wallboard with vapour control layer

Insulation between channel sections

Render finish

8 mm min. plywood sheathing

70 mm rigid insulation system surfaced for rendered finish

200 min.

Mineral wool sound insulation batt min. 50 mm thickness of density 33–60 kg/m³

19 mm plasterboard (horizontal)

12.5 mm plasterboard (vertical)

Channel section framing

Floorboarding

Structural floor system of channel sections or lattice joists shown

300 min.

Spaces between joists fire sealed

Party wall construction

Figure 3.10.3   Steel frame – further details.

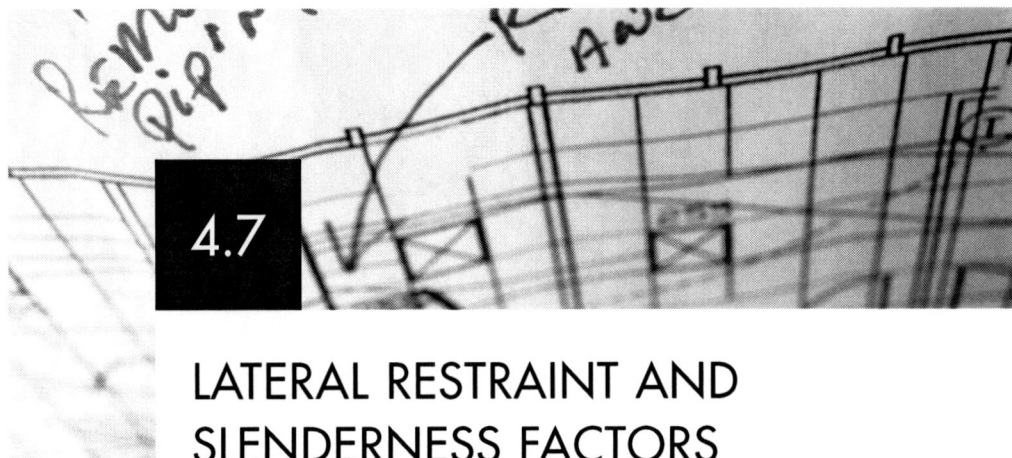

LATERAL RESTRAINT AND SLENDERNESS FACTORS

Walls have been designed such that their mass, together with the loads carried from floors and roofs, provide adequate resistance to buckling. Buckling can be controlled by using buttresses or piers, but these may encroach on space and be visually unattractive. Contemporary design favours more slender construction: therefore stability and resistance to tensile lateral forces such as wind, and possibly impact, is achieved by using support from the floor and roof (see Part 6).

Floor structures function as a stable horizontal platform supported by perimeter and intermediate walls. They complement that support by providing restraint and stability for the wall against lateral overturning forces, in conjunction with adequate structural connections. Connections to external, compartment (fire), separating (party), and internal loadbearing walls in houses where walls exceed 3 m length may be achieved by:

1. 90 mm minimum direct bearing of the floor by timber joists (see Fig. 4.3.5), or from a continuous concrete slab;
2. BS EN 845-1 approved galvanised steel restraint type joist hangers with a minimum 100 mm bearing, spaced at no more than 2 m;
3. galvanised steel purpose-made straps of minimum cross-section 30 mm × 5 mm, spaced at no more than 2 m, secured to the inner leaf of masonry and over at least 3 joists;
4. galvanised steel straps, as 3 above, applied to adjacent floors. Continuity of contact between the floor and wall is also acceptable.

[*Note*: Items 1 and 2 assume that joist spacing does not exceed 1.2 m and the house is not over two storeys. If over two storeys, supplementary strapping should be provided to joists in the longitudinal direction, as shown in Fig. 4.7.1.]

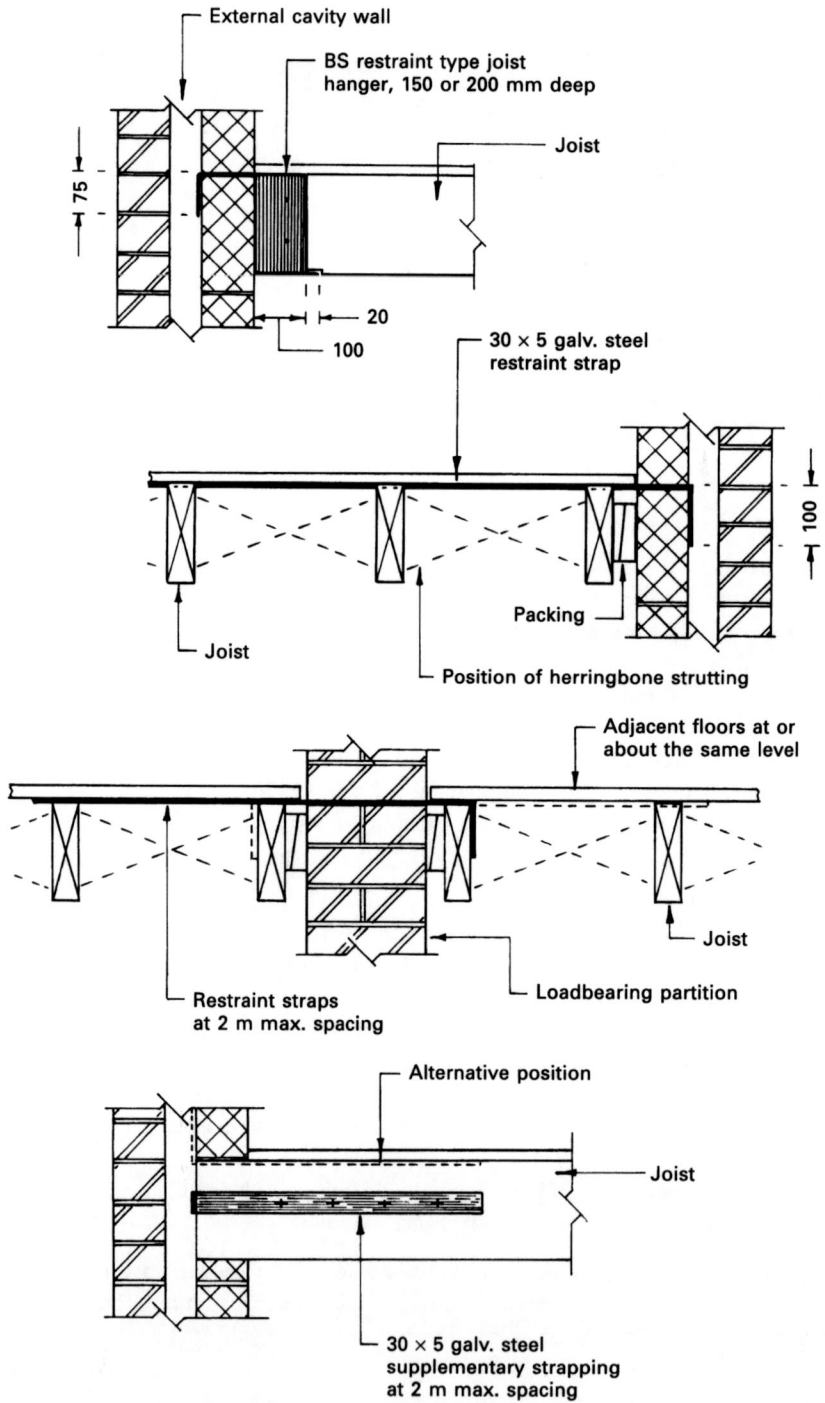

Figure 4.7.1   Lateral restraint connections between wall and floor.

Figure 4.7.2   Effective height (H) calculation.

▨▨■ SLENDERNESS RATIO

This is an acceptable standard for measuring dimensional stability. Actual wall height and thickness (see Chapters 3.1–3.5) can be varied for structural calculation purposes. This is known as the effective height or thickness and depends on the method (if any) of restraint. The effectiveness of connecting a wall to an adjacent structure is shown in Fig. 4.7.2.

Calculations to determine effective wall thickness are also possible for different wall constructions. Single leaf/solid walls without piers have an effective thickness equal to the actual thickness. Attached piers will cause some variation, and reference to BS 5628-1: *Structural use of unreinforced masonry* will provide appropriate coefficients. Cavity walls have an effective thickness equal to two-thirds of the sum of the actual thickness of both leaves, or the actual thickness of the thicker leaf (whichever is greater).

Effective length can also be important for structural calculations. This depends on the extent of support from abutments, as shown in Fig. 4.7.3.

Figure 4.7.3 Effective length (*L*) calculation.

EXAMPLE CALCULATION OF SLENDERNESS RATIO

A cavity wall consists of 102.5 mm brick outer leaf and 150 mm concrete block inner leaf. The wall height from floor to ceiling is 3 m, with floor joists built into the inner leaf (enhanced support).

Effective thickness = 0.67 (102.5 + 150) = 169 mm
Effective height   = 0.75 × 3000 = 2250 mm

$$\text{Slenderness ratio} \quad = \frac{\text{effective height}}{\text{effective thickness}} = \frac{2250}{169} = 13.30$$

Maximum acceptable slenderness ratios vary with applications in accordance with BS 5628-1: *Structural use of unreinforced masonry*. The main objective is to evaluate and compare numerically different construction methods: the lower the slenderness ratio, the less prone a structure is to buckling under load due to insufficient rigidity.

▨ ▧ ■ LATERAL RESTRAINT – RETRO-FIX

As shown in Fig. 4.7.1, lateral restraint from floors is necessary to stabilise adjacent walls (see Fig. 6.1.9 for roof lateral support). Many older buildings (mainly housing) have been constructed without strapping. Consequently, as these buildings age, there can be a tendency for their walls to show signs of outward bulging. Walls rarely bulge inwards, because the effect of thermal movement from the sun causes the outer surface to expand. Also, floor loads will tend to push outwards rather than inwards, particularly if there is an inner leaf carrying greater load. Wall bulging can also be caused where wall ties have failed because of corrosion.

REMEDIAL MEASURES

- Traditional through-tie (Fig. 4.7.4).
- Retro-strap (Fig. 4.7.5).
- Retro-stud (Fig. 4.7.6).
- Driven resin-fixed screw (Fig. 4.7.7).
- Self-tapping helix (Fig. 4.7.8).

Figure 4.7.4 Traditional through-tie.

Figure 4.7.5   Retro-strap.

Figure 4.7.6   Retro-stud.

Figure 4.7.7   Driven resin-fixed screw.

Figure 4.7.8   Self-tapping helix.

Figure 4.7.9 Standard spacing of polyurethane injection holes.

Notes:

1. At door and window openings, hole spacing is 300 mm vertically (200 mm horizontally from openings) and 400 mm horizontally above the opening.
2. At party walls, vertical holes are placed at 300 mm spacing, 300 mm from the party wall line.
3. Any unsleeved air bricks are replaced with sleeved, to prevent foam from leakage to where it is not required, e.g. under suspended floors.
4. At upper floor level, supplementary stainless steel anchors are positioned at 1000 mm horizontal intervals.

WALL TIE DECAY

Wall ties should be specified as manufactured from corrosion-resistant stainless steel. Historically, they have been produced from iron or steel, at best galvanised with a coating of zinc. Iron and steel ties can corrode and break, particularly where the zinc coating to steel is of poor quality, or it has been damaged during construction. Ties will have greater exposure to corrosion where pointing has broken down, and where old lime mortars have softened by decomposition due to atmospheric pollutants and frost damage. Inevitably there will be loss of stability between the two leaves of masonry wall, creating areas of outward bulging from the outer leaf.

A solution is to demolish the outer leaf, one small area at a time, and rebuild it complete with new ties. A simpler, less dramatic approach is to apply chemical cavity stabilisation. The material used is structural polyurethane foam of closed cell characteristic. The polyurethane is created by on-site mixing of an isocyanate with a resin to produce a liquid for injection by hand gun through 12 mm diameter holes. Holes are pre-drilled in the outer leaf at intervals as shown in Fig. 4.7.9. Within the cavity the fluid mix reacts and expands to produce a rigid foam mass. This foam combines as an adhesive agent and as an insulant.

ROOFS: TIMBER, FLAT AND PITCHED

■ ■ ■ TIMBER FLAT ROOFS

A flat roof is essentially a low-pitched roof, and is defined in BS 6100: *Glossary of building and civil engineering terms* as a pitch of 10° or less to the horizontal. Generally the angle of pitch is governed by the type of finish that is to be applied to the roof.

The functions of any roof are:

- to keep out rain, wind, snow and dust;
- to prevent excessive heat loss in winter;
- to keep the interior of the building cool in summer;
- to accommodate all stresses encountered;
- to accept movement due to changes in temperature and moisture content;
- to provide lateral restraint and stability to adjacent walls;
- to resist penetration of fire and spread of flame from external sources.

The simplest form of roof construction to fulfil these functions is a timber flat roof covered with an impervious material to prevent rain penetration. This form of roof is suitable for spans up to 4000 mm; spans over this are usually covered with a reinforced concrete slab or a patent form of decking.

The disadvantages of timber flat roofs are as follows:

- They have limited capacity for insulation.
- They may contrast in style with other buildings in the vicinity and, if an extension, the building to which it is attached.
- Unless they are properly designed and constructed, pools of water will collect on the surface causing local variations in temperature. This results in deterioration of the covering and, consequently, high maintenance costs.
- They have little or no space to accommodate services.

Firring pieces

Figure 6.1.1 Timber flat roof slope details.

CONSTRUCTION

The construction of a timber flat roof follows the same methods as those employed for the construction of timber upper floors. Suitable joist sizes can be obtained by design or by reference to tables in publications recommended in the Building Regulations, Approved Document A. The spacing of roof joists is controlled by the width of decking material to be used and/or the width of ceiling board on the underside. Timber flat roofs are usually constructed to fall in one direction towards a gutter or outlet. This can be achieved by sloping the joists to the required fall, but, as this would give a sloping soffit on the underside, it is usual to fix wedge shaped fillets called **firrings** to the top of the joists to provide the fall (see Fig. 6.1.1). The materials used in timber flat roof construction are generally poor thermal insulators, and therefore some form of non-structural material can be incorporated into the roof if it has to comply with Part L of the Building Regulations.

Decking materials

Timber

This can be in the form of softwood boarding, chipboard, oriented strand board or plywood. Plain-edge sawn softwood boards or tongued and grooved boards are suitable for joists spaced at centres up to 450 mm. Exterior grade water- and boil-proof (WBP) plywood is available in sheet form, which requires fixing on all four edges. This means noggins will be required between joists to provide the bearing for end fixings. Chipboard is also a suitable sheet material and is fixed in a similar manner to plywood. This material can be susceptible to moisture movement: therefore for roofing it should be specified 'moisture resistant to BS EN 312, type C3, C4 or C5'. Flat roofs must have the void between ceiling and decking ventilated to prevent condensation occurring. It is also advisable to use structural timbers that have been treated against fungal and insect attack. In certain areas treatment to prevent softwood infestation by the house longhorn beetle is a requirement under the Building Regulations. Details can be found in the Approved Document to support Regulation 7.

Compressed straw slabs

These are made from selected straw by a patent method of heat and pressure to a standard width of 1200 mm × 2400 mm length, the standard thickness being 58 mm, which gives sufficient strength for the slabs to span 600 mm. All edges of the slabs must be supported and fixed. Ventilation is of the utmost importance, and it is common practice to fix cross-bearers at right angles to and over the joists to give cross-ventilation. A bitumen scrim should be placed over the joints before the weathering membrane is applied.

Wood wool slabs

These are 610 mm wide slabs of various lengths, which can span up to 1200 mm. Thickness varies; for roof decking 51 mm is normally specified. The slabs are made of shredded wood fibres that have been chemically treated and are bound together with cement. The fixing and laying is similar to compressed straw slabs.

Insulating materials

There are many types of insulating material available, usually in the form of boards or quilts. Insulation boards laid over the decking create a **warm deck** roof, whereas quilted materials draped over the joists or placed between them, make a **cold deck**.

Boards

These originated from lightly compressed vegetable fibres, bonded with natural glues or resins. Compressed straw and wood wool slabs have been particularly successful as decking materials with the benefit of in-built insulation.

For insulation-only purposes, the most popular materials for roofing boards are high-density mineral wool with a tissue membrane bonded to one surface, expanded polystyrene, or polyurethane slabs. A warm deck roof has insulation board placed over the decking, but below the waterproof membrane. Conversely, an inverted warm deck has the insulation board above the waterproof membrane. The inverted warm deck insulation board must be unaffected by water and be capable of receiving a surface treatment of stone granules or ceramic pavings. With this technique, the waterproof membrane is protected from the stresses caused by exposure to weather extremes. Examples of the various forms of construction are shown in Fig. 6.1.2.

Quilts

These are made from mineral or glass wool that is loosely rolled, with the option of a kraft paper facing. The paper facing is useful as the wool is in fine shreds, which give rise to irritating scratches if handled. Quilts rely on the loose way in which the core is packed for their effectiveness, and therefore the best results are obtained when they are laid between joists.

A variety of loose fills are also available for placing between the joists and over the ceiling to act as thermal insulators. Existing flat roofs can have their resistance to heat loss improved by applying thermal insulation laminated plasterboard to the ceiling.

Weatherproof finishes

Suitable materials are asphalt, lead, copper, zinc, aluminium and built-up roofing felt; only the latter will be considered at this stage.

Built-up roofing felt

Most roofing felts consist essentially of a base sheet of glass fibre or polyester reinforcement, impregnated with hot bitumen during manufacture. This is coated on both sides with a stabilised weatherproof bitumen compound. The outer coating is dusted with sand while still hot and tacky. The underlayer may receive a thin layer of polythene to prevent the sheet from sticking to itself when rolled. After cooling the felt is cut to form rolls 1 m wide and 10 or 20 m long before being wrapped for dispatch.

BS 747: *Reinforced bitumen sheets for roofing. Specification* contains two types:

- Type 3: glass fibre reinforced;
- Type 5: polyester reinforced.

Both types have subdivisions relating to the surface finish. Other bituminous sheet materials are available that incorporate polymer modifications to the bitumen. These are styrene–butadiene–styrene (SBS) and atactic–polypropylene (APP). SBS improves the physical properties, and APP has a higher melting point, most suited to torch-on applications. Rag-fibre-reinforced bituminous felts are still available, but are no longer recommended for roofing habitable accommodation.

For flat roofs three layers of felt should be used, the first being laid at right angles to the fall, commencing at the eaves. If the decking is timber the first layer is secured with large flat-head felt nails, and the subsequent layers are bonded to it with a hot bitumen compound by a roll and pour method. This involves pouring molten bitumen on the decking or underlayer and unrolling the sheet over it. Torch-on is for specially made sheets which are heated to the underside to produce a wave of molten bitumen while the sheet is unrolled. If the decking is of a material other than timber, all three layers are bonded with hot bitumen compound. It is usually recommended that a vented first layer be used in case moisture is trapped during construction; this recommendation does not normally apply to roofs with a timber deck, as timber has the ability to 'breathe'. The minimum fall recommended for built-up roofing felt is 17 mm in 1000 mm or 1°.

In general the Building Regulations require a flat roof with a weatherproofing that has a surface finish of asbestos-based bituminous felt or is covered with a layer of stone chippings. The chippings protect the underlying felt, provide additional fire resistance, and give increased solar reflection. A typical application would be 12.5 mm stone chippings at approximately 50 kg to each 2.5 m^2 of roof area. Chippings of limestone, granite and light-coloured gravel would be suitable.

Vapour control layer/membrane

The problem of condensation should always be considered when constructing a flat roof. The insulation below the built-up roofing felt will not prevent condensation occurring, and as it is a permeable material water vapour will pass upwards through it and condense on the underside of the roofing felt. The drops of moisture so formed will soak into the insulating material, lowering its insulation value and possibly causing staining on the underside. To prevent this occurring a vapour control layer should be placed on the underside of the insulating material. Purpose-made plasterboard with a metallised polyester backing can be specified in this situation, to combine water vapour resistance with the ceiling lining. The inverted warm deck roof will not require a separate vapour control layer, as the waterproof membrane will provide this function. For typical timber flat roof details see Figs 6.1.1 and 6.1.2.

▨ ▨ ■ FLAT ROOF JOIST SIZING

Joist sizes can be determined by calculation or by reference to design tables. The calculation method for roof joists is in principle as shown in the example for floor joists in Chapter 4.3, with the exception of an imposed loading allowance for snow, i.e. $< 30°$ pitch, 1.5 kN/m^2; $> 30°$ pitch, 0.75 kN/m^2.

The sizing of flat roof timbers in accordance with Building Regulation A – Structure, is provided in the Approved Document *Span tables for solid timber members* published by the Timber Research and Development Association (TRADA). Table 6.1.1 gives some guidance for selection of commercial sawn timber sizes relative to span and loading.

▨ ▨ ■ TIMBER PITCHED ROOFS

The term **pitched roof** includes any roof whose angle of slope to the horizontal lies between 10° and 70°; below this range it would be called a flat roof and above 70° it would be classified as a wall.

The pitch is generally determined by the covering that is to be placed over the timber carcass, whereas the basic form is governed by the load and span. The terminology used in timber roof work and the basic members for various spans are shown in Figs 6.1.3 and 6.1.4.

The cost of constructing a pitched roof is greater than for a flat roof, but the pitch will create a useful void for locating cold water storage cisterns and for general storage. The timber used in roof work is structural softwood, the members being joined together with nails. The sloping components or rafters are used to transfer the covering, wind, rain and snow loads to the loadbearing walls on which they rest. The rafters are sometimes assisted in this function by struts and purlins in what is called a **purlin** or **double roof** (see Fig. 6.1.5). As with other forms of roof the spacing of the rafters and consequently the ceiling joists is determined by the module size of the ceiling boards that are to be fixed on the underside of the joists.

ROOF MEMBERS

- **Ridge**   This is the spine of a roof and is essentially a pitching plate for the rafters that are nailed to each other through the ridge board. The depth of ridge board is governed by the pitch of the roof: the steeper the pitch, the deeper will be the vertical or plumb cuts on the rafters abutting the ridge.

Figure 6.1.2 Timber flat roofs.

Table 6.1.1 Guide to span and loading potential for GS grade softwood timber flat roof joists (for timber grading categories, see Table 3.8.2).

Sawn size of joist (mm)	Dead weight of decking and ceiling, excluding self-weight of joist								
	< 50 kg/m² < 0.50 kN/m²			50–75 0.50–0.75			75–100 0.75–1.00		
	Spacing of joists mm (c/c)								
	400	450	600	400	450	600	400	450	600
	Maximum clear span (m)								
38 × 125	1.80	1.79	1.74	1.74	1.71	1.65	1.68	1.65	1.57
38 × 150	2.35	2.33	2.27	2.27	2.25	2.18	2.21	2.18	2.09
38 × 175	2.88	2.85	2.77	2.77	2.74	2.64	2.68	2.64	2.53
38 × 200	3.47	3.43	3.29	3.33	3.28	3.16	3.21	3.16	3.02
38 × 225	4.08	4.03	3.71	3.90	3.84	3.56	3.75	3.66	3.43
50 × 125	2.06	2.05	2.00	2.00	1.98	1.93	1.95	1.93	1.86
50 × 150	2.68	2.65	2.59	2.59	2.58	2.47	2.51	2.47	2.38
50 × 175	3.27	3.25	3.14	3.14	3.10	2.99	3.04	2.99	2.86
50 × 200	3.93	3.86	3.61	3.76	3.70	3.47	3.62	3.56	3.35
50 × 225	4.60	4.47	4.07	4.38	4.30	3.91	4.21	4.13	3.78
63 × 100	1.67	1.66	1.63	1.63	1.61	1.57	1.59	1.93	1.86
63 × 125	2.31	2.29	2.24	2.24	2.21	2.15	2.17	2.15	2.07
63 × 150	2.98	2.95	2.87	2.87	2.84	2.74	2.78	2.74	2.63
63 × 175	3.62	3.59	3.41	3.48	3.43	3.28	3.36	3.30	3.16
63 × 200	4.34	4.29	3.90	4.15	4.08	3.75	3.99	3.92	3.62
63 × 225	5.00	4.82	4.39	4.82	4.64	4.22	4.62	4.48	4.08
75 × 125	2.50	2.48	2.42	2.42	2.40	2.32	2.35	2.32	2.24
75 × 150	3.23	3.19	3.11	3.11	3.07	2.96	3.00	2.96	2.84
75 × 175	3.91	3.87	3.61	3.75	3.69	3.47	3.61	3.55	3.35
75 × 200	4.66	4.53	4.13	4.45	4.36	3.97	4.28	4.20	3.84
75 × 225	5.28	5.09	4.65	5.09	4.90	4.47	4.92	4.74	4.32

- **Common rafters** The main loadbearing members of a roof; they span between a wall plate at eaves level and the ridge. Rafters have a tendency to thrust out the walls on which they rest, and this must be resisted by the walls and the ceiling joists. Rafters are notched over and nailed to a wall plate situated on top of a loadbearing wall; the depth of the notch should not exceed one-third the depth of the rafter.
- **Jack rafters** These fulfil the same function as common rafters but span from ridge to valley rafter or from hip rafter to wall plate.
- **Hip rafters** Similar to a ridge but forming the spine of an external angle and similar to a rafter spanning from ridge to wall plate.
- **Valley rafters** As hip rafters but forming an internal angle.
- **Wall plates** These provide the bearing and fixing medium for the various roof members, and distribute the loads evenly over the supporting walls; they are bedded in cement mortar on top of the loadbearing walls.
- **Dragon ties** Ties placed across the corners and over the wall plates to help provide resistance to the thrust of a hip rafter.

Roofing terminology

Lean-to roof

Figure 6.1.3   Roofing terminology and lean-to roof.

32 thick ridge board

100 × 50 rafters
at 400 c/c

100 × 50 wall plate

3.600 max.

Couple roof

150 × 50 rafters
at 400 c/c

32 thick ridge
board

200 × 50 collars
or ceiling joists
at 400 c/c

100 × 50 wall plate

4.800 max.

Closed couple roof

32 thick ridge
board

125 × 50 rafters
at 400 c/c

150 × 50
collars at
400 c/c

h

$\frac{1}{3}h$

100 × 50
wall plate

5.500 max.

Collar roof

Figure 6.1.4 Pitched roofs for small spans.

Figure 6.1.5   Typical double or purlin roof details for spans up to 7200 mm.

Note: Mineral wool insulation (or equivalent) placed between and over ceiling joists or between rafters. Thickness in accordance with Building Regulations, Approved Document L

Labels in figure:
- 32 thick ridge board
- 100 × 50 rafters at 400 c/c
- Alternative purlin arrangement
- Struts, collars and hangers to every 4th pair of rafters
- Ventilation spacer
- Tilting fillet
- Open eaves detail
- 100 × 50 collar
- 25
- 100 × 50 rafters at 400 c/c
- 150 × 63 purlin
- 100 × 50 struts
- 100 × 50 hangers
- Fascia board
- 100 × 50 binder
- 100 × 50 wall plate
- Cement particle board cavity closer
- Ventilated soffit to closed eaves, fixed to cradling
- 100 × 50 wall plate bedded in cm. mt. (1:3)
- Loadbearing partition
- Insulated external cavity wall

- **Ceiling joists** These fulfil the dual function of acting as ties to the feet of pairs of rafters and providing support for the ceiling boards on the underside and any cisterns housed within the roof void.
- **Purlins** These act as beams, reducing the span of the rafters and enabling an economic section to be used. If the roof has a gable end they can be supported on a corbel or built in, but in a hipped roof they are mitred at the corners and act as a ring beam.
- **Struts** These are compression members that transfer the load of a purlin to a suitable loadbearing support within the span of the roof.
- **Collars** These are extra ties to give additional strength, and are placed at purlin level.
- **Binders** These are beams used to give support to ceiling joists and counteract excessive deflections, and are used if the span of the ceiling joist exceeds 2400 mm.
- **Hangers** Vertical members used to give support to the binders and allow an economic section to be used; they are included in the design if the span of the binder exceeds 3600 mm.

[*Note*: The arrangement of struts, collars and hangers occurs only on every fourth or fifth pair of rafters.]

PITCHED ROOF COMPONENT SIZING

The size of the principal timber members constituting a roof structure can be determined by calculation or from design tables as referred to under 'flat roof joist sizing'. Tables are extensive, to include the various roof components, grades of timber, different roof pitches and loadings. As an example, Table 6.1.2 is provided for guidance on selection of rafters for pitches between 30° and 45° with an imposed loading of 0.75 kN/m².

Table 6.1.2 Guide to span and loading potential for GS grade softwood timber rafters

Sawn size of rafter (mm)	Dead weight tiles, battens, etc., excluding self-weight of rafter								
	< 50 kg/m² < 0.50 kN/m²			50–75 0.50–0.75			75–125 0.75–1.25		
	Spacing of rafters (c/c)								
	400	450	600	400	450	600	400	450	600
	Maximum clear span (m)								
38 × 100	2.28	2.23	2.10	2.10	2.05	1.91	1.96	1.91	1.76
38 × 125	3.07	2.95	2.69	2.87	2.77	2.52	2.65	2.56	2.35
38 × 150	3.67	3.53	3.22	3.44	3.31	3.01	3.26	3.14	2.85
50 × 100	2.69	2.59	2.36	2.53	2.43	2.21	2.38	2.30	2.09
50 × 125	3.35	3.23	2.94	3.15	3.03	2.76	2.98	2.87	2.61
50 × 150	4.00	3.86	3.52	3.76	3.62	3.30	3.57	3.44	3.13

Note: Clear span is measured between wallplate and purlin and between purlin and ridge board.

EAVES

The eaves of a roof is the lowest edge that overhangs the wall, thus giving the wall a degree of protection; it also provides the fixing medium for the rainwater gutter. The amount of projection from the wall of the eaves is a matter of choice but is generally in the region of 300–450 mm.

There are two basic types of eaves finish: **open eaves** and **closed eaves**. The former is less expensive, with rafters left exposed on the underside and treated with preservative. With both, the space between the rafters and the roof covering receives insulation over the top of the wall. A 50 mm air space must remain above the insulation for free air circulation through the roof in order to prevent condensation from occurring. This is easily achieved with a proprietary eaves ventilator secured between the rafters. A continuous triangular tilting fillet is fixed over the backs of the rafters to provide support for the bottom course of slates or tiles. A closed eaves is one in which the feet of the rafters are boxed in using a vertical fascia board, with the space between the fascia and the wall containing a ventilated soffit board. In a cheaper variant, the rafters are cut marginally beyond the wall face to leave space for ventilation and only a fascia board fixed to the rafter ends. This is called a **flush eaves**. Figures 6.1.5 and 6.1.6 indicate various rafter finishes, with provision for adequate through-ventilation.

50 mm min. air space

25 mm min. continuous gap

< 15˚ pitch (i.e. flat)

10 mm min. continuous gap

> 15˚ pitch

5 mm min. continuous gap through purpose-made ridge tiles

50 mm min. air space

25 mm min. continuous gap

Roofs with insulation in slope (i.e. between rafters)

Note: Gaps need not be continuous, if staggered voids provide the equivalent area

Figure 6.1.6   Roof ventilation requirements.

TIMBER ROOF TRUSSES

These can be used on the larger spans in domestic work to give an area below the ceiling level free from loadbearing walls. Trusses are structurally designed frames based on the principles of triangulation, and serve to carry the purlins; they are spaced at 1800 mm centres with the space between being infilled with common rafters. It is essential that the members of a roof truss are rigidly connected together, as light sections are generally used. To make a suitable rigid joint, bolts and timber connectors are used. These are square- or circular-toothed plates; the teeth are pointed up and down and, when clamped between two members, bite into the surface, forming a strong connection and spreading the stresses over a greater surface area. A typical roof truss detail is shown in Fig. 6.1.7.

TRUSSED RAFTERS

This is another approach to the formation of a domestic timber roof giving a clear span; as with roof trusses it is based upon a triangulated frame, but in this case the members are butt jointed and secured with truss plates. All members in a trussed rafter are machined on all faces so that they are of identical thickness, ensuring a strong connection on both faces. The trussed rafters are placed at 600 mm centres and tied together over their backs with 38 mm × 25 mm tiling battens; no purlin or ridge is required. Stability is achieved from the tile battens and 100 mm × 25 mm diagonal wind braces from the bottom corner to a top corner. Also, two 100 mm × 25 mm longitudinal ties should run horizontally along the ceiling ties.

Truss manufacturers will design and prefabricate to the client's specification. This should include span, loading (type of tile), degree of exposure, pitch, spacing (if not 600 mm), and details of any special loadings such as water cistern location.

Truss or nail plates are generally of one or two forms:

- those in which holes are punched to take nails; suitable for site assembly using a nailing gun;
- those in which teeth are punched and bent from the plate; used in factory assembly using heavy presses.

In all cases truss plates are fixed to both faces of the butt joint.

Trussed rafters are also produced using gusset plates of plywood at the butt joints instead of truss plates; typical details of both forms are shown in Fig. 6.1.8.

LATERAL BRACING

Gable ladders and restraint straps secure pitched roofs to adjacent walls and, in turn, add stability to the wall. Figure 6.1.9 shows the application with straps at 2 m spacing. Straps may need to be more frequent, depending on building height and degree of exposure.

Trusses are symmetrical about ridge
except for hanger trusses spaced at
1.800 c/c infill 100 × 38 rafters at 450 c/c

25 thick ridge

100 × 38 rafter

75 × 38 hanger

2 no. 75 × 38 ties

38 thick packing between ties

125 × 50 binder

Joists lapped at centre

100 × 50 purlin

100 × 50 strut

75 × 50 strut notched under rafter and over joist

Ventilation spacer

Bolts and timber connection

125 × 50

100 × 38 tie or ceiling joist

100 × 50 wall plate

Hole for bolt

Typical timber connector

Ventilated soffit on cradling

Fascia

Figure 6.1.7   Typical truss details for spans up to 8000 mm.

Spikes cut and pressed from galvanised steel plate

Alternative truss plate

Alternative method: plywood gusset plates to both faces

Punched holes for sheradised twisted or annular threaded nails

Galvanised steel plate

Typical truss plate

Trussed rafters at 600 c/c

All members of trussed rafters machined on faces

Truss plates to both faces

Ventilated soffit fixed to wall batten

Fascia

Figure 6.1.8 Typical trussed rafter details for spans up to 11 000 mm.

Gable wall

End truss
or rafter

Strut or ladder

Barge board

Noggins or struts
between rafters
at strap locations

30 × 5 galv. steel restraint
straps – 2 m max. spacing
extending over 3 rafters

Restraint strap min.
1 m length anchored
to wall and rafter at
max. 2 m spacing

Gable
wall

Wallplate

Figure 6.1.9 Lateral restraint to gable walls.

BUILDING REGULATIONS

Regulation 7

This requires that any building work shall be carried out with proper materials and in a workmanlike manner. The Approved Document supporting this regulation defines acceptable levels of performance for materials that include products, fittings, items of equipment, and backfilling for excavations. The aids for establishing fitness of materials suggested in the Approved Document are:

- past experience – such as a building in use;
- Agrément certificates or equivalent European Technical Approvals;
- British Standards and European Community national standards;
- independent certification schemes to the National Accreditation Council for Certification Bodies (NACCB) requirements;
- quality assurance schemes complying with BS 5750 and BS EN ISO 9000–9004;
- test and calculations for materials only using the National Measurement Accreditation Service (NAMAS) scheme for testing laboratories.

The Approved Document supporting Regulation 7 lists certain geographical areas where the softwood timber used for roof construction should be adequately treated with a suitable preservative to prevent infestation by the house longhorn beetle. This is a wise precaution whether it is recommended or not.

Regulation B4 (Section 14)

This requires the roof to offer adequate resistance to the spread of fire over the roof. Table 17 in Approved Document B gives limitations on roof coverings for dwelling houses by designations and distance from the boundary, the designations being defined in Table A5.

Regulation C2

This requires that the roof of a building shall adequately resist the passage of moisture to the inside of the building.

Regulation L1

This states that reasonable provision shall be made for the conservation of fuel and power in buildings. To satisfy this requirement Approved Document L requires that the roof construction is enhanced with suitable insulation material (see Chapter 8.2 for more detail).

Regulation A

The selection of suitable structural timber members for roofs with various loadings and spans can be determined from publications recommended in Approved Document A of the Building Regulations.

ROOF TILING AND SLATING

A roof can be defined as the upper covering of a building, and in this position it is fully exposed to the rain, snow, wind, sun and general atmosphere: therefore the covering to any roof structure must have good durability to meet these conditions. Other factors to be taken into account are weight, maintenance and cost.

Roofs are subjected to wind pressures, both positive and negative, the latter causing uplift and suction, which can be overcome by firmly anchoring lightweight coverings to the structure or by relying upon the deadweight of the covering material. Domestic roofs are not usually designed for general access, and therefore the chosen covering material should be either very durable or easily replaceable. The total dead load of the covering will affect the type of support structure required and ultimately the total load on the foundations, so therefore careful consideration must be given to the medium selected for the roof covering.

In domestic work the roof covering usually takes the form of tiling or slating, because these materials economically fulfil the above requirements and have withstood the test of time.

▨▨■ TILING

Tiles are manufactured from clay and concrete to a wide range of designs and colours suitable for pitches from 15° to 45°, and work upon the principle of either double or single lap. The vital factor for the efficient performance of any tile or slate is the pitch, and it should be noted that the pitch of a tile is always less than the pitch of the rafters owing to the overlapping technique.

Tiles are laid in overlapping courses and rely upon the water being shed off the surface of one tile onto the exposed surface of the tile in the next course. The problem of water entering by capillary action between the tiles is overcome by the camber of the tile, by the method of laying, or by overlapping side joints. In all methods of tiling a wide range of fittings are produced to enable all roof shapes to be adequately protected.

PLAIN TILING

This is a common method in this country and works on the double lap principle. The tiles can be of handmade or machine-pressed clay, the process of manufacture being similar to that of brickmaking. The handmade tile is used mainly where a rustic or distinctive roof character is required, because they have a wide variation in colour, texture and shape. They should not be laid on a roof of less than 45° pitch because they tend to absorb water, and if allowed to become saturated they may freeze, expand and spall or fracture in cold weather. Machine-pressed tiles are harder, denser and more uniform in shape than handmade varieties and can be laid to a minimum pitch of 35°.

A suitable substitute for plain clay tiles is the concrete plain tile. These are produced in a range of colours to the same size specifications as the clay tiles and with the same range of fittings. The main advantage of concrete tiles is their lower costs; the main disadvantage is the extra weight. Plain clay tile details are specified in BS EN 1304 and BS EN 538. Concrete tiles have separate designation in BS EN 490 and 491.

Plain tiling, in common with other forms of tiling, provides an effective barrier to rain and snow penetration, but wind is able to penetrate into the building through the gaps between the tiling units: therefore a barrier in the form of boarding or sheeting is placed over the roof carcass before the battens on which the tiles are to be hung are fixed.

The rule for plain tiling is that there must always be at least two thicknesses of tiles covering any part of the roof, and bonded so that no 'vertical' joint is immediately over a 'vertical' joint in the course below. To enable this rule to be maintained shorter-length tiles are required at the eaves and the ridge; each alternate course is commenced with a wider tile of one-and-a-half tile widths. The apex or ridge is capped with a special tile bedded in cement mortar over the general tile surface. The hips can be covered with a ridge tile, in which case the plain tiling is laid underneath and mitred on top of the hip; alternatively a special bonnet tile can be used where the plain tiles bond with the edges of the bonnet tiles. Valleys can be formed by using special tiles or mitred plain tiles, or by forming an open gutter with a durable material such as lead. The verge at the gable end can be formed by bedding plain tiles face down on the gable wall as an undercloak and bedding the plain tiles in cement mortar on the upper surface of the undercloak. The verge tiling should overhang its support by at least 50 mm. Abutments are made watertight by dressing a flashing over the upper surface of tiling, between which is sandwiched a soaker. The soaker in effect forms a gutter. An alternative method is to form a cement fillet on top of the tiled surface, but this method sometimes fails by the cement shrinking away from the surface of the wall.

The support or fixing battens are of softwood extended over and fixed to at least three rafters, the spacing or gauge being determined by the lap given to the tiles thus:

Camber in length

Nail holes

10 to 15

265

165

Width for tile and half = 248 with 3 no. nibs length for eaves and top course tile = 190

Standard plain tiles

105° or 90°

200

Angle section

105°

200

Segmental section

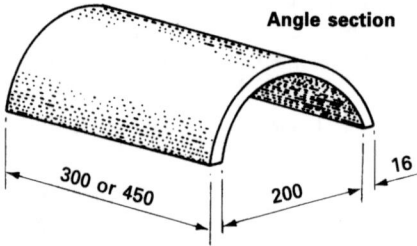

300 or 450

200

16

Half-round ridge tile

150

200

Hog back section

[Typical ridge tiles]

200 min.

300

Bonnet hip tile

Various angles

200 min.

225 min.

Angular hip tile

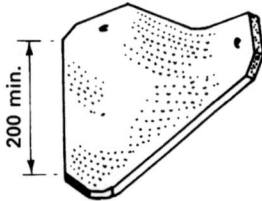

200 min.

Curved valley tile

265 min.

Angular valley tile

Figure 6.2.1   Standard plain tiles and fittings.

$$\text{Gauge} = \frac{\text{length of tile} - \text{lap}}{2}$$

$$\text{Gauge} = \frac{265 - 65}{2} = 100 \text{ mm.}$$

Plain tiles are fixed with two galvanised nails to each tile in every fourth or fifth course. Details of plain tiles, fittings and methods of laying are shown in Figs 6.2.1 to 6.2.5.

SINGLE-LAP TILING

Single-lap tiles are laid with overlapping side joints to a minimum pitch of 35° and are not bonded like the butt-jointed single-lap plain tiles; this gives an overall reduction in weight as fewer tiles are used. A common form of single-lap tile is the **pantile**, which has opposite corners mitred to overcome the problem of four tile thicknesses at the corners (see Fig. 6.2.6). The pantile is a larger unit than the plain tile and is best employed on large roofs with gabled ends, because the formation of hips and valleys is difficult and expensive. Other forms of single-lap tiling are Roman tiling, Spanish tiling and interlocking tiling. The latter types are produced in both concrete and clay and have one or two grooves in the overlapping edge to give greater resistance to wind penetration; they can generally be laid as low as 15° pitch (see Fig. 6.2.6).

■ ■ ■ SLATING

Slate is a naturally dense material, which can be split into thin sheets and used to provide a suitable covering to a pitched roof. Slates are laid to the same basic principles as double-lap roofing tiles except that every slate should be twice nailed. Slates come mainly from Wales, Cornwall and the Lake District and are cut to a wide variety of sizes – the Westmorland slates are harder to cut and are usually supplied in random sizes. Slates can be laid to a minimum pitch of 25° and are fixed by head nailing or centre nailing. Centre nailing is used to overcome the problem of vibration caused by the wind and tending to snap the slate at the fixing if nailed at the head; it is used mainly on the long slates and pitches below 35°.

The gauge of the battens is calculated thus:

$$\text{Head-nailed gauge} = \frac{\text{length of slate} - (\text{lap} + 25 \text{ mm})}{2}$$

$$= \frac{400 - (75 + 25)}{2} = 150 \text{ mm}$$

$$\text{Centre-nailed gauge} = \frac{\text{length of slate} - \text{lap}}{2}$$

$$= \frac{400 - 76}{2} = 162 \text{ mm.}$$

Roofing slates are covered by BS EN 12326-1, which gives details of standard sizes, thicknesses and quality. Typical details of slating are shown in Fig. 6.2.7.

Alternative fixing for under-ridge tile – hung on 38 × 32 batten

Plain tiles laid face down as undercloak

1:3 cm. mt. bed

Boxed fascia

Tile and half to complete bond

Verge detail

Ridge

Half-round ridge-capping bedded and jointed in cm. mt. (1:3)

Top course tile nailed to ridge

Insulation

Under-eaves course

Gauge

Margin

Lap

Undertiling felt

Cavity closer

Insulated cavity wall

Plain tiles on 38 × 25 battens, each tile in every 4th course nailed

Eaves course tile

Ventilated soffit

Figure 6.2.2 Plain tiling details.

Typical abutment detail (see also Fig. 5.1.1)

Ridge termination at gable end

Ridge junction with hipped end

Figure 6.2.3 Abutment and ridge details.

Bonnet hip tiles nailed
and bedded in cm. mt.
(1:3) to hip rafter

Tile slip

Plain tiles bonded with
bonnet hip tiles

Under-eaves tile course

Half-round hip capping
bedded in cm. mt. (1:3)

Galvanised hip
iron screwed to
top of hip rafter

Plain tiles mitred over hip
rafter under-hip capping

Figure 6.2.4 Hip treatments.

Figure 6.2.5 Valley treatments.

Figure 6.2.6 Examples of single-lap tiling.

Double course of slates at ridge

Clay angle ridge tile bedded in cm. mt. (1:3)

Ridge

Rafters

Typical ridge detail

Under-eaves slate 300 long (G + L + 25)

75 lap

200 margin

Undertiling felt

50×25 battens at 200 gauge

Insulation between ceiling joist

Wall plate

Fascia

Ventilated soffit

Head-nailed slating using 500 × 250 slates

Under-eaves slate 365 long

80 lap

260 margin

Undertiling felt

50×25 battens at 260 gauge

Insulation between ceiling joists

Wall plate

Cavity closer

40

Fascia

Ventilated soffit

Centre-nailed slating using 600 × 300 slates

Figure 6.2.7   Typical slating details.

▨▦▪ UNDERTILING FELTS

The object of undertiling felt is to keep out dust and the wind. It also provides a secondary waterproof layer for limited protection against rain if tiles are damaged. It consists basically of a bituminous impregnated matted fibre sheet, which can be reinforced with a layer of jute hessian embedded in the coating on one side to overcome the tendency of felts to tear readily. Undertiling felts are supplied in rolls 1 m wide and 10 or 20 m long depending upon type. They should be laid over the rafters and parallel to the eaves with 150 mm laps and temporarily fixed with large-head felt nails until finally secured by the battens. Traditional first-generation undertiling felts are also known as **sarking felts** and should conform to the requirements of BS 747. They should also be permeable to water vapour, to relieve any possibility of condensation in the roof space. Subsequently there has been a second generation of lightweight tiling underlays produced from reinforced plastics. As for traditional bituminous felt, there is a risk that condensation can form on the underside. Third-generation underlays are of triple-ply construction, comprising a waterproof and vapour-permeable core between layers of non-woven, spun-bonded polypropylene. In effect, they permit internal moisture to pass through but remain watertight to external conditions.

Figure 6.2.8   Plain tiled warm roof.

▓▓■ COUNTER BATTENS

If a roof is boarded before the roofing felt is applied the tiling battens will provide ledges on which dirt and damp can collect. To overcome this problem counter battens are fixed to the boarding over the rafter positions to form a cavity between the tiling battens and the boarding. Boarding a roof over the rafters is a method of providing a wind barrier and adding to the thermal insulation properties, but it is seldom used in new work because of the high cost.

Use of counter battening is common where pitched roofs are of warm construction, i.e. the insulation is above the roof slope to create a habitable room in the roof void. See Fig. 6.2.8. Cold roof construction with insulation at ceiling joist level is shown in Figs 6.2.2 and 6.2.7.

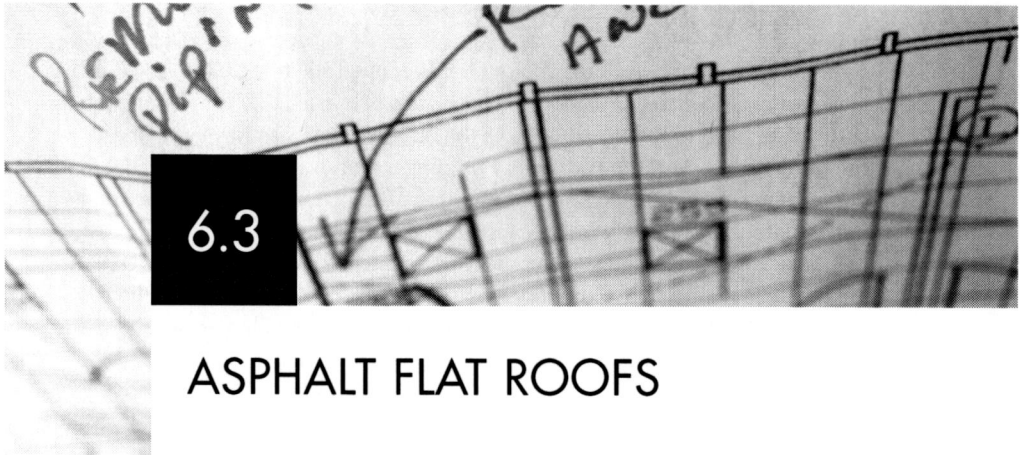

6.3

ASPHALT FLAT ROOFS

Flat roofs are often considered to be a simple form of construction, but unless correctly designed and constructed they can be an endless source of trouble. Flat roofs can have the advantage of providing an extra area to a building for the purposes of recreation and an additional viewpoint. Mastic asphalt provides an ideal covering material, especially where foot traffic is required.

Mastic asphalt consists of an aggregate with a bituminous binder, which is cast into blocks ready for reheating on site (see Chapter 7.8). The blocks are heated in cauldrons or cookers to a temperature of over 200 °C and are then transported in a liquid state in buckets for application to the roof deck by hand spreading. Once the melted asphalt has been removed from the source of heat it will cool and solidify rapidly: therefore the distance between the cauldron and the point of application should be kept to a minimum. Mastic asphalt can be applied to most types of rigid substructure and proprietary structural deckings. To prevent slight movements occurring between the substructure and the finish an isolating membrane should be laid over the base before the mastic asphalt is applied.

Roof work will often entail laying mastic asphalt to horizontal, sloping and vertical surfaces, and these are defined as follows:

- horizontal surfaces – up to 10° pitch;
- sloping surfaces – between 10° and 45° pitch;
- vertical surfaces – over 45° pitch.

The thickness and number of coats required will depend on two factors:

- surface type;
- substructure or base.

Horizontal surfaces with any form of rigid base should have a two-coat application of mastic asphalt laid breaking the joint and built up to a minimum total thickness of 20 mm. An isolating membrane of black sheathing felt complying with BS 747 Type 4A(i) should be used as an underlay laid dry over insulation boards with 50 mm lapped joints.

Vertical and sloping surfaces other than those with a timber base require a three-coat application built up to a 20 mm total thickness without an isolating membrane.

Timber substructures with vertical and sloping surfaces should have a three-coat 20 mm mastic asphalt finish applied to expanded metal lathing complying with BS 1369 fixed at 150 mm centres over an isolating membrane.

If the mastic asphalt surface is intended for foot traffic the total thickness of the two-coat application should be increased to a minimum of 25 mm.

Roofs with a mastic asphalt finish can be laid to falls so that the run-off of water is rapid and efficient. Puddles of water left on the roof surface will create small areas of different surface temperatures, which could give rise to local differential thermal movements and cause cracking of the protective covering. Depressions will also provide points at which dust and rubbish can collect: it is therefore essential that suitable falls be provided to direct the water to an eaves gutter or specific outlet points. The falls should be formed on the base or supporting structure to a gradient of not less than 1 in 80 (see typical details in Figs 6.3.1 and 6.3.2).

Alternatively the roof can be designed to act as a reservoir by a technique sometimes called **ponding**. The principle is to retain on the roof surface a 'pond' of water some 150 mm deep by having the surface completely flat, with high skirtings and outlets positioned 150 mm above the roof level. The main advantage is that differential temperatures are reduced to a minimum; the disadvantages are the need for a stronger supporting structure to carry the increased load, a three-coat 30 mm thick covering of mastic asphalt, and the need to flood the roof in dry hot weather to prevent the pond from completely evaporating away.

Resistance to heat loss can be achieved by incorporating within the structure a dry insulation such as cork slabs, wood fibre boards, glass or mineral fibre boards, rigid polyisocyanurate (Pi) foam board or rigid lightweight expanded polystyrene (EPS) board. This may be deployed to create warm or cold deck roof insulating principles as described in Chapter 6.1. If fixed over the roof structure it will reduce the temperature variations within the roof to a minimum and hence the risk of unacceptable thermal movements. A lightweight concrete screed will also prove a useful insulative supplement and a means of providing the roof slope. Suitable aggregates are furnace clinker, foamed blast furnace slag, pumice, expanded clay, sintered pulverised fuel ash, exfoliated vermiculite and expanded perlite. The thickness should not be less than 40 mm, and it may be necessary to apply to the screed a 1:4 cement:sand topping to provide the necessary surface finish. Mix ratios of 1:8–10 are generally recommended for screeds of approximately 1100 kg/m^3 density using foamed slag, sintered pulverised fuel ash and expanded clay, whereas a 1:5 mix is recommended for exfoliated vermiculite and expanded perlite aggregates giving a low density of under 640 kg/m^3. When mixing screeds containing porous aggregates, high water/cement ratios are required to give workable mixes, and therefore the screeds take a long time to dry out.

Moisture in the form of a vapour will tend to rise within the building and condense on the underside of the covering or within the thickness of the insulating

Figure 6.3.1 Timber flat roof with mastic asphalt covering.

Labels:

- Firring
- 13 mm layer of light-coloured stone chippings
- 2-coat 20 mm thick asphalt
- Isolating membrane
- Boarded deck
- 50 mm min. air space
- Metal trim
- Fascia
- 25 mm continuous ventilation gap
- Soffit
- 12 mm ventilation gap
- Code 4 lead flashing
- 150 × 100 timber fillet
- 3-coat 20 mm thick asphalt
- 2-coat angle fillet
- Expanded metal lathing
- Vapour control layer
- Insulation between joists
- Joist hanger
- 9.5 mm plasterboard

Mineral wool insulation board

13 mm layer of light-coloured stone chippings

Metal trim

Isolating membrane

2-coat 20 mm thick asphalt

Timber fillet

Cavity insulation

Skirting dressed into 25 × 25 chase

2-coat asphalt skirting keyed to brickwork

2-coat angle fillet

150 min.

Lightweight insulating screed laid to falls

Vapour control layer

RC roof slab

Figure 6.3.2 Reinforced concrete flat roof with mastic asphalt covering.

material. If an insulating material becomes damp its efficiency will decrease, and if composed of organic material it can decompose. To overcome this problem a vapour control layer of a suitable impermeable material such as polythene sheet or aluminium foil should be placed beneath the insulating layer. Care must be taken to see that all laps are complete and sealed and that the edges of the insulating material are similarly protected against the infiltration of moisture vapour. This is achieved by turning the vapour control layer around the edges of insulation board and bonding about 300 mm (min. 150 mm) to the top face of board.

The surface of a flat roof, being fully exposed, will gain heat by solar radiation and if insulated will be raised to a temperature in excess of the air or ambient temperature, as the transfer of heat to the inside of the building has been reduced by the insulating layer. The usual method employed to reduce the amount of solar heat gain of the covering is to cover the upper surface of the roof with light-coloured chippings to act as a reflective finish. Suitable aggregates are white spar, calcined flint, white limestone or any light-coloured granite of 12 mm size and embedded in a bitumen compound.

LEAD-COVERED FLAT ROOFS

Lead as a building material has been used extensively for over 5000 years, and is obtained mainly from the mineral galena, of which Australia, Canada, Mexico and the USA are the main producers. The raw material is mined, refined to a high degree of purity and then cast into bars or pigs, which can be used to produce lead sheet, pipe and extruded products.

Lead is a durable and dense material (11 340 kg/m³) of low strength but is very malleable and can be worked cold into complicated shapes without fracture. In common with other non-ferrous metals, lead oxidises on exposure to the atmosphere and forms a thin protective film or coating over its surface. When in contact with other metals there is seldom any corrosion by electrolysis, and therefore fixing is usually carried out by using durable copper nails.

For application to flat roofs, milled lead sheet should comply with the recommendations of BS EN 12588. The sheet is supplied in rolls of widths varying between 150 mm and 2400 mm, in 3 m and 6 m standard lengths. For easy identification, lead sheet carries a colour guide for each code number:

BS Code No.	Thickness (mm)	Weight (kg/m²)	Colour
3	1.32	14.97	green
4	1.80	20.41	blue
5	2.24	25.40	red
6	2.65	30.10	black
7	3.15	35.72	white
8	3.55	40.26	orange

The code number is derived from the former imperial notation of 5 lb/ft² = No. 5 lead.

The thickness or code number of lead sheet for any particular situation will depend upon the protection required against mechanical damage and the shape

Figure 6.4.1   Typical layout of lead flat roof.

required. The following thicknesses can therefore be considered as a general guide for flat roofs:

- small areas without foot traffic, No. 4 or 5;
- small areas with foot traffic, No. 5, 6 or 7;
- large areas with or without foot traffic, No. 5, 6 or 7;
- flashings, No. 4 or 5;
- aprons, No. 4 or 5.

Milled lead sheet may be used as a covering over timber or similar deckings and over smooth screeded surfaces. In all cases an underlay of felt or stout building paper should be used to reduce frictional resistances, decrease surface irregularities and, in the case of a screeded surface, isolate the lead from any free lime present that might cause corrosion. Provision must also be made for the expansion and contraction of the metal covering. This can be achieved by limiting the area and/or length of the sheets being used. The following table indicates the maximum recommended area and length for any one piece of lead:

BS Code No.	Max. length between drips (m)	Max. area (m^2)
3	Only suitable for soakers	—
4	1.50	1.13
5	2.00	1.60
6	2.25	1.91
7	2.50	2.25
8	3.00	3.00

Joints that can accommodate the anticipated thermal movements are in the form of rolls running parallel to the fall and drips at right angles to the fall positioned so that they can be cut economically from a standard sheet: for layout and construction details see Figs 6.4.1 and 6.4.2.

[*Note*: Current legislation will require these details to incorporate cavity insulation in the walls with an insulative concrete block inner leaf. Insulation must also be included within the roof construction, as shown in Chapter 6.1.]

Lead
flashing

1:3 cement/sand pointing

Lead wedges at 450 c/c

Clips hung
over top edge
of skirting

40
lap

Lead
sheeting

Wood
roll

Felt underlay

Skirting

Decking

Lead sheets
dressed as
underlay on
one roll and
as overlay on
next roll

Head roll

Bossed
end

**Typical
wood
roll**

45

50

25

40

50 mm
high
drip

Lead
underlay
close
copper
nailed
to roll

Anti-capillarity groove

Drip former batten

Felt underlay

Decking

Figure 6.4.2   Lead flat roof details.

COPPER-COVERED FLAT ROOFS

Copper, like lead, has been used as a building material for many centuries. It is obtained from ore deposits, which have to be mined, crushed, and ground to a fine powder. The copper dust, which is about 4% of the actual rock mined, is separated from the waste materials, generally by a system of flotation, and transferred to the smelting furnace and then cast into cakes of blister copper or thick slabs called **anodes**. The metal is now refined and formed into copper wire, strip, sheets and castings. Copper is also used to form alloys that are used in making components for the building industry. Common alloys are copper and zinc (forming brass) and copper and tin (forming bronze).

Copper is a dense material (8900 kg/m^3) that is highly ductile and malleable, and can be cold-worked into the required shape or profile. The metal hardens with cold-working, but its original dead soft temper can be restored by the application of heat with a blowlamp or oxyacetylene torch and quenching with water or by natural air cooling. If the dead soft temper is not maintained the hardened copper will be difficult to work and may fracture. On exposure to the atmosphere copper forms on its upper surface a natural protective film or patina, which varies in colour from green to black, making the copper beneath virtually inert.

For covering flat roofs rolled copper complying with the recommendations of BS 2870 is generally specified. Rolled copper is available in three forms:

- **Sheet** Flat material of exact length, over 0.15 mm up to and including 10.0 mm thick and over 450 mm in width.
- **Strip** Material over 0.15 mm up to and including 10.0 mm thick and any width, and generally not cut to length. It is usually supplied in coils but can be obtained flat or folded.
- **Foil** Material 0.15 mm thick and under, of any width supplied flat or in a coil; because of its thickness foil has no practical application in the context of roof coverings.

Figure 6.5.1 Typical layout of copper flat roof.

In general copper strip is used for flashings and damp-proof courses, whereas sheet or strip can be considered for general roof covering application; widths of 600 and 750 mm, according to thickness, are used with a standard length of 1.800 m.

The copper sheet or strip is laid in bays between rolls or standing seams to allow for the expansion of the covering. Standing seams are not recommended for pitches under 5° because they may be flattened by foot traffic and become a source of moisture penetration due to a capillary action. The recommended maximum bay widths for the common sheet thicknesses used are:

- 0.60 mm thick – maximum bay width 600 mm;
- 0.70 mm thick – maximum bay width 750 mm.

Transverse joints in the form of double lock welts should be used on all flat roofs. The welts should be sealed with a mastic or linseed oil before being folded together. Cross-welts may be staggered or continuous across the roof when used in conjunction with batten rolls (see Fig. 6.5.1).

An exception is the relatively new concept of long strip copper roofing. It uses special sheet lengths of up to 10 m in standard widths, without the need for cross-welts. Panels are machined together with standing welts/seams, which include sliding clips to allow for longitudinal movement. The process is less labour intensive than traditional, and therefore more economical to apply, and the roof appearance is smoother.

The substructure supporting the covering needs to be permanent, even, smooth, and laid to the correct fall of not less than 1:60 (40 mm in 2.400 m). With a concrete structural roof a lightweight screed is normally laid to provide the correct surface and fall; if the screed has a sulphate content it will require sealing coats of bitumen to prevent any moisture present from forming dilute acids which might react with the copper covering. The 50 mm × 25 mm dovetail battens inserted in the screed to provide the fixing medium for the batten rolls should be impregnated with a suitable wood preservative. Timber flat roofs should be wind tight and free from 'spring', and may be covered with 25 mm nominal tongued and grooved boarding laid with the fall or diagonally, or any other decking material that fulfils the general requirements given above.

On flat roofs, drips at least 65 mm high are required at centres not exceeding 3.000 m to increase the flow of rainwater across the roof to the gutter or outlet. To lessen the wear on the copper covering as it expands and contracts a separating layer of felt (BS 747 Type 4A(ii)) should be incorporated into the design. The copper sheet should be secured with copper wire nails not less than 2.6 mm thick and at least 25 mm long; the batten rolls should be secured with well countersunk brass screws. Typical constructional details are shown in Fig. 6.5.2.

[*Note*: For habitable accommodation current Building Regulations require the external walls to include a lightweight concrete block inner leaf and cavity insulation. The roof will also need insulating, as shown in Chapter 6.1.]

Figure 6.5.2   Copper flat roof details.

ROOFLIGHTS IN PITCHED ROOFS

Rooflights can be included in the design of a pitched roof to provide daylight and ventilation to rooms within the roof space, or to supplement the daylight from windows in the walls of medium- and large-span single-storey buildings.

In domestic work a rooflight generally takes one of two forms – the dormer window or skylight. A **dormer window** has a vertical sash, and therefore projects from the main roof; the cheeks or sides can be clad with a sheet material such as lead or tile hanging, and the roof can be pitched or flat of traditional construction (see Fig. 6.6.1).

A **skylight** is fixed in a trimmed opening and follows approximately the pitch of the roof. It can be constructed as an opening or dead light (see Fig. 6.6.2). In common with all rooflights in pitched roofs, making the junctions water- and weathertight present the greatest problems, and careful attention must be given to the detail and workmanship involved in the construction of dormer windows and rooflights.

Roofs of the type used on medium-span industrial buildings with coverings such as corrugated fibre cement sheeting supported by purlins and steel roof trusses require a different treatment. The amount of useful daylight entering the interior of such a building from windows fixed in the external walls will depend upon:

- the size of windows;
- the height of window above the floor level;
- the span of building.

Generally the maximum distance that useful daylight will penetrate is approximately 10.000 m; over this distance artificial lights or rooflights will be required during the daylight period. Three methods are available for the provision of rooflights in profiled sheeted roofs.

Special rooflight units of fibre cement consisting of an upstand kerb surmounted by either a fixed or opening glazed sash can be fixed instead of a standard profiled

Figure 6.6.1 Typical flat roof dormer window details.

Horizontal section through cheek

Timber studding and plasterboard to wall

Vapour-check lined plasterboard

Dormer window

Trimming rafter

Lead or similar cladding to dormer cheek (tiled or other vapour-permeable treatment preferred)

Plywood face

Studding to cheek

Timber facing

Timber beam over dormer opening

Dormer cheeks of timber studding

Dormer wall of timber studding

Skirting

Flooring and joists

Insulated timber studding

Vertical section

Tilting fillet

Sheet roof covering

Roof decking

Wrot timber beam with outside timber facing

Vapour-check lined plasterboard

Roof joists

Firring

Fillet

Fascia

Ventilation gap

Soffit

Casement window

Lead or similar flashing

Roof tiling

Hinges

Timber or metal tongue

Glass

Skylight framing

Lead gutter and apron lining

Lead clips

Lining

Insulation

Lead flashing and apron

Trimming

Vapour-check lined plasterboard

Packing

Control cord

Quadrant opening gear – alternative-teleflex gear

Trimmer

Alternative methods: preformed metal skylights; patent glazing and any combination

Typical section

Skylight framing

Lead gutter and apron lining

Lining

Glazing bar

Glass

Lead clips

Trimming rafter

Cover moulding

3 mm deep condensation groove

Bottom rail

Side detail

Bottom rail detail

Figure 6.6.2   Typical timber opening skylight.

sheet. These units are useful where the design calls for a series of small isolated glazed rooflights to supplement the natural daylight. An alternative is to use translucent profiled sheets that are of the same size and profile as the main roof covering. In selecting the type of sheet to be used the requirements of Part B of the Building Regulations must be considered. Approved Document B4 (Section 14) deals specifically with the fire risks of roof coverings, and refers to the designations defined in BS 476-3. These designations consist of two letters: the first letter represents the time of penetration when subjected to external fire, and the second letter is the distance of spread of flame along the external surface. Each group of designations has four letters, A–D, and in both cases the letter A has the highest resistance. Specimens used in the BS 476 test are tested for use on either a flat surface or a sloping surface, and therefore the material designation is preceded by either EXT. F or EXT. S.

Most of the translucent profiled sheets have a high light transmission, are light in weight, and can be fixed in the same manner as the general roof covering. It is advisable to weather-seal all lapping edges of profiled rooflights with silicon or mastic sealant to accommodate the variations in thickness and expansion rate of the adjacent materials. Typical examples are:

- **Polyester glass fibre sheets**   Made from polyester resins reinforced with glass fibre and nylon to the recommendations of BS 4154. These sheets can be of natural colour or tinted, and are made to suit most corrugated fibre cement and metal profiles. Typical designations are EXT. S.AA for self-extinguishing sheets and EXT. S.AB for general-purpose sheets.
- **Wire-reinforced PVC sheets**   Made from unplasticised PVC reinforced with a fine wire mesh to give a high resistance to shattering by impact. Designation is EXT. S.AA, and they can therefore be used for all roofing applications. Profiles are generally limited to Categories A and B defined in BS EN 494.
- **PVC sheets**   Made from heavy gauge clear unplasticised rigid PVC to the recommendations of BS 4203, they are classified as self-extinguishing when tested in accordance with method 508A of BS 2782: Part O, Annex C, and may be used on the roof of a building provided that part of the roof is at least 6.000 m from any boundary. If that part of the roof is less than 6.000 m from any boundary and covers a garage, conservatory or outhouse with a floor area of less than 40 m^2, or is on an open balcony, carport or the like, or a detached swimming pool, PVC sheets can be used without restriction. Table 6.3 of Approved Document B defines the use of these sheets for the roof covering of a canopy over a balcony, veranda, open carport, covered way or detached swimming pool.

As an alternative to profiled rooflights in isolated areas, continuous rooflights can be incorporated into a corrugated or similar roof covering by using flat-wired glass and patent glazing bars. The bars are fixed to the purlins and spaced at 600 mm centres to carry either single or double glazing. The bars are available as a steel bar sheathed in lead or PVC or as an aluminium alloy extrusion (see Fig. 6.6.3). Many sections with different glass-securing techniques are manufactured under the patents granted to the producers, but all have the same basic principles. The bar is generally an inverted 'T' section, the flange providing the bearing for the glass and the stem

Jointless lead sheath

Lead wings dressed onto glass

40 × 32 rolled steel bulb tee bar core

6 mm wired glass

Neoprene or rubber seal

Condensation channel

Crittall-Hope lead-clothed steel bar

PVC snap-on capping

40 × 32 rolled steel bulb tee bar core

White PVC sheath

6 mm wired glass

Neoprene or rubber seal

Condensation channel

Crittall-Hope polyclad bar

Aluminium alloy extruded bar

Wing fixing bolt

Aluminium wing bolted through bar

6 mm wired glass

Neoprene or rubber seal

Condensation channel

British Challenge aluminium bar

Aluminium alloy extruded bar

Aluminium alloy cover strip

6 mm wired glass

Neoprene or rubber seal

Condensation channel

Heywood Williams 'Aluminex' bar

Figure 6.6.3   Typical patent glazing bar sections.

Figure 6.6.4   Patent glazing and profiled roof covering connection details.

depth giving the bar its spanning properties. Other standard components are fixing shoes, glass weathering springs or clips, and glass stops at the bottom end of the bar (see Fig. 6.6.3).

As the glass and the glazing bar are straight they cannot simply replace a standard profiled sheet; they must be fixed below the general covering at the upper end and above the covering at the lower end to enable the rainwater to discharge onto the general roof surface. Great care must be taken with this detail and with the quality of workmanship on site if a durable and satisfactory junction is to be made. Typical details are shown in Fig. 6.6.4.

The total amount of glazing to be used in any situation involves design appreciation beyond the scope of this volume, but a common rule of thumb method is to use an area of glazing equal to 10% of the total roof area. The glass specified is usually a wired glass of suitable thickness for the area of pane being used. Wired glass is selected so that it will give the best protection should an outbreak of fire occur; the splinters caused by the heat cracking the glass will adhere to the wire mesh and not shatter onto the floor below. A successful alternative is laminated glass composed of two or more sheets of float glass with a plastic interlayer. Polyvinylbutyral (PVB) is the most common interlayer, which is bonded to the glass laminates by heat and pressure. If broken, the glass remains stuck to the PVB to provide the benefit of safety and security. It also remains intact following impact from bullets or explosive blasts.

As with timber skylights, provision should be made to collect the condensation that can occur on the underside of the glazing to prevent the annoyance of droplets of water falling to the floor below. Most patent glazing bars for single glazing have condensation channels attached to the edges of the flange, which directs the collected condensation to the upper surface of the roof below the glazing line (see Figs 6.6.3 and 6.6.4). Contemporary frames can be produced from uPVC or extruded aluminium. The latter is often coated in polyester powder for colour enhancement and protection. A double-glazed example is shown in Fig. 6.6.5. This applies the principle of tension between the glazing frame and glass for security of fit, with the ability to respond to thermal movement without loss of seal.

Figure 6.6.5 'Glidevale' patent double-glazing unit.

Polycarbonate (PC) can be an economic option in preference to glass, particularly for rooflight applications. It has the benefit of a double skin if required and, although produced in flat sheet format, can be moulded to domed profiles. Colour variants are possible, in addition to transparent, translucent and opaque composition. Dimensions, types and characteristics are defined in BS EN ISO 11963.

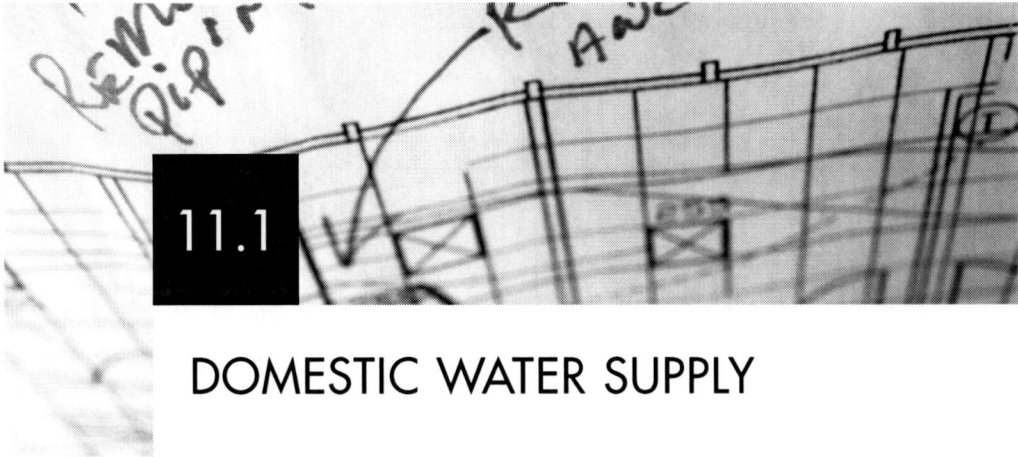

11.1

DOMESTIC WATER SUPPLY

An adequate supply of water is a basic requirement for most buildings, for reasons of personal hygiene or for activities such as cooking and manufacturing processes. In most areas a piped supply of water is available from the local utility company's water main.

Water is, in the first instance, produced by condensation in the form of clouds, and falls to the ground as rain, snow or hail; it then either becomes surface water in the form of a river, stream or lake, or percolates through the subsoil until it reaches an impervious stratum, or is held in a water-bearing subsoil.

The water authority extracts water from surface storage reservoirs, rivers or through boreholes into water-bearing subsoil. Thereafter it is filtered, chlorinated, aerated, and treated with fluoride for human consumption before distribution through a system of mains.

The water company's mains are laid underground at a depth where they will be unaffected by frost or traffic movement. The layout of the system is generally a circuit with trunk mains feeding a grid of subsidiary mains for distribution to specific areas or districts. The materials used for main pipes are cast iron and uPVC, which can be tapped while under pressure; a plug cock is inserted into the crown of the mains pipe to provide the means of connecting the communication pipe to supply an individual building.

Terminology
- **Main** A pipe for the general conveyance of water, as distinct from the conveyance to individual premises.
- **Service** A system of pipes and fittings for the supply and distribution of water in any individual premises.
- **Service pipe** A pipe in a service that is directly subject to pressure from a main, sometimes called the rising main, inside the building.

Figure 11.1.1   Supply pipe and copper pipe joint details.

- **Communication pipe**   That part of the service pipe that is vested in the water undertaking.
- **Distribution pipe**   Any pipe in a service conveying water from a storage cistern.
- **Cistern**   A container for water in which the stored water is under atmospheric pressure.
- **Storage cistern**   Any cistern other than a flushing cistern.
- **Tank**   A rectangular vessel completely closed and used to store water.
- **Cylinder**   A closed cylindrical tank.

▨▉▉ COLD WATER SUPPLY

The water company will provide from their mains tapping plug cock a communication pipe to a stop valve and protection chamber just outside the boundary; this is a chargeable item to the building owner. The gooseneck bend is included to relieve any stress likely to be exerted on the mains connection.

A service pipe is taken from this stop valve to an internal stop valve, preferably located just above floor level and housed under the sink unit. The stop valve should have a drain-off valve incorporated in it, or just above it, so that the service pipe or rising main can be drained.

Care must be taken when laying a service pipe that it is not placed in a position where it can be adversely affected by frost, heavy traffic or building loads. A minimum depth of 750 mm is generally recommended for supplies to domestic properties; where the pipe passes under a building it should be housed in a protective duct or pipe suitably insulated within 750 mm of the floor level (see Fig. 11.1.1).

Suitable materials for service pipes are copper, PVC, polythene and galvanised steel. Copper service pipes can be laid on and covered by a layer of sand to prevent direct contact with the earth, or wrapped with a suitable proprietary insulating material. Plastic-coated copper pipes are also available for underground pipework. Steel pipes should have a similar protection, but plastic pipes are resistant to both frost and corrosion and have largely superseded metal pipes in this situation.

WATER METER

These are a standard installation for all new buildings and conversions within buildings, as a resource conservation measure. Existing premises may have meters installed at the water authority's discretion. Where practicable, the meter is located on the service pipe, in a small compartment below ground and just inside the property boundary. If this proves impossible owing to lack of space, the meter may be positioned at the base of the rising main.

DIRECT COLD WATER SUPPLY

In this system the whole of the cold water to the sanitary fittings is supplied directly from the service pipe. The direct system is used mainly in northern districts where

Direct system of cold water supply

Indirect system of cold water supply

Note: All pipe sizes shown are standard copper outside diameters

Figure 11.1.2 Cold water supply systems.

large, high-level reservoirs provide a good mains supply and pressure. With this system only a small cold water storage cistern to feed the hot water tank is required; this can usually be positioned below the roof ceiling level, giving a saving on pipe runs to the roof space and eliminating the need to insulate the pipes against frost (see Fig. 11.1.2).

Another advantage of the direct system is that drinking water is available from several outlet points. The main disadvantage is the lack of reserve should the mains supply be cut off for repairs; also there can be a lowering of the supply during peak demand periods.

When sanitary fittings are connected directly to a mains supply there is always a risk of contamination of the mains water by back-siphonage. This can occur if there is a negative pressure on the mains and any of the outlets are submerged below the water level, such as a hand spray connected to the taps.

INDIRECT COLD WATER SUPPLY

In this system all the sanitary fittings, except for a drinking water outlet at the sink, are supplied indirectly from a cold water storage cistern positioned at a high level, usually in the roof space. This system requires more pipework, but it gives a reserve supply in case of mains failure, and it also reduces the risk of contamination by back-siphonage (see Fig. 11.1.2). Note that the local water authority determines the system to be used in the area.

PIPEWORK

Any of the materials that are suitable for the service pipe are equally suitable for distribution pipes, and the choice is very often based on individual preference, initial costs and possible maintenance costs.

Copper pipes

Copper pipes have a smooth bore, giving low flow resistance; they are strong, and easily jointed and bent. Joints in copper pipes can be made by one of three methods:

- **Manipulative compression joint** The end of the pipe is manipulated to fit into the coupling fitting by means of a special tool. No jointing material is required, and the joint offers great resistance to being withdrawn. It is usually a by-law requirement that this type of joint is used on service pipes below ground.
- **Non-manipulative compression joint** No manipulation is required to the cut end of the pipe; the holding power of the joint relies on the grip of a copper cone, ring or olive within the joint fitting.
- **Capillary joint** The application of heat makes the soft solder contained in a groove in the fitting flow around the end of the pipe, which has been cleaned and coated with a suitable flux to form a neat and rigid joint.

Typical examples of copper pipe joints are shown in Fig. 11.1.1.

Insulated rising main

Securely fitted cover

Filtered vent (0.65 mm max. opening)

Expansion pipe sleeve

Filtered 22 mm warning pipe

Service valve

20 min.
25 min.
50

Insulation jacket

Float valve

Boarded platform

100 × 50 bearers

Ceiling joist

22 mm cold feed

15 mm rising main

Insulation

Typical cold water storage cistern

Piston

Cap

Float arm

Lock nut

Outlet

Back nut

Piston float valve

Galvanised steel socket

Steel pipe

Tapered thread

Steel pipe joint

Nylon nozzle

Rubber diaphragm

Body

Plunger

Lock nut

Float arm

Back nut

End plate

Cap

Outlet may be at top of body, with a small pipe to direct flow downwards

Diaphragm float valve

Polythene pipe

Copper fitting

Copper liner

Cone wedge

Polythene pipe joint

Figure 11.1.3   Cisterns, float valves and joints.

Steel pipes

Steel pipes for domestic water supply can be obtained as black tube, galvanised or coated and wrapped for underground services. The joint is usually made with a tapered thread and socket fitting, and to ensure a sound joint, stranded hemp and jointing paste should be wrapped around the thread; alternatively a non-contaminating polytetrafluoroethylene (PTFE) seal tape can be used (see Fig. 11.1.3).

Polythene pipe

Polythene pipe is very light in weight, easy to joint, non-toxic, and is available in long lengths, which gives a saving on the number of joints required. Jointing of polythene pipes is generally of the compression type using a metal or plastic liner to the end of the tube (see Fig. 11.1.3). To prevent undue sagging, polythene pipes should be adequately fixed to the wall with saddle clips: recommended spacings are 14 times the outside diameter for horizontal runs and 24 times outside diameter for vertical runs.

Unplasticised PVC (uPVC)

This is plastic pipe for cold water services that is supplied in straight lengths up to 9000 mm long and in standard colours of grey, blue or black. Blue is the water authorities' preferred colour, for easy identification when buried. Jointing can be by a screw thread, but the most common method is by solvent welding. This involves cleaning and chamfering the end of the pipe, which is coated with the correct type of adhesive and pushed into a straight coupling that has been similarly coated. The solvent will set within a few minutes, but the joint does not achieve its working strength for 24 hours. Heat fusion is also used, but mainly for the larger-diameter water authority mains. Here the pipe spigot and the coupling are heated with circular dies to melt the uPVC and effect a push fit weld.

COLD WATER STORAGE CISTERNS

The size of cold water storage cisterns for dwelling houses will depend upon the reserve required and whether the cistern is intended to feed a hot water system. Minimum actual capacities recommended in model water by-laws are 115 litres for cold water storage only and 230 litres for cold and hot water services.

Cisterns should be adequately supported and installed in such a position as to give reasonable access for maintenance purposes. The cistern must be installed so that its outlets are above the highest discharge point on the sanitary fittings, as the flow is by gravity. If the cistern is housed in the roof the pipes and cistern should be insulated against possible freezing of the water; preformed casings of suitable materials are available to suit most standard cistern sizes and shapes. The inlet and outlet connections to the cistern should be on opposite sides to prevent stagnation of water. A securely fitting cover must be provided to prevent ingress of dust, dirt and insects. To prevent a vacuum occurring as water is drawn, the cover is fitted with a screened vent. It also has a moulded sleeve/boss for adapting the hot water expansion pipe. The overflow or warning pipe is also fitted with a filter. A typical cistern installation is shown in Fig. 11.1.3.

Plastic cisterns have many advantages over the traditional galvanised mild steel cisterns: they are non-corrosive, rot proof and frost resistant, and have good resistance to mechanical damage. Materials used are polythene, polypropylene and glass fibre: these cisterns are made with a wall thickness to withstand the water pressure, and have an indefinite life. Some forms of polythene cistern can be distorted to enable them to be passed through an opening of 600 mm × 600 mm, which is a great advantage when planning access to a roof space. However, it is always better to deposit the cistern within the roof structure during construction, rather than have access difficulties later!

Float valves

Every pipe supplying a cold water storage cistern must be fitted with a float valve to prevent an overflow. The float valve must be fitted at a higher level than the overflow to prevent it becoming submerged and creating the conditions where back-siphonage is possible. A float valve is designed to automatically regulate the supply of water by a floating ball closing the valve when the water reaches a predetermined level.

Two valves are in common use for domestic work, the piston valve and the diaphragm valve. The piston valve has a horizontal piston or plunger that closes over the orifice of a diameter to suit the pressure; high-, medium- and low-pressure valves are available (see Fig. 11.1.3). The diaphragm valve closes over an interchangeable nylon nozzle orifice. This type of valve is quieter in operation, easily adjustable, and less susceptible to the corrosion trouble caused by a sticking piston – this is one of the problems that can be encountered with the piston valve (see Fig. 11.1.3). Diaphragm valves now have the outlet at the top to increase the air gap between outlet and water level, thus reducing the possibility of back-siphonage if the cistern water level were to rise excessively.

▨▨■ HOT WATER SUPPLY

The supply of hot water to domestic sanitary fittings is usually taken from a hot water tank or cylinder. The source of heat is usually in the form of a gas-fired, oil-fired or solid-fuel boiler; alternatives are a back boiler to an open fire or an electric immersion heater fixed into the hot water storage tank. When a quantity of hot water is drawn from the storage tank it is immediately replaced by cold water from the cold water storage cistern. Two main systems are used to heat the water in the tank – these are called the **direct** and **indirect** systems. For any hot water system copper or steel pipes are generally used. These materials are satisfactory if used independently throughout the system, but they must not be mixed or interchanged within a system. This is due to the electrolytic attraction that dissimilar metals have in the presence of water, which eventually leads to corrosion. Copper and zinc are particularly renowned for this problem, as zinc is the protective plating given to steel pipes under the name of galvanising.

DIRECT HOT WATER SYSTEM

This is the simplest and cheapest system; the cold water flows through the water jacket in the boiler, where its temperature is raised and convection currents are induced, which causes the water to rise and circulate. The hot water leaving the boiler is replaced by colder water descending from the hot water cylinder or tank by gravity, thus setting up the circulation. The hot water supply is drawn off from the top of the cylinder by a horizontal pipe at least 450 mm long to prevent 'one pipe' circulation being set up in the vent or expansion pipe. This pipe is run vertically from the hot water distribution pipe to a discharge position over the cold water storage cistern (see Fig. 11.1.4).

The direct system is not suitable for supplying a central heating circuit or for hard water areas because the pipes and cylinders will become furred with lime deposits. This precipitation of lime occurs when hard water is heated to temperatures of between 50 and 70 °C, which is the ideal temperature range for domestic hot water supply.

INDIRECT HOT WATER SYSTEM

This system is designed to overcome the problems of furring, which occurs with the direct hot water system. The basic difference is in the cylinder design, which now becomes a heat exchanger. The cylinder contains a coil or annulus that is connected to the flow and return pipes from the boiler. A transfer of heat takes place within the cylinder, and therefore, after the initial precipitation of lime within the primary circuit and boiler, there is no further furring as fresh cold water is not being constantly introduced into the boiler circuit.

The supply circuit from the cylinder follows the same pattern as the direct hot water system, but a separate feed and expansion system is required for the boiler and primary circuit for initial supply, also for any necessary topping up due to evaporation. The feed cistern is similar to a cold water storage cistern but of a much smaller capacity. The water levels in the two cisterns should be equal so that equal pressures act on the indirect cylinder.

A gravity heating circuit can be taken from the boiler, its distribution being governed by the boiler capacity (see Fig. 11.1.4). Alternatively a small-bore forced system of central heating may be installed.

Hot water storage cylinders

Copper cylinders are produced to the recommendations of BS 1566. The Standard recommends sizes, capacities and positions for screwed holes for pipe connections.

To overcome the disadvantage of the extra pipework involved when using an indirect cylinder, a single-feed indirect or 'Primatic' cylinder can be used. This form of cylinder is entirely self-contained, and is installed in the same manner as a direct cylinder but functions as an indirect cylinder. It works on the principle of the buoyancy of air, which is used to form seals between the primary and secondary water systems. When the system is first filled with water the cylinder commences to

Technology & Design

216

Direct hot water system

Note: Not suitable in hard water areas

Indirect hot water system

Note: Pipe sizes shown are for standard copper outside diameters

Figure 11.1.4 Hot water system.

fill and fully charges the primary circuit to the boiler with water. When the cylinder water capacity has been reached two air seals will have formed, the first in the upper chamber of the primatic unit and the second in the air vent pipe. These volumes of air are used to separate the primary and secondary water. When the water is heated in the primary system expansion displaces some of the air in the upper chamber to the lower chamber. This is a reciprocating action: the seals transfer from chamber to chamber as the temperature rises and falls.

Any excess air in the primary system is vented into the secondary system, which will also automatically replenish the primary system should this be necessary. As with indirect systems careful control over the heat output of the boiler is advisable to prevent boiling and consequent furring of the pipework. Typical examples of cylinders are shown in Fig. 11.1.5.

Faults in hot water systems

Unless a hot water system is correctly designed and installed a number of faults may occur, such as airlocks and noises. Airlocks are pockets of trapped air in the system, which will stop or slow down the circulation. Air suspended in the water will be released when the water is heated, and rise to the highest point. In a good installation the pipes are designed to rise 25 mm in 3000 mm towards the vent where the air is released through the vent pipe. The most common positions for airlocks are sharp bends and the upper rail of a towel rail; the only cure for the latter position is for the towel rail to be vented.

Noises from the hot water system usually indicate a blocked pipe caused by excessive furring or corrosion. The noise is caused by the imprisoned expanded water, and the faulty pipe must be descaled or removed, or an explosion may occur.

Inadequate bracketing of pipes is another common cause of plumbing noise, particularly in the rising main, where pressures are higher than elsewhere. This is known as **water hammer**.

Mains supply hot water

This has become a popular alternative to the traditional installation. It is very economic in pipework, space requirements and installation time as conventional expansion facilities are not required. The system is mains fed and sealed, with expansion accommodated in a specially designed vessel containing an air 'cushion'. Safety facilities are essential and include both pressure and thermal relief valves. Figure 11.1.6 indicates the principles of operation.

114 litre indirect cylinder

Hot water supply outlet
Immersion heater connection
Secondary return inlet
Secondary water
Primary flow inlet
Copper cylinder
Primary water
Corrugated primary heater
Primary return outlet
Cold feed inlet
400
1.050

135 litre single-feed or 'Primatic' cylinder

Immersion heater connection
Hot water supply outlet
Air vent pipe
Air bubble
Copper cylinder
Level of secondary water
Secondary water
Level of primary water
Primary water
Primary flow inlet
Annular heater
Air locks
Cold feed inlet
Primary return outlet
450
1.050

Figure 11.1.5   Typical hot water cylinders.

Figure 11.1.6   Schematic of mains-fed hot water supply.

SANITARY FITTINGS AND PIPEWORK

Sanitary fittings or appliances can be considered under two headings:

- **Soil fitments**   Those that are used to remove soil water and human excreta such as water closets and urinals.
- **Waste water fitments**   Those that are used to remove the waste water from washing and the preparation of food including appliances such as wash basins, baths, showers and sinks.

All sanitary appliances should be made from impervious materials, be quiet in operation, easy to clean and of a convenient shape fixed at a suitable height. A number of materials are available for most domestic sanitary fittings.

Vitreous china

This is a white clay body that is vitrified and permanently fused with a vitreous glazed surface when fired at a very high temperature, generally to the recommendations of BS 3402. Appliances made from this material are non-corrosive, hygienic, and easily cleaned with a mild detergent or soap solution.

Glazed fireclay

This consists of a porous ceramic body glazed in a similar manner to vitreous china; it is exceptionally strong and resistant to impact damage but will allow water penetration of the body if the protective glazing is damaged. Like vitreous china, these appliances are non-corrosive, hygienic and easily cleaned.

Vitreous enamel

This is a form of glass that can be melted and used to give a glazed protective coating over a steel or cast iron base. Used mainly for baths, sinks and draining boards, it produces a fitment that is lighter than those produced from a ceramic material, is hygienic, easy to clean, and has a long life. The finish, however, can be chipped and is subject to staining, especially from copper compounds from hot water systems.

Plastic materials

Acrylic plastics, glass-reinforced polyester resins and polypropylene sanitary fittings made from these plastics require no protective coatings, are very strong, light in weight, and chip resistant, but generally cost more than ceramic or vitreous enamel products. Care must be taken with fitments made of acrylic plastics as they become soft when heated: therefore they should be used for cold water fitments or have thermostatically controlled mixing taps. Plastic appliances can be easily cleaned using warm soapy water, and any dullness can be restored by polishing with ordinary domestic polishes.

Stainless steel

This is made from steel containing approximately 18% chromium and 8% nickel, which gives the metal a natural resistance to corrosion. Stainless steel appliances are very durable and relatively light in weight; for domestic situations the main application is for sinks and draining boards. Two finishes are available, polished or 'mirror' finish and 'satin' finish: the latter has a greater resistance to scratching.

General considerations

The factors to be considered when selecting or specifying sanitary fitments are as follows:

- cost – outlay, fixing and maintenance;
- hygiene – inherent and ease of cleaning;
- appearance – size, colour and shape;
- function – suitability, speed of operation and reliability;
- weight – support required from wall and/or floor;
- design – ease with which it can be included into the general services installation.

Building Regulation G1 establishes requirements for sanitary conveniences, i.e. water closets, urinals and wash basins, and Regulation G2 extends coverage to bathrooms containing bath or shower installations. The quantity of WCs and sanitary appliances in various locations is detailed in BS 6465: *Sanitary installations*. This Standard is in two parts: Part 1 is the code of practice for provision and installation, and Part 2 relates to spatial layout and design for sanitary accommodation.

The subject of water conservation with respect to the use of sanitary fitments is very topical, with manufacturers endeavouring to adapt their products and develop new ideas in line with conservation and environmental issues. Building Research Establishment Information Paper ref. IP 8/97, Parts 1 and 2, provides further reading on this topic with application to the design of low-flush WCs.

BS EN 37 ceramic washdown WC pan

Typical siphonic WC pans

Bell-type cistern

Piston-type cistern

Figure 11.2.1   WC pans and cisterns.

▨ ▩ ■ WATER CLOSETS

Most water closets are made from a ceramic base to the requirements of BS EN 33 or 37 with a horizontal outlet. The complete water closet arrangement consists of the pan, seat, flush pipe and flushing cistern. The cistern can be fixed as high level, low level (BS EN 37) or closed coupled (BS EN 33); the latter arrangement dispenses with the need for a flush pipe. A typical arrangement is shown in Fig. 11.2.1. The British Standard water closet is termed a washdown type and relies on the flush of water to wash the contents of the bowl round the trap and into the soil-pipe. An alternative form is the siphonic water closet, which is more efficient and quieter in operation but has a greater risk of blockage if misused. Two types are produced – the single-trap and the double-trap.

The single-trap siphonic water closet has a restricted outlet that serves to retard the flow, when flushed, so that the bore of the outlet connected to the bowl becomes full and sets up a siphonic flushing action, completely emptying the contents of the bowl (see Fig. 11.2.1). With the double-trap siphonic pan the air is drawn from the pocket between the two traps; when the flushing operation is started this causes atmospheric pressure to expel the complete contents of the bowl through both traps into the soil pipe (see Fig. 11.2.1).

The pan should be fixed to the floor with brass screws and bedded on a suitable compressible material; the connection to the soil-pipe socket can be made with cement mortar or preferably a mastic to allow for any differential movement between the fitment and the structure. Connections to PVC soil pipes are usually made with compression rings. The flush pipe is invariably connected to the pan with a special plastic or rubber one-piece connector.

Flushing cisterns together with the flush pipes are usually constructed to the recommendations of BS 1125 and BS EN 997, and can be made from enamelled cast iron, enamelled pressed steel, ceramic ware or of plastic materials. Two basic types have been produced, the bell or cone and the piston. The former is now obsolete, but may still be found in service. It is activated by pulling a chain, which raises and lowers the bell or cone and in so doing raises the water level above the open end of the flush pipe, thus setting up a siphonic action. These cisterns are efficient and durable but are noisy in operation (see Fig. 11.2.1). The piston-type cistern is the one in general use, and is activated by a lever or button. When activated, the disc or flap valve piston is raised and with it the water level, which commences the siphonage (see Fig. 11.2.1). The level of the water in the cistern is controlled by a float valve, and an overflow or warning pipe of a larger diameter than the inlet is fitted to discharge so that it gives a visual warning, usually in an external position. The capacity of the cistern will be determined by local water board requirements, the most common being 6, 7.5 and 9 litres.

There is a wide range of designs, colours and patterns available for water closet suites, but all can be classified as one of the types described above.

FLUSHING VALVES

These have been a popular marine plumbing installation for many years. In compact lavatory compartments they have proved effective in restricted space, and they are

Overall size 457 × 635

Splashback

Overflow slot

Plug and chain

Grating

790

165

Back nut and washer

BS 3380 32 mm waste

Cantilever support bracket

40 or 75 mm seal 'P' trap

'S' traps also available

Plastic traps BS 3943

Cleaning eye

Typical lavatory basin details

Body

Overflow slot

Backnut

Waste connection nut

32 or 40 mm outlet

40 or 75 seal

Removable base for access

Overflow slot

635

457

838

Basin

Pedestal

High-density polythene bottle trap and standard BS 3380 waste

Typical pedestal basin

Figure 11.2.2   Basins, traps and wastes.

economic with the use of limited water resources. They are becoming a credible alternative for use in buildings, particularly where usage is frequent, as they can flush at any time without delay. They comprise a large equilibrium valve, which functions on the principle of water displacement and pressure equalisation limiting the flow. Current research and recommendations from the Water Regulations Advisory Committee (WRAC) to the government are likely to succeed in establishing these valves in the Water Supply Byelaws. See BRE IP 8/97 Part 2 for more detail.

WASH BASINS

Wash basins for domestic work are usually made from a ceramic material, but metal basins complying with BS 1329 are also available. A wide variety of shapes, sizes, types and colours are available, the choice usually being one of personal preference. BS 1188 and BS 5506 provide recommendations for ceramic wash basins and pedestals, and specify two basic sizes, 635 mm × 457 mm and 559 mm × 406 mm. Small wall-hung hand-rinse basins are also available for use in limited space. These are produced to BS EN 111. All these basins are a one-piece fitment, having an integral overflow, separate waste outlet and generally pillar taps (see Fig. 11.2.2).

Wash basins can be supported on wall-mounted cantilever brackets, leg supports or pedestals. The pedestals are made from identical material to the wash basin, and are recessed at the back to receive the supply pipes to the taps and the waste pipe from the bowl. Although pedestals are designed to fully support the wash basin, most manufacturers recommend that small wall-mounted safety brackets are also used.

BATHS AND SHOWERS

Baths are available in a wide variety of designs and colours, made from porcelain-enamelled cast iron, vitreous-enamelled sheet steel, 8 mm cast acrylic sheet, or 3 mm cast acrylic sheet reinforced with a polyester resin/glass fibre laminate. Most bath designs today are rectangular in plan and made as flat bottomed as practicable with just sufficient fall to allow for gravity emptying and resealing of the trap. The British Standards for the materials quoted above recommend a coordinating plan size of 1700 mm × 700 mm with a height within the range of $n \times 50$ mm, where n is any natural number including unity. Baths are supplied with holes for pillar taps or mixer fittings, and for the waste outlets. Options include handgrips, built-in soap and sponge recesses and overflow outlets. It is advisable always to specify overflow outlets as a precautionary measure to limit the water level and to minimise splashing; most overflow pipes are designed to connect with the waste trap beneath the bath (see Fig. 11.2.3). Support for baths is usually by adjustable feet for cast iron and steel and by a strong cradle for the acrylic baths. Panels of enamelled hardboard or moulded high-impact polystyrene or glass fibre are available for enclosing the bath. These panels can be fixed by using stainless steel or aluminium angles or direct to a timber stud framework.

Coordinating length 1.700
Work size 1.694
65
Overflow
Fall to outlet
100
$n \times 50$
Bath panel with toe recess
Adjustable feet or cradle support
Waste hole boss
100 to 170

Coordinating width = 700; work size = 697
Coordinating sizes can be varied within range of
$n \times 100$ mm, where n = any natural number including unity

BS 1189 (cast iron), BS 4305 (acrylic) and BS 1390 (vitreous enamelled steel) baths. Also, BS EN 60335–2–60 whirlpool baths.

Overflow outlet
Plug and chain
32 mm dia. flexible tube
Overflow pipe connected to trap opposite cleaning eye
40 mm dia. waste
75 mm seal trap
Waste pipe

Overflow outlet
Plug and chain
40 mm dia. waste outlet
75 mm seal trap
Waste pipe
Cleaning eye

Alternative overflow connections

Typical sizes

600 × 600 × 175 deep
760 × 760 × 175 deep
900 × 900 × 175 deep

Also available in enamelled steel and acrylic to BS 7015

Weir overflow
Outlet for waste and sealed trap connection

Typical fireclay shower tray

Figure 11.2.3   Baths and shower trays.

Shower sprays can be used in conjunction with a bath by fitting a rigid plastic shower screen or flexible curtain to one end of the bath. A separate shower fitment, however, is considered preferable. Such fitments require less space than the conventional bath, use less hot water, and are considered to be more hygienic as the used water is being continuously discharged. A shower fitment consists of the shower tray with a waste outlet, the impervious cubicle, and a door or curtain (see Fig. 11.2.3). Materials available are similar to those described for baths. The spray outlet is normally fixed to the wall, and is connected to a mixing valve so that the water temperature can be controlled.

▦▦◼ SINKS

Sinks are used mainly for the preparation of food, washing of dishes and clothes, and are usually positioned at the drinking water supply outlet. Their general design follows that described for basins, except that they are larger in area and deeper. Any material considered suitable for sanitary appliance construction can be used. Designs range from the simple Belfast sink with detachable draining boards of metal, plastic or timber to the combination units consisting of integral draining boards and twin bowls. Support can be wall-mounted cantilever brackets, framed legs or a purpose-made cupboard unit; typical details are shown in Fig. 11.2.4.

The layout of domestic sanitary appliances is governed by size of fitments, personal preference, pipework system being used and the space available. Building Regulations G1 and G2 detail requirements and minimum facilities to be made available in a dwelling, and the need for sanitary accommodation to be separated from kitchen areas.

▦▦◼ PIPEWORK

Building Regulations, Approved Document H1: *Sanitary pipework and drainage* sets out in detail the recommendations for soil pipes, waste pipes and ventilating pipes. These regulations govern such things as minimum diameters of soil pipes, material requirements, provision of adequate water seals by means of an integral trap or non-integral trap, the positioning of soil pipes on the inside of a building, overflow pipework, and ventilating pipes. The only pipework that is permissible on the outside of the external wall is any waste pipe from a waste appliance situated at ground floor level, provided such a pipe discharges into a suitable trap with a grating, and the discharge is above the level of the water but below the level of the grating.

PIPEWORK SYSTEMS

Three basic pipework systems have been used for domestic work:

- one-pipe system;
- two-pipe system;
- single-stack system.

Whichever system is adopted, the functions of quick, reliable and quiet removal of the discharges to the drains remain constant.

Weir overflow

Outlet for 40 mm waste and trap connection

BS 1206 fireclay sinks
Belfast pattern – wide range of sizes
from 457 × 380 × 200 deep up to
1.219 × 610 × 305 deep. Sinks
supported on cantilever brackets,
legs and bearers or on brick
dwarf walls. Fixing heights 850
to 920 to top of sink

Edge
lipping

Flutes

Clip-on draining boards
Reversible and available in
hardwood, stainless steel,
aluminium alloy and vitreous
enamel in range of sizes
from 560 × 406 to 762 × 457

Brackets
hook over
sink

Hole for
pillar tap

Overflow slot

Stainless steel sinks
Generally made to the
requirements of BS EN
13310 available with single
or double drainers in a
range of sizes from 1.070 ×
460 to 1.600 × 530. Sink
tops supported on
cantilever brackets

180 or 200
deep bowl

Single
drainer

Mixer taps

Sink units
Available in same plan sizes
as BS EN 13310 sinks to a general
work height of 910 mm. Sink
top can be of stainless steel
or vitreous enamel with a wide
choice of cabinet designs
and finishes

Toe
recess

Sliding
cupboard doors

Note: Waste fittings to BS EN 274-1

Figure 11.2.4   Sinks and draining boards.

One-pipe system

This consists of a single discharge pipe, which conveys both soil and waste water directly to the drain. To ensure that water seals in the traps are not broken, deep seals of 75 mm for waste pipes up to 65 mm diameter and 50 mm for pipes over 75 mm diameter are required. To allow for unrestricted layout of appliances most branch pipes will require an anti-siphon arrangement (see Fig. 11.2.5). The advantage of this system is the flexibility of appliance layout, the main disadvantage is cost, and generally the one-pipe system has been superseded by the more restricted but economic single-stack system described below.

Two-pipe system

As its name implies, this system consists of two discharge pipes: one conveys soil discharges and the other all the waste discharges. It is a simple, reliable and costly system, but has the advantages of complete flexibility in appliance layout and the fact that deep seal traps are not usually required. Like the one-pipe system, it has been largely superseded by the single-stack system. A comparison of the one- and two-pipe systems is shown in Fig. 11.2.5.

Single-stack system

This system was developed by the Building Research Establishment, and is fully described in their Digest No. 249. It is also fully detailed in BS EN 12056-2, and is now adapted into the Building Regulations, Approved Document H1. It is a simplification of the one-pipe system by using deep seal traps, relying on venting by the discharge pipe and placing certain restrictions on basin waste pipes, which have a higher risk of self-siphonage than other appliances. A diagrammatic layout is shown in Fig. 11.2.6.

Materials that can be used for domestic stack pipework include galvanised steel prefabricated stack units (BS 3868), cast iron (BS 416) and uPVC (BS 4514). The latter is standard contemporary practice, being light and easy to install with simple push-fit or solvent-weld joints. Branch waste pipes can be of a variety of plastics, including uPVC, polyethylene and polypropylene, or of copper.

Most manufacturers of soil pipes, ventilating pipes and fittings produce special components for various plumbing arrangements and appliance layouts. These fittings have the water closet socket connections, bosses for branch waste connections and access plates for cleaning and maintenance arranged as one prefabricated assembly to ease site work and ensure reliable and efficient connections to the discharge or soil pipe.

Figure 11.2.5   Comparison of one-pipe and two-pipe systems.

Soil and vent pipe

Perforated dome to svp termination above roof level

32 mm dia. waste with 75 mm min. seal trap

1.700 maximum

Up to 6.000

Slope determined by length – see BRE Digest No. 249 and Bldg Regs AD H1, Diagram 3

Basin

WC with 50 mm minimum seal

Bath

✳

3 m max. (40 mm waste)
4 m max. (50 mm waste)

Slope, 9 mm/m min.

50 mm swept radius at junction

40 mm dia. waste with 75 mm minimum seal trap

Soil and vent pipe

WC branch

200

Note: All sanitary appliances on the ground floor are connected independently to the manhole or drains as Fig. 11.2.5

50 mm radius

Large radius bends to foot of stack

Note: No connection to the stack to be made within the shaded portion to prevent backing up of WC discharge into bath waste. If 'S' trap is used on WC bath, waste could be a straight connection

Figure 11.2.6   Single-stack system.

Figure 11.2.7   Macerator/pump installation.

Small-diameter pumped discharge systems

A macerator and pump unit may be connected to the WC pan outlet to collect, process and discharge soil and waste from the WC and other sanitary appliances. The discharge is conveyed in a relatively small-diameter pipe to the nearest convenient soil stack. Figure 11.2.7 shows the possible installations from the box attachment at the back of a WC pan, through vertical and near-horizontal pipes. Structural disruption is minimal, and the small discharge pipes can be used for considerable distances between WC and stack.

Macerator installation is permitted in a dwelling only as a supplement to an existing gravity-discharging WC. See Building Regulation G: Hygiene, Approved Document G1, *Sanitary conveniences and washing facilities*. This requirement is a safeguard that, in the event of an electrical power failure, the conventional gravity-discharge WC will still function.

Most applications are to loft conversions, extensions and basements, or to other situations where it is impractical to install a normal discharge branch pipe. The Care Standards Act has also produced a need for additional facilities. Care home proprietors must provide their residents with access to suitable and sufficient conveniences. This places greater emphasis for en-suite facilities, particularly in care homes for elderly people.

Installation guidelines
■ By application to, and at the discretion of the local authority building control department.
■ Building Regulations approval will apply only where appliance specification satisfies strict test standards, such as that set by the British Board of Agrément (BBA).
■ Discharge pipework:
   ■ 22 or 28 mm outside diameter copper or equivalent in stainless steel or polypropylene.
   ■ Long radius 'pulled' bends at direction changes, not proprietary elbow fittings.
   ■ Minimum fall or gradient, 1 in 200.
   ■ Up to 50 m horizontally and 5 m vertically.
■ Not suitable for use with siphonic WC pans.
■ Short spigot, 100 mm diameter horizontal outlet pans to BS EN 33 or 37 required.
■ Electrical requirements:
   ■ 230 volts single phase.
   ■ 5 amp fused non-switched neon light spur box.
   ■ 450–650 watts pump specification.

1.3

SUBSOIL DRAINAGE

■■■ BUILDING REGULATION C2 Resistance to moisture

Subsoil drainage shall be provided if it is needed to avoid:

■ the passage of ground moisture to the interior of the building;
■ damage to the fabric of the building.

The ideal site (see Fig. 1.3.1) will not require any treatment, but sites with a high water table will require some form of subsoil drainage. The water table is the level at which water occurs naturally below the ground, and this level will vary with the seasonal changes.

The object of subsoil drainage is to lower the water table to a level such that it will comply with the above Building Regulation, i.e. not rise to within 0.25 m of the lowest floor of a building. It also has the advantage of improving the stability of the ground, lowering the humidity of the site, and improving its horticultural properties.

Figure 1.3.1   The ideal site.

MATERIALS

The pipes used in subsoil drainage are usually dry jointed and are either porous or perforated pipes. The porous pipes absorb the water through their walls and thus keep out the fine particles of soil or silt, whereas perforated pipes, which are laid with the perforations at the base, allow the water to rise into the pipe, leaving any silt behind.

Suitable pipes

- Perforated clayware: BS EN 295-5.
- Porous concrete: BS 5911-114.*
- Clayware field pipes: BS 1196.
- Profiled and slotted polypropylene or uPVC: BS 4962.
- Perforated uPVC: BS 4660.

Note: Porous concrete is rarely manufactured now, therefore the BS has been withdrawn.

Figure 1.3.2 Subsoil drainage systems and drains.

Ground
level

Concrete or brick bank protection

Drain to discharge above
water level

Timber or
metal baffle

Fall

Water level

Last 3.000 to
5.000 in proper
drainage to
prevent marshlike
soil at outfall

Protection to
opposite bank if
stream or river
is narrow

Figure 1.3.3 Outfall to stream or river.

Anti-flood valve
if stream or
river is tidal

1.000   1.000

Baffle

Subsoil drain to
discharge with the flow

Flow

Bank protection

2.000

Ground
level

Cast iron cover and frame

Brick levelling course

Precast concrete
cover

Reverse action
intercepting
trap

Brick-built
inspection
chamber

Flow

Rodding
eye

Surface water
drain or sewer

Subsoil
drain

Figure 1.3.4 Outfall to surface water sewer or drain.

DRAINAGE LAYOUTS

The pipes are arranged in a pattern to cover as much of the site as is necessary. Typical arrangements are shown on the plans in Fig. 1.3.2. Water will naturally flow towards the easy passage provided by the drainage runs. The system is terminated at a suitable outfall such as a river, stream or surface water sewer. In all cases permission must be obtained before discharging a subsoil system. The banks of streams and rivers will need protection against the turbulence set up by the discharge, and if the stream is narrow the opposite bank may also need protection (see Fig. 1.3.3). If discharge is into a tidal river or stream, precautions should be taken to ensure that the system will not work in reverse by providing an outlet for the rising tide. On large schemes sediment chambers or catch pits are sometimes included to trap some of the silt which is the chief cause of blockages in subsoil drainage work. The construction of a catch pit is similar to the manhole shown in Fig. 1.3.4 except that in a catch pit the inlet and outlet are at a high level; this interrupts the flow of subsoil water in the drains and enables some of the silt to settle on the base of the catch pit. The collected silt in the catch pit must be removed at regular intervals.

DRAINAGE

Drainage is a system of pipework, usually installed below ground level, to convey the discharge from sanitary fittings, rainwater gutters and downpipes to a suitable disposal installation. The usual method of disposal is to connect the pipework to the public sewer, which will convey the discharges to a local authority sewage treatment plant. Alternatives are a small self-contained treatment plant on site or a cesspool; the latter is a collection tank to hold the discharge until it can be collected in a special tanker lorry and taken to the local authority sewage treatment installation for disposal.

▓▓■ PRINCIPLES OF GOOD DRAINAGE

- Materials should have adequate strength and durability.
- Diameter of drain to be as small as practicable: for soil drains the minimum diameter allowed is 100 mm and for surface water the minimum diameter is 75 mm.
- Every part of a drain should be accessible for the purposes of inspection and cleansing.
- Drains should be laid in straight runs as far as possible.
- Drains must be laid to a gradient that will render them efficient. The fall or gradient should be calculated according to the rate of flow, the velocity required and the diameter of the drain. Individual domestic buildings have an irregular flow, and tables to accommodate this are provided in the Building Regulations, Approved Document H1. Alternatively, Maguire's rule can be used to give a gradient with reasonable velocity. This well-established rule of thumb calculates the gradient by dividing the pipe diameter (mm) by 2.5. Thus a 100 mm drain can have a fall of 1 in 40, a 150 mm drain 1 in 60, and so on. Velocity of flow should be at least 0.75 m/s to ensure self-cleansing with a drain capacity not more than 0.75 proportional depth to ensure clear flow conditions. For more detailed drainage calculations, see *Building Services, Technology and Design* by R. Greeno (Pearson Education and CIOB co-publishers).

- Every drain inlet should be trapped to prevent the entry of foul air into the building; the minimum seal required is 50 mm. The trap seal is provided in many cases by the sanitary fitting itself; rainwater drains need not be trapped unless they connect with a soil drain or sewer.
- A rodding access should be located at the head or start of each drain run.
- Inspection chambers, manholes, rodding eyes or access fittings should be placed at changes of direction and gradient if these changes would prevent the drain from being readily cleansed.
- Inspection chambers must also be placed at a junction, unless each run can be cleared from an access point.
- A change of drain pipe size will also require access.
- Junctions between drains must be arranged so that the incoming drain joints at an oblique angle in the direction of the main flow.
- Avoid drains under buildings if possible; if unavoidable they must be protected to ensure watertightness and to prevent damage. The usual protection methods employed are:
  - encase the drain with 100 mm (minimum) of granular filling;
  - use cast iron pipes under the building.
- Drains that are within 1 m of the foundations to the walls of buildings and below the foundation level must be backfilled with concrete up to the level of the underside of the foundations. Drains more than 1 m from the foundations are backfilled with concrete to a depth equal to the distance of the trench from the foundation less 150 mm.
- Where possible, the minimum invert level of a drain should be 450 mm to avoid damage by ground movement and 700 mm for traffic. The invert level is the lowest level of the bore of a drain.

▨▨■ DRAINAGE SCHEMES

The scheme or plan layout of drains will depend upon a number of factors:

- number of discharge points;
- relative positions of discharge points;
- drainage system and location of the local authority sewers;
- internal layout of sanitary fittings;
- external positions of rainwater pipes;
- disposition of buildings;
- topography of the area to be served.

Drainage systems must be designed within the limits of the terrain, so that the discharges can flow by gravity from the point of origin to the point of discharge. The pipe sizes and gradients must be selected to provide sufficient capacity to accommodate maximum flows, while at the other extreme they must have adequate self-cleansing velocity at minimum flows to prevent debris from accumulating. Economic and construction factors control the depth to which drains can be laid. Therefore, in flat and opposingly inclined areas it may be necessary to provide pumping stations to raise the drainage discharge to higher-level sewers.

There are three drainage systems used by local authorities in this country, and the method employed by any particular authority will determine the basic scheme to be used for the drain runs from individual premises.

COMBINED SYSTEM

All the drains discharge into a common or combined sewer. It is a simple and economic method as there is no duplication of drains. This method has the advantages of easy maintenance, all drains are flushed when it rains, and it is impossible to connect to the wrong sewer. The main disadvantage is that all the discharges must pass through the sewage treatment installation, which could be costly and prove to be difficult with periods of heavy rain.

TOTALLY SEPARATE SYSTEM

The most common method employed by local authorities; two sewers are used in this method. One sewer receives the surface water discharge and conveys this direct to a suitable outfall such as a river, where it is discharged without treatment. The second sewer receives all the soil or foul discharge from baths, basins, sinks, showers and toilets; this is then conveyed to the sewage treatment installation. More drains are required, and it is often necessary to cross drains one over the other. There is a risk of connection to the wrong sewer, and the soil drains are not flushed during heavy rain, but the savings on the treatment of a smaller volume of discharge leads to an overall economy.

PARTIALLY SEPARATE SYSTEM

This is a compromise of the other two systems, and is favoured by some local authorities because of its flexibility. Two sewers are used, one to carry surface water only and the other to act as a combined sewer. The amount of surface water to be discharged into the combined sewer can be adjusted according to the capacity of the sewage treatment installation.

Soakaways, which are pits below ground level designed to receive surface water and allow it to percolate into the soil, are sometimes used to lessen the load on the surface water sewers. Typical examples of the three drainage systems are shown in Fig. 11.3.1.

PRIVATE SEWERS

A sewer can be defined as a means of conveying waste, soil or rainwater below the ground that has been collected from the drains and conveying it to the final disposal point. If the sewer is owned and maintained by the local authority it is generally called a **public sewer**, whereas one owned by a single person or a group of people and maintained by them can be classed as a **private sewer**.

Figure 11.3.1   Drainage systems.

Surface water drain inspection chamber

Foul or soil drain inspection chamber

Foul sewer

Surface water sewer

Individual sewer connections involving opening up highway in each case to make connection

Individual drain and sewer connections

Surface water drain inspection chamber

Foul or soil drain inspection chamber

Rodding eye

Rodding eye

Foul sewer

Surface water sewer

Private sewer for foul drains

Private sewer for surface water drains

Single connections to public sewer

Note: Generally 20 houses can be connected to a 100 mm dia. private sewer at a gradient of 1:70 and 100 houses can be connected to a 150 mm dia. private sewer laid to a fall of 1:150

Figure 11.3.2   Example of a private sewer arrangement.

When planning the connection of houses to the main or public sewer one method is to consider each dwelling in isolation, but important economies in design can be achieved by the use of a private sewer. A number of houses are connected to the single sewer, which in turn is connected to the public sewer. Depending upon the number of houses connected to the private sewer, and the distance from the public sewer, the following savings are possible:

- total length of drain required;
- number of connections to public sewer;
- amount of openings in the roads;
- number of inspection chambers.

A comparative example is shown in Fig. 11.3.2.

DRAINAGE MATERIALS

Drain pipes are considered as either rigid or flexible according to the material used in their manufacture. Clay is a major material used for rigid drain pipes in domestic work, with cast iron as an expensive alternative. Flexible drain pipes are produced from unplasticised PVC.

Clay pipes

This is the traditional material used for domestic drainage, with current manufacturing standards in accordance with BS 65 and BS EN 295. These pipes were treated with a glazing of common salt, borax or boric acid during the firing process to render them impervious. Today's high standards of manufacture combined with quality dense materials no longer justify this process. Several qualities of pipes are produced, ranging from standard pipes for general use to surface water pipes and pipes of extra strength to be used where heavy loadings are likely to be encountered. The type and quality of pipes are marked on the barrel so that they can be identified after firing.

Clay pipes are produced in a range of diameters from 100 to 300 mm nominal bore for general building work. Lengths vary between manufacturers from 1300 to 1600 mm for plain-end pipes, with spigot and socketed pipes produced in shorter lengths down to 600 mm. They can be obtained with sockets and spigots prepared for rigid or flexible jointing. Rigid jointing is rarely used now, except perhaps for small repairs or alterations to an existing drain, as it is difficult to make a sound joint in wet trenches; also the system is unable to absorb movement without fracturing. Most pipes are supplied plain ended for use with push-fit polypropylene sleeve couplings. A wide variety of fittings for use with clay pipes are manufactured to give flexibility when planning drainage layouts and means of access. Typical examples of clay pipes, joints and fittings are shown in Figs 11.3.3 and 11.3.4.

Clay pipes are resistant to attack by a wide range of acids and alkalis: they are therefore suitable for all forms of domestic drainage.

Typical BS 65 clay drain pipe

Rigid joint
(Not recommended in AD, H)

Flexible 'O' ring joint

Flexible coupling joint

Flexible ring seal socket joint

Pitch fibre pipe joints
(Not recommended in AD, H)

Figure 11.3.3 Pipes and joints.

45° oblique junction

Eighth bend

$\frac{1}{4}$ $\frac{1}{6}$ $\frac{1}{12}$ $\frac{1}{16}$ $\frac{1}{24}$ and $\frac{1}{32}$ bends also available

$\frac{1}{2}$ and $\frac{3}{4}$ section channel junctions and bends similar

Yard gully with 'P' trap outlet

Access gully with 'Q' trap outlet

Back inlet with 'S' trap outlet

Reversible gully with 'P' trap outlet

All gullies can be supplied with 'P', 'Q', or 'S' trap outlets

Figure 11.3.4   Clay drain pipe fittings and gullies.

Cast iron pipes

These pipes are generally considered for domestic drainage only in special circumstances such as sites with unstable ground, drains with shallow inverts, and drains that pass under buildings. Like clay pipes, cast iron pipes are made with a spigot and socket for rigid or flexible joints. The rigid joint is made with a tarred gaskin and caulked lead, whereas the flexible joint has a sealing strip in the socket, allowing a 5° deflection. Lengths, diameters and fittings available are similar to those produced for clay pipes but to the recommendations of BS 437 and BS EN 598.

Cast iron pipes are given a protective coating of a hot tar composition or a cold solution of a naphtha and bitumen composition. This coating gives the pipes good protection against corrosion and reasonable durability in average ground conditions.

Pitch fibre pipes

Pitch fibre pipes and fittings preceded uPVC as a flexible drainage material. They are rarely used now, but will be found in many existing systems. They are made from preformed felted wood cellulose fibres thoroughly impregnated under vacuum and pressure, with at least 65% by weight of coal tar pitch or bituminous compounds. They have been used for all forms of domestic drainage, and because of the smooth bore with its high flow capacity could be laid to lower gradients than most other materials of their day. Sizes range from 50 to 225 mm nominal bore, with lengths generally 2400 and 3000 mm.

The original joints had a machined 2° taper on the ends of the pipe, which made a drive fit to machined pitch fibre couplings. These joints are watertight, but do not readily accommodate axial or telescopic movement. The snap joint used a rubber 'D' ring in conjunction with a polypropylene coupling, giving a flexible joint. Both methods are shown in Fig. 11.3.3.

Unplasticised PVC pipes

These pipes and fittings are made from polyvinyl chloride plus additives that are needed to facilitate the manufacture of the polymer and produce a sound, durable pipe. BS 3506 gives the requirements for pipes intended for industrial purposes, and BS 4660 covers the pipes and fittings for domestic use. Standard outside diameters are 110 and 160 mm (100 and 150 mm nominal bore) with non-standard outside diameters of 82, 200, 250 and 315 mm being available from most manufacturers. Long lengths of 3 m and 6 m can be easily cut by hacksaw. BS 5481 and BS EN 1401-1 are also available as specifications for uPVC sewer pipes in nominal diameters of 200–630 mm. The pipes are obtainable with socket joints for either a solvent-welded joint or a ring seal joint (see Fig. 11.3.3). Like pitch fibre pipes, uPVC pipes have a smooth bore, are light and easy to handle, long lengths reducing to a minimum the number of joints required; they can be jointed and laid in all weathers.

▨ ▥ ■ DRAIN LAYING

Domestic drains are laid in trenches that are excavated and if necessary timbered in a similar manner to that described for foundations; the main difference is that drain trenches are excavated to the required fall or gradient. It is good practice to programme the work to enable the activities of excavation, drain laying and backfilling to be carried out in quick succession so that the excavations remain open for the shortest possible time.

The technique used in the laying and bedding of drains will depend upon two factors:

- material – rigid or flexible;
- joint – rigid or flexible.

Approved Document H recommends drains to be of sufficient strength and durability and so jointed that the drain remains watertight under all working conditions, including any differential movement between the pipe and ground.

Many examples of traditional bedding and haunching in concrete will be found in existing drains, but this is no longer practised unless the drain requires a complete surround of concrete for total protection. The cost is prohibitive, the quality of concrete is difficult to control in wet trenches, and the system is prone to failure in ground movement and settlement. Both clay and uPVC drains can accommodate axial flexibility and extensibility by combining flexible jointing with a granular flexible bedding medium. Several examples of bedding specifications are provided in the Building Regulations, Approved Document H and BS EN 752-1 to 4: *Drain and sewer systems outside buildings*. Two popular applications are shown in Fig. 11.3.5.

The selected material required for granular bedding and for tamping around pipes laid on a jointed concrete base must be of the correct quality. Pipes depend to a large extent upon the support bedding for their strength and must therefore be uniformly supported on all sides by a material that can be hard compacted. Generally a non-cohesive granular material with a particle size of 5–20 mm is suitable, and if not present on site it will have to be 'imported'.

Pipes with socket joints are laid from the bottom of the drain run with the socket end laid against the flow, each pipe being aligned and laid to the correct fall. The collar of the socket is laid in a prepared 'hollow' in the bedding, and the bore is centralised. In the case of a rigid joint a tarred gaskin is used, which also forms the seal, whereas the mechanical or flexible joints are self-aligning. Most flexible joints require a special lubricant to ease the jointing process, and those that use a coupling can be laid in any direction.

MEANS OF ACCESS

Drains require access for testing, maintenance and clearance of blockages. Four possibilities exist:

- rodding eye;
- shallow access fitting;
- inspection chamber;
- manhole.

150 mm topsoil

Excavated spoil as backfill

Selected fill free from stones larger than 40 mm, lumps of clay over 100 mm, timber, frozen material and vegetable matter

Pea shingle or 20 mm max. granular fill

150

Pipe dia.

100

150 | Pipe dia. | 150

Normal backfill and topsoil

Selected fill as described above

Selected or granular fill free from stones larger than 40 mm

Granular fill conforming to BS 8301 (Appendix D)

300

100

Pipe dia.

100

150 | Pipe dia. | 150

Figure 11.3.5   Typical pipe bedding details.

When fitted with lightweight covers these should be secured by screws to deter unauthorised interference.

Rodding eyes

These generally locate at the head of a drain and are effectively a swept extension of the drain to surface level, with a sealed access plate. With local authority approval they can replace a more expensive inspection chamber to provide means for clearance in one direction only.

Shallow access fittings

These provide vertical access to both directions of a drain run that is not over 600 mm deep.

Inspection chambers

These are an enlarged version of the shallow access fitting, used to invert depths of up to 1 m. They provide for limited access, and contain facilities for a few junctions and branch connections. Materials include plastics, precast concrete and traditional brick masonry. Figure 11.3.6 shows examples of means of drain access, with the plastic inspection chamber containing optional adaptors, which can be cut to suit 100 or 150 mm pipes at various approach angles. The depth of these units is cut to suit drain trench levels, and a cast iron or aluminium frame and cover is fitted.

Manholes

These are inspection chambers over 1 m to invert. They are a compartment containing half or three-quarter section round channels to enable the flow to be observed, and to provide a drain access point for cleansing and testing. Both inspection chambers and manholes are positioned to comply with the access recommendations of Approved Document H (see Fig. 11.3.1).

Simple domestic drainage is normally concerned only with shallow manholes up to an invert depth of 1800 mm. The internal sizing is governed by the depth to invert, the number of branch drains, the diameter of branch drains, and the space required for a person to work within the manhole. A general guide to the internal sizing of inspection chambers and manholes is given in Approved Document H, Table 9.

Manholes can be constructed of brickwork or of rectangular or circular precast concrete units (see Fig. 11.3.7). The access covers used in domestic work are generally of cast iron or pressed steel, and are light duty as defined in BS EN 124. They have a single seal, which should be bedded in grease to form an airtight joint; double seal covers would be required if the access was situated inside the building. Concrete access covers are available for use with surface water manholes.

Plastic inspection chamber

Clay or plastic shallow access chamber

Rodding eye

Figure 11.3.6 Drains – means of access up to 1 m deep.

LOCATION OF DRAIN ACCESS POINTS

Access to drainage systems is required at various situations. These are outlined on page 579. Long straight drain runs must also be avoided, otherwise parts of the drain would be very difficult to access by cleaning rods in event of a blockage. For domestic drainage (up to 300 mm diameter) the maximum spacing between different means of access provision are as listed in Table 11.3.1.

VENTILATION OF DRAINS

To prevent foul air from soil and combined drains escaping and causing a nuisance, all drains should be vented by a flow of air. A ventilating pipe should be provided at or near the head of each main drain and any branch drain exceeding 10.000 in length. The ventilating pipe can be a separate pipe, or the soil discharge stack pipe

Shallow brick inspection chamber

Precast concrete inspection chamber (BS 5911-4 and BS EN 1917)

Figure 11.3.7 Typical shallow inspection chambers.

Table 11.3.1 Maximum spacing of drainage access (m)

From:	To: Small access fitting	Large access fitting	Junction	Inspection chamber	Manhole
Start of drain	12	12	–	22	45
Rodding eye	22	22	22	45	45
Small access fitting	–	–	12	22	22
Large access fitting	–	–	12	45	45
Inspection chamber	22	45	22	45	45
Manhole	–	–	–	45	90 (note 2)

Notes:
1. Small access fitting: 150 mm × 100 mm or 150 mm diameter. Large access fitting: 225 mm × 100 mm.
2. Up to 200 m is permitted if the manhole is of substantial proportions, i.e. sufficient to allow a person entry space to work.

can be carried upwards to act as a ventilating discharge stack or soil vent pipe. Ventilating pipes should be open to the outside air and carried up for at least 900 mm above the head of any window opening within a horizontal distance of 3.000 from the ventilating pipe, which should be finished with a cage or cover that does not restrict the flow of air.

Conventional venting through the stack is not always necessary. An air admittance valve can be fitted in up to four consecutive dwellings of no more than three storeys, if the fifth dwelling is conventionally vented. Systems with air admittance valves have the following advantages:

- Ventilating stack can terminate inside the building (above highest spillover level), typically in the roof space.
- Greater design flexibility.
- Adaptable to plastic or metal pipework.
- Visually unobtrusive as there is no projecting stack pipe.

The principles of application and operation are shown in Fig. 11.3.8. A discharge of water in the stack creates a slight negative pressure, sufficient to open the valve and admit air. After discharge a return to atmospheric pressure allows the spring to re-seal the unit to prevent foul air escaping. To satisfy building regulations, the device must have received design approval in accordance with the Board of Agrément.

RAINWATER DRAINAGE

A rainwater drainage installation is required to collect the discharge from roofs and paved areas, and convey it to a suitable drainage system. Paved areas, such as garage forecourts or hardstands, are laid to fall so as to direct the rainwater into a yard gully, which is connected to the surface water drainage system. A rainwater

Figure 11.3.8   Air admittance valve.

installation for a roof consists of a collection channel called a **gutter**, which is connected to vertical rainwater pipes. The rainwater pipe is terminated at its lowest point by means of a rainwater shoe for discharge to a surface water drain, or a trapped gully if the discharge is to a combined drain (see Fig. 11.3.9). If a separate system of drainage or soakaways is used it may be possible to connect the rainwater pipe direct to the drains, provided there is an alternative means of access for cleansing.

The materials available for domestic rainwater installations are galvanised pressed steel, cast iron and uPVC. The usual materials for domestic work are cast iron and uPVC, the latter being the usual specification for new work.

For details of eaves
construction see
Figs 6.1.5 and 6.2.2

Half-round section
rainwater gutter

Gutter brackets
fixed to fascia
at 1.000 c/c

112° offset or
swanneck

Pipe clip or holderbat

Rainwater pipe

Cavity insulation
and insulated
blockwork inner
leaf if habitable
accommodation

Rainwater pipe

Sealed access cover

Raising piece

To surface
water drain

Rainwater shoe

Rainwater pipe

Sealed access cover

To combined
drain

Back inlet access gully

Figure 11.3.9 Rainwater pipework and drainage.

Cast iron rainwater goods

Cast iron rainwater pipes, gutters and fittings are generally made to the requirements of BS 460, which specifies a half-round section gutter with a socket joint in diameters from 75 to 150 mm and an effective length of 1800 mm. The gutter socket joint should be lapped in the direction of the flow and sealed with either putty or an approved sealing compound before being bolted together. The gutter is supported at 1000–1800 mm centres by means of mild steel gutter brackets screwed to the feet of rafters for an open eaves or to the fascia board with a closed eaves.

Cast iron rainwater pipes are also produced to a standard effective length of 1800 mm with a socket joint that is sealed with putty, run lead or in many cases dry jointed – the pipe diameters range from 50 to 150 mm. The downpipes are fixed to the wall by means of pipe nails and spacers when the pipes are supplied with ears, or with split ring hinged holderbats when the pipes are supplied without ears cast on. A full range of fittings such as outlets, stopped ends and internal and external angles are available for cast iron half-round gutters, and, for the downpipes, fittings such as bends, offsets and rainwater heads are produced.

Unplasticised PVC rainwater goods

The advantages of uPVC rainwater goods over cast iron are:

- Easier jointing, gutter bolts are not required, and the joint is self-sealing, generally by means of a butyl or similar strip.
- Corrosion is eliminated.
- Decoration is not required; several standard colours are available including brown, black, white and grey.
- Breakages are reduced.
- Better flow properties usually enable smaller sections and lower falls.

Half-round gutters are supplied in standard effective lengths up to 6 m, with diameter ranging from 75 to 150 mm. Downpipes are supplied in two standard lengths of 2 and 4 m with diameters of 50, 63, 75 and 89 mm. The gutters, pipes and fittings are generally produced to the requirements of BS 4576 and BS 12200-1. Typical details of domestic rainwater gutter and pipework are shown in Fig. 11.3.9.

Sizing of pipes and gutters

The sizing of the gutters and downpipes to effectively cater for the discharge from a roof will depend upon:

- the area of roof to be drained;
- anticipated intensity of rainfall;
- material of gutter and downpipe;
- fall within gutter, usually in the range 1/150 to 1/600;
- number, size and position of outlets.

The requirements for Building Regulation H3 concerning rainwater drainage can be satisfied by using the design guide tables contained in Approved Document H, which gives guidance to sizing gutters, downpipes and selection of suitable materials.

▨ ■ ■ CONNECTIONS TO SEWERS

It is generally recommended that all connections to sewers shall be made so that the incoming drain or private sewer is joined to the main sewer obliquely in the direction of flow and that the connection will remain watertight and satisfactory under all working conditions. Normally sewer connections are made by the local authority or under their direction and supervision.

The method of connection will depend upon a number of factors:

- relative sizes of sewer and connecting drain or private sewer;
- relative invert levels;
- position of nearest inspection chamber on the sewer run;
- whether the sewer is existing or being laid concurrently with the drains or private sewers;
- whether stopped or joinder junctions have been built into the existing sewer;
- the shortest and most practicable route.

If the public sewer is of a small diameter, less than 225 mm, the practical method is to remove two or three pipes and replace with new pipes and an oblique junction to receive the incoming drain. If three pipes are removed it is usually possible to 'spring in' two new pipes and the oblique junction and joint in the usual manner, but if only two pipes are removed a collar connection will be necessary (see Fig. 11.3.10).

If new connections have been anticipated stopped junctions or joinder junctions may have been included in the sewer design. A stopped junction has a disc temporarily secured in the socket of the branch arm, whereas the joinder has a cover cap as an integral part of the branch arm. In both cases careful removal of the disc or cap is essential to ensure that a clean undamaged socket is available to make the connection (see Fig. 11.3.10).

Connections to inspection chambers or manholes, whether new or existing, can take several forms, depending mainly upon the differences in invert levels. If the invert levels of the sewer and incoming drain are similar, the connection can be made in the conventional way using an oblique branch channel. Where there is a difference in invert levels the following can be considered:

- a ramp formed in the benching within the inspection chamber;
- a backdrop manhole or inspection chamber;
- an increase in the gradient of the branch drain.

The maximum difference between invert levels that can be successfully overcome by the use of a ramp is a matter of conjecture. The old CP 2005 entitled *Sewerage*, since replaced by BS 8005: Part 1 and subsequently BS EN 752, gave a maximum difference of 1.800 m, whereas BS 8301, covering building drainage, gave 1.000 for external ramps at 45°. The generally accepted limit of invert level difference

Removing 3 No. pipes and inserting oblique junction

Removing 2 No. pipes and inserting oblique junction

Joinder junction   **Stopped junction**

Figure 11.3.10   Connections to small-diameter sewers (traditional rigid-jointed spigot and socket clay pipes).

Brick levelling course

600 × 600 cast iron cover
and frame to BS EN 124

Ramp formed in
concrete benching

100 mm precast
concrete slab

Flow

Wall in BS 3921
class B bricks
in cm. mt. (1:3)
laid to English
Bond

700 max.

Mass concrete
benching

Incoming
drain

Mass concrete base

Private or public sewer

Ramp connection

150 × 150 cast iron
cover and frame

60 × 600 cast iron cover
and frame to BS EN 124

Incoming
drain

Flow

100 mm precast
concrete slab

Galv. step irons
to BS 1247 every
4th course vertically
set staggered at
230 c/c horizontally
1st step 450 mm
below cover level

Double
square
junction

Lever
locking
stopper

Drop
pipe

Wall in BS 3921
class B bricks
in cm. mt. (1:3)
laid to English
Bond

150 mm min.
concrete
encasing

90° bend

Mass concrete
benching

Mass concrete base

Private or public sewer

Backdrop connection

Figure 11.3.11 Manhole and inspection chamber sewer connections.

for the use of internal ramps is 700 mm, which approximates to the figure quoted in the first edition of CP 301, later superseded by BS 8301. Typical constructional details are shown in Fig. 11.3.11.

Where the limit for ramps is exceeded, a backdrop manhole construction can be considered. This consists of a vertical 'drop' pipe with access for both horizontal and vertical rodding. If the pipework is of clay or concrete the vertical pipe should be positioned as close to the outside face of the manhole as possible and encased in not less than 150 mm of mass concrete. Cast iron pipework is usually sited inside the chamber and fixed to the walls with holderbolts. Whichever material is used the basic principles are constant (see Fig. 11.3.11).

Changing the gradient of the incoming drain to bring its invert level in line with that of the sewer requires careful consideration and design. Although simple in conception, the gradient must be such that a self-cleansing velocity is maintained and the requirements of Building Regulation Part H are not contravened.

Connections of small-diameter drains to large-diameter sewers can be made by any of the methods described above, or by using a saddle connection. A saddle is a short socketed pipe with a flange or saddle curved to suit the outer profile of the sewer pipe. To make the connection a hole must be cut in the upper part of the sewer to receive the saddle, ensuring that little or no debris is allowed to fall into the sewer. A small pilot hole is usually cut first, and this is enlarged to the required diameter by careful cutting and removing the debris outwards. The saddle connection is bedded onto the sewer pipe with a cement mortar, and the whole connection is surrounded with a minimum of 150 mm of mass concrete (see Fig. 11.3.12).

▨▦▉ DRAIN TESTING

To satisfy the Building Regulations requirements for watertightness of drains, reference to Approved Document H1 permits application of either a water or an air test. A smoke test could also be applied to determine the position of any apparent leakage revealed by the other tests. The Approved Document also makes reference to the recommendations contained in BS EN 752-3, 4 and 6.

The local authority will carry out drain testing after the backfilling of the drain trench has taken place: therefore it is in the contractor's interest to test drains and private sewers before the backfilling is carried out, as the detection and repair of any failure discovered after backfilling can be time-consuming and costly.

TYPES OF TEST

There are three methods available for the testing of drains:

■ **Water test**   The usual method employed; carried out by filling the drain run being tested with water under pressure and observing whether there is any escape of water (see Fig. 11.3.13).
■ **Smoke test**   This is a dated practice, but if required smoke can be pumped into the sealed drain run under test and any fall in pressure, as indicated by the fall of the float on the smoke machine, observed (see Fig. 11.3.14).

150 mm concrete encasing
to saddle connection

Shoulder of saddle
shaped to fit outside
diameter of sewer and
to form oblique
junction

Flow

Incoming
drain

Flow

Private or public sewer

Connection arrangement

Incoming drain

Rigid joint

Flow

Saddle bedded
in cm. mt. (1:3)

At least
half saddle
width to
bear on
sewer wall

45°   45°

Private or
public sewer

Note: Saddle connection should be made in
the crown of the sewer pipe within 45°
on either side of the vertical axis

Typical section

Figure 11.3.12   Saddle connections to sewers.

Cap

Expanding ring

Wing nut

Plates

Flat moulded rubber expanding ring

13 or 25 mm dia. brass threaded outlet

Brass cap

Brass wing nut

Galvanised iron plates

Pipe ₵ and plug

Typical drain plug details

Drain plug to lower end of run under test

Drain under test filled with water

Bedding

Temporarily jointed vertical length(s) of pipe to give required test head of 1.5 m, which should be held for 2 hours after initial drop in water level and subsequent topping up – measure leakage over a 30 minute period

Temporarily jointed bend

Figure 11.3.13   Water testing of drains.

Removable float guide

Copper cover or float

Square copper tank filled to within 6 mm of top with water

Steel tube outlet

Valve

Bellows handle with security chain

Leather-covered double-action bellows

502 × 228 × 223 overall frame

Smoke machine details

32 mm bore embedded wire rubber tube or 25 mm bore flexible metallic tube

Smoke testing machine

Expanding plug type connection

Drain under test filled with smoke

Bedding

Smoke is produced in the firebox by burning oily cotton waste or prepared smoke paper – after a few strokes of the bellows the float rises and will remain stationary if drain run is sound

Drain plug capped or stopper inflated when smoke has reached upper end of drain run

Figure 11.3.14 Smoke testing of drains.

■ **Air test**   This is not a particularly conclusive test, but it is sometimes used in special circumstances such as large-diameter pipes where a large quantity of water would be required. If a failure is indicated by an air test the drain should be retested using the more reliable water test (see Fig. 11.3.15).

The illustrations of drain testing have been prepared on the assumption that the test is being carried out by the contractor before backfilling has taken place.

In general the testing of drains should be carried out between manholes. Manholes should be tested separately, and short branches of less than 6.000 m should be tested with the main drain to which they are connected; long branches would be tested in the same manner as a main drain.

▨■■ SOAKAWAYS

A soakaway is a pit dug in permeable ground that receives the rainwater discharge from the roof and paved areas of a small building, and is so constructed that the water collected can percolate into the surrounding subsoil. To function correctly and efficiently a soakaway must be designed to take the following factors into account:

■ permeability or rate of dispersion of the subsoil;
■ area to be drained;
■ storage capacity required to accept sudden inflow of water, such as that encountered during a storm;
■ local authority requirements as to method of construction and siting in relation to buildings;
■ depth of water table.

Before any soakaway is designed or constructed the local authority should be contacted to obtain permission and ascertain its specific requirements. Some authorities will permit the use of soakaways only as an outfall to a subsoil drainage scheme.

The rate at which water will percolate into the ground depends mainly on the permeability of the soil. Generally, clay soils are unacceptable for soakaway construction, whereas sands and gravels are usually satisfactory. An indication of the permeability of a soil can be ascertained by observing the rate of percolation. A borehole 150 mm in diameter should be drilled to a depth of 1.000 m. Water to a depth of 300 mm is poured into the hole, and the time taken for the water to disperse is noted. Several tests should be made to obtain an average figure, and the whole procedure should be repeated at 1.000 m stages until the proposed depth of the soakaway has been reached. A suitable diameter and effective depth for the soakaway can be obtained from design guidance in Building Research Establishment Digest 365.

An alternative method, using a simple empirical formula, calculates the volume of a soakaway by allowing for a storage capacity equal to one-third of the hourly rain falling onto the area to be drained:

Figure 11.3.15 Air testing of drains.

$$C = \frac{AR}{3}$$

where
  C = capacity (m^3)
  A = area to be drained (m^2)
  R = rainfall (m/h)

For example:

  Area to be drained = 150 m^2
  stormwater allowance = 75 mm/h

therefore

$$C = \frac{150 \times 0.075}{3} = 3.75 \text{ m}^3$$

TYPES OF SOAKAWAY

A soakaway is constructed by excavating a pit of the appropriate size and either filling the void with selected coarse granular material or lining the sides of the excavation with brickwork or precast concrete rings (see Figs 11.3.16 and 11.3.17).

Filled soakaways are usually employed only for small capacities, because it is difficult to estimate the storage capacity, and the life of the soakaway may be limited by the silting-up of the voids between the filling material. Lined soakaways are generally more efficient, have a longer life, and if access is provided can be inspected and maintained at regular intervals.

Soakaways should be sited away from buildings so that foundations are unaffected by the percolation of water from the soakaway. The minimum 'safe' distance is often quoted as 5.000 m, but local authority advice should always be sought. The number of soakaways required can be determined only by having the facts concerning total drain runs, areas to be drained, and the rate of percolation for any particular site.

Surface water drain

Topsoil

500 approx.

Impervious layer

Large rubble at outlet

Coarse granular material with size range of 10 to 100 mm

Surface water drain

Topsoil

100 mm thick precast concrete cover slab

Large rubble at outfall

Coarse granular material with size range of 10 to 100 mm

Suitable coarse granular materials include broken bricks, crushed sound rock and hard clinker

Figure 11.3.16 Filled soakaways.

Brick-lined soakaway

Brick levelling courses

600 × 600 cast iron cover and frame

Surface water drain

100 mm thick precast concrete cover slab

Brick walls laid in honeycomb bond

Alternatives for walls – dry rubble walling and dry-jointed brickwork

Mass *in-situ* concrete strip

Brick levelling courses

Cast iron cover and frame

Drain

Precast concrete light duty chamber cover slab

600 min. diameter

Dry ogee joints

675 to 1.800 dia.

300 to 1.200 in multiples of 150 mm

Granular backfill

Precast concrete cylindrical chamber sections

75 mm dia. drainage holes

Mass *in-situ* concrete strip

Precast concrete soakaway

Figure 11.3.17 Lined soakaways.

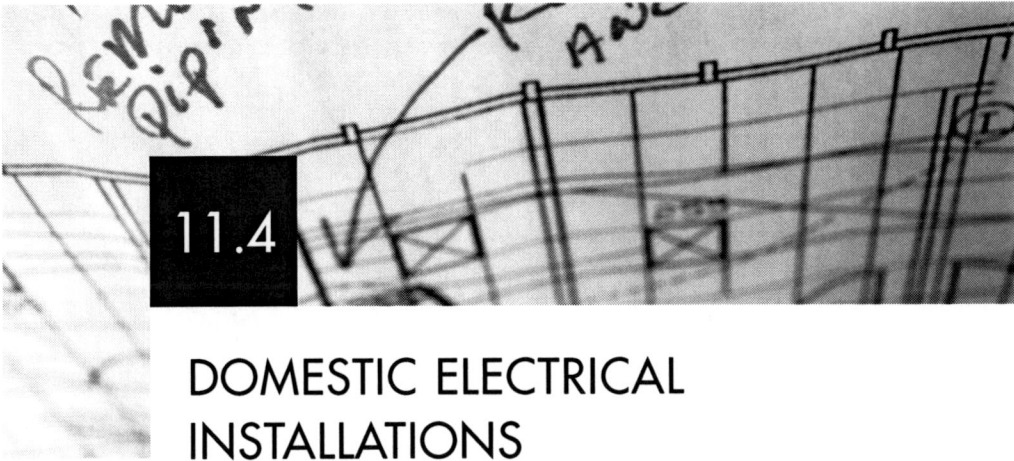

DOMESTIC ELECTRICAL INSTALLATIONS

A simple definition of the term **electricity** is not possible, but it can be considered as a form of energy due to the free movement of tiny particles called **electrons**. If sufficient of these free or loose electrons move, an electric current is produced in the material in which they are moving. Materials such as most metals and water which allow an electric current to flow readily are called **conductors** and are said to have a low resistance. Materials that resist the flow of an electric current such as rubber, glass and most plastics are called **insulators**.

For an electric current to flow there must be a complete path or circuit from the source of energy through a conductor back to the source. Any interruption of the path will stop the flow of electricity. The pressure that forces or pushes the current around the circuit is called the **voltage**. The rate at which the current flows is measured in **amperes**, and the resistance offered by the circuit to passage of electrons is measured in **ohms**. A **watt** is the unit of power, and is equal to the product of volts × amperes; similarly it can be shown that voltage is equal to the product of amperes × ohms.

Another effect of an electric current flowing through a conductor is that it will dissipate wasted energy in the form of heat according to the resistance of the conductor. If a wire of the correct resistance is chosen it will become very hot, and this heating effect can be used in appliances such as cookers, irons and fires. The conductor in a filament bulb is a very thin wire of high resistance and becomes white hot, thus giving out light as well as heat.

Most domestic premises receive a single-phase supply of electricity from an area electricity authority at a rating of 230 volts, and a frequency of 50 hertz. The area authority's cable, from which the domestic supply is taken, consists of four lines: three lines each carry a 230 volt supply, and the fourth is the common return line or neutral, which is connected to earth at the transformer or substation as a safety precaution should a fault occur on the electrical appliance. Each line or phase is tapped in turn together with the neutral to provide the single-phase 230 V supply. Electricity is generated and supplied as an **alternating current**, which means that the current flows first one way then the other; the direction change is so rapid that it is hardly discernible in fittings such as lights. The cycle of this reversal of flow is termed **frequency**.

Figure 11.4.1 shows a typical underground domestic electricity supply to an external meter box. The consumer unit should be located as close as possible to the intake on the inside of the cavity wall as shown, or on an adjacent partition.

The conductors used in domestic installations are called **cables,** and consist of a conductor of low resistance such as copper or aluminium surrounded by an insulator of high resistance such as rubber or plastic. Cable sizes are known by the nominal cross-sectional area of the conductor, and up to 2.5 mm^2 are usually of one strand. Larger cables consist of a number of strands to give them flexibility. All cables are assigned a rating in amperes, which is the maximum load the cable can carry without becoming overheated.

For domestic work, wiring drawings are not usually required; instead the positions of outlets, switches and lighting points are shown by symbols on the plans. Specification of fittings, fixing heights and cables is given either in a schedule or in a written document (see Fig. 11.4.2).

▨▨■ CIRCUITS

Domestic buildings are wired using a **ring circuit** as opposed to the older method of having a separate fused subcircuit to each socket outlet. Lighting circuits are carried out by using the **loop in** method.

The supply or intake cable will enter the building through ducts and be terminated in the area authority's fused sealing chamber, which should be sited in a dry accessible position. From the sealing chamber the supply passes through the meter, which records the electricity consumed in units of kilowatt/hours, to the consumer unit, which has a switch controlling the supply to the circuit fuses or miniature circuit-breakers. These fuses or circuit-breakers are a protection against excess current or overload of the circuit because, should overloading occur, the fuse or circuit-breaker will isolate the circuit from the supply.

The number of fuseways or miniature circuit-breakers contained in the consumer unit will depend upon the size of the building and the equipment to be installed. A separate ring circuit of 32 amp loading should be allowed for every 100 m^2 of floor area, and as far as practicable the number of outlets should be evenly distributed over the circuits. A typical domestic installation would have the following circuits from the consumer unit:

1. 6 amp: ground floor lighting up to 10 fittings or a total load of 6 amps;
2. 6 amp: upper floor lighting as above;
3. 16 amp: immersion heater;
4. 32 amp: ring circuit 1;
5. 32 amp: ring circuit 2;
6. 32 amp: ring circuit, kitchen;
7. 45 amp: cooker circuit.

[*Note*: A further 40 or 45 amp circuit-breaker or fuse may be installed for an electric shower unit.]

External
cavity wall

Consumer unit
(fuse box)

Plastic
meter cupboard

Phase and neutral
intake to sealing
chamber (see Fig. 10.4.4)

Ground floor

Plastic protective
conduit

450
min.

Figure 11.4.1   Underground domestic electrical supply.

Ground floor plan

Upper floor plan

Symbols		
✓ One-way switch	⚡ Pendant switch	☑ Consumer unit
⚡ Two-way switch	◯ Ceiling outlet	● Meter
▷— Switch socket outlet	⊙— Immersion heater	☐ Cooker control

Figure 11.4.2 Typical domestic electrical layout.

Main
switch

6 amp mcb – ground floor lighting circuit
6 amp mcb – upper floor lighting circuit
16 amp mcb – immersion heater
32 amp mcb – ring circuit, ground floor
32 amp mcb – ring circuit, upper floor
32 amp mcb – ring circuit, kitchen
45 amp mcb – cooker

Meter

Sealing
chamber

Supply
cable

Consumer
unit

Socket outlets

Line

Neutral

Earth

Earth terminal –
cable colour
green/yellow

Socket
outlet

Spur outlet

Cap
screw

BS 1363
plug

Cartridge
fuse – 3 amp for up to 720 watt rating
13 amp for up to 3,000 watt rating

Line terminal – cable
colour brown

Cable
grip

Neutral terminal – cable
colour blue

Figure 11.4.3   Ring circuits and plug wiring.

Figure 11.4.4   Split-load consumer unit.

The complete installation is earthed by connecting the metal consumer unit casing to the sheath of the supply cable, or by connection to a separate earth electrode. Figure 11.4.3 shows a standard consumer unit with disposition of fuseways or miniature circuit-breakers. A preferable alternative is the split-load consumer unit shown in Fig. 11.4.4. This contains specific protection to ground floor sockets that could have extension leads attached for use with portable garden equipment.

For lighting circuits using sheathed wiring a $1.5 \, mm^2$ conductor is required, and therefore a twin with earth cable is used. The loop-in method of wiring is shown diagrammatically in Fig. 11.4.5. It is essential that lighting circuits are properly earthed, as most domestic fittings and switches contain metal parts or fixings, which could become live should a fault occur. Lighting circuits using a conduit installation with single-core cables can be looped from switch to switch as shown in Fig. 11.4.5. Conduit installation consists of metal or plastic tubing together with various boxes for forming junctions and housing switches, which gives a protected rewireable system. If steel-screwed conduit is used it will also serve as the earth leakage path, but if plastic conduit is used, as it is non-conductive, the circuit must have an insulated earth conductor throughout.

A ring circuit for socket outlets consists of a twin $2.5 \, mm^2$ earthed cable starting from and returning to the consumer unit. The cables are looped into the outlet boxes, making sure that the correct cable is connected to the correct terminals (see Fig. 11.4.4). The number of outlets is unlimited if the requirement of one ring circuit per $100 \, m^2$ of floor area has been adopted. Spur outlets leading off the main ring circuit are permissible provided the limitations that not more than two outlet sockets are on any one spur, and that not more than half the socket outlets on the circuit are on spurs, are not exceeded. Socket outlets can be switched controlled and of single or double outlet; the double outlet is considered the best arrangement as it discourages the use of multiple adaptors. Fixed appliances such as wall heaters should be connected directly to a fused spur outlet to reduce the number of trailing leads. Movable appliances such as irons, radios and standard lamps should have a fused plug for connection to the switched outlet, conforming to the requirements of BS 1363. The rating of the cartridge fuse should be in accordance with rating

Line

Neutral

Earth

Light

Ceiling
rose or
outlet

Switch
line

One-way switch

'Loop-in' method of wiring using sheathed cable

Line

Neutral

Earth

Light

Ceiling
rose or
outlet

Switch
line

One-way switch

Single-core cable looped from switch to switch

Figure 11.4.5   Typical lighting circuits.

of the appliance. Appliances with a rating of not more than 720 watts should be protected by a 3 amp fuse and appliances over this rating up to 3000 watts should have a 13 amp fuse. As with the circuit, correct wiring of the plug is essential (see Fig. 11.4.3).

The number of outlets is not mandatory, but the minimum numbers recommended for various types of accommodation are:

- kitchens: 6 plus cooker control unit with one outlet socket;
- living rooms: 8;
- dining rooms: 4;
- bedrooms: 4;
- halls: 1;
- landings: 1;
- garages: 1;
- stores and workshops: 1.

The outlets should be installed around the perimeter of the rooms in the most convenient and economic positions to give maximum coverage with minimum amount of trailing leads.

Cables sheathed with PVC can be run under suspended floors by drilling small holes on the neutral axis of the joists; where the cables are to be covered by wall finishes or floor screed they should be protected either by oval conduit or by means of small metal cover channels fixed to the wall or floor. Systems using mineral-insulated covered cables follow the same principles. This form of cable consists of single strands of copper or aluminium, all encased in a sheath of the same metal, which is densely packed with fine magnesium oxide insulation around the strands. This insulating material is unaffected by heat or age and is therefore very durable, but it can absorb moisture. The sealing of the ends of this type of cable with special sealing 'pots' is therefore of paramount importance. Cables used in a conduit installation have adequate protection, but it is generally necessary to chase the walls of the building to accommodate the conduit, outlet socket boxes and switch boxes below the wall finish level. Surface run conduit is normally secured to the backing by using screwed shaped clips called **saddles**.

Guidance for the installation of electrical circuits and electrical equipment is provided in the Building Regulations, Approved Document P: Electrical safety. Further details are produced in the Institution of Electrical Engineers Regulations in accordance with BS 7671: *Requirements for electrical installations*.

With the exception of minor work such as replacement of socket outlets, switches, etc., all other proposed electrical work in dwellings requires notification to the local building control authority. Certification of a satisfactory installation is by:

- inspection by a qualified electrician appointed by the local building control office; or
- self-certification by a prescribed suitably qualified competent person.

DOMESTIC GAS INSTALLATIONS

Gas is a combustible fuel that burns with a luminous flame; it is used mainly in domestic installations as a source of heat energy in appliances such as room heaters, cookers and boilers. Historically, gas preceded electricity as a domestic energy utility, and it has been used to power washing machines, refrigerators and lighting.

BG Group plc supplies and processes gas for general distribution in the UK. It is stored in a liquid state in huge underground storage chambers, from where it is conveyed as a gas through a network of underground mains installed and maintained by the gas transporter, National Grid Transco Plc. Some gas is still stored in above-ground cylindrical holders, but these are gradually being phased out. Until the late 1960s a gas manufactured from coal known as **town gas** served domestic premises. The original pipework for conveying **town gas** was retained when supplies were changed to offshore gas supplies, which became known as **North Sea gas**. Offshore supply is a natural gas comprising about 90% methane, whereas coal gas had a hydrogen content of about 50%. Therefore, although pipework was unaffected, the different burning characteristics of the gases required major changes or replacements to domestic appliances. Table 11.5.1 shows a comparison of the calorific values of both gases and for bottled gases for use where mains gas is unavailable. Most domestic appliances manufactured for use with mains gas can be converted for bottled gas by changing the burners.

The installation of gas supplies can be considered in three stages:

1. **Main**   This is the part of the gas distribution system that is connected to form a grid. The grid is an interconnection of main pipes, normally located beneath roads or footways. The arrangement of pipes enables maintenance and repairs to be undertaken in isolation, without a major disruption of supply to a large community. For ease of identification, all new underground gas installation pipework is undertaken in a yellow-coloured plastic, not to be confused with water (blue), electricity (red) or drainage (orange).

2. **Service pipe** This is the connection between the main and the consumer control valve positioned just before the meter. For domestic installations the service pipe diameter is between 25 and 50 mm according to the number and type of appliances being installed. The pipeline should be as short as possible, at right angles to the main, and laid at least 375 mm below the surface to avoid damage. Figure 11.5.1 shows a typical domestic installation with meter details and accessories.

3. **Internal distribution** This commences at the consumer control valve and consists of a governor to stabilise gas pressure and volume, a meter to record the amount of gas consumed, and pipework to convey the gas supply to appliances. The meter and associated equipment are the property of the gas provider, but thereafter the installation is the responsibility of the building owner. A typical internal distribution to a house is shown in Fig. 11.5.2.

Table 11.5.1 Calorific values of gases for domestic appliances

Type of gas	Approx. calorific value (MJ/m^3)
Town gas	18
North sea gas	38
Bottled gas (Propane)	96
Bottled gas (Butane)	122

Notes:
1. Approximate values are given, as values will vary slightly depending on the source and quality.
2. Propane and butane are otherwise known as liquid petroleum gas (LPG). They are found under the North Sea bed and in other oil resources around the world. For transportation they are pressurised and liquefied to about 1/200 their gas volume.

███ PIPEWORK

Pipes for internal distribution can be of mild steel (not galvanised) or solid drawn copper. Flexible tubing of metal-reinforced rubber may be used for connection to cookers and portable appliances. The size of pipes will depend on such factors as gas consumption of appliances, frictional losses due to pipe length, and number of bends. A typical domestic installation is in 22 mm copper from the meter, with a 15 mm branch to a boiler and 10 mm to individual low-rated appliances. Pipes must not be accommodated in the cavity of a wall, but may pass through a wall provided a sleeve of non-corrodible material protects the pipe against any differential movement or settlement.

███ APPLIANCES

Gas appliances fall into two categories:

- gas supply only: cookers, radiant convector fires, decorative fuel effect fires;
- gas supply plus other services: central heating boilers, water heaters.

Figure 11.5.1 Domestic gas supply.

Figure 11.5.2 Internal distribution to appliances.

Gas radiant convector fires have a relatively low energy rating (generally < 3 kW). If less than 7 kW input rating, air for gas combustion can be taken from the room. They have a visible heat source as the gas burns through the fragile fireclay radiant. Gas fires can be set on a fireplace hearth with a closure back plate over the fire opening. A void in the plate allows for extraction of burnt gases directly up the chimney. Precast concrete flue blocks can also be used; see section on flue materials in Chapter 5.2.

Decorative fuel effect (DFE) fires are a popular adaptation within traditional fireplace openings. Log or coal effects are designed to resemble a real fire by burning gas and discharging the combusted products indirectly into the open flue. For efficient combustion, most DFE fires will require a room air vent of at least 10 000 mm^2 free area. The manufacturer's details should be consulted.

Gas cookers and instantaneous water heaters are an exception to the requirements for flues, but they should be installed and used only in well-ventilated rooms. The Building Regulations, Approved Document J, Section 3 should be consulted for minimum areas of air vents relative to room volume.

Room-sealed or balanced flue heaters are appliances that have the heat exchanger sealed from the room. Air for combustion of gas is drawn in from an external duct at the back of the unit, and burnt gases discharge through an adjacent flue: see Fig. 5.2.6. Acceptable locations for balanced flues are shown in Fig. 5.2.7 and Table 5.2.1.

Gas central heating consists of a wall-mounted or free-standing boiler connected to a flue (Chapter 5.2). This is the heat source for either a ducted fan-assisted warm air circulation system or a pump-circulated hot water system.

The Health and Safety Executive, through the Gas Safety (Installation and Use) Regulations, requires the installation and maintenance of gas fittings, appliances and storage vessels to be undertaken only by a competent and qualified person. A facility for assessing and accrediting individuals to undertake the various aspects of gas fitting and maintenance has been established by the Council for Registered Gas Installers (CORGI). Ref. Building Regulations, Approved Document J, Section 3.2.

The installation of gas services, like that of electricity, is a specialist subject not normally developed within the framework of construction technology. For a greater appreciation, see *Building Services, Technology and Design* by R. Greeno (Pearson Education and CIOB, co-publishers).

DOORS, DOOR FRAMES AND LININGS

▦▦▪ DOORS

A door is a screen used to seal an opening into a building or between rooms within a building. It can be made of timber, glass, metal or plastic or any combination of these materials. Doors can be designed to swing from one edge, slide, slide and fold, or roll to close an opening. The doors to be considered in this book are those made of timber and those made of timber and glass that are hung so that they swing from one edge. All doors may be classified by their position in a building, by their function, or by their method of construction.

EXTERNAL DOORS

These are used to close the access to the interior of a building and provide a measure of security. They need to be weather resistant, as in general they are exposed to the elements: this resistance is provided by the thickness, stability and durability of the construction and materials used, together with protective coatings of paint or polish. The external walls of a building are designed to give the interior of a building a degree of thermal and sound insulation; doors in such walls should therefore be constructed, as far as is practicable, to maintain the insulation properties of the external enclosure.

The standard sizes for external timber doors are 1981 mm high × 762 or 838 mm wide × 45 mm thick, which is a metric conversion of the old Imperial door sizes. Metric doors are produced so that, together with the frame, they fit into a modular coordinated opening size, and are usually supplied as door sets with the door already attached or hung in the frame.

INTERNAL DOORS

These are used to close the access through internal walls and partitions and to the inside of cupboards. As with external doors the aim of the design should be to

Figure 7.1.1   Purpose-made doors and mouldings.

maintain the properties of the wall in which they are housed. Generally, internal doors are thinner than their external counterparts as weather protection is no longer a requirement. Standard sizes are similar to those of external doors but with a wider range of widths to cater for narrow cupboard openings.

Purpose-made doors

The design and construction of these doors are usually the same as those of manufacturers' standard doors but to non-standard sizes, shapes or designs. Most door manufacturers produce a range of non-standard doors, which are often ornate and are used mainly for the front elevation doors of domestic buildings. Purpose-made doors are also used in buildings such as banks, civic buildings, shops, theatres and hotels to blend with or emphasise the external façade design or internal decor (see Fig. 7.1.1).

Methods of construction

The British Standard Code of Practice 151 covers all aspects of door construction. Unfortunately it is no longer published, but access to old copies will provide a useful reference for all doors of timber construction and their frames. British Standard 459 is published especially for matchboarded wooden doors for use externally.

Standard doors are used extensively because they are mass produced to known requirements, are readily available from stock and are cheaper than purpose-made doors.

Panelled and glazed wood doors

The Code of Practice gives a wide variety of types, all of which are based upon the one-, two-, three- or four-panel format. They are constructed of timber, which should be in accordance with the recommendations of BS 1186 and BS EN 942 with plywood or glass panels. External doors with panels of plywood should be constructed using an external-quality plywood (see Fig. 7.1.2).

The joints used in framing the doors can be a dowelled joint or a mortise and tenon joint. The dowelled joint is considered superior to the mortise and tenon joint and is cheaper when used in the mass production of standard doors. Bottom and lock rails have three dowels, top rails have two dowels, and intermediate rails have a single dowel connection (see Fig. 7.1.3). The plywood panels are framed into grooves with closely fitting sides with a movement allowance within the depth of the groove of 2 mm. The mouldings at the rail intersections are scribed, whereas the loose glazing beads are mitred. Weatherboards for use on external doors can be supplied to fit onto the bottom rail of the door, which can also be rebated to close over a water bar (see Fig. 7.1.2).

A fire door specification of FD 30 (see section headed: Flush fire doors) can be attained for 45 mm panelled doors by lining the existing panel with 6 mm glass-reinforced plasterboard or by replacing the panels with a double layer of 6 mm glass-reinforced plasterboard.

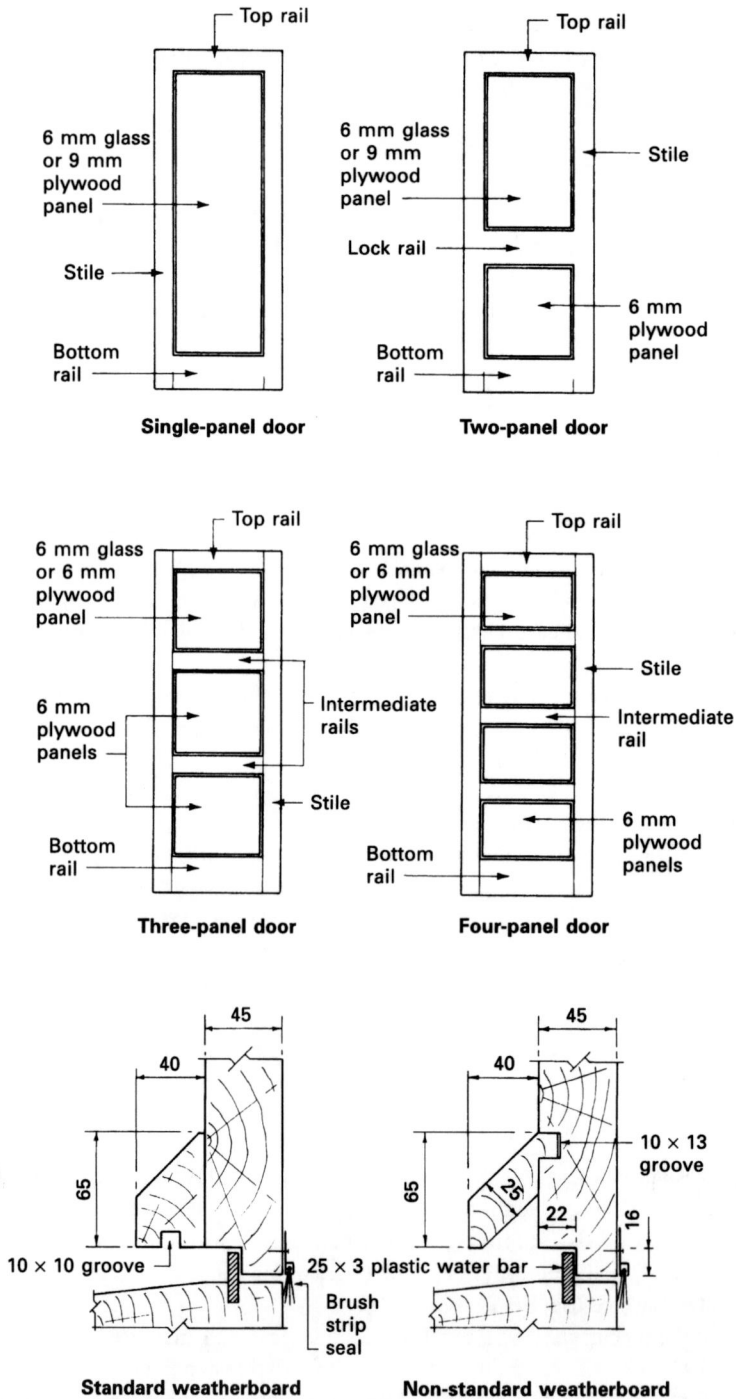

Figure 7.1.2 Standard panelled doors and weatherboards.

35 or
45

95 deep
top rail

Top rail

Scribed shoulder

Stile

16 mm dia. keyed
dowels stopped
25 mm from
outside edge
of stile

Typical dowelled joint

Glass panel bedded
in putty or leather

Glazing bead pinned to rail

95 × 35 or 45
intermediate rail

6 or 9 mm
plywood panel

Scribed
shoulder

Haunch

Top rail

Tenon

Stile

Mortise

Wedges

Typical mortise and tenon joint

195 × 35 or 45 bottom rail

Figure 7.1.3 Panelled door details.

Figure 7.1.4   Skeleton core flush doors.

Flush doors

This type of door has the advantage of a plain face that is easy to clean and decorate; it is also free of the mouldings that collect dust. Flush doors can be faced with hardboard, plywood or a plastic laminate, and by using a thin sheet veneer of good-quality timber the appearance of high-class joinery can be created.

The method of constructing flush doors is left to the manufacturer, which provides complete freedom for design. Therefore the forms of flush door construction are many and varied, but basically they can be considered as either skeleton core doors or solid core doors. The former consists of an outer frame with small-section intermediate members over which is fixed the facing material. The facing has a tendency to deflect between the core members, and this can be very noticeable on the surface, especially if the facing is coated with gloss paint. Solid core doors are designed to overcome this problem and at the same time improve the sound insulation properties of flush doors. They also provide a higher degree of fire resistance and security. Solid doors of suitably faced block or lamin board are available for internal and external use. Another method of construction is to infill the voids created by a skeleton core with a lightweight material such as foamed plastic, which will give support to the facings but will not add appreciably to the weight of the door.

The facings of flush doors are very vulnerable to damage at the edges: therefore a lipping of solid material should be fixed to at least the vertical edges (good-quality doors have lippings on all four edges).

Small glazed observation panels can be incorporated in flush doors when the glass panel is secured by loose fixing beads (see Figs 7.1.4 and 7.1.5).

Flush fire doors

These doors provide an effective barrier to the passage of fire for the time designated by a reference coding. They can be assessed in terms of stability and integrity in the presence of fire tests. For example, a coding of 30/30 indicates the time in minutes for which a door is 'stable' under simulated fire conditions and sufficiently 'integral' to resist the penetration of flame and hot gases. To achieve this they must be used in conjunction with the correct frame.

However, the term 'stability' is now considered less appropriate, and in accordance with BS 476-22: *Methods for determination of the fire resistance of non-loadbearing elements of construction*, integrity and insulation are sufficient criteria for grading (see BS 476-20 for test procedures). Furthermore, BS 5588: *Fire precautions in the design, construction and use of buildings* and the Building Regulations Approved Document B (see Appendix B, Table B1) designate fire doors by integrity performance only.

The performance of fire doors is simplified by expressing the category with the initials FD and the integrity in minutes numerically. For example, FD 60 indicates a fire door with 60 minute integrity, and if the coding is followed by the letter S it indicates the door or frame has a facility to resist the passage of smoke, i.e. FD 60S. Standard ratings are 20, 30, 60 and 90, but other ratings are available to order. A timber frame is unlikely to satisfy British Standard tests for a 120 rating.

Figure 7.1.5 Solid core doors.

Resistance to smoke penetration can be achieved by fitting a brush strip seal to the frame. These are primarily for draught-proofing, but will be effective in providing a barrier to cold smoke. A more effective barrier to smoke and flame is an intumescent strip fitted to the door edge or integral with the frame. The latter is usually the most practical, being secured in a frame recess with a rubber-based or PVA adhesive. At temperatures of about 150 °C the seal expands to prevent passage of fire and smoke for the designated period. The seal will not prevent door movement for access and escape of personnel.

Notes

1. Doorsets/hardware and glass must be selected with compatibility to the door specification (see BS 476-31 for conformity of doorsets).
2. A colour-coded plastic plug is fitted into the hanging style of the door to indicate fire resistance. For example:

   - blue core/white background:
     - FD 20 without intumescent strip in frame;
     - FD 30 with intumescent strip in frame;
   - red core/blue background:
     - FD 60 with two intumescent strips in frame.

   A full list of coloured core and background codes can be found in BS 8214, the *Code of practice for fire door assemblies* (see Table 1).
3. Half-hour fire-rated doors are hung using one pair of hinges, whereas one-hour doors require one-and-a-half pairs of hinges (see Fig. 7.1.6).
4. All fire doors should have an automatic self-closing device, except cupboards and accesses to service ducts that are normally kept locked.

Matchboarded doors

These doors can be used as external or internal doors and, as a standard door, take one of two forms, a ledged and braced door or a framed ledged and braced door, the latter being a stronger and more attractive version.

The face of the door is made from tongue-and-grooved boarding that has edge chamfers to one or both faces; these form a vee joint between consecutive boards. Three horizontal members called **ledges** clamp the boards together, and in this form a non-standard door, called a **ledged and battened door**, has been made. It is simple and cheap to construct but has the disadvantage of being able to drop at the closing edge, thus pulling the door out of square; the only resistance offered is that of the nails holding the boards to the ledges. The use of this type of door is limited to buildings such as sheds and outhouses and to small units such as trapdoors (see Fig. 7.1.7). In the standard door, braces are added to resist the tendency to drop out of square; the braces are fixed between the ledges so that they are parallel to one another and slope downwards towards the hanging edge (see Fig. 7.1.7).

In the second standard type a mortise and tenoned frame surrounds the matchboarded panel, giving the door added strength and rigidity (see Fig. 7.1.7). If wide doors of this form are required, the angle of the braces becomes too

838 or 914

83 × 38 framing

Lipping

59

25 × 35 planted stop

83

Intumescent strip

45

34

3 mm max. gap

Two-piece frame

45 mm deep rail

165 mm deep rail

9.5 mm plasterboard or 6 mm glass-reinforced plasterboard protective lining to both faces

3 mm plywood facing

Half-hour fire door and frame (FD 30)

838 or 914

83 × 38 framing

Lipping

59

35

92

Dual intumescent strip

54

34

3 mm max. gap

Solid frame

45 mm deep rail

165 mm deep rail

9.5 mm plasterboard or 6 mm glass-reinforced plasterboard protective lining to both faces

6 mm cement particle board to both faces

3 mm plywood facing

One-hour fire door and frame (FD 60)

Figure 7.1.6   Fire doors and frames.

16 mm matchboarding

150

95 × 22 ledge

95 × 22 brace

95 × 22 ledge

Hanging edge

95 × 22 brace

95 × 22 ledge

150

**Ledged and battened
(rear elevation)**

**Ledged and braced
(rear elevation)**

16 mm matchboarding

Brace

25

Ledge

95 × 45
framing

15

95 × 27
brace

Hanging
stile

15

146 × 27
middle rail

Alternative brace connection

95 × 27
brace

t

$5t$ max.

146 × 27 bottom rail

Bottom
rail

**Framed, ledged and braced
(rear elevation)**

Barefaced tenon

Figure 7.1.7 Matchboarded doors.

Figure 7.1.8   Matchboarded double doors.

low to be of value as an effective restraint, and the brace must therefore be framed as a diagonal between the top and bottom rails. Wide doors of this design are not covered by the British Standard but are often used in pairs as garage doors or as wide entrance doors to workshops and similar buildings (see Fig. 7.1.8).

The operation of fixing a door to its frame or lining is termed **hanging**, and entails: removing the protective horns from the top and bottom of the stiles; planing the stiles to reduce the door to a suitable width; cutting and planing the top and bottom to the desired height; marking out and fitting the butts or hinges that attach the door to the frame; and fitting any locks and door furniture that is required. The hinges should be positioned 225 mm from the top and bottom of the door; where one-and-a-half pairs of hinges are specified for heavy doors, the third hinge is positioned midway between the bottom and top hinges.

A door, irrespective of the soundness of its construction, will deteriorate if improperly treated during transportation and storage, and after hanging. It should receive a wood priming coat of paint before or immediately after delivery, and be stored in the dry and in a flat position so that it does not twist; it should also receive the finishing coats of paint as soon as practicable after hanging.

▨▨■ FRAMES AND LININGS

A door frame or lining is attached to the opening in which a door is to be fitted; it provides a surround for the door and is the member to which a door is fixed or hung. Door sets consisting of a storey-height frame with a solid or glazed panel over the door head are also available; these come supplied with the door ready hung on lift-off hinges (see Fig. 7.1.9).

TIMBER DOOR FRAMES

These are made from rectangular section timber in which a rebate is formed or to which a planted door stop is fixed to provide the housing for the door. Generally a door frame is approximately twice as wide as its thickness plus the stop. Frames are used for most external doors, heavy doors, doors situated in thin non-loadbearing partitions and internal fire doors.

A timber door frame consists of three or four members: the head, two posts or jambs, and a sill or threshold. The members can be joined together by wedged mortise and tenon joints, combed joints, or mortise and tenon joints pinned with a metal star-shaped dowel or a round timber dowel. All joints should have a coating of adhesive (see Fig. 7.1.10).

Door frames that do not have a sill are fitted with mild steel dowels driven into the base of the jambs and cast into the floor slab or, alternatively, grouted into preformed pockets as a means of securing the feet of the frame to the floor. If the frame is in an exposed position it is advisable to sit the feet of the jambs on a damp-proof pad such as lead or bituminous felt, to prevent moisture soaking into the frame and creating the conditions for fungal attack.

Lining head

25 or 32

Width of wall plus finishes

Housed joint

35 × 12 planted door stop

Lining jamb

Folding wedges behind jamb

Typical door lining

Combed joint

95 × 42 rebated head

Solid or glass panel

95 × 42 rebated transom

40 mm thick flush door

30 × 12 fixing bead

41.5 × 12 rebate

Lift-off hinge

Door size: 2.040 × 826
Overall frame: 2.376 × 890
to suit ceiling height
of 2.400 and opening
width of 900

95 × 42 rebated jamb

95 × 15 threshold

Typical door set

Figure 7.1.9   Door linings and door sets.

Horn built in or cut off

Mortise

85 × 57 splayed
and rebated
head

10 mm dia. wood
dowel

Tenon full
width of
jamb

3 No. corrugated
tee brackets
per jamb

16

25.5

51

52   48

1.5 mm
galvanised
mild steel

100

**External metal
door frame**

Metal fixing
cramp screwed
to back of frame

85 × 57 splayed and
rebated jamb

13 mm
deep
rebate
for
door

10 mm dia.
wood dowel

Tenon

Hole for
dowel

25 × 3
plastic water
bar

Mortise

10 mm throat

25 mm wide
bedding groove

121 × 45 hardwood
weathered sill

Figure 7.1.10   Door frames.

Door frames fitted with a sill are designed for one of two conditions:

- doors opening out;
- doors opening in.

In both cases the sill must be designed to prevent the entry of rain and wind under the bottom edge of the door. Doors opening out close onto a rebate in the sill, whereas doors opening in have a rebated bottom rail, and close over a water bar set into the sill (see Fig. 7.1.10).

Timber door frames can be fixed to a wall by the following methods:

- Built into the brick or block wall as the work proceeds by using L-shaped ties or cramps. The ties are made from galvanised mild steel with one end turned up 50 mm, with two holes for wood screws, the other end being 100–225 mm long and fish-tailed for building into brick or block bed joints. The ties are fixed to the back of the frame for building in at 450 mm centres.
- Fixed into a brick opening at a late stage in the contract to prevent damage to the frame during the construction period. This is a more expensive method and is usually employed only when high-class joinery using good-quality timber is involved. The frames are fixed to timber plugs inserted into the reveals with wood screws, whose heads are sunk below the upper surface of the frame; this is made good by inserting over the screw heads plugs or pellets of matching timber.

Timber door frames of softwood are usually finished with several applications of paint, whereas frames of hardwood are either polished or oiled. Frames with a factory coating of plastic are also available.

METAL DOOR FRAMES

These are made from mild steel pressed into one of three standard profiles, and are suitable for both internal and external positions. The hinges and striking plates are welded on during manufacture, and the whole frame receives a rust-proof treatment before delivery. The frames are fixed in a similar manner to timber frames using a tie or tee bracket, which fits into the back of the frame profile and is built into the bed joints of the wall (see Fig. 7.1.10). The advantage of this type of frame is that they will not shrink or warp, but they are more expensive than their timber counterparts.

DOOR LININGS

These are made from timber board 25 or 32 mm thick and as wide as the wall plus any wall finishes. They are usually specified only for internal doors. Door linings are not built in but are fixed into an opening by nailing or screwing directly into block walls, or into plugs in the case of brick walls. Timber packing pieces or folding wedges are used to straighten and plumb up the sides or jambs of the lining (see Fig. 7.1.9).

7.2

GLASS AND GLAZING

■■■ GLASS

Glass is made mainly from soda, lime, silica and other minor ingredients such as magnesia and alumina, to produce a material suitable for general window glazing. The materials are heated in a furnace to a temperature range of 1490–1550 °C, where they fuse together in a molten state; they are then formed into sheets by a process of drawing, floating or rolling. BS 952-1: *Glass for glazing* classifies glass for use in buildings by composition, dimensions, mass and available sizes.

DRAWN CLEAR SHEET GLASS

There are two principal methods of producing drawn clear sheet glass. The first is by vertical drawing from a pool of molten glass that, when 1 m or so above the pool level, is rigid enough to be engaged by a series of asbestos-faced rollers that continue to draw the ribbon of glass up a tower some 10 m high, after which the ribbon is cut into sheets and washed in a dilute acid to remove surface deposits. In the second method the glass is initially drawn in the vertical plane but is turned over a roller so that it is drawn in the horizontal direction for some 60 m and passes into an annealing furnace, at the cold end of which it is cut into sheets.

Clear sheet glass is a transparent glass with 85% light transmission, with a fire-finished surface, but because the two surfaces are never perfectly flat nor parallel there is always some distortion of vision and reflection.

The only thicknesses produced in the UK are 3 and 4 mm; 5 and 6 mm are available as an import.

FLOAT GLASS

This is gradually superseding the sheet glass process, and provides a glass with undistorted vision. It is formed by floating a continuous ribbon of molten glass over a bath of liquid metal at a controlled rate and temperature. A general glazing quality and a selected quality are produced in thicknesses ranging from 3 to 25 mm.

ROLLED AND ROUGH CAST GLASS

This is a term applied to a flat glass produced by a rolling process. Generally the glass produced in this manner is translucent, and transmits light with varying degrees of diffusion so that vision is not clear. A wired transparent glass with 80% light transmission is, however, produced generally in one thickness of 6 mm. The glass is made translucent by rolling onto one face a texture or pattern that will give 70–85% light transmission. Rough cast glass has an irregular texture to one side. Wired rough cast glass comes in two forms: Georgian wired, which has a 12 mm square mesh electrically welded wire reinforcement; and hexagonally wired, which is reinforced with hexagonal wire of approximately 20 mm mesh. Rough cast glass is produced in 5, 6 and 10 mm thicknesses and is made for safety and fire-resistant glazing purposes.

SPECIAL GLASS PRODUCTS

Numerous special glasses are available. Some of the most significant include:

- toughened glass;
- laminated glass;
- fire-resisting glass.

Toughened glass

Processed glass is subjected to heat and then cooled by jets of cold air. The effect is to create compressive stresses at the surface with balancing tensile stresses in the centre. The result is a glass of a strength 4–5 times greater than that of annealed glass. It can, however, still fracture under extreme bending loads or severe impact from a sharp implement. When broken it shatters into small blunt-edged fragments, which reduce the risk of personal injury. Because of its great strength and potential for large glazed areas it provides considerable scope for freedom of design.

Laminated glass

As the name suggests, laminated glass is built up in layers. It is composed of an outer and inner layer of annealed float glass with a heat and pressure-sealed intermediate bonding layer of polyvinylbutyral (PVB). Performance can be varied by changing the number and thickness of glass layers to provide a wide range of applications and purposes. These include rooflights, internal doors and partitions, noise and solar controls, as well as its suitability for security and safety situations due to its inherent resistance to bullets and explosives.

Table 7.2.1   Fire test performance of Pilkington Pyrodur and Pyrostop glass

Glass type	Thickness (mm)	Integrity (min.)	Insulation (min.)
Pyrodur	10	30	N/A
	13	60	N/A
Pyrostop	15	60	30
	21	60	60
	44	90	90
	50	120	120

Fire-resisting glass

Fire resistance can be measured in terms of **integrity** and **insulation**: see also Chapter 7.1. BS 476-20 defines integrity as 'the ability of a specimen of a separating element to contain a fire to specified criteria of collapse, freedom from holes, cracks and fissures and sustained flaming on the unexposed face'. Insulation is also defined in the same BS as 'the ability of a specimen of a separating element to restrict the temperature rise of the unexposed face to below specified levels'. 'Specified levels' means an average of no more than 140 °C and, in any specific position, 180 °C.

Wired glass, composed of an electrically welded mesh embedded centrally in rough glass during the rolling process, is well established as an effective means of resisting fire. It is frequently used in doors for security reasons and its ability to remain integral in fire for up to 2 hours. Although the glass fractures in heat, the close proximity of mesh retains the unit in one piece. Clear fire-resisting glass is produced by Pilkington UK Ltd under the trade names of Pyrodur and Pyrostop. Pyrodur is suitable for use internally or externally in doors and screens. Standard thicknesses are 10 and 13 mm, composed of three or four glass layers respectively. Interlayers are of intumescent material with an ultraviolet bonding laminate of polyvinylbutyral to ensure impact resistance performance. It is primarily intended to satisfy the Building Regulations' requirements for integrity, as shown in Table 7.2.1, although it has insulation properties for up to 22 minutes. Pyrostop is produced in two grades corresponding to internal or external application. For internal use it is made up of four glass layers with three intumescent interlayers. External specification has an additional glass layer and an ultraviolet filter interlayer positioned to the outside to protect the intumescent material against degradation. It is also produced in double-glazed format with an 8 mm air gap achieved with steel spacer bars. Overall thicknesses are 15, 21, 44 and 50 mm, to attain integrity and insulation for up to 2 hours.

▨▩▦ GLAZING

The securing of glass in prepared openings such as doors, windows and partitions is termed **glazing**. It is logical that, as the area of glass pane increases, so must its thickness: similarly, position, wind load and building usage must be taken into account.

Figure 7.2.1   Zones of safe glazing – shown shaded.

The Building Regulations effect suitable standards for the safe use and application of glass through Approved Document N. Position is very important, and critical locations are shown in Fig. 7.2.1. These are defined within 800 mm of the finished floor level and 1500 mm if in a door or adjacent side panel. Glass in critical locations must be classified as safe, which means it satisfies one of the following:

■ It conforms to the 'safe break' characteristics defined in BS 6206: *Specification for impact performance requirements for flat safety glass and safety plastics for use in buildings*.

■ Annealed glass within the limitations of Table 7.2.2. Small panes isolated or in groups separated by glazing bars: maximum pane width is 250 mm, maximum pane area is 0.5 m^2, nominal thickness minimum 6 mm.

■ A robust glass substitute material such as polycarbonate. It is permanently protected by a screen, as shown in Fig. 7.2.2.

The effect of wind loading on glazed area and glass thickness can be determined by reference to BS 6262: *Code of practice for glazing for buildings*. Tables and graphs

Table 7.2.2 Maximum dimensions of annealed glass panels

Annealed glass thickness (mm)	Maximum width (m)	Maximum height (m)
8	1.10	1.10
10	2.25	2.25
12	4.50	3.00
15	Any	Any

Figure 7.2.2 Screen protection to glazing.

permutate data for topography, ground roughness, life and glass factors to provide the recommended minimum glass thickness.

GLAZING WITHOUT BEADS

This is a suitable method for general domestic window and door panes. The glass is bedded in a compound, secured with sprigs, pegs or clips, and fronted with a weathered surface putty. Putty is a glazing compound that will require a protective coating of paint as soon as practicable after glazing. Two kinds of putty are in general use:

- **Linseed oil putty**   For use with primed wood members; made from linseed oil and whiting, usually to the recommendations of BS 544.
- **Metal casement putty**   For use with metal or non-absorbent wood members; made from refined vegetable drying oils and finely ground chalk.

[*Note*: A general-purpose putty is available that will satisfy application for both wood and metal glazing.]

12–20

Sprig

Back
putty

Glass

Front putty

Sprig

Spring clip

Back
putty

Wood frame

Metal frame

Glazing without beads

Glass

Internal bead
fixed with
cups and screws

External
bead

Bedding
material

Wood frame

Metal
frame

Mastic or sealant
recommended by manufacturer

Glazing with beads

Figure 7.2.3   Glazing details.

The glass pane should be cut to allow a minimum clearance of 2 mm all round for both wood and metal frames. Sufficient putty is applied to the rebate to give at least 2 mm of back putty when the glass is pressed into the rebate, any surplus putty being stripped off level or at an angle above the rebate. The glass should be secured with sprigs or clips at not more than 440 mm centres and finished off on the front edge with a weathered putty fillet so that the top edge of the fillet is at or just below the sightline (see Fig. 7.2.3).

Compounds and sealants

Putty has the disadvantage of setting after a period of time, which may be unsuitable for large glazed areas subject to thermal movement. Therefore several non-setting compounds and sealants are available. Rubberised compounds are usually in two parts for mixing on site and applying by hand or with an extruder gun. One-part sealants of polysulphide, silicone and urethane cure by chemical reaction with exposure to the atmosphere. They form a firm, resilient seal with a degree of flexibility. One-part sealants of butyl or acrylic do not cure, but remain soft and pliable. These are preferred for bedding glass and beads only, as they can deteriorate if exposed. Two-part polysulphide- or polyurethane-based sealants are mixed for application to cure into rubbery material within 14 days. These have excellent adhesion.

GLAZING WITH BEADS

For domestic work, glazing with beads is generally applied to good-class joinery. The beads should be secured with either panel pins or screws; for hardwoods it is usual to use cups and screws. The glass is bedded in a compound or a suitable glazing felt, mainly to prevent damage by vibration to the glass. Beads are usually mitred at the corners to give continuity of any moulding. Beads for metal windows are usually supplied with the surround or frame, and fixing of glass should follow the manufacturer's instructions (see Fig. 7.2.3).

DOUBLE GLAZING

Double glazing is now standard practice in window installation to satisfy UK Building Regulation requirements for energy conservation in external walls. Factory-made units contain two parallel glass panes sealed with an air gap between the glass. This not only reduces heat loss considerably but will also improve sound insulation and restrict surface condensation. Typical manufactured units comprise two panes with a dry air gap of between 3 and 20 mm. The greater the air space, the better the thermal insulation, although care must be observed when applied at extremes of atmospheric conditions as explosion or implosion may occur with wider-gapped units. Generally, the insulative effect is to reduce the thermal transmittance coefficient (U value) by about half, from approximately 5.6 $W/m^2 K$ for single glazing to approximately 2.8 $W/m^2 K$, depending on air gap and exposure. Some applications are shown in Fig. 7.2.4.

Figure 7.2.4 Double glazing.

LOW-EMISSIVITY GLASS

The use of low-emissivity or 'Low E' glass in double-glazed units can considerably enhance window insulation. Units are manufactured with a standard pane of float glass to the outside and a microscopic-metal-coated outer surface to the inner pane of glass, as shown in Fig. 7.2.5.

The effect is to permit short-wave radiation such as sunlight to pass through the glazed unit, while reflecting long-wave radiation such as internal heat from radiators and fires back into the room. Using argon gas, which has lower thermal conductivity than air, between the panes will also reduce heat losses. Table 7.2.3 compares the insulation properties of glazed systems.

Figure 7.2.5 'Low E' double glazing.

Table 7.2.3 Typical U values based on 6 mm thick glass and a 12 mm void in double glazing.

Glazing system	Void	U value (W/m^2 K)
Single glazing	–	5.6
Double glazing:		
Float glass × 2	air	2.8
Float glass × 2	argon	2.7
Float glass + 'Low E'	air	1.9
Float glass + 'Low E'	argon	1.6

▨▨■ GLASS BLOCK WALLING

Glass blocks are produced in a variety of sizes, colour tones and surface finishes. They can be used for non-loadbearing partitioning, particularly in offices where a degree of separation is required while still retaining access for light. They are also acceptable as a light source through external walling, provided they are within a structural support frame.

Standard units are shown in Fig. 7.2.6. These are manufactured in two halves, rather like square ash trays, of 10 mm thick glass and then heat-fused together to make a hollow block. The periphery is sprayed with a white adhesive textured finish to bond with mortar. Blocks can be staggered or stretcher-bonded like traditional brickwork. For aesthetic reasons they are usually laid with continuous vertical and horizontal joints, i.e. stack bonded with steel wire reinforced bed joints.

EXTERNAL APPLICATION

Blocks are laid and tied to a structural support frame of maximum area 9 m^2 and 3 m in any direction, as shown in Fig. 7.2.7. The lowest course is laid on a bituminous bed and mortar. The mortar to this and subsequent courses comprises

80 or 100 mm thickness

Textured finish for mortar key

Clear, ribbed or frosted surface to blocks of nominal size: 150 mm × 150 mm, 200 mm × 200 mm, 300 mm × 300 mm, 100 mm × 200 mm or 150 mm × 200 mm

Heat-fused joint

Figure 7.2.6   Standard glass block.

Lintel

Polyethylene foam expansion strip to sides and head

Perforated metal straps secured to head and jambs every second joint

Max. 3000 mm

Wire reinforcement in bed joints

Silicon pointing

Glass block panel

Figure 7.2.7   Typical glass block framing and laying.

1 part white Portland cement, 0.5 part lime and 4 parts white quartzite or silver sand, measured by volume. A waterproofing agent is added to the mix. Pointing can be with a weather-resistant silicon sealant. To accommodate expansion and contraction, a polyethylene foam strip is located around the periphery of blocks at the sides and head of the support frame. 9 gauge (3.7 mm) steel reinforcement in ladder pattern is placed in every horizontal course with 300 mm blocks, every other course with 200 mm blocks and every third course with 150 mm blocks (sizes nominal).

7.3

WINDOWS

The primary function of a window is to provide a means for admission of natural daylight to the interior of a building. A window can also serve as a means of providing the necessary ventilation of dwellings, as required under Building Regulation F1, by including opening lights in the window design.

Windows, like doors, can be made from a variety of materials, or a combination of these materials, such as timber, metal and plastic. They can also be designed to operate in various ways by arranging the sashes to slide, pivot or swing, or hang as a casement to one of the frame members.

■ ■ ■ BUILDING REGULATIONS

Approved Document F details the requirements for ventilating habitable rooms, kitchens, utility rooms, bathrooms and sanitary accommodation in domestic buildings. A habitable room is defined as a room used for dwelling purposes but not a kitchen. A habitable room must have ventilation openings unless it is adequately ventilated by mechanical means.

Passive stack ventilation (PSV) is an acceptable alternative in some rooms (see Section 1, Approved Document F). This is a simple system of ducts used to convey air by natural movement to external terminals. Non-domestic buildings have different requirements to suit various purposes, with criteria applied to occupied rooms instead of habitable rooms and greater emphasis on mechanical ventilation and floor areas (see Section 2, Approved Document F).

A ventilation opening includes any permanent or closable means of ventilation that opens directly to the external air. Included in this category are openable parts of windows, louvres, air bricks, window trickle ventilators and doors that open directly to the external air. The three general objectives of providing a means of ventilation are:

■ to extract moisture from rooms where it is produced in significant quantities, such as kitchens and bathrooms;

Figure 7.3.1   Traditional timber casement window.

- to provide for occasional rapid ventilation where moisture presence is likely to produce condensation;
- to achieve a background ventilation that is adequate without affecting the comfort of the room.

Guidance in the Approved Document allows for a variety of means to achieve these objectives. These range from simple trickle-type ventilators (see Fig. 7.3.3) to opening sashes, mechanical extract fans and fully ducted air ventilation systems. The minimum height for ventilators is 1.700 m from finished floor level.

Unless a mechanical system of air movement is used throughout a dwelling, background ventilation through trickle vents of minimum equivalent area of 6000 mm^2 is required in all habitable rooms. Additionally, these rooms should have rapid or purge ventilation by opening sash or an extract fan with a capability of at least 4 room air changes per hour. Intermittent use of mechanical fan extract ventilation is also required for the following specific situations:

- kitchen – minimum 60 litres per second; 30 l/s if adjacent to hob;
- utility room – 30 l/s;
- bathroom – 15 l/s;
- sanitary accommodation – 6 l/s.

If any of the above situations is without a window with an opening sash, a combined light/extract fan switch should be fitted with an over-run facility for the fan. A gap of at least 10 mm should be provided between the door and floor finish.

▨▨■ TRADITIONAL CASEMENT WINDOWS

Figure 7.3.1 shows a typical arrangement and details of this type of window. A wide range of designs can be produced by using various combinations of the members, the only limiting factor being the size of glass pane relevant to its thickness.

The general arrangement of the framing is important; heads and sills always extend across the full width of the frame and in many cases have projecting horns for building into the wall. The jambs and mullions span between the head and sill; these are joined to them by a wedged or pinned mortise and tenon joint. This arrangement gives maximum strength, as the vertical members will act as struts; it will also give a simple assembly process.

The traditional casement window frame has deep rebates to accommodate the full thickness of the **sash**, which is the term used for the framing of the opening ventilator. If fixed glazing or lights are required it is necessary to have a sash frame surround to the glass, because the depth of rebate in the window frame is too great for direct glazing to the frame.

STANDARD WOOD CASEMENT WINDOWS

BS 644: *Timber windows. Factory assembled windows of various types. Specification* provides details of the quality, construction and design of a wide range of wood casement windows. The frames, sashes and ventlights are made from standard sections of softwood timbers arranged to give a variety in design and size. The

External elevation (309 CVC window)

Mullion section

Jamb section

Vertical section

Figure 7.3.2   Typical modified BS casement window (see Figure 7.3.3 for double-glazed vertical section).

sashes and ventlights are designed so that their edges rebate over the external face of the frame to form a double barrier to the entry of wind and rain. The general construction is similar to that described for traditional casement windows, and the fixing of the frame into walls follows that described for door frames.

Most joinery manufacturers produce a range of modified standard casement windows following the basic principles set out in BS 644 but with improved head, sill and sash sections. The range produced is based on brick modules to avoid unnecessary cutting and disturbance to the masonry appearance. Window types are identified by a notation of figures and letters, for example

212 CV

where   2 = width divided into two units
      12 = 1200 mm height
      C = casement
      V = ventlight

For typical details see Figs 7.3.1–7.3.3.

Figure 7.3.3   Double-glazed casement window.

External elevation (18 FCT 11 RH window)

Mullion section

Vertical section

Jamb section

Figure 7.3.4 Typical steel window details.

STEEL CASEMENT WINDOWS

These windows are produced to conform to the recommendations of BS 6510, which gives details of construction, sections, sizes, composites and hardware. The standard range covers fixed lights, hung casements, pivot casements and doors. They are produced in dimensions to suit both imperial and metric applications, the latter conforming to the basic space first preference of 300 mm, giving the following range (in mm):

500; 600; 800; 900; 1200; 1500; 1800.

Frame heights are based upon basic spaces for the preferred head and sill heights for public sector housing, giving the following sizes (in mm):

200; 500; 700; 900; 1100; 1300; 1500.

Steel windows, like wood windows, are identified by a notation of numbers and letters:

- Prefix number: × 100 = basic space length.
- Code letters: F = fixed light.
  C = side-hung casement opening out.
  V = top-hung casement opening out and extending full width of frame.
  T = top-hung casement opening out and extending less than full width of frame.
  B = bottom casement opening inwards.
  S = fixed sublight.
- Suffix number: × 100 = basic space height.
- Suffix code: RH = right-hand casement as viewed from outside.
  LH = left-hand casement as viewed from outside.

The basic range of steel windows can be coupled together to form composite frames by using transom and mullion coupling sections without increasing the basic space module of 100 mm. The actual size of a steel frame can be obtained by deducting the margin allowance of 6 mm from the basic space size.

All the frames are made from basic rolled steel sections, which are mitred and welded at the corners to form right angles; the internal bars are tenoned and riveted to the outer frame and to each other. The completed frame receives a hot-dip galvanised protective finish after manufacture and before delivery.

Steel windows can be fixed into an opening by a number of methods, such as direct fixing to the structure or by using a wood surround that is built into the reveals and secured with fixing ties or cramps. The wood surround will add 100 or 50 mm to the basic space size in each direction using either a nominal 75 mm × 75 mm or 50 mm × 75 mm timber section. Typical details of steel windows, couplings and fixings are shown in Figs 7.3.4 and 7.3.5.

The main advantage of steel windows is the larger glass area obtained for any basic space size, because of the smaller frame sections used. The main disadvantage is the condensation that can form on the frames because of the high thermal conductivity of the metal members.

Figure 7.3.5 Steel window couplings and fittings.

ALUMINIUM HOLLOW PROFILE CASEMENT WINDOWS

Extruded aluminium profiles can be designed for use in window and door framing. The main advantages over other materials in these applications are high strength and durability relative to light weight, and very little maintenance except for occasional cleaning. The aluminium is protected from surface oxidisation and corrosive atmospheres with a coloured polyester powder coating. Standard colours are white or dark brown, but other options are available to order.

Metals are very poor thermal insulators, but the overall thermal performance of aluminium profiled casements can be considerably improved by specifying a closed cell foam infill to the hollow sections. Cold or thermal bridging and associated condensation is prevented by incorporating a thermal barrier or break between internal and external components. The thermal break is produced from a high strength two–part polyurethane resin.

Typical section details are shown in Fig. 7.3.6.

Figure 7.3.6 Aluminium casement window.

Figure 7.3.7   Bay window types and corner posts.

UPVC HOLLOW PROFILE CASEMENT WINDOWS

uPVC (or PVC-U) window components are produced in similar sectional profiles to that shown for hollow section aluminium windows. Plastic is an excellent thermal insulating material, so there is no need to incorporate a thermal break. uPVC has lower strength characteristics than aluminium: therefore manufacturers include box sections of aluminium or galvanised steel within the profiles of larger framing members.

uPVC windows are very popular in both new build and the refurbishment housing market. Manufacturers' designs can emulate most traditional features associated with timber casements, with the added advantage of excellent thermal insulation, improved security and a maintenance-free finish. Pigmenting in the plastic provides for a variety of colour options, generally white, light or dark brown.

■■■ BAY WINDOWS

Any window which projects in front of the main wall line is considered to be a bay window; various names are, however, given to various plan layouts (see Fig. 7.3.7). Bay windows can be constructed of timber, and/or metal and designed with casement or sliding sashes; the main difference in detail is the corner post, which can be made from the solid, jointed or masked in the case of timber and tubular for metal windows (see Fig. 7.3.7).

The bay window can be applied to one floor only or continued over several storeys. Any roof treatment can be used to cover in the projection and weather seal it to the main wall (see Fig. 7.3.8). No minimum headroom heights for bay windows or habitable rooms are given in the Building Regulations but 2.000 in bay windows and 2.300 in rooms would be considered reasonable. A bay window which occurs only on upper storeys is generally called an oriel window.

■■■ DOUBLE-HUNG SASH WINDOWS

These windows are sometimes called **vertical sliding sash windows** and consist of two sashes sliding vertically over one another. They are costly to construct, but are considered to be more stable than side-hung sashes and have a better control over the size of ventilation opening, thus reducing the possibility of draughts.

In timber, two methods of suspension are possible:

■ weight-balanced type;
■ spring-balanced type.

The former is the older method, in which the counterbalance weights suspended by cords are housed in a boxed framed jamb or mullion. It has been generally superseded by the metal spring balance, which uses a solid frame and needs less maintenance (see Figs 7.3.9 and 7.3.10).

Double-hung sashes in metal are supported and controlled by spring balances or by friction devices, but the basic principles remain the same.

Figure 7.3.8   Typical existing bay window roofs.

Figure 7.3.9 Traditional double-hung weight-balanced sliding sash windows.

40 mm min. horn projection

Dowelled mortise and tenon joint

114 × 33 solid head

19 × 14 removable bead

48 × 21 head outside lining

21 × 8 parting bead

48 × 41 upper sash framing

21 × 28 parting bead

114 × 33 solid stile

19 × 14 removable bead

Spring balance

48 × 21 outside lining

38 × 24 splayed end rebated meeting rails

Fixing hole

Tube housing coil spring

Rotating nylon bush

Variable twisted rod

Bracket

48 × 14 lower sash framing

33 × 19 draught stop

135 × 60 flush sill

57 × 41 bottom rail

'Unique' spiral balance

Note: If 114 × 60 solid stiles are used, balances can be housed in grooves within the stile thickness

Figure 7.3.10   Double-hung spring-balanced sash windows.

▨ ▨ ▨ PIVOT WINDOWS

The basic construction of the frame and sash is similar to that of a standard casement frame and sash. The sash can be arranged to pivot horizontally or vertically on friction pivots housed in the jambs or in the sill and head. These windows give good adjustment for ventilation purposes, and in the main both faces of the glazing can be cleaned from the inside of the building.

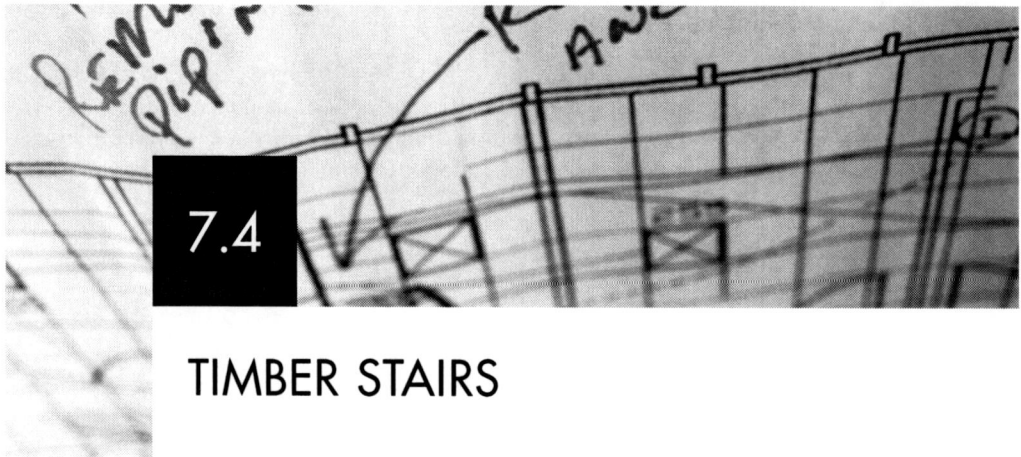

7.4

TIMBER STAIRS

A stair is a means of providing access from one floor level to another. Modern stairs with their handrails are designed with the main emphasis on simplicity, trying to avoid the elaborate and costly features used in the past.

The total rise of a stair – that is, the distance from floor finish to floor finish in any one storey height – is fixed by the storey heights and floor finishes being used in the building design: therefore the stair designer has only the total going or total horizontal distance with which to vary the stair layout. It is good practice to keep door openings at least 450 mm away from the head or the foot of a stairway, and to allow at least the stair width as circulation space at the head or foot of the stairway.

Stairs can be designed as one straight flight between floor levels, which is the simplest and cheapest layout; alternatively they can be designed to turn corners by the introduction of quarter space (90°) or half space (180°) intermediate landings. Stairs that change direction of travel use tapered steps or are based on geometrical curves in plan. Irrespective of the plan layout, the principles of stair construction remain constant, and are best illustrated by studying the construction of simple straight-flight stairs in this volume.

Terminology

- **Stairwell**   The space in which the stairs and landings are housed.
- **Stairs**   The actual means of ascent or descent from one level to another.
- **Tread**   The upper surface of a step on which the foot is placed.
- **Nosing**   The exposed edge of a tread, usually projecting with a square, rounded or splayed edge.
- **Riser**   The vertical member between two consecutive treads.
- **Step**   Riser plus tread.
- **Going**   The horizontal distance between two consecutive risers or, as defined in Approved Document K, the horizontal dimensions from front to back of a tread less any overlap with the next tread above.

- **Rise**   The vertical height between two consecutive treads.
- **Flight**   A series of steps without a landing.
- **Newel**   Post forming the junction of flights of stairs with landings or carrying the lower end of strings.
- **Strings**   The members receiving the ends of steps, which are generally housed to the string and secured by wedges, called wall or outer strings according to their position.
- **Handrail**   Protecting member usually parallel to the string and spanning between newels. This could be attached to a wall above and parallel to a wall string.
- **Baluster**   The vertical infill member between a string and handrail.
- **Pitch line**   A line connecting the nosings of all treads in any one flight.

Building Regulations Part K

Approved Document K defines three categories of stairs:

1. **Private**: intended for use solely in connection with one dwelling.
2. **Institutional** and assembly: serves one place in which a substantial number of people will gather.
3. **Other**: serves in buildings other than dwellings, institutional and assembly.

The practical limitations applicable to each of these three categories are shown in Table 7.4.1.

Table 7.4.1   Stairs (Approved Document K)

Category	Rise (mm)		Going (mm)
Private	155–220 or 165–200 with		245–260 or 223–300
Institutional and assembly*	135–180	with	280–340
Other*	150–190	with	250–320

* Subject to requirements for access for disabled people. See Building Regulations, Approved Document M, Section 3.51 (max. rise 170 mm, min. going 250 mm).

▨▨■ CONSTRUCTION AND DESIGN

It is essential to keep the dimensions of the treads and risers constant throughout any flight of steps to reduce the risk of accidents by changing the rhythm of movement up or down the stairway. The height of the individual step rise is calculated by dividing the total rise by the chosen number of risers. The individual step going is chosen to suit the floor area available so that it, together with the rise, meets the requirements of the Building Regulations (see Fig. 7.4.1). It is important to note that in any one flight there will be one more riser than treads, as the last tread is in fact the landing.

Stairs are constructed by joining the steps into the spanning members or strings by using housing joints, glueing and wedging the steps into position to form a complete and rigid unit. Small angle blocks can be glued at the junction of tread

Private stairways

Continuous handrail
if total rise is over
600 mm and to both
sides if stairs over
1.000 wide

900 min.
900 min.
1.000 max.
900 min.
2.000 min.

Going
220 min.

No riser
16 min.

Pitch
line

Pitch
line

Rise
220 max.

42°
max.

Sum of going + twice rise = 550 min. to 700 max.
in any flight all risers of equal height and all
goings of equal width

Continuous handrail
above 2 bottom steps
and to both sides if
stairs over
1.100 wide

1.100 min.
1.100 min.
900 min.
1.000 max.
2.000 min.

Going
280* (250)
min.

No riser
16 min.

Pitch
line

Pitch
line

Rise
180 (190) max.

* 250 mm if the
floor area < 100 m²

Sum of going + twice rise = 550 min. to 700 max.
in any flight all risers of equal height and all
goings of equal width

Institutional and assembly and (other) stairways

Figure 7.4.1   Timber stairs and Approved Document K.

and riser in a step to reduce the risk of slight movement giving rise to the annoyance of creaking. The flight can be given extra rigidity by using triangular brackets placed under the steps on the centreline of the flight. A central beam or carriage piece with rough brackets as a support is used only on wide stairs over 1200 mm, especially where they are intended for use as a common stairway (see Fig. 7.4.2).

Stairs can be designed to be fixed to a wall with one outer string, fixed between walls, or free standing; the majority have one wall string and one outer string. The wall string is fixed directly to the wall along its entire length, or is fixed to timber battens plugged to the wall, the top of the string being cut and hooked over the trimming member of the stairwell. The outer string is supported at both ends by a newel post: in the case of the bottom newel this rests on the floor; in the case of the upper newel, it is notched over and fixed to the stairwell trimming member. If the upper newel is extended to the ground floor to give extra support, it is called a **storey newel post**. The newel posts also serve as the termination point for handrails that span between them and are then infilled with balusters, balustrade or a solid panel to complete the protection to the sides of the stairway (see Fig. 7.4.3).

If the headroom distance is critical it is possible to construct a bulkhead arrangement over the stairs, as shown in Fig. 7.4.4; this may give the increase in headroom required to comply with the Building Regulations. The raised floor in the room over the stairs can be used as a shelf or form the floor of a hanging cupboard.

LAYOUT ARRANGEMENTS

A stair flight incorporating landings or tapered steps will enable the designer to economise with the space required to accommodate the stairs. Landings can be quarter space, giving a 90° turn, or half space, giving a 180° turn: for typical arrangements see Fig. 7.4.5. The construction of the landing is similar to that of a timber upper floor except that, with the reduced span, joist depths can be reduced (see Fig. 7.4.5). The landing can be incorporated in any position up the flight, and if sited near the head may well provide sufficient headroom to enable a cupboard or cloakroom to be constructed below the stairs. A dog-leg or string over string stair is economical in width, as it will occupy a width less than two flights, but this form has the disadvantage of a discontinuous handrail because this abuts to the underside of the return or upper flight.

TAPERED STEPS

Prior to the introduction of the Building Regulations tapered steps or winders were frequently used by designers to use space economically, because three treads occupied the area required for the conventional quarter space landing, which is counted as one tread. These steps had the following disadvantages:

- hazard to the aged and very young, because of the very small tread length at or near the newel post;
- difficult to carpet, requiring many folds or wasteful cutting;
- difficult to negotiate with furniture owing to a rapid rise on the turn;
- expensive to construct.

Figure 7.4.2   Stair construction details.

70 × 45 handrail

Cap

Mortise and housing for handrail

90

100

Outer string

20 × 20 balusters

100 × 100 newel post

25 mm thick string capping

100 × 100 newel post

Dowel hole

Plasterboard soffit

Stairs

Mortise and housing for string

Lead or similar pad

Housing for treads and risers

Bottom riser turned into newel

Typical detail at bottom newel

Newel notched 15 mm over trimmer

20 × 20 balusters

Skirting

T & G flooring

90

Wall string hooked over trimmer

Joist

Rebated nosing

Ceiling finish

Stairs

Trimmer

Packing

Pendant

Trimmer

Stairs

Ceiling finish

Outer string

Typical details at landing

Figure 7.4.3 Stair support and fixing details.

Typical stairwell finishes

Baluster or infill panel
Rebated nosing to match treads
Apron lining
Floor finish
Ceiling finish
Trimming joist
Cover moulding

Baluster or infill panel
Rebated capping
Apron lining
Floor finish
Ceiling finish
Trimming joist

Typical bulkhead over stairs

Timber studding or lightweight blockwork
Wall finish
Skirting
T & G flooring
100 × 50 joists at 400 c/c
Trimmer
Ceiling finish
Timber studding or lightweight blockwork
Line of minimum headroom
Apron lining to match stairwell finish
Upper floor construction

Figure 7.4.4 Stairwell finishes and bulkhead details.

Straight flight — Bullnose step

Quarter turn — 'D' step

Quarter turn — Tapered steps, Splay step

Dog-leg or string-over-string — Half-space landing, Newel post

Open well or open newel — Half-space landing

Open well or open newel — Quarter-space landings

Landing details — Rebated nosing, Skirting, Riser, 100 × 50 joists at 400 c/c, 100 × 75 trimmer, Tread, Wall string, Flooring

Figure 7.4.5 Typical stair layouts.

With the introduction of the Building Regulations special attention has been given to the inclusion of tapered steps in Approved Document K, which makes the use of tapered steps less of an economic proposition and more difficult to design (see Fig. 7.4.6).

A popular space-saving variation is the application of continuous tapered steps to create a spiral stair. The example illustrated in Fig. 7.4.7 can be in hard or softwood timber, but contemporary design versions are produced in stainless steel or in any combination of steel, timber and plastic. With spiral stairs every tread has a continuous taper, and the arrangement of these treads to produce a stairway should comply with the safety in use requirements indicated in the Building Regulations. Approved Document K1 of these regulations gives a specific reference for spiral stairs as conforming to BS 5395-2: *Stairs, ladders and walkways. Code of practice for the design of helical and spiral stairs.* Joinery manufacturers can be expected to adhere to these recommendations to ensure that there is a market for their product. However, before specifying a particular type, the details should be checked with the local authority building control department. Any structural alteration to the floor and landing will also require approval.

Spiral stair units are generally produced as a kit for site assembly of simple fit components about a central column or continuous newel post. The column is centralised over a lower-floor secured pattress, from which are placed alternate spacers and treads. Balusters fit to the periphery of the treads and provide support to the helical spire handrail. On plan, overall diameters from outside of tread to outside of tread are 1200 and 1400 mm at 14 treads per 360° turn, and 1600 and 2200 mm at 16 treads per 360° turn. Ascent may be clockwise or anti-clockwise.

OPEN-TREAD STAIRS

These are a contemporary form of stairs used in homes, shops and offices based on the simple form of access stair, which has been used for many years in industrial premises. The concept is simplicity with the elimination of elaborate nosings, cappings and risers. The open tread or riserless stair must comply fully with Part K of the Building Regulations and in particular Approved Document K, which recommends a minimum tread overlap of 16 mm. Where they are likely to be used by children under 5 years, i.e. dwellings, pre-school nurseries, etc., the opening between treads must contain a barrier sufficient to prevent a 100 mm sphere passing through.

Four basic types of open-tread stairs can be produced, as described below.

Closed string

This will terminate at the floor and landing levels and be fixed as for traditional stairs. The treads are tightly housed into the strings, which are tied together with long steel tie bars under the first, last and every fourth tread. The nuts and washers can be housed into the strings and covered with timber inserts (see Fig. 7.4.8).

Max. going + twice rise
= 700

Headroom
clearance
measured
from notional
width line

230

Note: Going
and rise
measured
on centreline
for stairs of
less than
1.000 wide

50

50

Pitch
lines

50

Min. going +
twice rise
= 550

100 × 100
newel

270

270

Width
1.000 or more

℄ Handrail

Wall string

Outer string

Tapered
steps

Newel post

Easing to take
bottom edge of riser

Note: Other tapered
step arrangements
are possible within
the requirements
of the Building
Regulations

Wall
string

Figure 7.4.6 Tapered steps for private stairways.

Upper newel post

Helical handrail

Landing

Central column

Balusters

Lower newel post

Tapered treads

Annular spacer

Floor pattress

Figure 7.4.7 Timber spiral stair.

Balustrading to landing

Top newel post notched over trimmer

Plank balustrade fixed to face of newel

Skirting to landing

Wall string hooked over trimmer

Treads housed into strings

Apron lining

Stairwell trimmer

Outer string

Bottom newel post

Typical arrangement

Exposed bolt head

Tread

String

12 mm deep housing

Tie bar every 4th tread

Wood cover insert often diamond shape for neat appearance

Alternative tie bar arrangements

Figure 7.4.8   Closed string open tread stairs.

Stepped rebated nosing

Wrot-faced trimmer

Handrail to landing

Gluelam timber handrail

Tread

Cut string or carriage

Timber knee board

Metal standards or balusters

Fixing bracket

Typical arrangement

Stepped rebated nosing

Treads cantilevered 225 mm over carriage at ends

Wrot-faced trimmer

Carriage housed into trimmer

Figure 7.4.9   Cut string open tread stairs.

Cut strings or carriages

These are used to support cantilever treads, and can be worked from the solid or of laminated construction. The upper end of the carriage can be housed into the stairwell trimming member, with possible additional support from metal brackets. The foot of the carriage is housed in a purpose-made metal shoe or fixed with metal angle brackets (see Fig. 7.4.9).

Mono-carriage

Sometimes called a spine beam, this employs a single central carriage with double cantilever treads. The carriage, which is by necessity large, is of laminated construction and very often of a tapered section to reduce the apparently bulky appearance. The foot of the carriage is secured with a purpose-made metal shoe in conjunction with timber connectors (see Fig. 7.4.10).

Alternating tread stairs

These make economic use of space and are frequently applied to loft conversions. They have a pitch of about 60° and paddle-shaped treads, which are both controversial issues in the interests of user safety. However, the Building Regulations, Approved Document K, accepts 'familiarity and regular use' as a reasonable safety argument provided the stair accesses only one habitable room. Additional requirements include a non-slip surface, handrails both sides, a minimum going of 220 mm with a maximum rise of 220 mm, and a gap between treads of no more than 100 mm if likely to be used by children under 5 years (see Fig. 7.4.11).

Treads

These must be of adequate thickness, because there are no risers to give extra support; usual thicknesses are 38 and 50 mm. To give a lighter appearance it is possible to taper the underside of the treads at their cantilever ends for a distance of 225–250 mm. This distance is based on the fact that the average person will ascend or descend a stairway at a distance of about 250 mm in from the handrail.

Balustrading

Together with the handrail, balustrading provides both the visual and the practical safety barrier to the side of the stair. Children present special design problems, because they can and will explore any gap big enough to crawl through. BS 5395 for wood stairs recommends that the infill under handrails should have no openings that would permit the passage of a sphere 90 mm in diameter, a slight reduction on the 100 mm stated in Approved Document K1, Section 1.29, to the Building Regulations. Many variations of balustrading are possible, ranging from simple newels with planks to elaborate metalwork of open design (see Figs 7.4.8, 7.4.9 and 7.4.10).

Stepped
rebated nosing

Handrail to landing

Wrot-faced
trimmer

Timber or
metal
handrail

Tread

Laminated timber
mono-carriage
housed into trimmer

Metal balustrade

Typical arrangement

Fixing
shoe

Laminated
timber
carriage

Purpose-
made cast
iron or steel
shoe

Holes for through bolt
using single-toothed
timber connectors
between shoe and
carriage

Holes for
holding-down bolts

Figure 7.4.10   Mono–carriage open tread stairs.

Plan

220 min.

Non-slip
surface

220 max.

Up to 63°-30'

Figure 7.4.11　Alternating tread stairs.

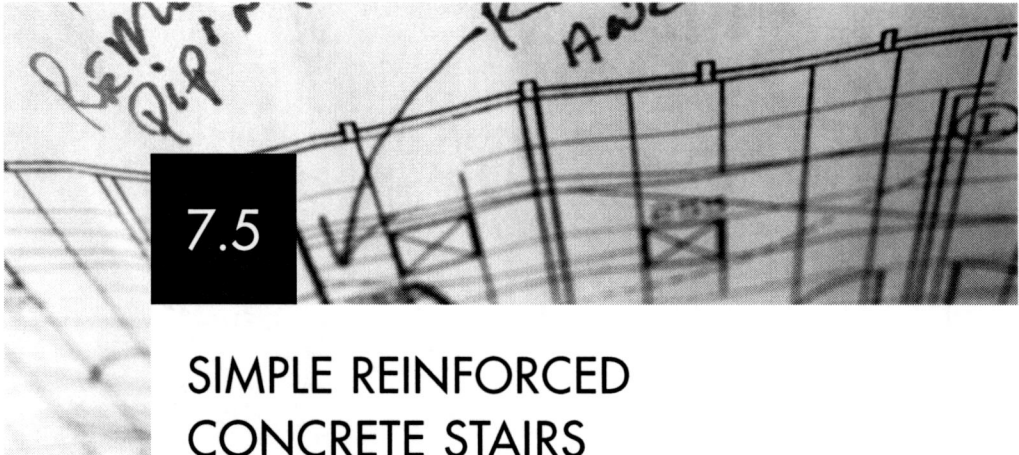

7.5

SIMPLE REINFORCED CONCRETE STAIRS

The functions of any stairway are:

- to provide for the movement of people from one floor level to another;
- to provide a degree of sound insulation where part of a separating element between compartments in a building (Building Regulations, Parts E1 and E3);
- to provide a suitable means of escape in event of fire (Building Regulations, Part B1).

A timber stairway will maintain its strength and integrity for a reasonable period during an outbreak of fire. However, timber is combustible and will contribute to the fire spread, thus increasing the hazards that could be encountered along an escape route. It is for this reason that application of timber stairs is limited by the Building Regulations to certain domestic and some other small building types. Stairs in this category are not normally in a protected shaft, and therefore not part of a specifically planned escape route.

Stairs, other than the exceptions given above, must therefore be constructed of non-combustible materials, but combustible materials are allowed to be used as finishes to the upper surface of the stairway or landing. Reinforced concrete stairs are non-combustible, strong and hard wearing. They may be constructed *in-situ* or precast in sections ready for immediate installation and use when delivered to site. The general use of cranes on building sites has meant that many of the large flight arrangements, which in the past would have been cast *in-situ*, can now be precast under factory-controlled conditions.

Many variations of plan layout and spanning direction are possible, but this study will be confined to the simple straight flight spanning from floor to floor or from floor to intermediate landing. The designer will treat the stairs as being an inclined slab spanning simply between the supports, the steps being treated as triangular loadings evenly distributed over the length. Where intermediate landings are included in the design the basic plan is similar to the open well or newel timber stairs. Difficulty is sometimes experienced with the intersection of the upper and lower flight soffits with the landing. One method of overcoming this problem is to have, in plan, the top and bottom steps out of line so that the soffit intersections form a straight line on the underside of the landing (see Fig. 7.5.1). The calculations to determine the rise, going and number of steps are the same as those used for timber stairs; it should be noted that the number of risers in each flight must not exceed 16. To achieve a greater tread length without increasing the actual horizontal going it is common to use a splayed riser face giving a 25 mm increase to the tread length.

The concrete specification should be very strong, with a mix ratio of 1:1.5:3–10 mm aggregate or 25–30 N/mm^2 compressive strength. Water/cement ratio is no greater than 0.5, otherwise concrete will flow over the formwork riser boards. Concrete cover to reinforcement is at least 15 mm or the bar diameter, whichever is the greater. This cover is sufficient for one-hour fire resistance in most buildings, but will need to be increased for buildings in certain purpose groups: see Table A2 in Appendix A of Approved Document B to the Building Regulations. The thickness of concrete required is dependent on the loading and span, but is not generally less than 100 mm or more than 150 mm measured across the waist, which is the distance from the soffit to the intersection of tread and riser (see Fig. 7.5.1).

Mild steel or high-yield steel bars can be used to reinforce concrete stairs, the bars being lapped to starter bars at the ground floor and taken into the landing or floor support slab. The number, diameter and spacing of the main and distribution reinforcement must always be calculated for each stairway.

Handrails and balustrading must be constructed of a non-combustible material, continuous and to both sides if the width of the stairs exceeds 1.0 m. The overall height of the handrail up the stairs should be between 900 and 1000 mm measured vertically and have a height above the floor of 1.1 m minimum. The capping can be of a combustible material such as plastic provided that it is fixed to or over a non-combustible core. Methods of securing balustrades and typical handrail details are shown in Fig. 7.5.2. Flights of over 1.8 m width in public buildings should have a centrally dividing handrail. Widths of stairs designated for fire escape purposes should be determined by reference to tables and calculations in Section 5 of the Building Regulations, Approved Document B1.

A wide variety of finishes can be applied to the tread surface of the stairs. If the appearance is not of paramount importance, such as in a warehouse, a natural finish could be used, but it would be advisable to trowel into the surface some carborundum dust to provide a hard-wearing non-slip surface. Alternatively, rubber or carborundum insert strips could be fixed or cast into the leading edges of the treads. Finishes such as PVC tiles, rubber tiles and carpet mats are applied and fixed in the same manner as for floors. The soffits can be left as struck from the formwork and decorated, or finished with a coat of spray plaster or a skim coat of finishing plaster.

Figure 7.5.1 Simple reinforced concrete *in-situ* stairs.

Removable plastic handrail cover

Moulded and polished hardwood handrail screwed from underside of metal rail

8 mm dia. set screw

Convex metal handrail

Metal top rail

8 mm dia. set screw

Metal standards or baluster section to design

Typical handrails

Metal rails slotted to take standards fillet-welded on underside

Alternative – cover plate

Cover plate welded to standards

Direct screw or bolt fixings

Matching cement mortar filling

Run lead or cement grout

Ragged end

Pocket formed in concrete

Typical fixing methods

Figure 7.5.2 Handrails and balustrades.

200 × 38 wall board fixed to wall

75 × 50 hanger

50 × 32 struts

21 mm plywood soffit board

150 × 50 joists

75 × 32 ribbon piece

15 mm plywood cut string

21 mm plywood risers

Alternative wall support – reversed cut string

Wall board

Hangers

Riser boards

21 mm plywood soffit to landing

Joists supported by adjustable steel props

2 No. 150 × 75 carriage pieces

Joists

Sole plate

Cut string

Figure 7.5.3 Typical formwork to reinforced concrete *in-situ* stairs.

▩ ▨ ▉ FORMWORK

The basic requirements are the same as for formwork to a framed structure. The stair profile is built off an adequately supported soffit of sheet material by using a cut string. Riser boards are used to form the leading face of the steps; these should have a splayed bottom edge to enable complete trowelling of the tread surfaces and to ensure that air is not trapped under the bottom edge of the riser board, thus causing voids. If the stair abuts a vertical surface two methods can be considered to provide the abutment support for the riser boards: a reverse-cut string or a wall board with hangers (see Fig. 7.5.3). Wide stairs can have a reverse-cut string as a central support to the riser boards to keep the thickness of these within an acceptable coat limit.

7.6

SIMPLE PRECAST CONCRETE STAIRS

Precast concrete stairs can be designed and constructed to satisfy a number of different requirements. They can be a simple inclined slab, a cranked slab, open riser stairs, or constructed from a series of precast steps built into, and if required cantilevered from, a structural wall.

The design considerations for the simple straight flight are the same as those for *in-situ* stairs of comparable span, width and loading conditions. The fixing and support, however, require a different approach. Bearings for the ends of the flights must be provided at the floor or landing levels in the form of a haunch, rebate or bracket, and continuity of reinforcement can be achieved by leaving projecting bars and slots in the floor into which they can be grouted (see Fig. 7.6.1).

Ideally the delivery of precast stairs should be arranged so that they can be lifted, positioned and fixed direct from the delivery vehicle, thus avoiding double handling. Precast components are usually designed for 2 conditions:

- lifting and transporting;
- final fixed condition.

It is essential that the flights are lifted from the correct lifting points, which may be in the form of loops or hooks projecting from or recessed into the concrete member, if damage by introducing unacceptable stresses during lifting is to be avoided.

Balustrade and handrail requirements, and the various methods of fixing, are as described for *in-situ* reinforced concrete stairs. Any tread finish that is acceptable for an *in-situ* stair will also be suitable for the precast alternative.

The use of precast concrete steps to form a stairway is limited to situations such as short flights between changes in floor level and external stairs to basements and areas. They rely on the loadbearing wall for support and, if cantilevered, on the downward load of the wall to provide the necessary reaction. The support wall has to provide this necessary load and strength, and at the same time it has to be bonded or cut around the stooled end(s) of the steps. It is for these reasons that the application of precast concrete steps is restricted.

Precast concrete flight of stairs

Projecting bonding
or continuity bars

Projecting
bonding or
continuity bars

Chases to receive
bonding bars

Rebate for precast
concrete flight

Chases in floor
made good with
matching grout

RC
floor
slab

RC edge
beam

Flight in position

RC landing

RC edge beam

Simple precast concrete stairs

Square or
stooled end
built into
wall

Cantilever step

Support wall

Precast concrete
cantilever steps
built into wall
forming stairs

Simple precast concrete steps

Figure 7.6.1   Precast concrete stairs and steps.

7.7

PARTITIONS

Internal walls that divide the interior of a building into areas of accommodation and circulation are called **partitions**, and these can be classified as loadbearing or non-loadbearing partitions.

▨▨■ LOADBEARING PARTITIONS

These are designed and constructed to receive superimposed loadings and transmit these loads to a foundation (see Fig. 4.1.2). Generally, loadbearing partitions are constructed of bricks or blocks bonded to the external walls (see Figs 3.3.1 and 3.3.2). Openings are formed in the same manner as for external walls; a lintel spans the opening, carrying the load above to the reveals on either side of the opening. Fixings can usually be made direct into block walls, whereas walls of bricks require to be drilled and plugged to receive nails or screws. Apart from receiving direct fixings, block partitions are lighter, cheaper, quicker to build and have better thermal insulation properties than brick walls, but their sound insulation values are slightly lower. For these reasons blockwork is usually specified for loadbearing partitions in domestic work. Loadbearing partitions, because of their method of construction, are considered to be permanently positioned.

▨▨■ NON-LOADBEARING PARTITIONS

These partitions, like loadbearing partitions, must be designed and constructed to carry their own weight and any fittings or fixings that may be attached to them, but they must not, in any circumstances, be used to carry or assist in the transmission of structural loadings. They must be designed to provide a suitable division between internal spaces and be able to resist impact loadings on their faces, also any vibrations set up by doors being closed or slammed.

Bricks or blocks can be used for the construction of non-loadbearing partitions. They may be built directly off a concrete floor with a thickened slab or steel reinforcement to support the wall's self-weight. At ceiling level stability is obtained by bracketing between or to the joists above. If the partition is built off a suspended timber floor a larger joist section or two joists side by side must be used to carry the load of the partition to the floor support walls. Openings are constructed as for loadbearing walls; alternatively a storey-height frame could be used.

Timber stud partitions with suitable facings are lighter than brick or block partitions but are less efficient as sound or thermal insulators. However, a high standard of sound and thermal insulation and fire resistance can be achieved by facing with plasterboard, filling the voids between studs and noggins with glass or mineral wool. They are easy to construct and provide a good fixing background, and because of their lightness are suitable for building off a suspended timber floor. The basic principle is to construct a simple framed grid of timber to which a dry lining such as plywood, plasterboard or hardboard can be attached. The lining material will determine the spacing of the uprights or studs to save undue wastage in cutting the boards to terminate on the centre line of a stud. To achieve a good finish it is advisable to use studs that have equal thicknesses, because the thin lining materials will follow any irregularity of the face of the studwork. Openings are formed by framing a head between two studs and fixing a lining or door frame into the opening in the stud partition; typical details are shown in Fig. 7.7.1. Where plasterboard is the specified facing/lining material, the extent of nailing will depend on the stud spacing, the facing thickness and its width. Table 7.7.1 provides guidance when using galvanised steel taper head nails at 150 mm spacing.

Proprietary partitions of plasterboard bonded on either side of a strong cellular core to form rigid panels are suitable as non-loadbearing partitions. These are fixed to wall and ceiling battens and supported on a timber sole plate. Timber blocks are inserted into the core to provide the fixing medium for door frames or linings and skirtings (see Fig. 7.7.2). This form of partition is available with facings suitable for direct decoration, plastercoat finish or with a plastic face as a self-finish.

Compressed strawboard panels provide another alternative method for non-loadbearing partitions. The storey-height panels are secured to a sole plate and a head plate by skew or tosh nailing through the leading edge. The 3 mm joint between consecutive panels is made with an adhesive supplied by the

Table 7.7.1   Guidance when using galvanised steel taper nails

Plasterboard thickness	Plasterboard width	Stud or batten spacing	Nails
9.5	900	450	2×30 long
	1200	400	2×30 long
12.5	600	600	2×40 long
	900	450	2×40 long
19.0	1200	600	2.6×40 long
	600	600	2.6×40 long

Note: All dimensions in millimetres.

Head plate

Head to opening

Noggins

Studs

Jambs to opening

Folding wedges

Sole plate

Typical arrangement

95 × 70 jamb to opening

12 mm deep housing

90 × 45 head plate fixed to joists

Tenon

Wedge

Mortise

95 × 70 head to opening

Rebated door lining

Architrave

Skirting

Lining

95 × 45 studs at 400 c/c

90 × 45 sole plate bolted to floor

Figure 7.7.1 Typical timber stud partition.

Figure 7.7.2   Typical preformed partitions.

manufacturer. Openings are formed by using storey-height frames fixed with 100 mm screws direct into the edge of the panel. The joints are covered with a strip of hessian scrim, and the whole partition is given a skim coat of board plaster finish (see Fig. 7.7.2).

Partially prefabricated partitions, such as the plasterboard and strawboard described above, can be erected on site without undue mess. Being mainly a dry construction they reduce the drying time required with the traditional brick and block walls. They also have the advantage, like timber stud partitions, of being capable of removal or repositioning without causing serious damage to the structure or without causing serious problems to a contractor.

FINISHES: FLOOR, WALL AND CEILING

▪▪▪ FLOOR FINISHES

The type of floor finish to be applied to a floor will depend upon a number of factors such as type of base, room usage, degree of comfort required, maintenance problems, cost, appearance, safety and individual preference.

Floor finishes can be considered under three main headings:

- *in-situ* floor finishes – those finishes that are mixed on site, laid in a fluid state, allowed to dry, and set to form a hard jointless surface;
- applied floor finishes – those finishes that are supplied in tile or sheet form and are laid onto a suitably prepared base;
- timber floor finishes – boards, sheets and blocks of timber laid on or attached to a suitable structural frame or base.

IN-SITU FLOOR FINISHES

Mastic asphalt – BS 6925 and BS 8204-5

This is a naturally occurring bituminous material obtained from asphalt lakes like those in Trinidad; it can also be derived from crude oil residues. Trinidad lake asphalt is used as a matrix or cement to a suitably graded mineral aggregate to form mastic asphalt as a material suitable for floor finishing. When laid, mastic asphalt is impervious to water and is ideal for situations such as sculleries, wash rooms and balconies. It also forms a very good surface on which to apply thin tile and sheet finishes (for example, PVC), and will at the same time fulfil the function of a damp-proof membrane or waterproof decking.

Mastic asphalt is a thermoplastic material and has to be melted before it can be applied to form a jointless floor finish. Hot mastic asphalt is applied by means of a float at a temperature of between 180 and 210 °C in a single 13 mm coat as a base for applied finishes or in a 16 mm single coat for a self-finish. Any sound and rigid subfloor is suitable, but a layer of ordinary black sheathing felt should be included between the subfloor and mastic asphalt to overcome the problems caused by differential movement. The finish obtained is smooth and hard, but the colour range is limited to dark colours such as red, brown and black. A matt surface can be produced by giving the top surface a dusting of sand or powdered stone.

Pitch mastic

Pitch mastic is a similar material to mastic asphalt but is produced from a mixture of calcareous and/or siliceous aggregates bonded with coal tar pitch. It is laid to a similar thickness and in a similar manner to mastic asphalt with a polished or matt finish. Pitch mastic floors are resistant to water but have a better resistance to oil and fats than mastic asphalt, and are therefore suitable for sculleries, washrooms and kitchens.

Granolithic

This is a mixture of Portland cement and granite chippings, which can be applied to a 'green' concrete subfloor or to a cured concrete subfloor. **Green concrete** is a term used to describe newly laid concrete that is not more than 3 hours old. A typical mix for granolithic is 1 part cement: 1 part sand: 2 parts granite chippings (5–10 mm free from dust) by volume. The finish obtained is very hard wearing, noisy and cold to touch; it is used mainly in situations where easy maintenance and durability are paramount, such as a common entrance hall to a block of flats.

If granolithic is being applied to a green concrete subfloor as a topping it is applied in a single layer approximately 20 mm thick in bay sizes not exceeding 28 m^2, and trowelled to a smooth surface. This method will result in a monolithic floor and finish construction.

The surface of mature concrete will need to be prepared by hacking the entire area and brushing well to remove all the laitance before laying a single layer of granolithic, which should be at least 40 mm thick. The finish should be laid, on a wet cement slurry coating or PVA bonding agent to improve the bond, in bay sizes not exceeding 14 m^2.

Magnesium oxychloride

This is a composition flooring that is sometimes used as a substitute for asphalt, as it has similar wearing and appearance properties. It is mixed on site using a solution of magnesium chloride with burned magnesite and fillers such as wood flour, sawdust, powdered chalk or limestone. It is essential that the ingredients are thoroughly mixed in a dry state before the correct amount of solution is added. The mixed material is laid in one or two layers, giving a total thickness of approximately 20 mm. The subfloor must be absolutely dry, otherwise the finish will lift and crack: therefore a damp-proof membrane in the subfloor is essential.

APPLIED FLOOR FINISHES

Many of the applied floor finishes are thin flexible materials, and should be laid on a subfloor with a smooth finish. This is often achieved by laying a cement/sand bed or screed with a steel float finish to the concrete subfloor. The usual screed mix is 1:3 cement/sand, and great care must be taken to ensure that a good bond is obtained with the subfloor. If the screed is laid on green concrete a thickness of 12 mm is usually specified, whereas screeds laid on mature concrete require a thickness of 40 mm. A mature concrete subfloor must be clean, free from dust, and dampened with water to reduce the suction before applying the bonding agent to receive the screed. To reduce the possibility of drying shrinkage cracks, screeds should not be laid in bays exceeding 15 m^2 in area. Screeds laid directly over rigid insulation should be at least 50 mm in thickness, reinforced with light steel mesh (chicken wire).

Flexible PVC tiles and sheet – BS EN 649 and BS 8203

Flexible PVC is a popular hardwearing floor finish produced by a mixture of polyvinyl chloride resin, pigments, mineral fillers and plasticisers to control flexibility. It is produced as 300 mm × 300 mm square tiles or in sheet form up to 2400 mm wide with a range of thicknesses from 1.5 to 4.5 mm. The floor tiles and sheet are fixed with an adhesive recommended by the manufacturer, and produce a surface suitable for most situations. PVC tiles, like all other small unit coverings, should be laid from the centre of the area towards the edges, so that if the area is not an exact tile module an even border of cut tiles is obtained.

Thermoplastic tiles

These are sometimes called **asphalt tiles** and are produced from coumarone-indene resins, fillers and pigments; the earlier use of asphalt binders limited the range of colours available. These tiles are hardwearing and moisture resistant, and are suitable for most situations, being produced generally as a 225 mm square tile either 3 or 4.5 mm thick. To make them pliable they are usually heated before being fixed with a bituminous adhesive. As they age they can become brittle and fracture, detaching from their base adhesive. The development of PVC tiles has largely displaced thermoplastic tiles as they are more resilient and offer a brighter colour range.

Rubber tiles and sheet – BS 1711 and BS 3187

Solid rubber tiles and sheet are produced from natural or synthetic rubber compounded with fillers to give colour and texture, the rubber content being not less than 35%. The covering is hardwearing, quiet and water resistant, and suitable for bathrooms and washrooms. Thicknesses range from 3 to 6.5 mm with square tile sizes ranging from 150 to 1200 mm; sheet widths range from 900 to 1800 mm. Fixing is by rubber-, epoxy- or neoprene-based adhesives, as recommended by the manufacturer, to a smooth surface.

Linoleum – BS EN 12104

Linoleum is produced in sheet or tile form from a mixture of drying oils, resins, fillers and pigments, which is pressed onto a hessian or bitumen-saturated felt paper backing. Good-quality linoleum has the pattern inlaid or continuing through the thickness, whereas the cheaper quality has only a printed surface pattern. Linoleum gives a quiet, resilient and hardwearing surface suitable for most domestic floors. Thicknesses vary from 2 to 6.5 mm for a standard sheet width of 1800 mm; tiles are usually 300 mm square with the same range of thicknesses. Fixing of linoleum tiles and sheet is by adhesive to any dry smooth surface, although the adhesive is sometimes omitted with the thicker sheets.

Carpet – BS 4223, BS 5808 and BS 5325

The chief materials used in the production of carpets are nylon, acrylics and wool, or mixtures of these materials. There is a vast range of styles, types, patterns, colours, qualities and sizes available for general domestic use in dry situations, as the resistance of carpets to dampness is generally poor. To obtain maximum life carpets should be laid over an underlay of felt or latex and secured by adhesives, nailing around the perimeter or being stretched over and attached to special edge-fixing strips. Carpet is supplied in narrow or wide rolls. Carpet squares (600 mm × 600 mm × 25 mm thick) are also available for covering floors without the use of adhesives; these rely on the interlocking of the edge fibres to form a continuous covering.

Cork tiles and carpet – BS EN 12104

Cork tiles are cut from baked blocks of granulated cork; the natural resins act as the binder. The tiles are generally 300 mm square with thicknesses of 5 mm upwards according to the wearing quality required, and are supplied in three natural shades. They are hardwearing, quiet and resilient but, unless treated with a surface sealant, they may collect dirt and grit. Fixing is by manufacturer's adhesive.

Cork carpet is a similar material, but it is made pliable by bonding the cork granules with linseed oil and resins onto a jute canvas backing. It is laid in the same manner as described above for linoleum, and should be treated with a surface sealant to resist dirt and grit penetration.

Quarry tiles – BS 6431

The term 'quarry' is derived from the Italian word *quadro* meaning square; it does not mean that the tiles are cut or won from an open excavation or quarry. They are made from ordinary or unrefined clays worked into a plastic form, pressed into shape, and hard burnt. Being hardwearing and with a good resistance to water they are suitable for kitchens and entrance halls, but they tend to be noisy and cold. Quarry tiles are produced as square tiles in sizes ranging from 100 mm × 100 mm × 20 mm to 225 mm × 225 mm × 32 mm thick.

Three methods of laying quarry tiles are recommended to allow for differential movement due to drying shrinkage or thermal movement of the screed. The first method is to bed the tiles in a 10–15 mm thick bed of cement mortar over a separating layer of sheet material such as polythene, which could perform the dual function of damp-proof membrane and separating layer. To avoid the use of a separating layer the 'thick bed' method can be used. With this method the concrete subfloor should be dampened to reduce suction and then covered with a semi-dry 1:4 cement/sand mix to a thickness of approximately 40 mm. The top surface of the compacted semi-dry 'thick bed' should be treated with a 1:1 cement/sand grout before tapping the tiles into the grout with a wood beater. Alternatively a dry cement may be trowelled into the 'thick bed' surface before bedding in the tiles. Special cement-based adhesives are also available for bedding tiles to a screed, and these should be used in accordance with the manufacturer's instructions to provide a thin bed fixing.

Clay tiles may expand, probably as a result of physical adsorption of water and chemical hydration, and for this reason an expansion joint of compressible material should be incorporated around the perimeter of the floor (see Fig. 7.8.1). In no circumstances should the length or width of a quarry tile floor exceed 7500 mm without an expansion joint. The joints between quarry tiles are usually grouted with a 1:1 cement/sand grout and then, after cleaning, the floor should be protected with sand or sawdust for 4 or 5 days. There is a wide variety of tread patterns available to provide a non-slip surface; also a wide range of fittings are available to form skirtings and edge coves (see Fig. 7.8.1).

Plain clay or ceramic floor tiles – BS 6431

These are similar to quarry tiles but are produced from refined natural clays, which are pressed after grinding and tempering into the desired shape before being fired at a high temperature. Plain clay floor tiles, being denser than quarry tiles, are made as smaller and thinner units ranging from 50 mm × 50 mm to 300 mm × 300 mm in thicknesses of 9.5–13 mm.

Laying, finishes and fittings available are all as described for quarry tiles.

TIMBER FLOOR FINISHES

Timber is a very popular floor finish with both designer and user because of its natural appearance, resilience and warmth. It is available as a board, strip, sheet or block finish, and if attached to joists, as in the case of a suspended timber floor, it also acts as the structural decking.

Timber boards

Softwood timber floorboards are joined together by tongued and grooved joints along their edges, and are fixed by nailing to the support joists or fillets attached to a solid floor. The boards are butt-jointed in their length, the joints being positioned centrally over the supports and staggered so that butt joints do not occur in the

Figure 7.8.1   Typical quarry tile floors.

same position in consecutive lengths. The support spacing will be governed by the spanning properties of the board (which is controlled by its thickness), and supports placed at 400 mm centres are usual for boards 19 and 22 mm thick. The tongue is positioned slightly off centre, and the boards should be laid with the narrow shoulder on the underside to give maximum wear. It is essential that the boards are well cramped together before being fixed to form a tight joint, and that they are laid in a position where they will not be affected by dampness. Timber is a hygroscopic material and will therefore swell and shrink as its moisture content varies; ideally this should be maintained at around 12%.

Timber strip

These are narrow boards, being under 100 mm wide to reduce the amount of shrinkage and consequent opening of the joints. Timber strip can be supplied in softwood or hardwood, and is considered to be a superior floor finish to boards. Jointing and laying is as described for boards, except that hardwood strip is very often laid one strip at a time and secret-nailed (see Fig. 7.8.2).

Timber sheet floor finish – BS EN 312

Chipboard is manufactured from wood chips or shavings bonded together with thermosetting synthetic resins, and forms rigid sheets 18 and 22 mm thick, which are suitable as a floor finish. The sheets are fixed by nailing or screwing to support joists or fillets. If the sheet is used as an exposed finish a coating of sealer should be used. Alternatively chipboard can be used as a decking to which a thin tile or carpet finish can be applied.

Tongued and grooved boards of 600 mm width are also available as a floor-decking material that does not need to be jointed over a joist.

Wood blocks

These are small blocks of timber, usually of hardwood, which are designed to be laid in set patterns. Lengths range from 150 to 300 mm with widths up to 89 mm; the width is proportional to the length to enable the various patterns to be created. Block thicknesses range from 20 to 30 mm, and the final thickness after sanding and polishing is about 5–10 mm less.

The blocks are jointed along their edges with a tongued and grooved joint, and have a rebate, chamfer or dovetail along the bottom longitudinal edges to take up any surplus adhesive used for fixing. Two methods can be used for fixing wood blocks: the first uses hot bitumen and the second a cold latex bitumen emulsion. If hot bitumen is used, the upper surface of the subfloor is first primed with black varnish to improve adhesion, and then, before laying, the bottom face of the block is dipped into the hot bitumen. The cold adhesive does not require a priming coat to the subfloor. Blocks, like tiled floors, should be laid from the centre of the floor towards the perimeter, which is generally terminated with a margin border.

Figure 7.8.2 Typical timber floor finishes.

To allow for moisture movement a cork expansion strip should be placed around the entire edge of the block floor (see Fig. 7.8.2).

Parquet

This is a superior form of wood block flooring made from specially selected hardwoods chosen mainly for their decorative appearance. Parquet blocks are generally smaller and thinner than hardwood blocks and are usually fixed to a timber subfloor that is level and smooth. Fixing can be by adhesives or secret nailing; alternatively they can be supplied as a patterned panel fixed to a suitable backing sheet in panel sizes from 300 to 600 mm square.

Wood veneer and laminate

These finishes are achieved with a tongued and grooved interlocking composite strip floor finish system. Strips are generally 1200 mm long, in widths of 60–200 mm and thicknesses between 10 and 15 mm depending on the quality. Some systems are glued along the t & g and others simply snap-lock together. End jointing is staggered between adjacent strips to avoid continuity of joints.

Veneered floors have a thin hardwood facing bonded to an HDFB core with a paper underlayer. Laminate floors comprise a thin but dense aluminium oxide clear protective surface over a photographic image of wood, an HDFB core and a paper backing. If damaged, veneers can be sanded to some extent, but laminated artificial veneers are less easily repaired.

- **Underlay**   Damp-proof plastic foil of 0.15 mm minimum thickness, with damp-proof adhesive-taped joints. Treated cork or foam alternatives are also available.
- **Sublayer**   Structural concrete or screed must dry out and be level; suspended timber must be stable and level, i.e. floor boards screwed to joists and surface irregularities sanded.
- **Movement**   An 8–10 mm expansion gap is required between strips and room periphery. With new build this gap can be accommodated under the skirting board. Where there is an existing skirting a moulding is used to cover the gap.

▨▧▩■ WALL FINISHES

External brickwork with an exposed face of facing bricks is a self-finish and requires no further treatment. External walls of common bricks or blocks can be treated to give an acceptable appearance by the application of paint or an applied wall finish such as rendering, or can be clad with boards or tiles. Internal walls or partitions can be built with a fair face of natural materials such as bricks or stone, but generally it is cheaper to use a material such as blocks with an applied finish such as plaster, drylining or glazed tiles.

EXTERNAL RENDERING – BS 5262

This is a form of plastering using a mixture of cement and sand, or cement, lime and sand, applied to the face of a building to give extra protection against the penetration of moisture or to provide a desired texture. It can also be used in the dual capacity of providing protection and appearance.

The rendering must have the properties of durability, moisture resistance and an acceptable appearance. The factors to be taken into account in achieving the above requirements are mix design, bond to the backing material, texture of surface, degree of exposure of the building, and the standard of workmanship in applying the rendering.

Cement and sand mixes will produce a strong moisture-resistant rendering, but one that is subject to cracking because of high drying shrinkage. These mixes are used mainly on members that may be vulnerable to impact damage, such as columns. Cement, lime and sand mixes have a lower drying shrinkage but are more absorbent than cement and sand mixes; they will, however, dry out rapidly after periods of rain and are therefore the mix recommended for general use.

The two factors that govern the proportions to be used in a mix are:

- background to which the rendering is to be applied;
- degree of exposure of the building.

The two common volume mix ratios are:

- $1:\frac{1}{2}:4-4\frac{1}{2}$ cement:lime:sand, which is used for dense, strong backgrounds of moderate to severe exposure and for application to metal lathing or expanded metal backgrounds. Equivalent cement and sand with a plasticiser is 1:3–4.
- 1:1:5–6 cement:lime:sand, which is for general use. Equivalent cement and sand with a plasticiser is 1:5–6.

If the rendering is to be applied in a cold, damp situation the cement content of the mix ratio should be increased by 1. The final coat is usually a weaker mix than the undercoats: for example, when using an undercoat mix 1:1:6 (1:5–6 cement: sand with plasticiser), the final coat mix ratio should be 1:2:9 (1:7–8 cement:sand with plasticiser), to reduce the amount of shrinkage in the final coat. The number of coats required will depend upon the surface condition of the background and the degree of exposure. Generally a two-coat application is acceptable, except where the background is very irregular or the building is in a position of severe exposure, when a three-coat application would be specified. The thickness of any one coat should not exceed 15 mm, and each subsequent coat thickness is reduced by approximately 3 mm to give a final coat thickness of 6–10 mm. Wood float treatment produces a smooth flat surface, which may be treated with a felt-coated float or lamb's wool roller to raise the surface texture and provide better resistance to cracking.

Various textured surfaces can be obtained on renderings by surface treatments such as scraping the surface with combs, saw blades or similar tools to remove a surface skin of mortar. These operations are carried out some 3–4 hours after the initial application of the rendering and before the final set takes place.

Alternative treatments are as follows:

- **Roughcast**   A wet plaster mix of 1 part cement: $\frac{1}{2}$ part lime: $1\frac{1}{2}$ parts shingle:3 parts sand, which is thrown onto a porous coat of rendering to give an even distribution.
- **Pebble or dry dash**   Selected aggregate such as pea shingle is dashed or thrown onto a rendering background before it has set, and is tamped into the surface with a wood float to obtain a good bond.
- **Spattered finishes**   These are finishes applied by a machine (which can be hand operated), guns or sprays using special mixes prepared by the machine manufacturers.

PLASTERING

Plastering, like brickwork, is one of the oldest-established crafts in this country, having been introduced by the Romans. The plaster used was a lime plaster, which generally has been superseded by gypsum plasters. The disadvantages of lime plastering are:

- drying shrinkage, which causes cracking;
- slow drying-out process, which can take several weeks, causing delays for the following trades;
- need to apply lime plaster in several coats, usually termed render, float and set, to reduce the amount of shrinkage.

Any plaster finish must smooth out irregularities in the backing wall, provide a continuous surface that is suitable for direct decoration, and be sufficiently hard to resist damage by impact upon its surface; gypsum plasters fulfil these requirements.

Gypsum is a crystalline combination of calcium sulphate and water. Deposits of suitable raw material are found in several parts of England, and after crushing and screening the gypsum is heated to dehydrate the material. The amount of water remaining at the end of this process defines its class under BS 1191: *Specification for gypsum building plasters*. If powdered gypsum is heated to about 170 °C it loses about three-quarters of its combined water and is called hemihydrate gypsum plaster, but is probably better known as **Plaster of Paris**. If a retarder is added to the hemihydrate plaster a new class of finishing plaster is formed to which the addition of expanded perlite and other additives will form a one-coat or universal plaster, a renovating-grade plaster or a spray plaster for application by a spray machine.

BS 1191 establishes four classes of plaster:

- Class A – Plaster of Paris;
- Class B – retarded hemihydrate gypsum plaster in two categories:
  (a) undercoat plasters;
  (b) finish coat plasters;
- Class C – anhydrous gypsum plaster (completely dehydrated gypsum);
- Class D – Keene's plaster (completely dehydrated gypsum, very slow set, high-quality finish).

Table 7.8.1   Categories of plaster

Gypsum-based plasters	BS ref.	Trade name
Class A:		
Plaster of Paris hemihydrate	BS 1191-1	
Class B:		
Retarded hemihydrate	BS 1191-1	
Undercoats:		
Browning	– section a1	Thistle browning
		Thistle slow set
		Thistle fibred
Metal lathing	– section a2	Thistle metal lathing
Finishes:		
Finish	– section b1	Thistle finish, Sirapite B
Board finish	– section b2	Thistle board finish
Class C:		
Anhydrous finish only	BS 1191-1	Sirapite
Class D:		
Keene's plaster	BS 1191-1	Standard Keene's
		Fine, polar
		white cement
Premixed lightweight	BS 1191-2	
Undercoats:		
Browning	– section a1	Carlite browning
		Carlite browning (HSB)
Metal lathing	– section a2	Carlite metal lathing
Bonding	– section a3	Carlite bonding
		Carlite welter-weight bonding
Finishes:		
Finish	– section b1	Carlite finish, Limelight finishing

Table 7.8.1 lists British Standard plaster classifications, but omits non-standard plasters for special applications. These include:

■ Thin-wall plasters – for skimming and filling. These may contain organic binders that could be incompatible with some backgrounds. Check with manufacturer before application.
■ Projection plasters – for spray machine application.
■ X-ray plasters – contain barium sulphate aggregate. This is a heavy metal with salts that provide a degree of exposure protection.
■ Acoustic plaster – contain porous gaps, which will absorb sound. Surface treatments that obscure should be avoided.
■ Resinous plaster – 'Proderite' formula S, a cement-based plaster especially formulated for squash courts as a substitute for Class D – Keene's plaster.

Gypsum plasters are not suitable for use in temperatures exceeding 43 °C, and should not be applied to frozen backgrounds. However, plasters can be applied under frosty conditions provided the surfaces are adequately protected from freezing after application.

Gypsum plasters are supplied in multi-walled paper sacks, which require careful handling. Damage to the bags will admit moisture and initiate commencement of the setting process. Plaster in an advanced state of set will have a short working time and may lack considerable strength. Characteristics are manifested in lack of bond and surface irregularities. Plaster should be stored in a dry location on pallets or other means of avoiding the ground. The dry, bagged plaster in store will be unaffected by low temperatures. Deterioration with age must also be avoided by regular checks on the manufacturer's date stamps, and by applying a system of strict rotation.

The plaster should be mixed in a clean plastic or rubber bucket using clean water only. Cleanliness is imperative, because any set plaster left in the mixing bucket from a previous mixing will shorten the setting time, which may reduce the strength of the plaster when set.

Premixed plasters incorporate lightweight aggregates such as expanded perlite and exfoliated vermiculite. Perlite is a glassy volcanic rock combining in its chemical composition a small percentage of water. When subjected to a high temperature the water turns into steam, thus expanding the natural perlite to many times its original volume. Vermiculite is a form of mica with many ultra-thin layers, between which are minute amounts of water, which expand or exfoliate the natural material to many times its original volume when subjected to high temperatures by the water turning into steam and forcing the layers of flakes apart. The density of a lightweight plaster is about one-third that of a comparable sanded plaster, and it has a thermal value of about three times that of sanded plasters, resulting in a reduction of heat loss, less condensation, and a reduction in the risk of pattern staining. It also has superior adhesion properties to all backgrounds including smooth dry clean concrete.

The choice of plaster mix, type and number of coats will depend upon the background or surface to which the plaster is to be applied. Roughness and suction properties are two of the major considerations. The roughness can affect the keying of the plaster to its background. Special keyed bricks are available for this purpose (see Fig. 3.2.3); alternatively the joints can be raked out to a depth of 15–20 mm as the wall is being built. *In-situ* concrete can be cast using sawn formwork giving a rough texture, and hence forming a suitable key. Generally all lightweight concrete blocks provide a suitable key for the direct application of plasters. Bonding agents in the form of resin emulsions are available for smooth surfaces; these must be applied in strict accordance with the manufacturer's instructions to achieve satisfactory results.

The suction properties of the background can affect the drying rate of the plaster by absorbing the moisture of the mix. Too much suction can result in the plaster failing to set properly, thus losing its adhesion to its background; too little suction can give rise to drying shrinkage cracks due to the retention of excess water in the plaster.

Undercoat plasters are applied by means of a wooden float or rule worked between dots or runs of plaster to give a true and level surface. The runs or rules and dots are of the same mix as the backing coat and are positioned over the background at suitable intervals to an accurate level so that the main application of plaster can be worked around the guide points. The upper surface of the undercoat plaster should be scored or scratched to provide a suitable key for the finishing coat. The thin finishing coat of plaster is applied to a depth of approximately 3 mm and finished

Ceiling joists

Cross-joints
staggered

Square-edge
plasterboard

Galvanised
nail fixings
at 150 c/c

Jute scrim or
metal bead at
junction

100 mm wide jute
scrim or paper
tape over joints

3–5 mm single-coat board-finish plaster

2-coat plaster finish to wall

100 × 50 ceiling joists at 400 c/c

32 mm long galv.
nails at 150 c/c

9.5 mm plasterboard

3–5 mm single-coat
board-finish plaster

6.3 mm thick plasterboard
cove moulding fixed
with adhesive

83

83

Figure 7.8.3   Plasterboard ceilings.

with a steel float to give a smooth surface. In hot and dry conditions care must be taken to ensure that water is not allowed to evaporate from the mix. Water is very important in the setting process, and if applied plaster is allowed to dry too quickly, loss of strength, surface adhesion and surface irregularities will become apparent.

Most paints and wall coverings are compatible with plaster finishes, provided the plaster is thoroughly dried out prior to application. This normally takes several months: therefore, as an interim measure, permeable water-based emulsion paint could be used.

Guidance in application and standards of workmanship can be found in BS 5492: *Code of practice for internal plastering* and BS 8000-10: *Workmanship on building sites. Code of practice for plastering and rendering.*

DRYLINING TECHNIQUES

External walls or internal walls and partitions can be drylined with a variety of materials, which can be self-finished, ready for direct decoration, or have a surface suitable for a single final coat of board finish plaster. The main advantages of drylining techniques are: speed; reduction in the amount of water used in the construction of buildings, thus reducing the drying out period; and in some cases increased thermal insulation.

Suitable materials are hardboard, plywood, chipboard and plasterboard. Hardboard, plywood and chipboard are fixed to timber battens attached to the wall at centres to suit the spanning properties and module size of the board. Finishing can be a direct application of paint, varnish or wallpaper, but masking the fixings and joints may present problems. As an alternative the joints can be made a feature of the design by the use of edge chamfers or by using moulded cover fillets.

Plasterboard consists of an aerated gypsum core encased in and bonded to specially prepared bonded paper liners. The grey-coloured liner is intended for a skim coat of plaster, and the ivory-coloured liner is for direct decoration.

Gypsum plasterboards are manufactured in a variety of specifications to suit numerous applications. They are generally available in metric coordinated widths of 900 and 1200 mm with coordinated lengths from 1800 to 3000 mm in thicknesses of 9.5 and 12.5 mm. Boards can be obtained with a tapered edge for a seamless joint or a square edge for cover fillet treatment. Some variants are listed in Table 7.8.2.

Baseboard is produced with square edges as a suitable base for a single coat of board finish plaster. One standard width is manufactured with a thickness of 9.5 mm; lengths are 1200, 1219 and 1372 mm. Before the plaster coat is applied the joints should be covered with a jute scrim 100 mm wide (see Fig. 7.8.3).

Plasterboard lath is a narrow plasterboard with rounded edges, which removes the need for a jute scrim over the joints. The standard width is 406 mm, with similar lengths to baseboard and thicknesses of 9.5 and 12.5 mm.

The fixing of drylinings is usually by nails to timber battens suitably spaced, plumbed and levelled to overcome any irregularities in the background. Fixing battens are placed vertically between the horizontal battens fixed at the junctions of the ceiling and floor with the wall. It is advisable to treat all fixing battens with an insecticide and a fungicide to lessen the risk of beetle infestation and fungal attack.

Table 7.8.2   Common types of plasterboard

Type	Thickness (mm)	Width (mm)	Application
Plank	19	600	Sound insulation
Moisture resistant	9.5 and 12.5	1200	Bathroom/kitchen
Contoured	6	1200	Curved surfaces
Vapour check	9.5 and 12.5	900 and 1200	External wall/roof
Firecheck	12.5	900 and 1200	Fire cladding
Lath	9.5 and 12.5	400 and 600	Ceiling lining
Thermal	12.5*	1200	Thermal insulation
Glass reinforced	4–35	Various	Fire protection

* Overall thickness, including laminates of expanded polystyrene, extruded polystyrene or phenolic foam, can be between 25 and 50 mm.

The spacing of the battens will be governed by the spanning properties of the lining material: fixing battens at 450 mm centres are required for 9.5 mm thick plasterboards and at 600 mm centres for 12.5 mm thick plasterboards, so placed that they coincide with the board joints.

12.5 mm plasterboard can also be fixed to brick or block masonry with dabs of plaster. Dabs of board-finish plaster about 50–75 mm wide by 250 mm long are close spaced vertically at a horizontal spacing (max. 600 mm) to suit the board width. Intermediate dabs are similarly spaced with a continuous spread at ceiling and ground levels. The plasterboard is then placed in position, tapped and horizontally aligned with a spirit level until it is firmly in contact with the dabs. Double-headed (duplex) nails can be used to secure the boards temporarily while the dabs set, after which they are removed and joints are made good. It is recommended that tapered edge boards are used for this method of fixing.

GLAZED WALL TILES

Two processes are used in the manufacture of these hard glazed tiles. First, the body or 'biscuit' tile is made from materials such as china clay, ball clay, flint and limestone, which are mixed by careful processes into a fine powder before being heavily pressed into the required shape and size. The tile is then fired at a temperature of up to 1150 °C. Second, glazing is applied in the form of a mixed liquid consisting of fine particles of glaze and water. The coated tiles are then fired for a second time at a temperature of approximately 1050 °C, when the glazing coating fuses to the surface of the tile. Gloss, matt and eggshell finishes are available, together with a wide choice of colours, designs and patterns.

A range of fittings with rounded edges and mitres are produced to blend with the standard 150 mm × 150 mm square tiles, 5 or 6 mm thick; also a similar range of fittings are made for the 108 mm × 108 mm, 4 or 6 mm thick, square tiles. The appearance and easily cleaned surface of glazed tiles makes them suitable for the complete or partial tiling of bathrooms and the provision of splashbacks for sinks and basins.

Tiles are fixed with a suitable adhesive, which can be of a thin bed of mastic adhesive or a bed of a cement-based adhesive; the former requires a flat surface such as a mortar screed. Ceramic or glazed tiles are considered to be practically inert: therefore careful selection of the right adhesive to suit the backing and final condition is essential. Manufacturer's instructions or the recommendations of BS 5385 should always be carefully followed.

Glazed tiles can be cut easily using the same method as employed for glass. The tile is scored on its upper face with a glass cutter; this is followed by tapping the back of the tile behind the scored line over a rigid and sharp angle such as a flat straight edge.

▨▨■ CEILING FINISHES

Ceilings can be finished by any of the drylining techniques previously described for walls. The usual method is a plasterboard base with a skim coat of plaster. The plasterboards are secured to the underside of the floor or ceiling joists with galvanised plasterboard nails to reduce the risk of corrosion to the fixings. At the abutment of boards, a 3–5 mm gap is filled with jointing plaster and bridged with jute scrim or special jointing tape. The most vulnerable point in a ceiling to cracking is at the junction between the ceiling and wall; this junction should be strengthened with a jute scrim or jointing tape around the internal angle (see Fig. 7.8.3); alternatively the junction can be masked with a decorative plasterboard or polystyrene cove moulding.

The cove moulding is made in a similar manner to plasterboard and is intended for direct decoration. Plasterboard cove moulding is jointed at internal and external angles with a mitred joint and with a butt joint in the running length. Any clean, dry and rigid background is suitable for the attachment of plasterboard cove, which can be fixed by using a special water-mixed adhesive applied to the contact edges of the moulding, which is pressed into position; any surplus adhesive should be removed from the edges before it sets. A typical plasterboard cove detail is shown in Fig. 7.8.3.

Many forms of ceiling tiles are available for application to a joisted ceiling or solid ceiling with a sheet or solid background. Fixing to joists should be by concealed or secret nailing through the tongued and grooved joint. If the background is solid such as a concrete slab then dabs of a recommended adhesive are used to secure the tiles. Materials available include expanded polystyrene, mineral fibre, fibreboard and glass fibre with a rigid vinyl face.

Other forms of finish that may be applied to ceilings are sprayed plasters, which can be of a thick or thin coat variety. Spray plasters are usually of a proprietary mixture, applied by spraying apparatus directly on to the soffit, giving a coarse texture which can be trowelled smooth, patterned with combs or stippled with a stiff brush (Artexing). Application can be with a brush if preferred. Various patterned ceiling papers are produced to give a textured finish. These papers are applied directly to the soffit or over a stout lining paper. Some ceiling papers are designed to be a self-finish but others require one or more coats of emulsion paint.

INTERNAL FIXINGS AND SHELVES

▨▦■ INTERNAL FIXINGS

These consist of trims, in the form of skirtings, dado rails, frieze or picture rails, architraves and cornices, whereas fittings would include such things as cupboards and shelves.

SKIRTINGS

A skirting is a horizontal member fixed around the skirt or base of a wall, primarily to mask the junction between the wall finish and the floor. It can be an integral part of the floor finish, such as quarry tile or PVC skirtings, or it can be made from timber, metal or plastic. Timber is the most common material used, and is fixed by nails direct to the background, but if this is a dense material that will not accept nails, plugs or special fixing bricks can be built into the wall. External angles in skirtings are formed by mitres, but internal angles are usually scribed (see Fig. 7.9.1).

ARCHITRAVES

These are mouldings cut and fixed around door and window openings to mask the joint between the wall finish and the frame. Like skirtings the usual material is timber, but metal and plastic mouldings are available. Architraves are fixed with nails to the frame or lining, and to the wall in a similar manner to skirtings if the architrave section is large (see Fig. 7.9.1).

DADO RAILS

These are horizontal mouldings fixed in a position to prevent the walls from being damaged by the backs of chairs pushed against them. They are very seldom used

Figure 7.9.1   Typical wood trim details.

today, as modern chair design renders them unnecessary. If used, they are fixed by nails directly to the wall or to plugs inserted in the wall.

PICTURE RAILS

These are moulded rails fixed horizontally around the walls of a room, from which pictures may be suspended, and are usually positioned in line with the top edges of the door architrave. They can be of timber or metal and, like the dado rail, are very seldom used in modern domestic buildings. They would be fixed by nails in the same manner as dado rails and skirtings; a typical picture rail moulding is shown in Fig. 7.9.1.

CORNICES

Cornices are timber or plaster ornate mouldings used to mask the junction between the wall and ceiling. These are very seldom used today, having been superseded by the cove mouldings.

CUPBOARD FITTINGS

These are usually supplied as a complete fitting and only require positioning on site; they can be free standing or plugged and screwed to the wall. Built-in cupboards can be formed by placing a cupboard front in the form of a frame across a recess and then hanging suitable doors to the frame. Another method of forming built-in cupboards is to use a recessed partition wall to serve as cupboard walls and room divider, and attach to this partition suitable cupboard fronts and doors.

SHELVES

Shelves can be part of a cupboard fitting or can be fixed to wall brackets or bearers that have been plugged and screwed to the wall. Timber is the usual material for shelving; this can be faced with a large variety of modern plastic finishes. Shelves are classed as solid or slat: the latter are made of 45 mm × 20 mm slats, spaced about 20 mm apart, and are used mainly in airing and drying cupboards. Typical shelf details are shown in Fig. 7.9.2.

■■■ KITCHEN FITTINGS

Kitchen cupboards and drawer units are manufactured in preassembled or flat pack form. Flat pack is more convenient for storage and delivery, but requires time for site assembly before fitting. Materials vary; they may be selected timber or its less expensive derivatives and composites of plywood, chipboard or medium-density fibreboard. Purpose-made plastic and metal brackets are used to assemble the components.

Disposition of fitments and general design layout is a specialist area of design for the application of standardised metric units shown in Fig. 7.9.3. Special

20 mm gap

45 × 20 slats fixed
to bearers

45 × 20 bearer to
each end fixed
to wall

Solid shelf out
of t & g boarding

45 × 20 bearer to
each end fixed
to wall

Solid chipboard
shelf

45 × 20
back
bearer

Rebated
timber
edging

45 × 20 bearer to
each end fixed
to wall

Solid blockboard
shelf

Timber
brackets
fixed to
wall

Typical
pressed
steel bracket

Figure 7.9.2 Shelves and supports.

Figure 7.9.3 Standard kitchen units (dimensions in mm).

components such as corner pieces and purpose-made base units, e.g. wine racks, are not included. These vary in style and measurements between manufacturers, but retain overall dimensions to coordinate with the standard range.

Heights of floor-supported units are nominal, with adjustable legs fitted as standard. Surfaces or worktops are secured to the base units with small angle brackets. The worktops are available in laminates of solid timber (usually beech), although the less expensive pattern and/or grain effect plastic-faced particle board is most often used. Thickness varies between 28 and 40 mm, with the option of a rounded edge or wood trimming.

IRONMONGERY

Ironmongery is a general term that is applied to builder's hardware and includes such items as nails, screws, bolts, hinges, locks, catches, window and door fittings.

▨▨■ NAILS

A nail is a fixing device that relies on the grip around its shank and the shear strength of its cross-section to fulfil its function. It is therefore important to select the right type and size of nail for any particular situation. Nails are specified by their type, length and diameter range given in millimetres. The diameter range is comparable to the old British Standard Wire Gauge. The complete range of nails is given in BS 1202. Steel is the main material used in the manufacture of nails; other metals used are copper and aluminium alloy.

Nails in common use are:

- **Cut clasp nails** These are made from black rolled steel and are used for general carcassing work.
- **Cut floor brads** These are made from black rolled steel and are used mainly for fixing floorboards, because their rectangular section reduces the tendency of thin boards to split.
- **Round plain head** Also known as round wire nails, these are made in a wide variety of lengths. They are used mainly for general carpentry work, but have a tendency to split thin members.
- **Oval brad head** These are made with an oval cross-section to lessen the risk of splitting the timber members. They are used for the same purpose as round wire nails but have the advantage of being able to be driven below the surface of the timber. A similar nail with a smaller head is also produced and is called an oval lost head nail.

- **Clout nails** Also called slate nails, these have a large flat head and are used for fixing tiles and slates. The felt nail is similar but has a larger head and is only available in lengths up to 38 mm.
- **Panel pins** These are fine wire nails with a small head that can be driven below the surface. They are used mainly for fixing plywood and hardboard.
- **Plasterboard nails** The holding power of these nails, with their countersunk head and jagged shank, makes them suitable for fixing ceiling and similar boards.

▨▨▨ WOOD SCREWS

A wood screw is a fixing device used mainly in joinery, and relies upon its length and thread for holding power and resistance to direct extraction. For a screw to function properly it must be inserted by rotation and not be driven in with a hammer. It is usually necessary to drill pilot holes for the shank and/or core of the screw.

Wood screws are manufactured from cold-drawn wire, steel, brass, stainless steel, aluminium alloy, silica bronze and nickel–copper alloy. In addition to the many different materials a wide range of painted and plated finishes are available, such as an enamelled finish known as black japanned. Plated screws are used mainly to match the fitting that they are being used to fix, and include such finishes as galvanised steel, copper plated, nickel plated and bronze metal antique.

Screws are specified by their material, type, length and gauge. The screw gauge is the diameter of the shank, and is designated by a number, but unlike the gauge used for nails the larger the screw gauge number the greater the diameter of the shank. Various head designs are available for all types of wood screw, each having a specific purpose:

- **Countersunk head** This is the most common form of screw head, and is used for a flush finish, the receiving component being countersunk to receive the screw head.
- **Raised head** This is used mainly with good-quality fixtures; the rounded portion of the head with its mill slot remains above the surface of the fixture, ensuring that the driving tool does not come into contact with the surface, causing damage to the finish.
- **Round head** The head, being fully exposed, makes these screws suitable for fittings of material that is too thin to be countersunk.
- **Recessed head** Screws with a countersunk head and a recessed cruciform slot, giving a positive drive with a specially shaped screwdriver.
- **Coach screws** These are made of mild steel with a square head for driving in with the aid of a spanner, and are used mainly for heavy carpentry work.

▨▨▨ CAVITY FIXINGS

Various fixing devices are available for fixing components to thin materials of low structural strength, such as plasterboard and hardboard. Cavity fixings are designed to spread the load over a wide area of the board. Typical examples are as follows:

- **Steel spring toggles**   Spring-actuated wings open out when the toggle fixing has been inserted through a hole in the board and spread out on the reverse side of the board. Spring toggles are specially suited to suspending fixtures from a ceiling.
- **Steel gravity toggles**   When inserted horizontally into a hole in the board the long end of the toggle drops and is pulled against the reverse side of the board when the screw is tightened.
- **Rubber cavity fixings**   A rubber or neoprene sleeve, in which a nut is embedded, is inserted horizontally through a hole in the board; the tightening of the screw causes the sleeve to compress and grip the reverse side of the board. This fixing device forms an airtight, waterproof and vibration-resistant fixing.

Typical examples of nails, screws and cavity fixings are shown in Fig. 7.10.1.

▨ ▨ ■ HINGES

Hinges are devices used to attach doors, windows and gates to a frame, lining or post so that they are able to pivot about one edge. It is of the utmost importance to specify and use the correct number and type of hinges in any particular situation to ensure correct operation of the door, window or gate. Hinges are classified by their function, length of flap, material used and sometimes by the method of manufacture. Materials used for hinges are steel, brass, cast iron, aluminium and nylon with metal pins. Typical examples of hinges in common use are as follows:

- **Steel butt hinge**   These are the most common type in general use, and are made from steel strip, which is cut to form the flaps and is pressed around a steel pin.
- **Steel double-flap butt hinge**   Similar to the steel butt hinge but made from two steel strips to give extra strength.
- **Rising butt hinge**   This is used to make the door level rise as it is opened, to clear carpets and similar floor coverings. The door will also act as a gravity self-closing door when fitted with these butts, which are sometimes called skew butt hinges.
- **Parliament hinge**   This is a form of butt hinge with a projecting knuckle and pin, enabling the door to swing through 180° to clear architraves and narrow reveals.
- **Tee hinge**   Sometimes called a cross garnet, this type of hinge is used mainly for hanging matchboarded doors, where the weight is distributed over a large area.
- **Band and hook**   A stronger type of tee hinge made from wrought steel and used for heavy doors and gates. A similar hinge is produced with a pin that projects from the top and bottom of the band, and is secured with two retaining cups screwed to the post; these are called reversible hinges.

Typical examples of common hinges are shown in Fig. 7.10.2.

Figure 7.10.1 Nails, screws and cavity fixings.

Figure 7.10.2   Typical hinges.

Figure 7.10.3   Door and window ironmongery.

▨▨■ LOCKS AND LATCHES

Any device used to keep a door in the closed position can be classed as a lock or latch. A lock is activated by means of a key, whereas a latch is operated by a lever or bar. Latches used on lightweight cupboard doors are usually referred to as catches. Locks can be obtained with a latch bolt so that the door can be kept in the closed position without using a key; these are known as **deadlocks**.

Locks and latches can be fixed to the face of the door with a staple or kept fixed to the frame, when they are termed **rim locks or latches**. Alternatively they can be fixed within the body of the door, when they are called **mortise locks or latches**. When this form of lock or latch is used, the bolts are retained in mortises cut behind the striking plate fixed to the frame (see Fig. 7.10.3).

Cylindrical night latches are fitted to the stile of a door, and a connecting bar withdraws the latch when the key is turned. Most night latches have an internal device to stop the bolt from being activated from outside by the use of a key.

Door handles, cover plates and axles used to complete lock or latch fittings are collectively called **door furniture** and are supplied in a wide range of patterns and materials.

▨▨■ DOOR BOLTS

Door bolts are security devices fixed to the inside faces of doors, and consist of a slide or bolt operated by hand to locate in a keep fixed to the frame. Two general patterns are produced: the **tower bolt**, which is the cheaper form; and the stronger, but dearer, **barrel bolt**. The bolt of a tower bolt is retained with staples or straps along its length, whereas in a barrel bolt it is completely enclosed along its length (see Fig. 7.10.3).

▨▨■ CASEMENT WINDOW FURNITURE

Two fittings are required for opening sashes: the **fastener**, which is the security device; and the **stay**, which holds the sash in the opened position. Fasteners operate by the blade being secured in a mortise cut into the frame, or by the blade locating over a projecting wedge or pin fixed to the frame (see Fig. 7.10.3). Casement stays can be obtained to hold the sash open in a number of set positions by using a pin fixed to the frame and having a series of locating holes in the stay, or they can be fully adjustable by the stay sliding through a screw-down stop fixed to the frame (see Fig. 7.10.3).

Shootbolt multi-point espagnolette locking systems provide improved security for window casements. They can also be used for securing doors. They have two or three bolt functions (number depends on casement size) operating through one application of the casement fastener or lock mechanism. The bolts slide within a recess in the casement sash and lock into corresponding keeps secured to the casement frame. Figure 7.10.4 illustrates the principle.

Figure 7.10.4   Shootbolt multi-point espagnolette casement fastener.

▨ ▩ ▇ LETTER PLATES

These are the hinged covers attached to the outside of a door, which cover the opening made to enable letters to be delivered through the door. The minimum opening size for letter plates recommended by the postal services is 200 mm × 45 mm; the bottom of the opening should be sited not lower than 750 mm from the bottom edge of the door and not higher than 1450 mm to the upper edge of the opening. A wide range of designs are available in steel, aluminium alloy and plastic, some of which have a postal knocker incorporated in the face design (see BS EN 13724).

BS EN 1906 and BS EN 12209 cover builder's hardware for housing, and give recommendations for materials, finishes and dimensions to a wide range of ironmongery items not covered by a specific standard. These include such fittings as finger plates, cabin hooks, gate latches, cupboard catches and drawer pulls.

PAINTING AND DECORATING

The application of coats of paint to the elements, components, trims and fittings of a building has two functions. The paint will impart colour and, at the same time, provide a protective coating that will increase the durability of the member to which it has been applied. The covering of wall and ceiling surfaces with paper or fabric is basically to provide colour, contrast and atmosphere. To achieve a good durable finish with any form of decoration the preparation of the surface and the correct application of the paint or paper are of the utmost importance.

■■■ PAINT

Paint is a mixture of a liquid or medium and a colouring or pigment. Mediums used in paint manufacture range from thin liquids to stiff jellies, and can be composed of linseed oil, drying oils, synthetic resins and water. The various combinations of these materials form the type or class of paint. The medium's function is to provide the means of spreading and binding the pigment over the surface to be painted. The pigment provides the body, colour and durability of the paint. White lead is a pigment that gives good durability and moisture resistance, but it is poisonous: therefore its use is confined mainly to priming and undercoating paints in situations where it is not exposed to human contact. Paints containing a lead pigment are required by law to state this fact on the can. The general pigment used for finishing paint is titanium dioxide, which gives good obliteration of the undercoating but is not poisonous.

OIL-BASED PAINTS

Priming paints

These are first-coat paints used to seal the surface, protect the surface against damp air, act as a barrier to prevent any chemical action between the surface and the finishing coats, and give a smooth surface for the subsequent coats. Priming paints are produced for application to wood, metal and plastered surfaces.

Undercoating paints

These are used to build up the protective coating and to provide the correct surface for the finishing coat(s). Undercoat paints contain a greater percentage of pigment than finishing paints, and as a result have a matt or flat finish. To obtain a good finishing colour it is essential to use an undercoat of the type and colour recommended by the manufacturer.

Finishing paints

A wide range of colours and finishes including matt, semi-matt, eggshell, satin, gloss and enamel are available. These paints usually contain a synthetic resin that enables them to be easily applied, be quick drying, and have good adhesive properties. Gloss paints have less pigment than the matt finishes and consequently less obliterating power.

POLYURETHANE PAINTS

These are quick-drying paints based on polyurethane resins giving a hard, heat-resisting surface. They can be used on timber surfaces as a primer and undercoat, but metal surfaces will require a base coat of metal primer; the matt finish with its higher pigment content is best for this 'one paint for all coats' treatment. Other finishes available are gloss and eggshell.

WATER-BASED PAINTS

Most of the water-based paints in general use come under a general classification of emulsion paints: they are quick drying and can be obtained in matt, eggshell, semi-gloss and gloss finishes. The water medium has additives such as polyvinyl acetate and alkyd resin to produce the various finishes. Except for application to ironwork, which must be primed with a metal primer, emulsion paints can be used for priming, undercoating and as a finishing application. Their general use is for large flat areas such as ceilings and walls.

VARNISHES AND STAINS

Varnishes form a clear, glossy or matt, tough film over a surface, and are a solution of resin and oil, their application being similar to that of oil-based paints. The type of resin used, together with the correct ratio of oil content, forms the various durabilities and finishes available.

Stains can be used to colour or tone the surface of timber before applying a clear coat of varnish; they are basically a dye in a spirit and are therefore quick drying.

PAINT SUPPLY

Paints are supplied in metal and plastic containers of 5 litres, 2.5 litres, 1 litre, 500 millilitres and 250 millilitres capacity. They are usually in one of the 100 colours recommended for building purposes in BS 4800. BS 381C is also a useful reference, giving 91 standard colours for special purposes such as determining colours used by HM services. The colour range in BS 381C can be used for purposes other than paint identification.

The British Standard colour range is derived from the Munsell scale of colours and includes black and white. The Munsell system is used internationally to provide an accurate definition of colours. It is based on hue (base colour), value (light or darkness) and chroma (intensity compared with greyness).

KNOTTING

Knots or streaks in softwood timber may exude resins, which may soften and discolour paint finishes; generally an effective barrier is provided by two coats of knotting applied before the priming coats of paint. Knotting is a uniform dispersion of shellac in a natural or synthetic resin in a suitable solvent. It should be noted that the higher the grade of timber specified, with its lower proportion of knots, the lower will be the risk of resin disfigurement of paint finishes.

■ ■ ■ WALLPAPERS

Most wallpapers consist of a base paper of 80% mechanical wood pulp and 20% unbleached sulphite pulp printed on one side with a colour and/or design. Papers with vinyl plastic coatings making them washable are also available, together with a wide range of fabrics suitably coated with vinyl to give various textures and finishes for the decoration of walls and ceilings.

The preparation of the surface to receive wallpaper is very important; ideally a smooth clean and consistent surface is required. Walls that are poor can be lined with a lightweight lining paper for traditional wallpaper and a heavier esparto lining paper for the heavier classes of wallpaper. Lining papers should be applied in the opposite direction to the direction of the final paper covering.

Wallpapers are attached to the surface by means of an adhesive such as starch/flour paste or cellulose pastes, which are mixed with water to the manufacturer's recommendations. Heavy washable papers and woven fabrics should always be hung with an adhesive recommended by the paper manufacturer. New plaster and lined surfaces should be treated to provide the necessary 'slip' required for successful paper hanging. A glue size is usually suitable for a starch/flour paste, whereas a diluted cellulose paste should always be used when a cellulose paste is used as the adhesive.

Standard wallpapers are supplied in rolls with a printed width of 530 mm and a length of 10 m, giving an approximate coverage of 4.5 m^2; the actual coverage will be governed by the 'drop' of the pattern, which may be as much as 2 m. Decorative borders and motifs are also available for use in conjunction with standard wallpapers.

TYPES OF WALLPAPER

Underlayers

Lining paper is used to provide uniform suction on uneven surfaces and to reinforce cracked plaster before applying decorative wallpaper finishes. The quality varies from common pulp for normal use to a stronger brown paper for badly cracked surfaces. A pitch-impregnated lining paper is also available for damp walls, but it is not intended as a substitute for remedial treatment to a source of dampness. Cotton-backed paper is produced for use on boarded backgrounds that are likely to move. Lining papers are manufactured 11 m long by 560 or 760 mm in width.

Finishes

- **Flocks**   These are manufactured with a raised pile pattern produced by blowing coloured wool, cotton or nylon fibres onto an adhesive printed pattern.
- **Metallic finishes**   Paper coated with metal powders or a metal foil sheet material.
- **Moires**   A watered silk effect finish.
- **Ingrained**   An effect produced by incorporating sawdust or other fibres in the paper surface (wood-chip).
- **Textured effect**   An imitation texture achieved by embossing the surface.
- **Washable papers**   These include varnish- and plastic-coated paper, in addition to expanded PVC foam and textured PVC sheet.
- **Relief papers**   These are in two categories – high relief (Anaglypta) and low relief (Lincrusta). Anaglypta is a quality wallpaper moulded while wet to provide embossed patterns that give the paper strength and resilience. The depressions on the back of the paper can be filled with a paste/sawdust mix to resist impact damage. Lincrusta is a paper composed of whiting, wood flour, lithopone, wax, resin and linseed oil, which is superimposed hot on kraft paper. The result is a relatively heavy paper requiring a dense paste for adhesion to the wall.

8.1

SOUND INSULATION

�▰▰ THE DEFINITION OF SOUND

Anything that can be heard is a sound, whether it is made by conversation, machinery, or walking on a hard surface. All sounds are produced by a vibrating object that moves rapidly to and fro, causing movement of the tiny particles of air surrounding the vibrating source. The displaced air particles collide with adjacent particles, setting them in motion and in unison with the vibrating object. Air particles move only to and fro, but the sound wave produced travels through the air until at some distance from the source the movement of the particles is so slight that the sound produced is inaudible.

For a sound to be transmitted over a distance a substance, called the **sound medium**, is required. It can be shown by experiments that sound cannot travel through a vacuum, but it can be transmitted through solids and liquids.

Sounds can differ in two important ways: by loudness and by pitch. The loudness of a sound depends on the distance through which the vibrating object moves to and fro as it vibrates – the greater the movement the louder the sound. The loudness with which a sound is heard depends upon how far away from the source the receiver or ear is. The unit of subjective loudness is a **phon,** and the objective unit is called a **decibel** (dB). Although the loudness of a sound will vary with the frequency of the note, for practical building purposes the phon and the decibel are considered to be equal over the range of 0 phons, the threshold of hearing, to 130 phons, the threshold of painful hearing.

The pitch of a sound depends on the rate at which the vibrating object oscillates. The number of vibrations in a second is called the **frequency**, and the higher the frequency the higher the pitch. The lowest-pitched note that the human ear can hear has a frequency of approximately 16 hertz (Hz, cycles per second) whereas the highest-pitched note that can be heard by the human ear has a frequency of approximately 20 000 Hz.

Airborne sounds   **Impact sounds**

Internal noise sources

Sound reduction through open flue, 30 dB

Sound reduction through concrete roof, 45 dB

Sound reduction through tiled roof, 35 dB

Sound reduction through open window, 10 dB

Sound reduction through closed single-glazed window, 20–25 dB

Sound reduction through brick cavity wall, 45–50 dB, but whole wall is affected by proportion of window glazing

External noise sources

Figure 8.1.1   Sources of noise within and around buildings.

When a sound is produced within a building three reactions can occur:

1. The pressure or sound waves can come into contact with the walls, floor and ceiling and be reflected back into the building.
2. Some of the sound can be absorbed by these surfaces and/or the furnishes. Note that sound absorption normally benefits only the occupants of the room in which the sound is generated, as its function is to reduce the amount of reflected sound.
3. The sound waves upon reaching the walls, floor and ceiling can set these members vibrating in unison and thus transmit the sound to adjacent rooms.

Note also that sounds can enter a building from external sources such as traffic and low-flying aircraft (see Fig. 8.1.1).

Sounds may be defined as either **impact sounds,** caused by direct contact with the structure such as footsteps or hammering on walls, which will set that part of the structure vibrating, or **airborne sounds,** such as conversation or radio, which sets the structure vibrating only when the sound waves emitted from the source reach the structural enclosure.

A noise can be defined as any undesired sound, and may have any one of the following effects:

- annoyance;
- disturbance of sleep;
- interference with the ability to hold a normal conversation;
- damage to hearing.

It is difficult to measure annoyance, as it is a subjective attitude and will depend upon the mental and physical well-being of the listener, together with the experience of being subjected to such types of noise. Damage to hearing can be caused by a sudden noise, such as a loud explosion, or by gradual damage resulting from continual noise over a period of years.

The solution to noise or sound problems can only therefore be reasonable to cater for the average person and conditions. The approach to solving a noise problem can be threefold:

- Reduce the noise emitted at the source, by such devices as attenuators, or by mounting machinery on resilient pads;
- Provide a reasonable degree of sound insulation to reduce the amount of sound transmitted;
- Isolate the source and the receiver.

▨▧▣ SOUND INSULATION

The most effective barrier to the passage of sound is a material of high mass. With modern materials and methods this form of construction is both impracticable and uneconomic. Unfortunately modern living with its methods of transportation and entertainment generates a considerable volume of noise, and therefore some degree of sound insulation in most buildings is not only desirable but also mandatory under building law.

Figure 8.1.2 Separating walls.

▨ ▥ ▦ BUILDING REGULATIONS

Parts E1 to E3 of the Building Regulations consider sound insulation to all types of dwelling. This includes hostels, hotels, student accommodation, nurses' homes and homes for the elderly, but excludes hospitals and prisons. Part E4 is specifically to control acoustic conditions in new schools, i.e. between rooms, from external noise and to create appropriate sound reverberation characteristics for clarity of speech.

The Approved Documents supporting these regulations are as follows:

- E1 *Protection against sound from adjoining dwellings or buildings etc.*;
- E2 *Protection against sound within a dwelling etc.*;
- E3 *Reverberation in the common internal parts of buildings containing dwellings etc.*;
- E4 *Acoustic conditions in schools.*

PROTECTION AGAINST SOUND FROM ADJOINING DWELLINGS OR BUILDINGS (FIGS 8.1.2 AND 8.1.3)

This will be satisfied with separating elements of structure (walls, floors and stairs between dwellings and residential buildings) having the following minimum standards of sound insulation:

- dwellings purpose built:
  - airborne sound 45 dB, impact sound (floors/stairs) 62 dB;
- dwellings created by change of use:
  - airborne sound 43 dB, impact sound (floors/stairs) 64 dB;
- residential purpose built:
  - airborne sound (walls) 43 dB, impact sound (walls) n/a;
  - airborne sound (floors/stairs) 45 dB, impact sound (floors/stairs) 62 dB;
- residential created by change of use:
  - airborne sound (walls) 43 dB, impact sound (walls) n/a;
  - airborne sound (floors/stairs) 43 dB, impact sound (floors/stairs) 64 dB.

PROTECTION AGAINST SOUND WITHIN A DWELLING

This applies specifically to: walls (it should also apply to floors) between a WC compartment and habitable rooms; walls between bedrooms, and between bedrooms and other rooms; and floors between bedrooms and other bedrooms and other rooms. Performance is satisfied if the minimum airborne sound insulation between these walls, floors and stairs is 40 dB. This is verified by types of construction assembled, tested and measured in laboratory-controlled conditions. Examples include:

- walls:
  - timber (75 mm min.) or metal stud (45 mm min.) framing with two layers of plasterboard (min. mass 9 kg/m^2 per sheet) each side;
  - concrete blockwork (min. mass 120 kg/m^2) with plaster or plasterboard finish both sides;

Type 1
- 4.5 mm min. soft floor covering
- Solid concrete floor, or precast concrete beams
- Reinforcement
- Plasterboard (min. mass 9 kg/m² on battens.

Concrete floors (min. mass of floor = 365 kg/m² inc. any screed).
Plasterboard to precast floors secured to resilient metal bars
with void filled with mineral wool (10 kg/m³)

Type 2
Floating screed
- Any floor finish
- 65 mm min. wire-reinforced screed (min. 80 kg/m²)
- 25 mm min. mineral wool quilt, density 36 kg/m³
- Structural floor as above inc. bonded screed, min. mass 300 kg/m²
- Plasterboard as above

Type 2 alternative
Floating timber raft
- Timber boarding nailed to 50 × 38 timber battens
- 25 mm min. mineral wool quilt capable of retaining resilience under impact, density 36 kg/m³
- Structural floor and plasterboard finish as above

Type 3
Timber floating floor
- 21 mm t & g wood boarding nailed to 45 × 45 timber battens
- Resilient quilt as above or 25 mm thick strip of 80 to 140 kg/m³ density
- Dry sand or similar pugging on 19 mm thick plasterboard + 6 mm plywood with polythene under joists; mass of pugging not less than 80 kg/m²
- Joist min. 45 mm width

Type 3 alternative
- 19 mm chipboard floating layer t & g glue jointed and spot-bonded to 19 mm plasterboard
- 25 mm resilient mineral fibre, 80–100 kg/m³
- 12 mm timber or particle board
- 100 mm rock fibre min. 10 kg/m³
- 30 mm plasterboard
- 45 mm min. wide joist

Figure 8.1.3 Separating floors.

- floors:
  - timber joists with wood board (min. mass 15 kg/m^2) upper surface, plasterboard (min. mass 9 kg/m^2) ceiling and 100 mm mineral wool (min. density 10 kg/m^3) in void;
  - 40 mm min. screed over precast concrete beams and infill blocks (min. mass exc. screed 220 kg/m^2) with timber battens and plasterboard (min. mass 9 kg/m^2) soffit.

PROTECTION AGAINST NOISE FROM EXTERNAL SOURCES

This requirement is generally satisfied where external elements are constructed in accordance with structural and thermal insulation requirements (Building Regulations A and L respectively). For example, brick and block cavity masonry or brick-clad timber-framed walls, tiled or slated roof containing insulation and 12.5 mm plasterboard ceiling, double-glazed windows with trickle vents (see additional section headed EXTERNAL NOISE on this page).

REVERBERATION IN THE COMMON INTERNAL PARTS OF BUILDINGS CONTAINING DWELLINGS

This is satisfied by applying absorptive materials, e.g. carpet, as a surface finish. Different applications, i.e. entrance halls, corridors, etc., will have suitable coefficients of sound absorption depending on the building purpose. These are listed in the Approved Document to the Building Regulations and correspond to a range of octave frequencies. Worked examples are also shown.

ACOUSTIC CONDITIONS IN SCHOOLS

Standards of construction should be adequate to satisfy guidelines for sound insulation, reverberation time and internal noise as determined in the publications:

Building Bulletin 87 – *Guidelines for Environmental Design in Schools*, and Building Bulletin 93 – *Acoustic Design of Schools*.

Both are produced by the DfES and published by the Stationery Office.

[*Note*: Where the local building control authority or other control body is required to determine conformity to standards, random sample testing of some houses on an estate development is deemed adequate. Site equipment is a simple hand-held meter, which can be used to indicate the sound level from an established noise source on one side of a separating element and that occurring on the other. Variations in air pressure are converted to a metered scale in volts, which are depicted in units of decibels as the **root mean square (RMS)** of the sound. The RMS of sound is a type of uniform average.]

◼◼◼ EXTERNAL NOISE

The main barrier to external noise is provided by the shell or envelope of the building, the three main factors being:

- the mass of the enclosing structure;
- the continuity of the structure;
- isolation by double-leaf construction when using lightweight materials.

Generally the main problem for insulation against external noise is the windows, particularly if these can be opened for ventilation purposes. Windows cannot provide the dual function of insulation against noise and ventilation, because the admission of air will also admit noise. Any type of window when opened will give a sound reduction of about 10 dB as opposed to the 45–50 dB reduction of the traditional cavity wall. A closed window containing single glazing will give a reduction of about 20 dB, or approximately half that of the surrounding wall. It is obvious that the window-to-wall ratio will affect the overall sound reduction of the enclosing structure.

Double glazing can greatly improve the sound insulation properties of windows provided the following points are observed:

- Sound insulation increases with the distance between the glazed units; for a reduction of 40 dB the airspace should be 150–200 mm wide.
- If the double windows are capable of being opened they should be weather-stripped.
- Sound insulation increases with glass thickness, particularly if the windows are fixed; this may mean the use of special ventilators having specific performances for ventilation and acoustics.

Double glazing, designed specifically to improve the thermal properties of a window, has no real value for sound insulation except by increasing the mass of resistance.

Roofs of traditional construction and of reinforced concrete generally give an acceptable level of sound insulation, but the inclusion of rooflights can affect the resistance provided by the general roof structure. Lightweight roofing such as profiled steel or fibre cement will provide only a 15–20 dB reduction, but is generally acceptable on industrial buildings where noise is generated internally by the manufacturing process. Furthermore, the mandatory inclusion of thermal insulation in the roof slope will benefit sound reduction by its inherent absorbing properties. The inclusion of rooflights in this type of roof generally has no adverse effects in an uninsulated roof, as the sound insulation values of the rooflight materials are similar to those of the coverings. However, this is not so if the main elements of the roof are insulated.

Modern buildings can be designed to give reasonable sound insulation and consequent comfort to the occupiers, but improvements and upgrading to existing properties can present practical problems. In addition to the Building Regulations, Approved Documents E1 to E5, the following provide a useful source of information on reducing noise in existing buildings:

- BS 8233: *Sound insulation and noise reduction for buildings. Code of practice*;
- BRE Report 238: *Sound control for homes*;
- BRE Digest 293: *Improving the sound insulation of separating walls and floors* (see also Digests 333 and 334);
- BRE Information Paper 6/88: *Methods for improving the sound insulation between converted flats.*

THERMAL INSULATION

Thermal insulation may be defined as a barrier to the natural flow of heat from an area of high temperature to an area of low temperature. In buildings this flow is generally from the interior to the exterior. Heat is a form of energy consisting of the ceaseless movement of tiny particles of matter called molecules; if these particles are moving fast they collide frequently with one another and the substance becomes hot. Temperature is the measure of hotness and should not be confused with heat.

The transfer of heat can occur in three ways:

- **Conduction**   Vibrating molecules come into contact with adjoining molecules and set them vibrating faster: hence they become hotter. This process is carried on throughout the substance without appreciable displacement of the particles.
- **Convection**   Transmission of heat within a fluid (gas or liquid) caused by the movement of particles. The fluid becomes less dense when heated and rises, thus setting up a current or circulation.
- **Radiation**   The transmission of thermal energy by electromagnetic waves from one body to another. The rate at which heat is emitted and absorbed will depend on the respective surface temperatures.

In a building all three methods of heat transfer can take place, because the heat will be conducted through the fabric of the building and dissipated on the external surface by convection and/or radiation.

The traditional thick and solid building materials used in the past had a natural resistance to the passage of heat in large quantities, whereas the lighter and thinner materials used today generally have a low resistance to the transfer of heat. Therefore to maintain a comfortable and healthy internal temperature the external fabric of a building must be constructed of a combination of materials that will provide an adequate barrier to the transfer of heat.

Figure showing building section with U values:

$U = 0.25$ (pitched roof apex)
$U = 0.25$ (pitched roof slope left)
Windows, doors, roof windows and rooflights, $U = 2.20$
Pitched roof
Flat roof $U = 0.25$
Exposed walls $U = 0.35$
Exposed floors $U = 0.25$
$U = 0.25$
$U = 0.35$
Ground floor $U = 0.25$
Garage (unheated)

Limiting area weighted elemental U values for dwellings

Note: Area-weighted average allows for individual areas of components.
e.g. 1, glass: frame area in window frames.
e.g. 2, openings in walls such as meter cupboards.

Limiting individual sub-elemental U values:
Wall, 0.70 (e.g. meter cupboard recess)
Floor, 0.70
Roof, 0.35
Windows, etc., 3.30

Objective insulation values:

Element	U value (W/m² K)
Pitched roof (insulation between rafters)	0.15
Pitched roof (insulation between joists)	0.15
Flat roof	0.15
External wall	0.28
Floor (ground & exposed)	0.20
Windows, doors, roof windows and rooflight*	1.80 (area weighted ave.)**

*   Should not exceed 25% of the dwelling total floor area.
**   Alternatively, a window energy rating of not less than −30 may be acceptable.
      Ref. British Fenestration Rating Council. website: www.bfrc.org.

Figure 8.2.1   Insulation to dwellings.

Thermal insulation of buildings will give the following advantages:

■ reduction in the rate of heat loss;
■ lower capital costs for heating equipment;
■ lower fuel costs;
■ reduction in the risk of pattern staining;
■ reduction of condensation and draughts, thus improving the comfort of the occupants;
■ less maintenance and replacement costs of heating equipment;
■ conservation of diminishing fossil fuel reserves;
■ reduction of atmospheric pollution, greenhouse effect and ozone depletion.

▨▮▮ BUILDING REGULATIONS

The Building Regulations Part L the states that reasonable provision shall be made for the conservation of fuel and power in dwellings. The requirements of this regulation can be partly satisfied by limiting the areas of windows, doors and rooflights and by not exceeding the limiting U value standards for elements, which are given in Fig. 8.2.1. U values are expressed in W/m^2 K, which is the rate of heat transfer in watts (joules/sec.) through 1 m^2 of the structure for one unit of temperature difference between the air on the two sides of the structure.

To calculate a U value the complete constructional detail must be known, together with the following thermal properties of the materials and voids involved:

■ **Thermal conductivity**   This is represented by the symbol λ (lambda). It is the measure of a material's ability to transmit heat, and is expressed as the energy flow in watts per square metre of surface area for a temperature gradient of one Kelvin per metre thickness, i.e. W/m K.
■ **Thermal resistance**   This is symbolized by the letter R, as representative of a material's thermal resistance achieved by dividing its thickness in metres by its thermal conductivity, i.e. $R = m/\lambda$ or m^2 K/W.
■ **Surface or standard resistances**   These are values for surface and air space (cavity) resistances. They vary with direction of energy flow, building elevation, surface emissivity and degree of exposure. They are expressed in the same units as thermal resistance. In calculations they are represented by:
  ■ R_{si} = surface resistance inside (typical value 0.12 m^2 K/W)
  ■ R_{so} = surface resistance outside (typical value 0.06 m^2 K/W)
  ■ R_a = surface resistance of the air space (typical value 0.18 m^2 K/W)

[*Note*: Values for λ and R can be obtained by reference to tables published by the Chartered Institution of Building Services Engineers or from listings in product manufacturer's catalogues.] See also Figs. 8.2.2 to 8.2.5.

The method for calculating the U value of any combination of materials will depend on the construction. For example, a traditional rendered and plastered one-brick wall is consistent: therefore the U value is expressed as the reciprocal of

Figure 8.2.2 Calculation of U value through an external insulated cavity wall.

the summation of resistances, i.e. $U = 1/\Sigma R$. ΣR comprises internal surface resistance (R_{si}), thermal resistance of materials [R_1 = plaster, R_2 = brickwork (inc. mortar) and R_3 = render] and external surface resistance (R_{so}). If an element of structure is inconsistent, e.g. lightweight concrete blockwork with dense mortar joints, or timber framing with insulation infilling, cold bridging will occur through the denser parts. Inconsistencies can be incorporated into the calculation using the Combined Method from BS EN ISO 6946: *Building components and building elements. Thermal resistance and thermal transmittance. Calculation method.*

Cavity wall U value calculation (ref. Fig. 8.2.2):

1. Butterfly pattern twisted wire wall ties can be used where the gap between masonry leaves does not exceed 75 mm. With these ties no allowance for thermal conductivity or bridging is considered necessary. In Fig. 8.2.2 where the gap exceeds 75 mm, vertical twist pattern ties are generally specified and an allowance of 0.02 W/m² K should be added to the U value calculation.
2. As the thermal resistances of brick and mortar are similar, i.e. < 0.1 m² K/W, the outer leaf is considered consistent and unbridged.
3. Fractional area of bridged layer:

Standard block nominal area	= 450 × 225 =	101 250 mm²
Standard block format area	= 440 × 215 =	94 600 mm²
Difference or mortar area	=	6 650 mm²

Block format = 94 600 /101 250 = 0.934 or 93.4%
Mortar area = 6650/101 250 = 0.066 or 6.6%

4. The example shown has only one bridged layer, the mortar joints in the inner leaf of brickwork.

Material	*Thermal resistance (R)*
Internal surface	0.120
Plaster	0.081
Blockwork – mortar (6.6%)	0.188
Blockwork – blocks (93.4%)	1.364
Insulation	1.818
Cavity	0.180
Brickwork (inc. mortar)	0.121
External surface	0.060
	3.932 m² K/W

5. Upper resistance limit:
   Heat energy loss has two paths in the wall, through the blocks and through the mortar.

   (a) Resistance through blocks, $3.932 - 0.188 = 3.744$ m² K/W [R_1]. Fractional area, 93.4% or 0.934 [F_1]
   (b) Resistance through mortar, $3.932 - 1.364 = 2.568$ m² K/W [R_2]. Fractional area, 6.6% or 0.066 [F_2]

$$\text{Upper limit of resistance} = \frac{1}{\dfrac{F_1}{R_1} + \dfrac{F_2}{R_2}} = \frac{1}{\dfrac{0.934}{3.744} + \dfrac{0.066}{2.568}}$$

$$= 3.634 \text{ m}^2 \text{ K/W}$$

6. Lower limit of resistance is a summation of resistance of all parts of the wall:

Internal surface	= 0.120
Plaster	= 0.081
Blockwork $1/[(0.934/1.364) + (0.066/0.188)]$	= 0.965
Insulation	= 1.818
Cavity	= 0.180
Brickwork	= 0.121
External surface	= 0.060
	3.345 m² K/W

7. The total resistance of the wall is the average of upper and lower resistances:

   $(3.634 + 3.345)/2 = 3.489$ m² K/W
   U value $= 1/R = 1/3.489 = 0.286$ W/m² K

   To this value, add 0.020 (wall tie allowance) $= 0.306$ W/m² K

Figure 8.2.3 Wall construction, typical U values (W/m^{2}K).

The thermal insulation of roofs can be effected between and/or over the rafters beneath the covering or at ceiling level. Generally rafter level insulation will use more materials but can be applied as a combined roofing felt and insulation to economise in application costs. The roof void will be warm, and on sheltered sites it should not be necessary to protect the water cistern and pipework against frost. Applying the insulation at ceiling level is simpler, but as the roof void is unheated the plumbing housed within this space will require insulation from frost damage. Cold roofs will need ventilation to prevent condensation in accordance with Building Regulation C2 and BS 5250: *Code of practice for control of condensation in buildings.*

Notes:
1. U values will vary significantly for different floor area and perimeter ratios. See data/tables in insulation manufacturers' publications.
2. Rigid insulation boards may be produced from extruded polystyrene, polyisocyanurate, urethane or phenolic materials (conductivity λ range, 0.02 to 0.03).

Figure 8.2.4 Floor construction, typical U values (W/m^{2}K).

Vapour-permeable tile underlay

Rigid insulation board* ($\lambda = 0.02$) over rafters

Tile batten

Rafter

50 × 50 mm counter battens above rafters

12.5 mm plasterboard ($\lambda = 0.16$)

Roof space

*60 mm, $U = 0.30$
100 mm, $U = 0.20$

Air space above insulation

Vapour-permeable tile underlay

Rigid insulation board* ($\lambda = 0.02$) between rafters ($\lambda = 0.13$)

Tile batten

*80 mm, $U = 0.30$
130 mm, $U = 0.20$

12.5 mm plasterboard

Roof space

Mineral fibre quilt insulation between and over ceiling joists ($\lambda = 0.04$)

Roof space

200 mm, $U = 0.20$
150 mm, $U = 0.30$

Ceiling joist

12.5 mm vapour-check plasterboard ceiling

Figure 8.2.5 Roof construction, typical U values (W/m^2 K).

■■■ ENERGY RATING OF DWELLINGS

Part L of the Building Regulations requires new build homes and refurbishment projects such as house conversions to flats to be assessed in terms of energy efficiency and performance of the whole building. Calculation of U values of the elements of construction is an important contributory factor, but the overall objective is to satisfy energy performance targets for building type and size relative to atmospheric contamination by carbon dioxide (CO_2) expressed in kg per m^2 of floor area.

DER, TER AND SAP

The measure of CO_2 is known as the **dwelling emissions rate (DER)**. All new homes are built to an acceptable DER measured against a **target emissions rate (TER)**. Methods and formulae for calculation are published in the government's Standard Assessment Procedure for Energy Rating of Dwellings, known as SAP. SAP incorporates a number of considerations relating to energy consumption. In addition to U values and type of insulation, these include the effect of incidental solar gains, ventilation characteristics, boiler type, hot water and heating systems, energy controls and accessories, amount and orientation of glazing, fuel prices and chosen fuel.

Part L also places emphasis on:

- quality of construction and workmanship;
- external lighting;
- interior fixed lighting;
- heating and hot water equipment;
- solar overheating;
- thermal bridges.

Quality of construction and workmanship

This is essential to minimise energy loss due to air leakage through the structure. Areas most vulnerable are the construction interface between wall and floor, wall and roof, wall and window, etc. For guidance, Robust Details (RDs) are published to supplement the Building Regulation Approved Documents. RDs include criteria such as density and thickness of materials and application of sealants at junctions and openings (see Chapter 8.4). Where RDs are specified, a sample of finished dwellings is subject to air pressure test. Where alternative construction to RDs is used, pre-completion air pressure testing is applied to a greater proportion of houses. For all new dwellings the worst acceptable air permeability is 10 $m^3/h/m^2$ envelope area at 50 pascals (Pa) pressure. Objective to be less than 7$m^3/h/m^2$.

External lighting

The maximum rating of each light fitting/luminaire is 150 watts, with an efficacy greater than 40 lumens per circuit watt. Control should be with an automatic light detector (photoelectric cell) and time switch to extinguish the light when not required. The recommended type of lamp is compact fluorescent and not the standard tungsten filament pattern.

Interior fixed lighting

In most-used locations, such as the living room, light fittings/luminaires should also be fitted with lamps of minimum efficacy, 40 lumens per circuit watt. See Table 8.2.1.

Table 8.2.1 Guide to disposition of efficient lights.

No. of rooms in a dwelling	Minimum no. of efficient lights
1–3	1
4–6	2
7–9	3
10–12	4

Garage and outbuilding not included.
Hall, stairs and landing regarded as one room.

Heating and hot water equipment

All new installations must have high-efficiency boilers, graded on the SEDBUK scale at A or B energy rating. (SEDBUK is the acronym for Seasonal Efficiency of a Domestic Boiler in the United Kingdom.) All manufacturers' boilers are listed on a database developed by the government's Energy Efficiency Best Practice programme. This provides an impartial comparison of different manufacturers' models (see the website, www.boilers.org.uk). Boilers rated at levels A or B are over 86% efficient, i.e. not more than 14% fuel energy potential is lost in converting the fuel to heat energy in water. These high-efficiency boilers are otherwise known as **condensing boilers** and operate on the principle of a double heating effect. After the initial heat exchange from burning the fuel, the flue gases are circulated by fan around the outside of the heat exchanger for a secondary effect before discharging to atmosphere.

Other considerations include solar heating and insulation of pipes and ducting.

Solar overheating

Solar overheating in summer must be avoided in the interests of comfort, otherwise high-energy-consuming air conditioning may be an option, which contradicts the principles of conserving energy. Control can be achieved by limiting window areas, installing awnings and shading systems, and limiting glazing exposed to the south.

Thermal bridges

Thermal bridges must be avoided. See Chapter 8.3. RSDs can be consulted.

House builders and designers now have far more to consider when specifying the construction of new dwellings. No longer can energy efficiency be determined by insulation alone. There are now many other factors to consider, creating many benefits in terms of greater flexibility of design. CO_2 reduction is the key, and this may be achieved by including renewable energy technologies into the construction as a trade off against perhaps limited glazing area or extensive insulation, for example. Photovoltaic solar panels and heat pumps rate highly in SAP terms, but even if these save energy in the long term, there is an inevitable initial increase in capital costs of construction. Designing new houses to be energy efficient is a complex and specialised exercise.

▨ ▨ ■ INSULATING MATERIALS

When selecting or specifying thermal insulation materials the following must be taken into consideration:

■ Thermal resistance of the material.
■ Need for a vapour control layer, because insulating materials that become damp or wet, generally from condensation, rapidly lose their insulation properties: therefore, if condensation is likely to occur, a suitable vapour control layer should be included in the detail. Vapour control layers should always be located on the warm side of the construction.
■ Availability of material chosen.
■ Ease of fixing or including the material in the general construction.
■ Appearance if visible.
■ Cost in relation to the end result and ultimate savings on fuel and/or heating installation.
■ Fire risk: all wall and ceiling surfaces must comply with the requirements of Building Regulation B2: *Internal fire spread (linings)*.

Insulating materials are made from a wide variety of materials and are available in a number of forms, as follows.

INSULATING CONCRETE

Basically a concrete of low density containing a large number of voids. This can be achieved by using lightweight aggregates such as clinker, foamed slag, expanded clay, sintered pulverised fuel ash, exfoliated vermiculite and expanded perlite, or alternatively an aerated concrete made by the introduction of air or gas into the mix. No fines concrete made by using lightweight or gravel aggregates between 20 and 10 mm size and omitting the fine aggregate is suitable for loadbearing walls. Generally lightweight insulating concrete is used in the form of an *in-situ* screed to a structural roof or as lightweight concrete blocks for walls.

LOOSE FILLS

Materials that can be easily poured from a bag and levelled off between the joists with a shaped template. Materials include exfoliated vermiculite, fine glass fibrewool, mineral wool and cork granules. The depth required to satisfy current legislation is usually well above the top level of ceiling joists: therefore this type of insulation is now better used as a vertical fill between stud framing to dormer windows and walls in loft conversions. Most loose fills are rot and vermin proof as well as being classed as non-combustible.

BOARDS

Used mainly as drylinings to walls and ceilings, either for self-finish or for direct decoration. Types include metallised polyester-lined plasterboard, woodwool slabs, expanded polystyrene boards, thermal-backed (expanded polystyrene/extruded polystyrene) plasterboard and fibreboards. Insulating fibreboards should be conditioned on site before fixing to prevent buckling and distortion after fixing. A suitable method is to expose the boards on all sides so that the air has a free passage around the sheets for at least 24 hours before fixing. During this conditioning period the boards must not be allowed to become wet or damp.

QUILTS

Made from glass fibre or mineral wool bonded or stitched between outer paper coverings for easy handling. The quilts are supplied in rolls from 6.000 to 13.000 m long and cut to suit standard joist spacings. They are laid between and over the ceiling joists and can be obtained in two thicknesses, 100 mm for general use and 150 mm for use in roof spaces. They can be placed in two layers, the lower layer between the joists with another superimposed at right angles to the joists.

INSULATING PLASTERS

Factory-produced premixed plasters that have lightweight perlite and vermiculite expanded minerals as aggregates, and require only the addition of clean water before application. They are only one-third the weight of sanded plasters, have three times the thermal insulation value and are highly resistant to fire. However, they can only be considered as a supplement to other insulation products as they have insufficient thickness to provide full insulation.

FOAMED CAVITY FILL

A method of improving the thermal insulation properties of an external cavity wall by filling the cavity wall with urea–formaldehyde resin foamed on site. The foam is formed using special apparatus by combining urea–formaldehyde resin, a hardener, a foaming agent and warm water. Careful control with the mixing and application is of paramount importance if a successful result is to be achieved; specialist contractors are normally employed. The foam can be introduced into the cavity by means of 25 mm boreholes spaced 1.000 m apart in all directions, or by direct introduction into the open end of the cavity. The foam is a white cellular material containing approximately 99% by volume of air with open cells. The foam is considered to be impermeable, and therefore unless fissures or cracks have occurred during the application it will not constitute a bridge of the cavity in the practical sense. Non-combustible water-repellent glass or rock wool fibres are alternative cavity fill materials. Manufacturer's approved installers use compressors to blow the fibres into new or existing cavity walls where both inner and outer leaves are constructed of masonry. The application of cavity fill must comply with the requirements of Building Regulation D1.

The most effective method of improving thermal comfort conditions within a building is to ensure that the inside surface is at a reasonably high temperature, and this is best achieved by fixing insulating materials in this position.

Thermal insulation for buildings other than dwellings is also contained in the Building Regulations under Part L2. This is considered in *Advanced Construction Technology*.

8.3

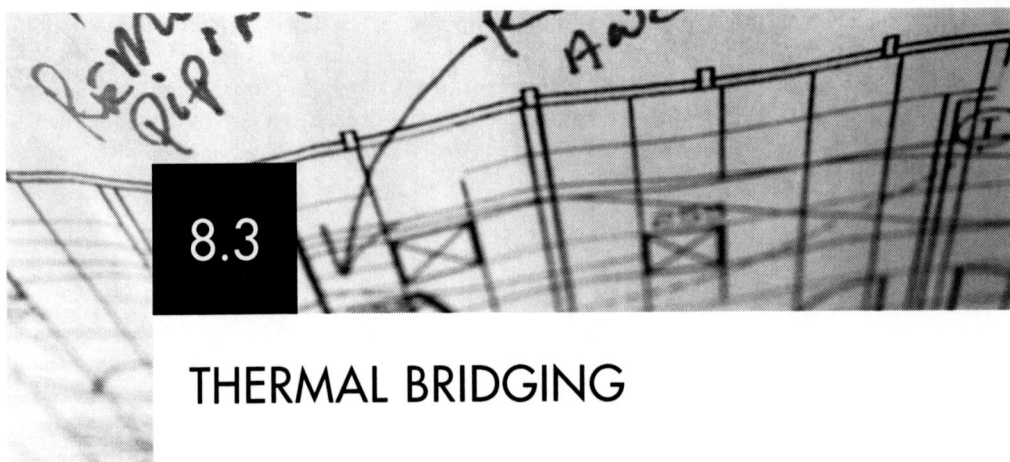

THERMAL BRIDGING

Consistency of construction in the external elements is desirable to achieve a uniform heat transfer. It is, nevertheless, impractical to build in uniform layers, and the routine is interrupted with 'bridges' between air voids and across solids such as timber in framed walls. This results in variations in thermal transmittance values (see proportional area calculation – previous chapter), which should be avoided as much as possible. Examples include metal or dense concrete lintels, and gaps in the continuity of cavity insulation. Where this does occur, the thermal or cold bridge will incur a cooler surface temperature than the remainder of the wall, greater heat loss at this point and a possible dew-point temperature manifesting in water droplets or condensation. The moisture will attract dust and dirt to contrast with adjacent clean areas. This is known as **pattern staining**.

The Approved Document to Part L of the Building Regulations makes specific reference to thermal bridging, indicating the areas most exposed. Further reference to the Building Regulations support document, *Thermal insulation: avoiding risks* (2nd edition), provides numerous examples of acceptable forms of construction at vulnerable places.

Apart from examples of bad practice, such as using bricks to make up coursing in lightweight insulating concrete block inner leaf walls, the most common areas for thermal bridging are around door and window openings, at junctions between ground floor and wall, and the junction between wall and roof. These are shown in Fig. 8.3.1.

Attention to detail at construction interfaces is the key to preventing thermal bridging. The details shown in Fig. 8.3.2 incorporate the necessary features to promote good practice.

Eaves

Window sill

Door or window head

Ground floor and wall

Door or window jamb

Figure 8.3.1   Thermal bridging – areas for concern.

Figure 8.3.2 Thermal bridging – treatment at openings and junctions.

8.4

DRAUGHT-PROOFING AND AIR PERMEABILITY

Draught-proofing is required to prevent the infiltration of cold external air through leakage in the building envelope. It is also to limit heat losses through breaks in the continuity of construction.

The areas most exposed occur at the junction of different components in the same element, e.g. door and window abutments with walls, access hatches into the roof space or eaves cupboards. The fit between window sashes and frames, and between doors and frames, is also very vulnerable to air leakage. The closeness of fit should be the subject of quality control at the point of manufacture, but this alone is insufficient to satisfy Part L of the Building Regulations. All opening units should have purpose-made seals or draught excluders.

Particular attention must be provided at the points where service pipes and ducts penetrate the structure. Gaps must be made good with appropriate filling and a flexible sealant applied between pipe or duct and adjacent filling. Drylinings, too, must receive special attention. It is not sufficient to secure these to background walls with only plaster dabs. Continuous plaster seals are required at abutments with walls, floors, ceilings and openings for services, windows and doors. Some areas and methods of treatment are shown in Fig. 8.4.1.

Other areas vulnerable to air permeability occur at junctions between different elements of construction, particularly where materials with differing movement characteristics meet, e.g. timber and masonry. A specific area for attention in where floor joists build into the inner leaf of external cavity walls. See Fig. 8.4.2.

Applied plaster finish

Plaster dabs

Door frame sealed to brickwork

Plasterboard dry lining

Insulated cavity closer (see also Ch. 3.5)

Mastic/silicone sealant

Sash-frame compressible seal

Door-frame compressible seal

Continuous ribbons of plaster adhesive

Window jamb

Door jamb (drylined wall)

Plasterboard drylining

Continuous ribbon of plaster adhesive

Adhesive sealant tape under skirting

Cavity insulation

Pipe or duct

Insulation support batten

Cement and sand filler

Mastic/silicone sealant

Suspended floor (drylined wall)

Service access

Insulated access cover

Ceiling joist

Insulation between joists

Latch compresses seal

Vapour-check plasterboard ceiling

Compressible sealant tape

Loft hatch

Figure 8.4.1   Prevention of air infiltration.

Figure 8.4.2   Air permeability seal at junction of floor joists and external wall.

ACCESSIBILITY

All new, refurbished and adapted dwellings must have reasonable provisions to allow accessibility for disabled persons. The objective is to provide wheelchair users with an easily negotiable approach from the point of alighting a vehicle to the dwelling entrance.

■■■ STEPPED APPROACHES

Steps are to be avoided. However, if the site has a gradient exceeding 1 in 15, steps designed to suit ambulant disabled persons may be acceptable. Figure 9.1.1 shows external step profiles that satisfy the Building Regulations.

Additional requirements for steps:

- unobstructed width, min. 900 mm;
- flight rise between landings, max. 1800 mm;
- landing length, min. 900 mm;
- tapered treads to be avoided, but if used dimension for tread measured 270 mm from the inside of tread;
- for three or more risers, a handrail should be provided between 850 and 1000 mm above the step pitch line (an imaginary line linking the tread nosings);
- handrail to extend 300 mm beyond top and bottom nosings. Figure 9.1.2 shows acceptable design limitations for handrails.

■■■ LEVEL OR RAMPED APPROACH

A level approach from a parked vehicle should satisfy the following:

- gradient not greater than 1 in 20;
- surface firm, even and not containing any loose shingle or other unstable material;
- unobstructed width not less than 900 mm.

280 min.

Pitch line

75–150

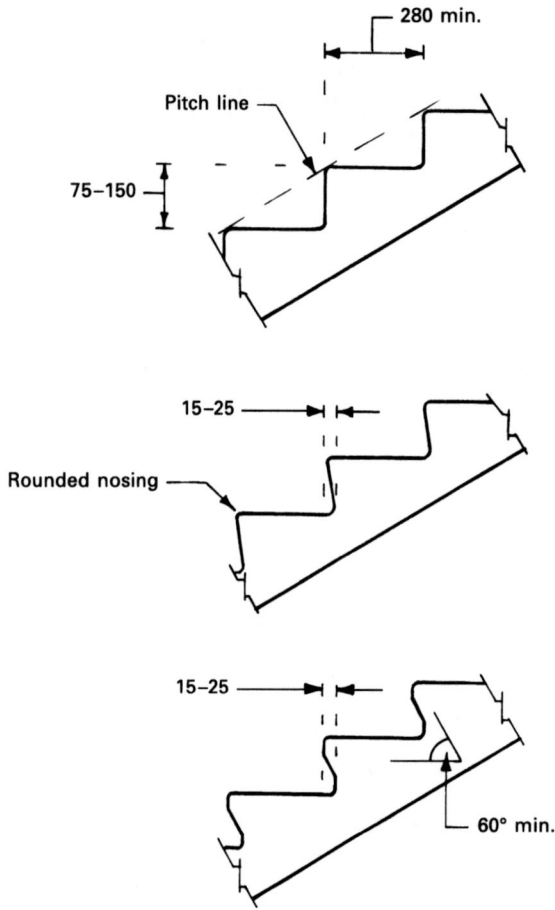

Figure 9.1.1 Acceptable external step profiles.

15–25

Rounded nosing

15–25

60° min.

Figure 9.1.1 Acceptable external step profiles.

50–60

40–50 dia. hardwood rail

**Alternative 50 wide
elliptical profile**

50 min.

15 min. radius

**Ramped or
stepped access**

**Height above pitch
line 850–1000**

50 max.

Rigid fixing — └ St/st bracket

Figure 9.1.2 Handrail design.

A ramped approach from a parked vehicle to dwelling access is defined as having a measured slope greater than 1 in 20, but not greater than 1 in 15 overall. A ramp should have:

- a firm and even surface, free of loose shingle or other unstable material;
- unobstructed width of not less than 900 mm;
- maximum flight length of 10 m for gradients not greater than 1 in 15;
- maximum flight length of 5 m where a gradient within the overall plot is not steeper than 1 in 12;
- horizontal landings at top, bottom and if necessary at intermediate points at least 1200 mm long, not including the passage of any door opening onto the landing.

[*Note*: Crossfalls to level and ramped approaches should not exceed 1 in 40.]

■■■ DWELLING ACCESS

Stepped thresholds should be avoided. For ease of wheelchair manoeuvring at entrances, the maximum recommended vertical projection is 15 mm. However, if a step is unavoidable owing to specific site circumstances, a rise at the threshold not exceeding 150 mm may be considered. Figure 3.5.9 shows a means for facilitating wheelchair entry with a drainage slot to convey rainwater from the door face.

■■■ DWELLING ENTRANCE DOOR

The minimum acceptable width of door opening for wheelchairs is 775 mm.
As shown in Fig. 9.1.3, this is measured from the face of the door stop, latch side of the frame, to the face of the door opened at 90° to the frame.

Figure 9.1.3   Entrance door.

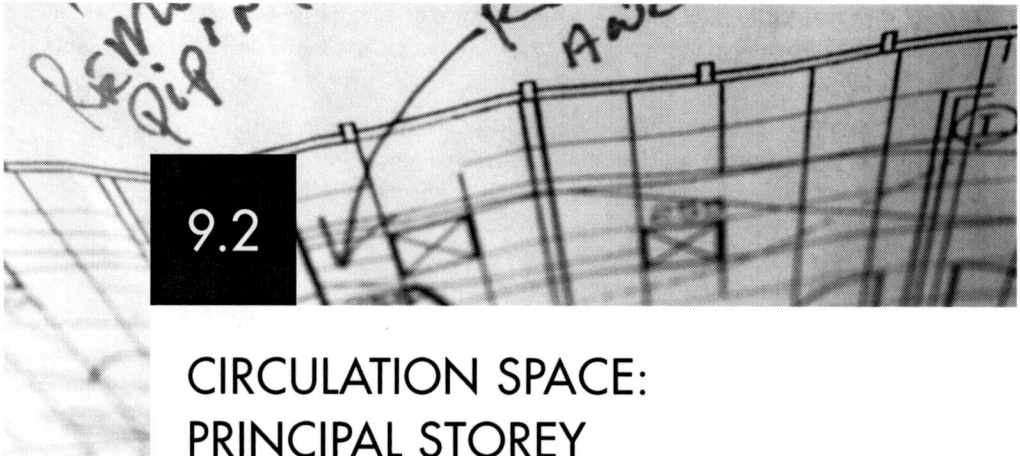

CIRCULATION SPACE: PRINCIPAL STOREY

The principal storey within a dwelling is usually the entrance storey. At this level the objective is to provide access into habitable rooms and a WC compartment.

■■■ CORRIDORS

An adequate means of passage is required within the entrance storey to permit unobstructed circulation by a wheelchair user. Allowance for normal projections such as shelves and radiators should be considered when designing for minimum acceptable corridor width. The passageway widths given in Table 9.2.1 can be reduced to 750 mm for a distance of no more than 2 m, where a necessary permanent obstruction such as a radiator cannot be avoided. This relaxation is not acceptable where it would impede a wheelchair user from turning into or out of a room, as shown in Fig. 9.2.1.

Rooms and facilities off a room must also be unobstructed and wheelchair accessible. Internal door openings should have sufficient width to accommodate the manoeuvring of a wheelchair from corridors and passageways. Table 9.2.1 indicates the spatial requirements for internal doors relative to corridor width and direction of approach.

Table 9.2.1 Passageway and door width dimensions

Internal doorway width (mm) See Fig. 9.2.1	Unobstructed passageway width (mm) minimum
≥ 750	900 (direct approach)
750	1200 (oblique approach)
775	1050 (oblique approach)
800	900 (oblique approach)

Figure 9.2.1   Corridors and passageways.

▨▣■ STEPS

Where the slope of a site is considerable, it may be necessary to incorporate a stepped change of level into the entrance storey. A slight slope is preferred, but where steps are unavoidable a stair should have a clear width of at least 900 mm. If the stair has three or more rises, a continuous handrail is required both sides of the flight. Step rise and going should satisfy the private stair provisions in Approved Document K of the Building Regulations. See Chapter 7.4.

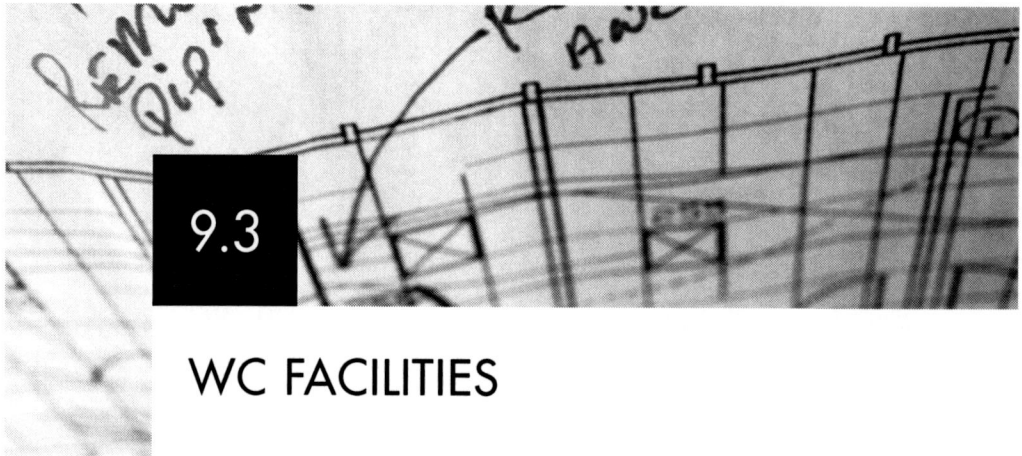

WC FACILITIES

In addition to a WC and bathroom that may be located elsewhere in a dwelling, a WC is required at the entrance storey containing a habitable room. If there are no habitable rooms in the entrance storey, a WC can be still provided here as well as within the principal storey. The WC does not have to be independent; it may be part of a bathroom suite. Access from habitable rooms to the WC compartment should avoid negotiation of stairs. To maximise space for a wheelchair user, an outward-opening door will provide clear access to the WC. The minimum widths of door openings are defined in Table 9.2.1. A basin of the hand wash type should be of minimal dimensions so as not to impede access to the WC. Clear space requirements in the vicinity of a WC are indicated in Fig. 9.3.1.

Figure 9.3.1 WC access for a wheelchair user.

References:

BS 8300: Design of buildings and their approaches to meet the needs of disabled people. Code of practice.

Building Regulations Part M and Approved Document: Access to and use of buildings.

Disability Discrimination Act.

9.4

ACCESSIBILITY IN FLATS, COMMON STAIRS AND LIFTS

The objective is to provide disabled people with a reasonable means of access to any storey in a block of flats. A lift is the most desirable and suitable means for vertical transportation, but this will not always be provided. A common stairway is essential for general use and as a means of fire escape. It should be designed with regard for the ambulant disabled and in particular for people with limited vision.

▨▨■ STAIRS

The following guidelines should be incorporated into the design:

- Landings provided at the top and bottom of a stair flight. Minimum length not less than stair width and without permanent obstruction.
- Handrail on both sides of the flight and landings, where there are two or more rises. See Fig. 9.4.1.
- Any door that opens onto a landing must leave at least 400 mm clear space across the width of the landing.
- Uniform rise of step, maximum 170 mm.
- Risers full, i.e. no gaps under tread.
- Uniform going of tread, minimum 250 mm.
- Tapered treads to be avoided, but if used, going measured 270 mm from inside of tread.
- Tread nosing profiles as shown in Fig. 9.4.1.
- Nosings made prominent with contrasting colour and brightness.

▨▨■ LIFTS

Dimensions in and around lifts should be sufficient for the convenience of an unaccompanied wheelchair user. Control facilities should also be designed to be

Figure 9.4.1 Step profiles for common stairs.

accessible and usable from a wheelchair and by people with a visual impairment. The following provides some design guidance:

- Lift door opening and closing time adequate for a wheelchair to access without contacting closing doors. Door fully open for at least 3 seconds.
- Minimum car load capacity of 400 kg.
- Landing space in front of lift doors, minimum 1500 mm × 1500 mm.
- Door opening width, minimum 800 mm.
- Lift car dimensions, minimum 900 mm wide × 1250 mm deep.
- Controls at landings and in car, minimum 900 mm, maximum 1200 mm above floor levels. Within car, minimum 400 mm from the front wall.
- Controls prominent/projecting to provide a tactile facility, i.e. floor numbers profiled.
- Visual indication that a lift is responding to a call.
- Over three storeys, visual and audible indication of floor level reached.

9.5

SWITCHES, SOCKETS AND GENERAL CONTROLS

This requirement covers a range of control devices normally installed within a dwelling, i.e. light switches, power sockets, telephone sockets, entry telephones, heating thermostats and radiator valves. It should also include door furniture and ironmongery. The objective is to provide these means of control at a level readily accessible for people with reach limitations. In addition to the registered disabled, this category will also include the elderly and infirm. Design of controls should facilitate ease of operation and prominent visibility, e.g. large rocker-type electrical switches and contrasting colours respectively. Interior design and layout of premises should ensure that control facilities are not impeded by obstructions.

A suitable wall mounting height for controls is recommended as between 450 and 1200 mm above finished floor level. Ceiling string pull switch pendants should also terminate within this range. Door handles align with switch controls as shown in Fig. 9.5.1.

Figure 9.5.1 Recommended accessibility for domestic controls.

Chapter five Moments of forces

The concept of the turning effect or moment of forces is explained in this chapter. The principle of the moment is then applied to the solution of problems connected with the equilibrium of a system of non-concurrent forces, including parallel forces (e.g. beam reactions, couples, etc.).

It is common knowledge that a small force can have a big turning effect or leverage. In mechanics, *moment* is commonly used instead of *turning effect* or *rotational effect*. The word moment is usually thought of as having some connection with time. Moment, however, derives from a Latin word meaning movement and moments of time refer, of course, to movement of time. Similarly, the **moment of a force** can be thought of as the movement of a force, although a more exact definition is 'turning effect of a force'. In many types of problem, there is an obvious **turning point** (or hinge or pivot or fulcrum) about which the body turns or tends to turn as a result of the effect of the force (see Fig. 5.1(a)–(e)). In other cases, where the principle of moments may be used to obtain solutions to problems, there may not be any obvious turning points.

Fig. 5.1 Different forms of moment: (a) anticlockwise; (b) clockwise; (c) and (d) anticlockwise; (e) clockwise at A, anticlockwise at B

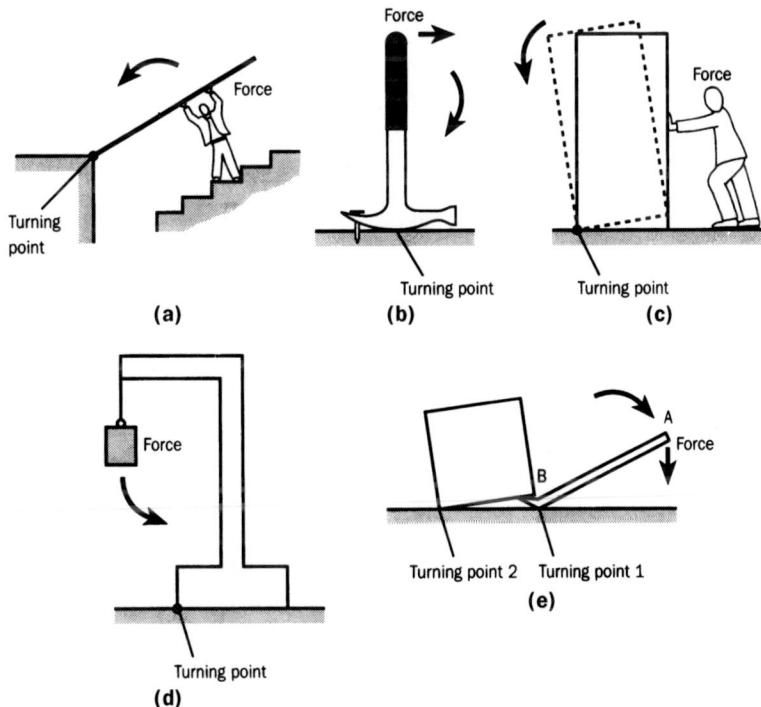

To solve problems by the use of the principle of moments, the effect of the forces must be considered in relation to the direction in which the body turns or tends to turn around the given point. In Fig. 5.1(a) the turning effect or moment of the force is anticlockwise; in (b) the moment is clockwise; and in (c) and (d) the moments are anticlockwise. There are two turning points in Fig. 5.1(e). Considering the point where the crowbar touches the ground (point 1), the moment of force at A is clockwise. At B, the bar applies a force to the stone and causes it to turn about point 2. The moment of force applied to the stone at B is therefore anticlockwise.

If the line of action of a force passes through a point it can have no turning effect (moment) about that point. For example, a door cannot be opened by pushing at the hinge. Further examples are given in Fig. 5.2. The given forces have no moments about points O.

Fig. 5.2 These forces have no moment about point O

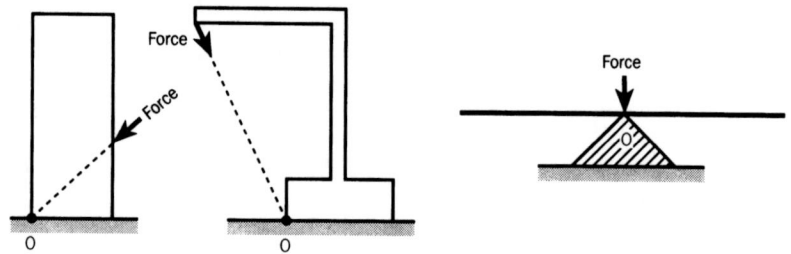

Measurement of moments

Figure 5.3(a) represents a uniform rod which balances on a fulcrum placed halfway along the length of the rod. If a force of 25 N is suspended at 0.3 m from the fulcrum it will be found that a force of 15 N is required at 0.5 m from the fulcrum on the other side in order to maintain equilibrium. Instead of 15 N at 0.5 m from the fulcrum we could place 12.5 N at 0.6 m or 7.5 N at 1.0 m. The results of the experiments would show that the force causing a clockwise moment multiplied by its distance from the turning point equals the force causing an anticlockwise moment multiplied by its distance from the turning point. For example, referring to Fig. 5.3(a), the clockwise moment of the 15 N force is 15 N × 0.5 m or 7.5 N m.

Moments are always expressed in force-length units such as N m, N mm, kN m, etc. A little consideration should show that this must be so, because the turning effect of a force depends on distance as well as on the magnitude of the force.

The distance from the force to the turning point is often called the **lever arm** of the force. In Fig. 5.3(a) the lever arm of the 15 N force is 0.5 m and the lever arm of the 25 N force is 0.3 m. It should be noted that the lever arm should be measured from the turning point to the point where it intersects the line of action of the force at right angles. In Fig. 5.3(a) the lines of action of the weights are vertical and the lever arms are horizontal. In Fig. 5.3(b) the lever arms of the forces are AO and BO respectively and for equilibrium $T \times$ AO must equal $P \times$ BO. The reason for measuring the lever arms in this way will be made clear in Example 5.3 on page 73.

Further demonstrations of the principle of moments can be arranged quite easily with the aid of a fulcrum, a rod and a few weights. In Fig. 5.3(c)

Fig. 5.3 Measurement of the 'lever arm' of a force

(a)

(b)

(c)

the rod itself, since it is supported at its centre of gravity, has no resultant turning effect, clockwise or anticlockwise:

$$\text{anticlockwise moments} = \text{clockwise moments}$$

$$(75 \times 300) + (45 \times 240) = (150 \times 150) + (30 \times 360)$$

$$33\,330 \text{ N mm} = 33\,300 \text{ N mm}$$

Example 5.1

A plank of uniform cross-section 4 m long and weighing 300 N has a support placed under it at 1.2 m from one end as shown in Fig. 5.4(a). Calculate the magnitude of the weight W required to cause the plank to balance.

Solution

It was stated on page 69 that, when considering the equilibrium of forces, the whole weight of a body can be assumed to act at its centre of gravity. In the case of a uniform rod or beam, this is halfway along the rod. Taking moments about the fulcrum or turning point,

$$1.2W \text{ N m} = 300 \times 0.8 \text{ N m}$$

$$W = \frac{240 \text{ N m}}{1.2 \text{ m}} = 200 \text{ N}$$

The whole weight of the plank is not, of course, concentrated at its centre of gravity. Each little particle of the plank is being attracted downwards by the earth and the 1.2 m length of the plank to the left of the fulcrum is exerting an anticlockwise moment, while the 2.8 m length of the plank to the right of the fulcrum is exerting a clockwise moment. The total net effect is, however, the same as if the whole of the weight were acting at 0.8 m to the right of the fulcrum.

For example, assume the plank is divided into 0.4 m lengths, each length weighing 30 N, and assume that each 30 N weight acts halfway along its 0.4 m length (Fig. 5.4(b)).

Fig. 5.4 Example 5.1:
(a) moment due to a uniform
plank; (b) proof that the whole
weight of a body acts at its centre

(a)

Loads in newtons
(b)

Taking moments about the fulcrum

$$30 \times (0.2 + 0.6 + 1.0) + 1.2W = 30 \times (0.2 + 0.6 + 1.0 + 1.4 \\ + 1.8 + 2.2 + 2.6)$$

$$(54 + 1.2W)\,\text{N m} = 294\,\text{N m}$$

$$1.2W\,\text{N m} = 240\,\text{N m}$$

$$W = 200\,\text{N}$$

If the plank is divided into a thousand lengths, each length weighing 0.3 N, and moments are taken about the fulcrum, the answer will be the same, so there need be no hesitation in assuming the whole weight of a body to act at its centre of gravity.

Example 5.2

A uniform rod weighing 50 N and carrying weights, as shown in Fig. 5.5(a), is hinged at A. The rod is supported in a horizontal position by a vertical string at B. Calculate the tension in the string and the reaction at the hinge.

Fig. 5.5 Example 5.2: (a) load
diagram; (b) free-body diagram

(a)

(b)

Solution

The free-body diagram is given in Fig. 5.5(b).

If the string were to be cut, all the weights would pull the rod downwards in a clockwise direction about the hinge. The string exerts a counterbalancing anticlockwise moment.

Taking moments about the hinge, assuming T newtons to be the tension in the string:

$$375T = (60 \times 200) + (50 \times 300) + (20 \times 600)$$

$$375T = 39\,000$$

$$T = 39\,000/375 = 104\,\text{N}$$

The total downward force is $60 + 50 + 20$, i.e. 130 N. Since the string is only holding up with a vertical force of 104 N, the reaction at the hinge must be $130 - 104$, i.e. 26 N acting upwards.

Example 5.3

A horizontal rod has a weight of 100 N suspended from it as shown in Fig. 5.6(a). Calculate the tension in the string and the reaction at the hinge, ignoring the weight of the rod.

Fig. 5.6 Example 5.3, Solution 1: (a) load diagram; (b) free-body diagram; (c) total reaction at hinge

Solution 1

Let the tension in the string be represented by T newtons and resolve this force into its vertical and horizontal components. This may be done by calculation or by drawing a line 10 units long to represent T (Fig. 5.6(b)).

It is found that the vertical component V is 5 units long, i.e. $0.5T$, and that the horizontal component H is 8.66 units long, i.e. $0.866T$. The line of action of the horizontal component of the tension in the string passes through the hinge and therefore has no moment about this point. Taking moments about the hinge:

$$\text{anticlockwise moment} = \text{clockwise moment}$$

$$0.5\,T \times 1\text{ m} = 100 \times 0.5\text{ m}$$

$$0.5\,T = 50$$

$$T = 50/0.5 = 100\text{ N} = \text{tension in string}$$

Reaction at hinge: the total downward force is 100 N. The vertical component of the tension in the string is $0.5T$, i.e. 50 N. (The horizontal component of the tension in the string is ineffective in holding up the suspended weight.) Since there is 100 N pulling down, there must be 100 N pushing up, therefore the hinge must supply a vertical reaction in the upward direction of 50 N. But the string has also a horizontal component of $0.866T$, i.e. 86.6 N, tending to pull the rod away horizontally from the hinge. The hinge must resist this pull. Therefore there must be a horizontal force acting at the hinge in addition to a vertical force.

The total reaction at the hinge is given in Fig. 5.6(c) and may be found from a scale drawing, or, if R is the reaction at the hinge,

$$R^2 = 50^2 + 86.6^2 = 10\,000$$

$$R = \sqrt{10\,000} = 100\text{ N}$$

In Fig. 5.7, which may be drawn to scale, produce the line of action of the string and draw a line AO at right angles, then taking moments about O,

$$T \times OA \times 100 \times 0.5$$

$$T \times 0.5 = 50$$

$$T = 100 \text{ N}$$

This method is not as convenient as Solution 1 for determining the reaction at the hinge.

Fig. 5.7 Example 5.3, Solution 2

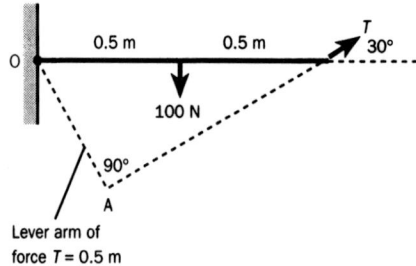

Lever arm of
force $T = 0.5$ m

Since there are only three forces in this problem, the triangle of forces law can be applied (see page 37), and this method may be quicker for problems in which the forces are inclined.

Example 5.4 A ladder rests against a smooth vertical wall and a man weighing 750 N stands on it as indicated in Fig. 5.8. Neglecting the weight of the ladder, determine the reactions at the wall and at the ground.

This problem is identical with that of Example 4.2 on page 52 but it is now being solved by using the principle of moments. Since the wall is smooth, the reaction at A is horizontal. There may not appear to be any obvious turning point but B can be considered to be one. (If the wall were to collapse, the ladder would swing round B in an anticlockwise direction due to the force of 750 N. If one could imagine the force at A to be increased above that necessary to maintain equilibrium, it would turn the ladder round B in a clockwise direction.) By taking moments about B, the reaction at B can be ignored since it passes through this point and therefore has no moment about it.

$$\text{reaction at A} \times \text{distance CB} = 750 \text{ N} \times \text{distance DB}$$

$$R_A \times 6 = 750 \times 1$$

$$R_A = 750/6 = 125 \text{ N}$$

Reaction at B (R_B): since the wall is smooth, it cannot help at all in holding *up* the ladder, therefore the whole weight of 750 N is taken at B. There is therefore an upward reaction at B of 750 N. There must also be a horizontal reaction to prevent the foot of the ladder from moving outwards. This horizontal reaction equals the force at A, i.e. 125 N, therefore the total reaction at B, which can be obtained graphically or by calculation, is 760 N.

Lever arm for
force of 750 N

Fig. 5.8 Example 5.4

Conditions of equilibrium

The above example is an illustration of the application of the three **laws of equilibrium** which apply to a system of forces acting in one plane. These laws are:

1   The algebraic sum of the vertical forces must equal zero, i.e. if upward forces are called positive and downward forces are called negative, then a force of $+750$ N must be balanced by a force of -750 N and the algebraic sum of the two forces is equal to zero. This can also be expressed by

$$\sum V = 0$$

where $\sum$ is the Greek letter sigma (letter S) and in this connection means 'the sum of', while V represents 'the vertical forces', upward forces being plus and downward forces being minus.

2   The algebraic sum of the horizontal forces must equal zero, i.e. the sum of the horizontal forces acting towards the left (plus forces) must equal the sum of the horizontal forces acting towards the right (minus forces), or

$$\sum H = 0$$

3   The algebraic sum of the moments of the forces must equal zero, i.e. if clockwise moments are called plus and anticlockwise moments are called minus then

$$\sum M = 0$$

Example 5.5

A vertical pole (Fig. 5.9(a)) is supported by being hinged in a socket at B and by a smooth ring which can give no vertical reaction at A. Calculate the reactions at A and B neglecting the weight of the pole.

Solution

First, resolve the pull of 5 kN into its vertical and horizontal components as shown in Fig. 5.9(b) and take moments about B.

Fig. 5.9 Example 5.5: (a) load diagram; (b) free-body diagram; (c) total reaction at point B; (d) total reaction at point A.

$\sum M = 0$ or clockwise moments equal anticlockwise moments:

$$4.33 \times 4.5 = R_A \times 1.5$$
$$R_A = 13.0 \text{ kN}$$

(Note that the vertical component of 2.5 kN has no moment about B since its line of action passes through B.)

$$\sum V = 0$$

The vertical component of the reaction at B must equal the vertical component of the pull at the top of the pole since the support of A can only *hold back* and cannot *hold up*. The vertical component of the reaction at B therefore equals 2.5 kN and acts upwards.

$$\sum H = 0$$

The horizontal force at the top of the mast is 4.33 kN acting $\rightarrow$ and the reaction at A is acting $\leftarrow$. There must be, therefore, a horizontal force at B acting $\rightarrow$ equal to $13.0 - 4.33$, i.e. 8.67 kN. The complete reaction at B is given by Fig. 4.9(c). Note that, if the pole itself weighs, say, 0.5 kN, this weight would be taken entirely at B (since the pole is vertical) and the vertical component of the reaction at B would be 3 kN instead of 2.5 kN as shown in Fig. 5.9(c). The complete reaction at B would then be

$$R_B = \sqrt{(8.67^2 + 3^2)} = 9.2 \text{ kN}$$

Another method of finding the reaction at A (neglecting the weight of the pole) is shown in Fig. 5.9(d).

$$5 \text{ kN} \times \text{distance BC} = R_A \times 1.5 \text{ m}$$

Note also that the triangle of forces principle could be applied to determine both reactions.

Example 5.6

A cantilever truss (Fig. 5.10(a)) is supported at A and B in such a manner that the reaction at A is horizontal. Neglecting the weight of the truss, calculate the reactions at A and B.

Fig. 5.10 Example 5.6: (a) load diagram; (b) total reaction at point B

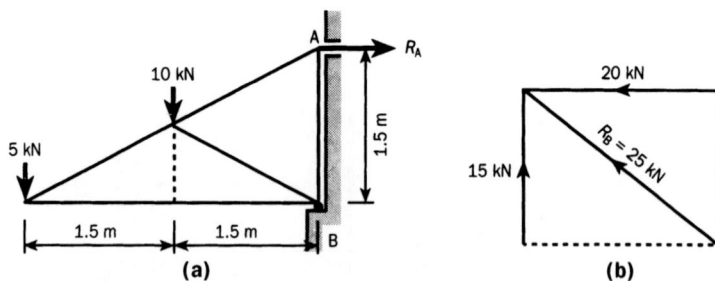

Solution

Take moments about B to determine the reaction at A:

$$\sum M = 0$$
$$1.5 R_A = 10 \times 1.5 + 5 \times 3$$
$$R_A = 20 \text{ kN acting towards the right}$$

$\Sigma H = 0$, therefore horizontal component of reaction at B is 20 kN, acting towards the left.

$\Sigma V = 0$, therefore vertical component of reaction at B is 15 kN acting upwards.

Referring to Fig. 5.10(b):

$$R_B = \sqrt{(20^2 + 15^2)} = \sqrt{625} = 25 \text{ kN}$$

Resultant of parallel forces

It was stated in Chapter 3 in connection with concurrent forces that the resultant of a given number of forces is the single force which, when substituted for the given forces, has the same effect on the *state of equilibrium* of the body. This definition applies also to parallel forces.

Consider Fig. 5.11(a) which represents a beam of negligible weight supporting three vertical loads of 13, 18 and 27 kN respectively.

The force in the vertical cable can be obtained by taking moments about the hinge, i.e.

$$F \times 3 \text{ m} = 13 \times 1.4 + 18 \times 2.4 + 27 \times 3.3$$

$$= 150.5 \text{ kN m}$$

$$F = 150.5/3 = 50.2 \text{ kN}$$

Now, if one force (the resultant) is substituted for the three downward loads without altering the state of equilibrium, its magnitude must be $13 + 18 + 27 = 58$ kN, and if the reaction in the cable is to remain as before, i.e. 50 kN, the moment of the single resultant force about the hinge must equal the sum of the moments of the forces taken separately.

Referring to Fig. 5.11(b), the moment of the resultant force about the hinge is $58x$ kN m, and this must equal 150.5 kN m, therefore

$$58x = 150.5$$

$$x = 15.5/58 = 2.59$$

The resultant of the three forces is, therefore, a single force of 58 kN acting at 2.59 m from the hinge. The reactions in the cable and at the hinge will be the same for this one force as for the three forces.

Fig. 5.11 Resultant of parallel forces: (a) load diagram; (b) free-body diagram.

Calculate the magnitude and position of the resultant of the system of forces shown in Fig. 5.12(a) and determine where a fulcrum must be placed to maintain equilibrium. (Neglect the weight of the rod.)

Fig. 5.12 Example 5.7: (a) load diagram; (b) free-body diagram

(a)   (b)

This is an example of a system of *unlike parallel forces* since all the forces are not acting in the same sense. The moment of this resultant about *any point* must equal the algebraic sum of the moments of the separate forces. Taking moments about end A,

$$150x = 25 \times 2 - 50 \times 3 + 75 \times 4$$
$$= 50 - 150 + 300$$
$$x = 200/150 = 1.33 \text{ m}$$

The fulcrum must therefore be placed at this point in order to maintain the rod in balance (and the reaction at the fulcrum = 150 N).

The same answer would be obtained by taking moments about any point, as for example, the point P, 2 m from A (see Fig. 5.12(b)).

$$150y = 100 \times 2 + 25 \times 4 - 50 \times 5 + 75 \times 6$$
$$= 200 + 100 - 250 + 450$$
$$y = 500/150 = 3.33 \text{ m}$$

The position of the resultant is therefore 3.33 m from P or 1.33 m from A. Problems can often be simplified by working with a resultant instead of with a number of separate forces. This is demonstrated in the following example.

Calculate the resultant of the three downward forces of Fig. 5.13(a), then use the triangle of forces principle to determine the reaction in the cable and the reaction at the hinge.

The resultant of the three downward forces is 6 kN and, taking moments about the hinge,

$$6x = 3 \times 0.6 + 1 \times 1.2 + 2 \times 2.5$$
$$x = 8/6 = 1.33 \text{ m}$$

Now, using the method of Example 4.2, page 52, the reactions can be found as shown in Fig. 5.13(b) and (c).

Fig. 5.13 Example 5.8:
(a) load diagram;
(b) free-body diagram;
(c) force diagram at point O

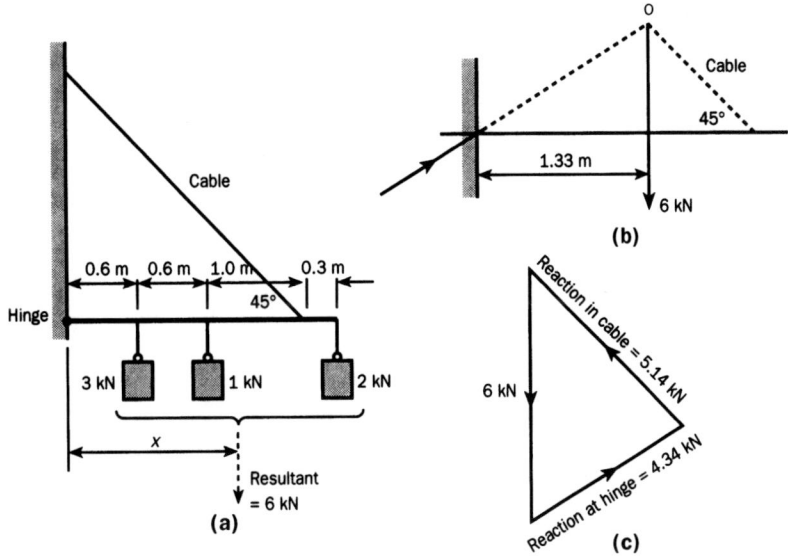

Couples

Two equal, unlike (i.e. acting in opposite directions) parallel forces are said to form a **couple**.

Imagine a rod resting on a smooth table, as shown in Fig. 5.14(a), and assume that two equal unlike parallel forces of 20 N are applied horizontally as shown. The rod will rotate in a clockwise direction, and the moment causing this rotation is obtained by multiplying *one* of the forces by the distance AB between the two forces. The perpendicular distance AB is called the arm of the couple or, in general terms, the **lever arm**, l_a. Therefore

$$\text{moment of couple} = 20\text{ N} \times 150\text{ mm}$$
$$= 3000\text{ N mm}$$

No matter about what point the moment is considered, the answer is equal to $W \times$ AB. For example, taking moments about any point O between the two forces (Fig. 5.14(b)), the moment causing rotation is

$$(W \times \text{AO}) + (W \times \text{BO})$$

Fig. 5.14 Couples: (a) load diagrams; (b) and (c) considering moments about different points

Fixing moment or couple applied by base to the mast

Fig. 5.15 Fixing moment

This equals
$$W(AO + BO) = W \times AB$$

In Fig. 5.14(c) the clockwise moment about O is $W \times AO$, and the anti-clockwise moment about O is $W \times BO$.

The net moment causing rotation is
$$W \times AO - W \times BO = W(AO - BO)$$
$$= W \times AB$$

Note that a couple acting on a body produces rotation and the forces cannot be balanced by a single force. To produce equilibrium another couple of equal and opposite moment is required.

Figure 5.15 represents a mast fixed at its base. The moment tending to break the mast at its base is
$$[2(x + 1) - 2x]\,kN\,m = 2x + 2 - 2x = 2\,kN\,m$$

No matter what the distance x may be, the moment at the base will be 2 kN m. This moment or couple is resisted by the fixing moment or couple applied by the base to the mast.

A knowledge of the principles of couples is useful in understanding beam problems (see Chapter 11).

Beam reactions

The application of the principle of moments of forces to the calculation of beam reactions can be verified by means of the following experiment.

A beam of wood, a little longer than 1.2 m and weighing 15 N, has weights suspended from it as shown in Fig. 5.16(a). It is required to determine the reactions at supports A and B.

Fig. 5.16 Beam reactions:
(a) balance attached at point B;
(b) balance attached at point A

If a spring balance is attached to the beam at B, the beam can be lifted just clear of the support and it will be observed that the reading on the balance is 32.5 N. When the balance is released so that the beam rests again on block B, it follows that the beam must be pushing down on the support with a force of 32.5 N. Similarly, the upward reaction of the support on the beam is 32.5 N.

If the hand holding the balance is moved up and down, the beam will turn round the point where it is supported at A. Taking moments about this point, representing the reaction at B by R_B,

$$R_B \times 1.2 \text{ m (anticlockwise about A)}$$
$$= 35 \times 0.4 + 15 \times 0.6 + 20 \times 0.8$$

therefore

$$1.2R_B = 39 \quad \text{and} \quad R_B = \frac{39}{1.2} = 32.5 \text{ N}$$

If the balance is transferred to A and the beam lifted off its support, the balance will read 37.5 N (Fig. 5.16(b)).

By calculation, taking B as the turning point,

$$R_A \times 1.2 = 20 \times 0.4 + 15 \times 0.6 + 35 \times 0.8$$

$$\text{clockwise} = \text{anticlockwise}$$

$$R_A = \frac{45}{1.2} = 37.5 \text{ N}$$

Note that the sum of the reactions is 70 N and that this is also the sum of the downward forces ($\Sigma V = 0$).

Note also that to determine the reaction at A, moments are taken about B, i.e. B is considered as the turning point and the moment of each force or load is the force multiplied by its distance from B.

Similarly, to determine the reaction at B, moments are taken about A, i.e. A is considered as the turning point.

The two weights of 35 N and 20 N in the discussion above are **point loads** or **concentrated loads**, since they act at definite points on the beam. The beam itself is a **uniformly distributed load (UDL)** since its weight is spread uniformly over its whole length. Figure 5.17(a) represents the test beam supporting a block of lead 0.4 m long of uniform cross-section and weighing 30 N. For calculating the reactions at the supports, the whole of this uniformly distributed weight can be assumed to act at its centre of gravity.

Taking moments about A:

$$1.2R_B = 30 \times 0.4 + 15 \times 0.6$$

$$R_A = \frac{21}{1.2} = 17.5 \text{ N}$$

Similarly, taking moments about B:

$$1.2R_A = 1.5 \times 0.6 + 30 \times 0.8$$

$$R_A = \frac{33}{1.2} = 27.5 \text{ N}$$

$$R_A + R_B = 17.5 + 27.5 = 45 \text{ N} = \text{ total load}$$

Fig. 5.17 Uniformly distributed loads: (a) load diagram; (b) and (c) representations of a UDL

(a)

(b)

(c)

These calculated values of the reactions can be verified by means of the spring balances.

Instead of drawing the beam every time, a free-body diagram can be drawn as in Fig. 5.17(b) and (c) where two methods of indicating uniformly distributed loads are shown.

Further experiments can be performed with the simple apparatus shown in Fig. 5.17 by placing the supports at different points. Figure 5.18 shows the supports placed 0.8 m apart. In this case, to determine experimentally the reaction at A, the spring balance must be connected to a point on the beam directly above A.

Fig. 5.18 Combination of point and uniformly distributed loads

Taking moments about B, the reaction at A produces a clockwise moment and all the loads anticlockwise moments.

$$0.8R_A = 30 \times 0.2 + 15 \times 0.6 + 20 \times 1.2$$

$$R_A = 39/0.8 = 48.75 \text{ N}$$

Taking moments about A, both the reactions at B and the load of 20 N produce anticlockwise moments:

$$0.8R_B = 20 \times 0.4 = 15 \times 0.2 + 30 \times 0.6$$

$$0.8R_B = 3.0 + 18.0 - 8.0$$

$$R_B = \frac{13}{0.8} = 16.25 \text{ N}$$

$$R_A + R_B = 48.75 + 16.25 = 65 \text{ N}$$

$$= \text{sum of the vertical loads}$$

Practical cases

In buildings, point loads on beams are usually due to loads from other beams or from columns, and uniformly distributed loads are due to floors, walls and partitions and the weights of the beams themselves.

In Fig. 5.19(a), assume that the beam AB weighs 10 kN and that it supports two beams which transmit loads of 60 kN and 90 kN respectively to beam AB. In addition, a column transmits a load of 240 kN. The reactions are usually taken as acting at the middle of the bearing area supplied by the supporting brickwork or column. Figure 5.19(b) shows the free-body diagram.

Taking moments about B:

$$6R_A = 90 \times 2.0 + 10 \times 3.0 + 240 \times 3.5 + 60 \times 4.0$$

$$= 180 + 30 + 840 + 240$$

$$R_A = \frac{1290}{6} = 215 \text{ kN}$$

Since the total load on the beam is 400 kN, the reaction at B is $400 - 215$, i.e. 185 kN. It is advisable, however, to determine the reaction

Fig. 5.19 Practical example: (a) loading of beam; (b) free-body diagram

Column supporting 240 kN

60 kN from beam

90 kN from beam

A   Beam weight 10 kN   B

2.0 m   0.5 m   1.5 m   2.0 m

R_A (a) R_B

2.0 m   60 kN 0.5 m 240 kN   1.5 m   90 kN   2.0 m

A   UDL of 10 kN   B

6.0 m   c.g. of beam

R_A R_B

(b)

at B by taking moments about A and thereby to obtain a check on the calculations.

Example 5.9

A beam weighing 9.6 kN supports brickwork 225 mm thick weighing 20 kN/m³ as indicated in Fig. 5.20(a). Calculate the reactions at the supports.

Solution

Both the brickwork and the beam are uniformly distributed loads.

$$\text{volume of brickwork} = 5.0 \times 2.5 \times 0.225 = 2.8125 \text{ m}^3$$
$$\text{weight of brickwork} = 2.8125 \times 20 = 56.25 \text{ kN}$$
$$\text{weight of beam} = 9.60 \text{ kN}$$
$$\text{total weight} = 65.85 \text{ kN}$$

The free-body diagram is shown in Fig. 5.20(b).

Fig. 5.20 Example 5.9: (a) load diagram; (b) free-body diagram

Taking moments about B,

$$3.5R_A = 65.85 \times 2$$
$$R_A = \frac{131.70}{3.5} = 37.63 \text{ kN}$$
$$R_B = 65.85 - 37.63 = 28.22 \text{ kN}$$

or R_B can be obtained by taking moments about A, thus providing a useful check.

Summary

Moment The turning effect of a force.

- Moments are considered in relation to a turning point, real or imaginary.
- A moment is always obtained by multiplying a force by a distance and this distance must be measured from the turning point to where it cuts the line of action of the force at right angles.
- Moments are expressed in force-length units such as newton metre (N m), newton millimetre (N mm), etc.
- If the line of action of a force passes through a given point, it can have no moment about that point.

Conditions of equilibrium For a system of forces acting in one plane, conditions of equilibrium are:

$$\sum V = 0 \quad \sum H = 0 \quad \sum M = 0$$

Resultant For a number of parallel forces the resultant is their algebraic sum. Its position can be found by taking moments about *any point* and moment of resultant equals the algebraic sum of moments of the individual forces.

Couple Two equal unlike parallel forces. The distance between the forces is called the arm of the couple, and the moment of a couple equals one of the forces multiplied by the arm of the couple.

Exercises

1 A uniform rod is in equilibrium under the action of weights as shown in Fig. 5.Q1. Calculate the value of W and the reaction at the fulcrum, ignoring the weight of the rod.

100 mm 100 mm 50 mm 75 mm 175 mm

35 N 25 N 15 N W 20 N

Fig. 5.Q1

2 Calculate the value of x metres so that the uniform rod of Fig. 5.Q2 will balance.

2 m

1 m 1 m x m

25 N 25 N 50 N

Fig. 5.Q2

3 A uniform rod weighing 100 N and supporting 500 N is hinged to a wall and kept horizontal by a vertical rope (Fig. 5.Q3). Calculate the tension in the rope and the reaction at the hinge.

1.3 m 0.7 m Rope

500 N

Fig. 5.Q3

4 A uniform rod weighing 40 N is maintained in equilibrium as shown in Fig. 5.Q4. Calculate the distance x and the reaction at the fulcrum.

200 mm 100 mm

x

25 N 200 N

Fig. 5.Q4

5 A uniform rod 0.4 m long weighing 10 N supports loads as shown in Fig. 5.Q5. Calculate the distance x if the rod is in equilibrium.

Fig. 5.Q5

6 A uniform horizontal beam 1.3 m long and weighing 200 N is hinged to a wall and supported by a vertical prop as shown in Fig. 5.Q6. Calculate the reactions at the prop and hinge.

Fig. 5.Q6

7 Calculate the reaction at the prop and hinge in Fig. 5.Q7. The uniform beam weighs 200 N.

Fig. 5.Q7

8 A compound lever is shown in Fig. 5.Q8. Each of the horizontal rods weighs 50 N and the vertical rod weighs 40 N. Calculate the value of the force W which is required for equilibrium, and calculate the reactions at the fulcrums. (First take moments about A to find the force in the vertical rod, then take moments about B.)

Fig. 5.Q8

9 Solve Exercises 1 to 13 of Chapter 4, with the aid of the principle of moments.

10 Determine the tension in the chain and the reaction at the hinge (Fig. 5.Q10). The uniform rod weighs 500 N.

Fig. 5.Q10

11 The horizontal cable in Fig. 5.Q11 is attached to the rod halfway along its length. The uniform rod weighs 250 N. Calculate the tension in the cable and the reaction at the hinge.

Fig. 5.Q11

12 Calculate the tension in the guy rope of Fig. 5.Q12, then use the triangle of forces law to determine the forces in the mast, tie and jib. Neglect the weight of the members.

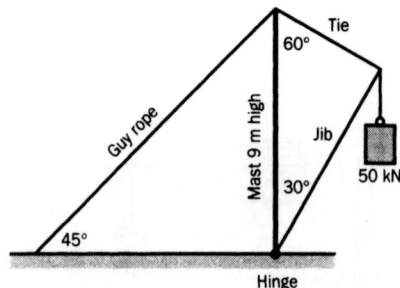

Fig. 5.Q12

13 A uniform rod weighing 50 N is loaded as shown in Fig. 5.Q13. Calculate the tension in the cable and the reaction at the hinge.

Fig. 5.Q13

14 Two uniform rods each 3 m long and weighing 250 N are connected by a link bar (Fig. 5.Q14). Calculate the tensions in the link bar and chain neglecting their weights.

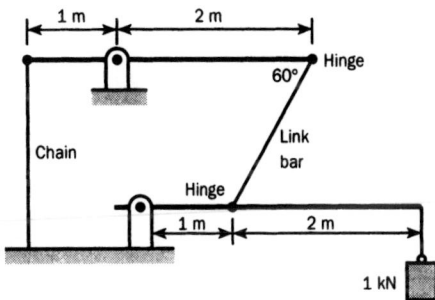

Fig. 5.Q14

15 For each of the structures shown in Fig. 5.Q15(a), (b) and (c) determine the position of the resultant of the vertical loads; then, by using the triangle of forces, determine the tension in the cable and the reaction at the hinge. Neglect the weight of the rod.

(a)

(b)

(c)

Fig. 5.Q15

16 The weights of the structures shown in Fig. 5.Q16(a), (b), (c) and (d) may be neglected. In each case the reaction at A is horizontal, and B is a hinge. Determine the position of the resultant of the vertical loads; then, by applying the principle of the triangle of forces, determine the reactions at A and B.

(a)   (b)

(c)   (d)

Fig. 5.Q16

17 The roof truss of Fig. 5.Q17 is supported on rollers at B and the reaction at B is therefore vertical. Determine the resultant of the four wind loads, then use the triangle of forces to determine the reactions at A and B.

Fig. 5.Q17

18 Reduce the system of forces shown in Fig. 5.Q18 to a couple. Determine the arm and moment of the couple.

Fig. 5.Q18

19 Calculate the reactions at A and B due to the given point loads in Fig. 5.Q19(a) to (e). The loads are in kilonewtons (kN).

(a)

(b)

(c)

(d)

(e)

Fig. 5.Q19

20 Calculate the reactions at A and B due to the given system of loads in Fig. 5.Q20(a) to (g).

(a)

(b)

(c)

(d)

(e)

(f)

(g)

Fig. 5.Q20

21 A beam AB carries two point loads and is supported by two beams CD and EF as shown in plan in Fig. 5.Q21. Neglecting the weights of the beams, calculate the reactions at C, D, E and F.

Fig. 5.Q21

22 A reinforced concrete bridge between two buildings spans 8 m. The cross-section of the bridge is shown in Fig. 5.Q22. The brickwork weighs 20 kN/m³, the reinforced concrete weighs 23 kN/m³, and the stone coping weighs 0.5 kN/m. The floor of the bridge has to carry a uniformly distributed load of 1.5 kN/m² in addition to its own weight. Calculate the force on the supporting buildings from one end of each beam.

Fig. 5.Q22

Chapter eight Shear force and bending moment

In this chapter the twin effects of the action of applied loads on beams are investigated in terms of the shear force and bending moment. The plotting of shear force diagrams (SFDs) and bending moment diagrams (BMDs) is demonstrated, and the significance of the position of the points of zero shear (maximum bending moment M_{max}) and zero bending (contraflexure) is explained.

When a beam is loaded, the applied loads have a tendency to cause failure of the beam, and whether or not the beam actually does fail depends obviously upon the extent or amount of loading and on the size and strength of the beam in question.

It is necessary to provide a beam that will safely carry the estimated loading with a reasonable factor of safety, and which will at the same time be light enough for economy and shallow enough to avoid unnecessary encroachment upon headroom.

In order to calculate the stresses that loading will induce into the fibres of a beam's cross-section, and to compare them with the known safe allowable stress for the material of which the beam is made, it is necessary to study the ways in which loading *punishes* a beam, and to assess the degree of *punishment*.

Loading tends to cause failure in two main ways:

• By 'shearing' the beam across its cross-section, as shown in Fig. 8.1(a).
• By bending the beam to an excessive amount, as shown in Fig. 8.1(b).

These two tendencies to failure or collapse do occur simultaneously, but for a clearer understanding of each they will be examined separately.

Shear force

Consider the portion of beam shown in Fig. 8.2(a). For simplicity of explanation the weight of the beam itself has been ignored.

Figure 8.2(b) shows how the beam would tend to shear at point A. The only load to the left of A is the left-hand (l.h.) reaction (acting upwards) of 55 kN and there is therefore a resultant force of 55 kN tending to shear the portion of beam to the left of A upwards as shown. Note that the loads to the right of A are 70 kN downwards and reaction 15 kN upwards, so that there is also a resultant of 55 kN tending to shear the portion of beam to the right of A downwards.

This 55 kN upwards to the left, and 55 kN downwards to the right, constitutes the shearing force at the point A.

It follows from the above that **shear force** may be defined as the algebraic sum of the loads to the left or to the right of a point.

Fig. 8.1 Failure caused by loading: (a) shearing; (b) bending

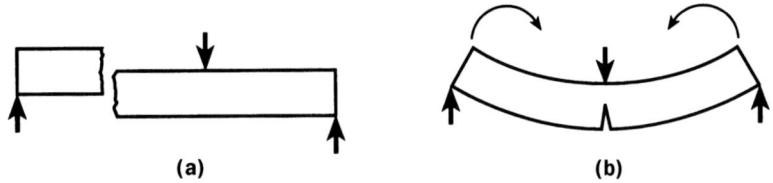

(a)   (b)

This type of shearing force, where the resultant shear is upwards to the left and downwards to the right, may be called **positive** shear.

Consider now the point B as shown in Fig. 8.2(c). The resultant shear to the left is seen to be $55 - 40 = 15$ kN upwards to the left, and $30 - 15 = 15$ kN downwards to the right (again positive shear). At point C in Fig. 8.2(d), the shear to the left is $30 + 40 - 55 = 15$ kN down, and to the right equals the r.h. reaction of 15 kN upwards. This type of shear, down to the left and up to the right, is called **negative** shear.

The above example of shear force ignored the weight of the beam and the only loading consisted of point loads – that is to say the loading was considered to be applied at a definite point along the span. Loads in actual fact are rarely applied in this fashion to structural members, but many loads applied to beams approximate to point loading and in design are considered as concentrated loads. The main beam shown in Fig. 8.3, for example, carries the reaction from one secondary beam and in addition has sitting on its top flange a short steel post; both these loads are applied to such a short length of the beam that they may be considered as point loads.

On the other hand, there are many cases where the loading is applied at a more or less uniform rate to the span of the beam. Such an example is found where a brick wall is carried on the top flange of a beam, or when a reinforced concrete slab sits upon a steel or reinforced concrete beam. Now, shear force has been described as the algebraic summation of loads to the left (or to the right) of a point. Therefore, the shear alters in such cases only where another

Fig. 8.2 Shear force in a beam

Fig. 8.3 Shear forces considered as point loads

point load occurs. When the loading is uniformly distributed, however, as in Fig. 8.4, then the shear force will vary at a uniform rate also and a sudden jump in the value will only occur at the point of application of the one point load. The shear at point A (Fig. 8.4(a)) upwards to the left will be

$$140 \text{ kN up} - 30 \text{ kN down} = +110 \text{ kN}$$

Similarly the shear at point B (Fig. 8.4(b)) upwards to the left is

$$140 \text{ kN up} - 60 \text{ kN down} = 80 \text{ kN (again positive)}$$

The shear just to the left of C (Fig. 8.4(c)) is

$$140 - 90 = 50 \text{ kN positive}$$

while just to the right of C when the 40 kN point load is included it is

$$140 - (90 + 40) = 10 \text{ kN positive}$$

Thus it will be seen that uniform loads cause gradual and uniform change of shear whereas point loads bring about a sudden change in the value of the shear force.

Fig. 8.4 Shear force due to uniform loading

Bending moment   The degree of punishment in bending is measured as bending moment, and the amount of bending tendency is dependent upon the loads and upon the distance between them.

For example, the beam shown in Fig. 8.5(a) tends to split in bending under the 30 kN load because the l.h. reaction of 15 kN acting 1.5 m to the left has a clockwise bending tendency of $15 \times 1.5 = 22.5$ kN m, at the point where splitting of this type would most easily occur in this case.

If the beam had been of 10 m span instead of only 3 m the l.h. reaction (ignoring for a while the self-weight of the beam) would still be only 15 kN, but this time the bending tendency at the point of maximum stress would be $15 \times 5 = 75$ kN m.

Reverting to the beam shown in Fig. 8.5(a), which we have seen has a clockwise bending tendency to the left of point C of 22.5 kN m, there is also an anticlockwise bending tendency to the right of C of $15 \times 1.5 = 22.5$ kN m caused by the action of the r.h. reaction. At *any point* along the span of a simple beam of this type supported at its ends, the bending tendency to the left will always be clockwise, and that to the right anticlockwise but of the same amount. Thus at any point of such a beam the bending will be of the *sagging* type as shown in Fig. 8.1(b), and the fibres towards the lower face of the section will be subjected to tension.

There are types of beams that bend in the opposite way. For example, a cantilever as shown in Fig. 8.5(b) has a *hogging* rather than a sagging tendency and obviously the moments in this type must be anticlockwise to the left and clockwise to the right.

To distinguish between these two types of bending it is normal to describe sagging as positive and hogging as negative.

From the foregoing example, which has been of the very simplest nature, it follows that **bending moment** may be described as the factor which measures the bending effect at any point of a beam's span due to a system of loading. The amount of bending moment is found by taking the moments acting to the left *or* to the right of the point concerned. The beam discussed and shown in Fig. 8.5(a) had only one load acting to the left of the point C at which the bending moment was calculated; where there is more than one load on the portion of beam concerned – as for example in the portion of beam shown in Fig. 8.6(a) – then taking moments to the left of point C, the reaction has a clockwise bending effect and the two downward loads have anticlockwise bending tendency. The net bending moment at C will be the

Fig. 8.5 Bending moments:
(a) sagging of beam; (b) hogging
of beam

22.5 kN m   22.5 kN m
30 kN
15 kN R_L R_R 15 kN
1.5 m |C
Beam fibres
tear at point
of maximum
bending moment
(a)

Beam fibres tear at point of
maximum bending moment
when this moment is greater
than the beam resisting
bending moment
40 kN m   2 m
|C
20 kN
(b)

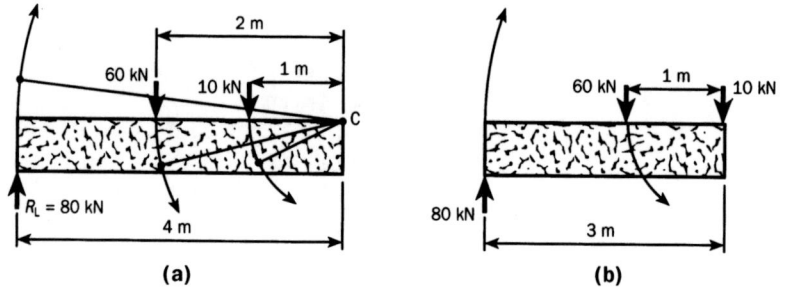

Fig. 8.6 Example of bending moments

difference between these two types of moment, i.e. their algebraic sum. The bending moment at any point is, therefore, defined as the algebraic sum of the moments caused by the forces acting to the left or to the right of that point.

In Fig. 8.6(a), the l.h. reaction exerts a clockwise moment of 80 kN × 4 m = 320 kN m about point C and the downward loads exert moments in an anticlockwise direction equal to 60 kN × 2 m = 120 kN m and 10 kN × 1 m = 10 kN m. Thus the bending moment at C is

$$+80 \times 4 - 60 \times 2 - 10 \times 1 = 320 - 120 - 10 = 190 \text{ kN m}$$

The bending moment at the point of the 10 kN load in the above beam would be

$$80 \times 3 \text{ m} - 60 \text{ kN} \times 1 \text{ m} = 240 - 60 = 180 \text{ kN m}$$

as shown in Fig. 8.6(b). Note that in this case the 10 kN load is ignored, as, passing through the point concerned, it does not exert a moment about that point.

When, on the other hand, a uniformly distributed load is applied to the beam, the punishment caused is less than that exerted by a comparable point load. Therefore, it would be most uneconomical in design to treat such loads as being concentrated at their midpoint.

Where such uniform rate of loading occurs, as in the case of the portion of beam shown in Fig. 8.7 for example, only that portion of loading which lies to the left of the point C (shown shaded) need be considered when the moment at that point to the left is being calculated. The shaded portion of load is 30 kN/m × 4 m = 120 kN, and its resultant lies halfway along its length (2 m from C). Therefore the moment about C of the uniform load is 120 kN × 2 m = 240 kN m and the total bending moment at point C is

$$200 \times 4 - 120 \times 2 = 800 - 240 = 560 \text{ kN m}$$

Fig. 8.7 Bending moments due to uniform loading

<table>
<tr><td>

Shear force and bending moment diagrams

</td><td>

Shear force and bending moment have been described in general terms and it will have been seen that the values of both vary at different points along the span.

It is often desirable to show this variation by means of diagrams, which are really graphs, and these diagrams are called shear force diagrams and bending moment diagrams.

The following examples will serve to show how the diagrams of this type may be constructed for simple and more complex cases.

</td></tr>
</table>

Simply supported beam with point load

Figure 8.8(a)(i) shows a simply supported beam of span l carrying one point load of W kN at the centre of the span. Since the loading is symmetrical the reactions must be equal to each other, and each reaction will be $\frac{1}{2}W$ kN. Ignoring the self-weight of the beam, at any point C at x m from the left-hand reaction, the shear force to the left will be simply the value of the l.h. reaction, i.e. $\frac{1}{2}W$ kN upwards to the left, and wherever point C lies between the l.h. end and the load, the shear will still be $\frac{1}{2}W$ kN.

Similarly at any point to the right of the load as at point D, the shear to the left of D is $\frac{1}{2}W$ kN downwards and $\frac{1}{2}W$ kN upwards, which is equal to $\frac{1}{2}W$ kN down to the left or $\frac{1}{2}W$ kN up to the right (negative shear). These variations of the shear values are shown to scale on the **shear force diagram (SFD)** (Fig. 8.8(a)(ii)). The vertical ordinate of the diagram at any point along the span shows the shear force at that point, and the diagram is drawn to two scales: a vertical scale of 1 mm = a suitable number of kilonewtons, and a horizontal scale of 1 mm = a suitable number of metres, being the same scale as that used in showing the span of the beam.

Fig. 8.8 Shear force and bending moments: (a)(i) beam with a single central load point, (ii) shear force diagram (SFD), (iii) bending moment diagram (BMD); (b)(i) beam with a single non-central load point, (ii) SFD, (iii) BMD

Figure 8.8(a)(iii) shows the variation of bending moment and constitutes a **bending moment diagram (BMD)**.

Obviously the moment at each end is zero, and at any point C at x m from the l.h. end the bending moment (summation of moments to the left) is simply $\frac{1}{2}W \times x = \frac{1}{2}Wx$ kN m. This moment increases as x increases, and will reach a maximum amount of $\frac{1}{2}W \times \frac{1}{2}l = \frac{1}{4}Wl$ at the centre of span as shown.

Again the diagram is drawn horizontally to the same scale as the span of the beam, but this time vertically to a scale of 1 mm = a suitable number of kN m or Nm m, and the vertical ordinate at any point along the span represents the bending moment at that point.

Comparing the two diagrams, it will be seen that the bending moment everywhere on the span is positive, and that the shear force changes its type from positive to negative at the point along the span where the bending moment reaches its maximum amount.

Figure 8.8(b)(i) shows a simply supported beam loaded with one single non-central point load, at distance a from one end and at b from the other.

Taking moments about the l.h. end,

$$\text{r.h. reaction} \times l = W \times a$$

$$\text{r.h. reaction} = Wa/l$$

Similarly, taking moments about the r.h. end,

$$\text{l.h. reaction} \times l = W \times b$$

$$\text{l.h. reaction} = Wb/l$$

At any point between the l.h. end and the point load,

$$\text{shear to the left} = \text{l.h. reaction} = Wb/l \text{ (positive)}$$

Similarly, at any point between the load and the r.h. end,

$$\text{shear to the right} = \text{r.h. reaction of } Wb/l$$
$$\text{(up to the right, thus negative shear)}$$

Thus the shear changes sign from positive to negative at the point load as in the previous example, and the SFD is as shown in Fig. 8.8(b)(ii).

As before, the bending moment is zero at the l.h. end, and at any point between that end and the load is equal to

$$R_L \times x = (Wb/l) \times x = Wbx/l$$

This reaches a maximum value of Wab/l at the point load (where $x = a$).

Also, at any point between the load and the r.h. end, at a distance of y from the r.h. reaction,

$$\text{bending moment} = \text{r.h. reaction} \times y = Way/l$$

and this also reaches a maximum at the point load (where $y = b$) of Wab/l.

The full bending moment diagram (Fig. 8.8(b)(iii)) is thus a triangle with a maximum vertical height of Wab/l at the load, and the bending moment at any point along the span may thus be scaled from the diagram to the same scale as was used in setting up the maximum ordinate of Wab/l.

Simply supported beam with uniformly distributed load

The next case will deal with a simply supported beam of span l carrying a uniformly distributed load of intensity w kN/metre run (Fig. 8.9(a)). The span consists of l m of load, and thus the total load is wl kN, and, as the beam is symmetrical, each reaction will be half of the total load:

$$R_L = R_R = \tfrac{1}{2}wl \text{ kN}$$

The shear (up to the left) at a point just in the span and very very near to R_L is quite obviously simply the l.h. reaction of $\frac{1}{2}wl$.

When the point concerned is, say, 1 m from R_L, however, the shear to the left (summation of loads to the left of the point) is then

$$\tfrac{1}{2}wl \text{ upwards} + 1 \text{ m of load } w \text{ downwards}$$
$$= \tfrac{1}{2}wl - w$$

Similarly when the point concerned is 2 m from R_L, the shear up to the left is

$$\tfrac{1}{2}wl \text{ upwards} - 2w \text{ (2m of load) downwards}$$
$$= \tfrac{1}{2}wl - 2w$$

Fig. 8.9 Simply supported beam carrying a uniform load: (a) load diagram; (b) SFD; (c) BMD

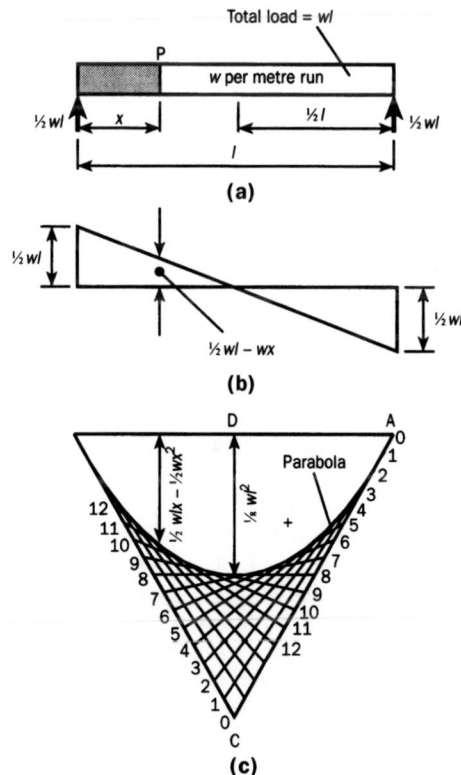

Putting this in general terms, the shear at any point P on the span at distance x from R_L is

$$\tfrac{1}{2}wl - x \text{ metres of uniform load} = \tfrac{1}{2}wl - wx$$

This will give a positive result wherever x is less than $\tfrac{1}{2}l$, and a negative result where x exceeds $\tfrac{1}{2}l$, so the shear will 'change sign' where $x = \tfrac{1}{2}l$ (at the point of midspan), and the SFD will be as shown in Fig. 8.9(b).

Referring again to Fig. 8.9(a), the bending moment at the l.h. end is again zero, and at a point 1 m from R_L, the bending moment (summation of moment to the left) is simply the algebraic sum of:

- the clockwise moment of the l.h. reaction ($\tfrac{1}{2}wl \times l$)
- the anticlockwise moment from 1 m of downward load ($w \times l \times \tfrac{1}{2} = \tfrac{1}{2}w$).

Thus, the bending moment $= \tfrac{1}{2}wl - \tfrac{1}{2}w$.

If the bending moment is required at a point P, at x m from R_L, then the bending moment is the algebraic sum again of:

- the clockwise moment of the l.h. reaction ($\tfrac{1}{2}wl \times x$)
- the anticlockwise moment of x m of load ($wx \times \tfrac{1}{2}x$).

Thus, the bending moment $= \tfrac{1}{2}wlx - \tfrac{1}{2}wx^2$.

This bending moment will be positive for any value of x, and will reach a maximum value of

$$\tfrac{1}{2}(wl \times \tfrac{1}{2}l) - \tfrac{1}{2}w(\tfrac{1}{2}l)^2 = \tfrac{1}{4}wl^2 - \tfrac{1}{8}wl^2 = \tfrac{1}{8}wl^2$$

It should be most carefully noted that the maximum bending moment (M_{max}) is $\tfrac{1}{8}wl^2$, where w is the amount of uniform load per metre.

Sometimes it is more convenient to think in terms of the *total load W* (i.e. capital W), and in this case $W = wl$, and M_{max} in terms of the total load will then be

$$\tfrac{1}{8}wl \times l = \tfrac{1}{8}Wl$$

If the values of this bending moment at points along the span are plotted as a graph, the resulting BMD will be a parabola with a maximum ordinate of $\tfrac{1}{8}wl^2$ or $\tfrac{1}{8}Wl$ as shown in Fig. 8.9(c). Where the diagram has to be drawn, it will be necessary only to draw a parabola having a central height of $\tfrac{1}{8}Wl$, and any other ordinates at points away from the centre may be scaled or calcu‐lated as required.

Shear force diagrams

It is advisable, at this stage, to study the shear force diagrams already drawn carefully and to note that these diagrams are drawn on a horizontal base. The upward loads (reactions) are projected upwards on this base, and at the point loads, the SFD drops vertically by the amount of the point load.

Where a uniform load occurs, however, the SFD slopes down at a uni‐form rate, dropping for each metre of span an amount equal to the amount of uniform load per metre as shown in Fig. 8.10. It should be observed that in every case, the value of the bending moment has been a maximum at the point where the shear force changes its sign (generally referred to as the point of zero shear).

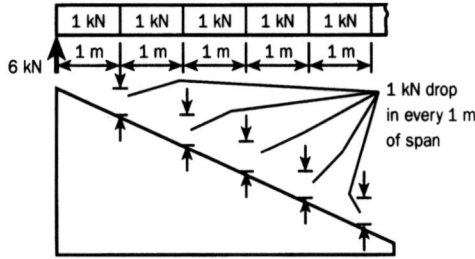

Fig. 8.10 Slope of SFD due to
uniform loading

Bearing this in mind, it is common practice to draw the shear force diagram simply to discover where the maximum bending moment occurs. This is quite unnecessary, as will be seen from consideration of the two cases shown in Fig. 8.11.

In Fig. 8.11(a), the l.h. reaction is 130 kN, and the shear force will change sign at the point of M_{max} where the downward loads starting from the l.h. end just equal 130 kN.

From A to C, the downward uniform load is 2 m at 15 kN/m = 30 kN. Then at the point load there is a further drop of 70 kN, making a drop in the shear diagram from A to C of 100 kN.

Hence, if D is the point of M_{max} (zero shear) then the portion of load shown shaded must equal $130 - 100 = 30$ kN, so that the downward loads up to D equal the l.h. reaction.

Thus, if the distance from C to D is x, then x m at 15 kN/m must equal 30 kN so $15x = 30$, i.e. $x = 2$ m and the maximum bending moment occurs at $2 + 2 = 4$ m from R_L.

Similarly in the case shown in Fig. 8.11(b) the load from the l.h. end up to and including the 70 kN point load is $2 \times 15 + 70 = 100$ kN.

Therefore, a further $145 - 100 = 45$ kN of load is required beyond C to D, the point of maximum bending moment. Therefore

$$15 \times x = 45 \text{ kN}$$

$$x = \frac{45}{15} = 3 \text{ m}$$

and M_{max} occurs at point D which is $2 + 3 = 5$ m from the l.h. end.

Fig. 8.11 SFDs for beams
carrying uniform loads

(a)   (b)

It will be seen that where the loading is uniform, the position of the maximum bending moment (M_{max}) occurs at a point on the span such that the sum of the downward loads from the l.h. end exactly equals the l.h. reaction.

Similarly, the downward loads taken from the r.h. end will equal the r.h. reaction at this point.

Uniformly distributed and point loads

When the loading includes point loading, however, as it does in the example shown in Fig. 8.12, it may well be that the point at which the bending moment is a maximum coincides with the position of a point load – and in the beam illustrated in Fig. 8.12 the maximum value occurs at the 40 kN load.

Summing up the loads (starting from the l.h. end) it will be seen that just to the left of the 40 kN load they are $30 \times 1.7 + 10 = 61$ kN, that is just less than R_1.

Immediately to the right of the 40 kN load they add up to $30 \times 1.7 + 10 + 40 = 101$ kN which is more than R_1.

The rule for finding the position of the **maximum bending moment** may therefore be stated as follows: add the downward loads together, starting from one reaction to the point where they equal (or suddenly become greater than) that reaction. This is the point of zero shear, and the point of maximum bending moment.

Cantilever

A beam which is supported at one end only by being firmly built into a wall, or which is held horizontally at one end only by other means, is called a **cantilever**. Figure 8.13(a)(i) shows such a cantilever AB having a length of *l* m and loaded with one point load of *W* kN at the free end B.

The only downward load is *W* kN, so for equilibrium the l.h. upward reaction will also be *W* kN, but in addition, to prevent the beam from rotating, the wall or other form of restraint at the fixed end A must exert a moment of *Wl* in an anticlockwise direction.

Fig. 8.12 SFD for a beam carrying uniform and point loads

Fig. 8.13 SFDs and BMDs for cantilever beams: (a)(i) point load, (ii) SFD, (iii) BMD; (b)(i) uniformly distributed load, (ii) SFD, (iii) BMD

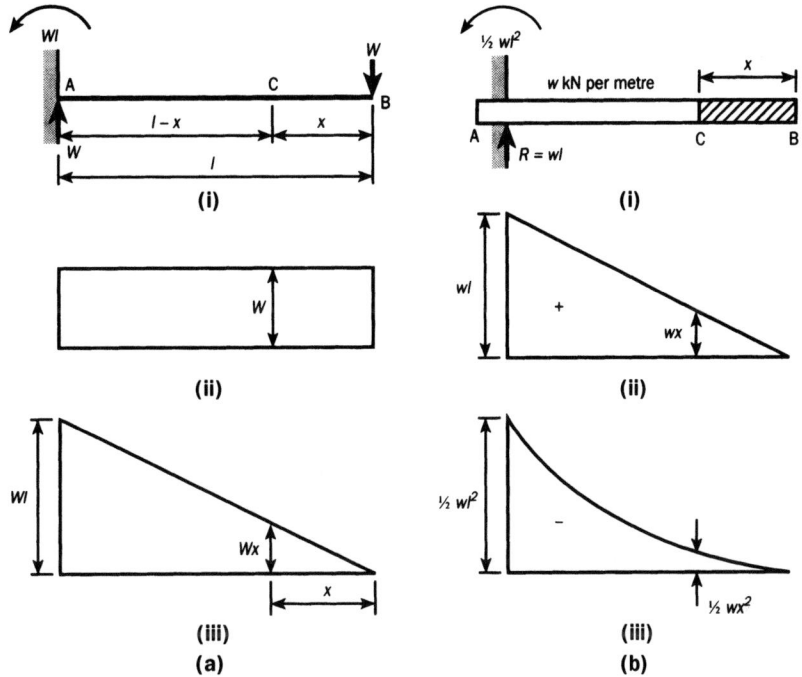

The shear at any point C between A and B (sum of the loads to the left or to the right of C) will be W kN down to the right, or W kN up to the left. This is positive shear, and the value remains the same at all points along the span, so that the SFD is a rectangle as shown in Fig. 8.13(a)(ii).

The bending moment (taken as the sum of moments to the right) at any point C, distance x m from the free end B, will be the downward load of W multiplied by x m.

Thus the bending moment at any point is Wx kN m. This is a negative or hogging bending moment and its value varies directly as the value of x varies, so that the BMD will be a triangle as shown in Fig. 8.13(a)(iii).

The maximum value will occur at the fixed end when $x = l$, and its amount is Wl kN m.

Note: The previous rule (page 153) for finding the position of M_{max} will not apply to cantilevers. In the case of cantilevers M_{max} will always occur at the fixed end.

Cantilever with uniformly distributed load

Figure 8.13(b)(i) shows a cantilever with a uniformly distributed load of w kN/m. The total load will be $w \times l = wl$ kN and the upward reaction at A will also be wl kN.

The moment of the downward load wl about the support A is

$$wl \times \tfrac{1}{2}l = \tfrac{1}{2}wl^2 \text{ kN m}$$

Thus the wall (or other form of restraint) at A must exert an anticlockwise moment of $\tfrac{1}{2}wl^2$ on the beam to prevent its rotating under the couple formed by the upward reaction and the resultant of the downward load.

The shear at any point C at distance x from the free end will be the portion of load to the right of C which is x m at w kN/m $= wx$ kN (positive shear). This varies at the same rate as x varies, and so the shear force diagram will be a triangle having a maximum value at the reaction (where $x = l$) of wl kN, as shown in Fig. 8.13(b)(ii).

Similarly the bending moment at C will be the moment (clockwise) of the portion of load to the right of C, which is $(wx) \times \frac{1}{2}x = \frac{1}{2}wx^2$ kN m (negative or sagging moment).

This again reaches a maximum value of $\frac{1}{2}wl^2$ kN m at the fixed end A where $x = l$ and the rate of increase will be found to form a parabola as shown in the BMD in Fig. 8.13(b)(iii).

Note: If the total load W is used instead of the value of the load per metre run, w, then $W = wl$, and the maximum bending moment will be $\frac{1}{2}Wl$ kN m.

Draw the SFD and BMD for the cantilever shown in Fig. 8.14(a) indicating all important values.

Reaction
There is only one reaction, R_L at A:

$$R_L = 30 + 20 + 10 = 60 \text{ kN}$$

Shear force
At any point between A and C, the shear downwards to the right is the sum of the three downward loads, which is 60 kN positive.

Similarly between C and D the shear is the sum of the two loads to the right, which is 30 kN positive. Between D and the free end B the shear is the single load of 10 kN positive.

This is shown in the SFD constructed in Fig. 8.14(b).

Fig. 8.14 Example 8.1: (a) load diagram; (b) SFD; (c) BMD

Bending moment

The BMD is most easily drawn by treating the three loads separately: the 10 kN load produces a bending moment of $10 \times 4 = 40$ kN m at A and the BMD for this load alone is the triangle 1 shown in Fig. 8.20(c).

The 20 kN load causes a bending moment at A of $20 \times 3 = 60$ kN m and the BMD for this load alone is the triangle 2.

Finally, the 30 kN load causes a $30 \times 1 = 30$ kN m bending moment at A and the BMD for this load is the triangle 3.

As in fact all three loads are on the beam at the same time, then the final BMD is the sum of the three triangles 1, 2 and 3 as shown in Fig. 8.14(c).

Example 8.2

Draw the SFD and BMD for the beam loaded as shown in Fig. 8.15(a)(i) indicating all important values.

Solution

Reactions

Taking moments about A:

$$R_R \times 4 = 20 \times 4 \times \tfrac{1}{2} \times 4 + 40 \times 0.8 + 30 \times 16 + 20 \times 32$$

$$= 160 + 32 + 48 + 64 = 304$$

$$R_R = 76 \text{ kN}$$

and

$$R_L = 80 + 40 + 30 + 20 - 76 = 94 \text{ kN}$$

Shear force

Note: It should be obvious by now that SFDs represent all point loads as vertical lines – upward in the case of reactions, and downward in the case of downward loads.

Downward uniform loads are shown as sloping lines (gradual change in the value of the shear force) and therefore the SFD may be plotted quickly from a horizontal base by merely plotting the loads in this way as they occur.

The horizontal base is shown as line A1–B1 in Fig. 8.15(a)(ii). The procedure is as follows:

1 Draw up from A1 the vertical reaction R_L of 94 kN (A1–F).
2 Draw the gradual change of (20×0.8) kN between A and C as the sloping line F–G.
3 Draw G–H of 40 kN vertically downwards to represent the sudden change of shear at the 40 kN load at point C.
4 Draw the gradual change of 16 kN between C and D as the sloping line H–J.
5 Draw J–K of 30 kN vertically downwards to represent the sudden change of shear at the 30 kN load at point D.
6 Draw the gradual change of (20×1.6) kN between D and E as the sloping line K–L.
7 Draw L–M of 20 kN vertically downwards to represent the sudden change of shear at the 20 kN point load at E.
8 Draw the gradual change of 16 kN between E and B as the sloping line M–P.
9 Finally draw the vertical right hand reaction of 76 kN upward from P to join the horizontal base at B1.

Figure 8.15(a)(ii) shows the construction of this SFD, and the final diagram with its important values is shown in Fig. 8.15(a)(iii).

Bending moment

The bending moment at any point or the maximum bending moment may be calculated in the usual way by taking moments to the left or to the right of that point. But if the final BMD is required (as it is in this example) then it may be drawn by constructing separately:

- the BMD for the uniformly distributed load (above baseline – Fig. 8.15(b)(i)
- the BMD for the point loads (below baseline – Fig. 8.15(b)(ii).

Fig. 8.15 Example 8.2: (a)(i) shear force load diagram, (ii) construction of SFD, (iii) final SFD; (b)(i) BMD for uniformly distributed loads, (ii) BMD for point loads, (iii) addition of BMDs, (iv) final BMD

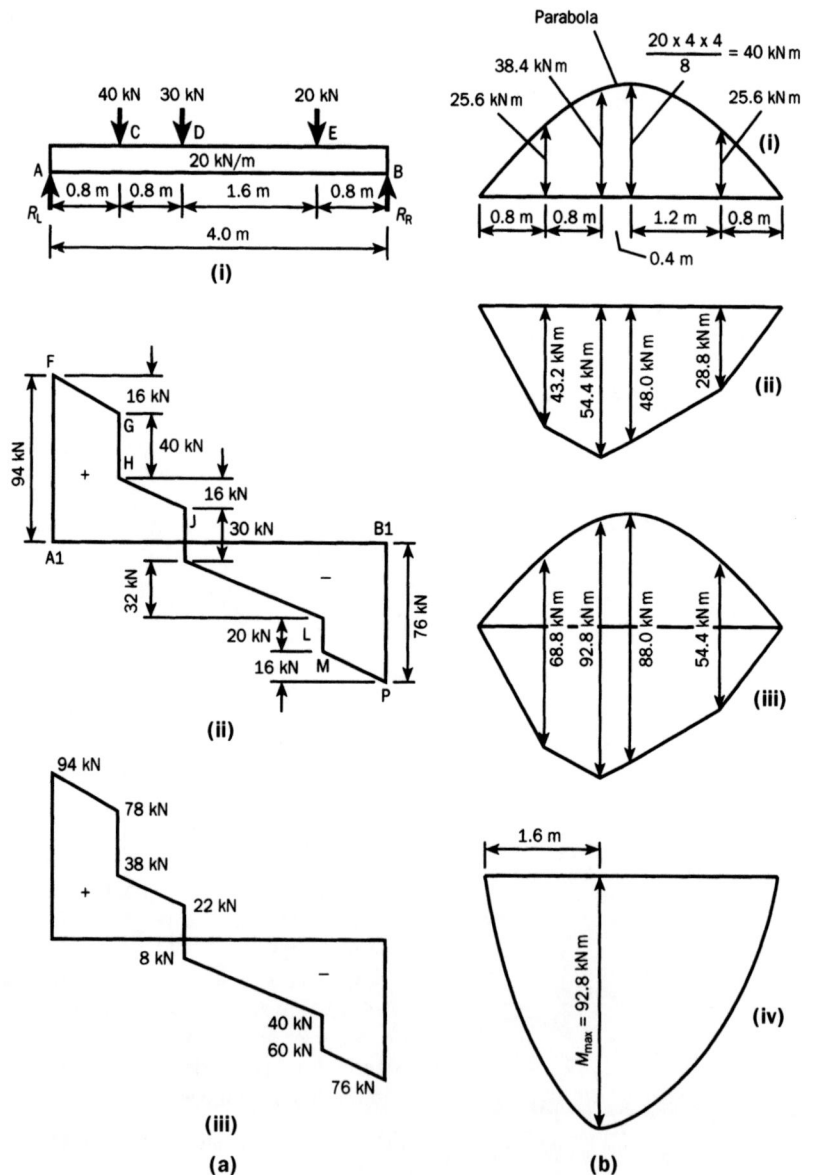

Then, by adding the calculated ordinates (Fig. 8.15(b)(iii)), the final BMD may be drawn, as shown in Fig. 8.15(b)(iv).

The value of the bending moment at any point may also be obtained by computing the area of the SFD to the left or to the right of that point.

Consider the bending moment at the centre of the span. The positive shear force area is

$$\tfrac{1}{2}(94 + 78) \times 0.8 + \tfrac{1}{2}(38 + 22) \times 0.8$$

$$= 68.8 + 24.0 = 92.8 \text{ kN m}$$

To obtain the negative shear force area, it is necessary to determine the value of the shear force at the centre of the span which is 0.4 m to the right of the 30 kN point load.

So, the shear force at the centre of span is

$$8 + 20 \times 0.4 = 16 \text{ kN}$$

Hence the negative shear force area to the left of the centre of the span is

$$\tfrac{1}{2}(8 + 16) \times 0.4 = 4.8 \text{ kN m}$$

Thus the bending moment at the centre of the span is

$$92.8 - 4.8 = 88.0 \text{ kN m}$$

Example 8.3

Draw the SFD for the beam shown in Fig. 8.16, and calculate the value of M_{max}. Determine also the bending moment at a point C at 2 m from the l.h. reaction.

Solution

Taking moments about A to determine reactions:

$$R_R \times 9 = 30 \times 9 \times (\tfrac{1}{2} \times 9) + 60 \times 6 \times (\tfrac{1}{2} \times 6)$$

$$= 1215 + 1080 = 2295 \text{ kN}$$

$$R_R = 255 \text{ kN}$$

and

$$R_L = 60 \times 6 + 30 \times 9 - 255 = 375 \text{ kN}$$

Fig. 8.16 Example 8.3: (a) load diagram; (b) SFD

M_{max} will occur at x m from A where

$$x \text{ m} \times (60 \times 30) \text{ kN/m} = R_L = 375 \text{ kN}$$

$$x = \frac{375}{60 + 30} = 4.167 \text{ m}$$

The value of M_{max} will, therefore, be

$$M_{max} = 375 \times 4.167 - ((60 + 30) \times 4.167) \times (\tfrac{1}{2} \times 4.167)$$

$$= 1562.50 - 781.25 = 781.25 \text{ kN m}$$

or by computing the areas of the SFD

$$M_{max} = 375 \times (\tfrac{1}{2} \times 4.167) = 781.25 \text{ kN m (as before)}$$

Bending moment at C, 2 m from R_L, is

$$375 \times 2 - (30 + 60) \times 2 \times (\tfrac{1}{2} \times 2) = 570 \text{ kN m}$$

If a BMD is required, bending moment values may be calculated at several points of the span and these values drawn to scale vertically from a horizontal line representing the span of the beam. The BMD is obtained by joining the tops of these lines.

Example 8.4

Draw the SFD for the loaded beam shown in Fig. 8.17, and determine the position and amount of the maximum bending moment (M_{max}).

Solution

Taking moments about A to determine reactions:

$$R_R \times 12 = 36 \times 3 \times 1.5 + 18 \times 12 \times 6 + 12 \times 3 \times 10.5$$

$$= 162 + 1296 + 378 = 1836$$

$$R_R = 153 \text{ kN}$$

Fig. 8.17 Example 8.4: (a) load diagram; (b) SFD

and

$$R_L = 36 \times 3 + 18 \times 12 + 12 \times 3 - 153$$
$$= 108 + 216 + 36 - 153$$
$$= 207 \text{ kN}$$

Position of M_{max}
At point C, 3 m from l.h. end, downward load from l.h. end is

$$(36 + 18) \times 3 = 162 \text{ kN}$$

M_{max} will occur where this has increased to 207 kN. Thus the M_{max} will occur at point D where the amount of load between C and D (shown shaded) is

$$207 - 162 = 45 \text{ kN}$$

Thus

$$\text{distance } v \times 18 \text{ kN/m} = 45 \text{ kN}$$
$$v = 45/18 = 2.5 \text{ m}$$

Therefore M_{max} occurs at D at $(3.0 + 2.5) = 5.5$ m from the l.h. end

$$M_{max} = 207 \times 55 - 162 \times (2.5 - (\tfrac{1}{2} \times 3.0))$$
$$- 18 \times 2.5 \times \tfrac{1}{2} \times 2.5$$
$$= 1138.5 - 648 - 56.25$$
$$= 434.25 \text{ kN m}$$

Check by shear force areas:

$$M_{max} = \tfrac{1}{2}(207 + 45) \times 3 + 45 \times \tfrac{1}{2} \times 2.5$$
$$= 378 + 56.25$$
$$= 434.25 \text{ kN m}$$

Example 8.5

Draw the SFD and BMD for the beam shown in Fig. 8.18(a), and determine the position and amount of the maximum bending moment.

Solution

Taking moments about A:

$$R_R \times 1.8 = 45 \times 0.6 + 54 \times 1.2 + 18 \times 2.4$$
$$= 27.0 + 64.8 + 43.2$$
$$= 135$$
$$R_R = 75 \text{ kN}$$

and

$$R_L = 45 + 54 + 18 - 75 = 42 \text{ kN}$$

Fig. 8.18 Example 8.5: (a) load diagram; (b) SFD; (c) BMD; (d) deflected shape of beam

(a)

(b)

(c)

(d)

The shear force diagram is as shown in Fig. 8.18(b). The values of bending moments at

$$45 \text{ kN load} = 42 \times 0.6 = 25.2 \text{ kN m} \quad (+)$$

$$54 \text{ kN load} = 42 \times 1.2 - 45 \times 0.6 = 23.4 \text{ kN m} \quad (+)$$

$$\text{r.h. support} = 42 \times 1.8 - 45 \times 1.2 - 59 \times 0.6$$

$$= 10.8 \text{ kN m}$$

The bending moment diagram is as shown in Fig. 8.18(c).

Note that, due to the overhanging of the r.h. end, part of the beam is subjected to negative bending moment.

There are, therefore, two points of zero shear: one at C which marks the point of maximum positive moment, and one at E where the maximum negative moment occurs. The absolute maximum bending moment is thus 25.2 kN m at C, and the shape of the deflected beam is as shown in Fig. 8.18(d).

The point at which the negative bending moment changes to positive (and vice versa) is called the **point of contraflexure**. The value of the bending moment at that point is zero.

Example 8.6

Draw the SFD and BMD for the beam shown in Fig. 8.19(a) and determine the position and amount of the maximum bending moment.

Solution

Since the loading and the beam are symmetrical, the reactions are each equal to $\frac{1}{2}(20 + 70 + 20) = 55$ kN.

$$\text{Bending moment at D} = 55 \times 1.3 - 20 \times 2.3$$
$$= 71.5 - 46.0$$
$$= 25.5 \text{ kN m } (+)$$
$$\text{Bending moment at C} = -20 + 1.0$$
$$= -20.0 \text{ kN m } (-)$$

Fig. 8.19 Example 8.6: (a) load diagram; (b) SFD; (c) BMD; (d) deflected shape of beam

Example 8.7

A beam 4 m long carrying a uniformly distributed load of 60 kN/m cantilevers over both supports as shown in Fig. 8.20(a). Sketch the SFD and BMD and determine the position of the point of contraflexure.

Fig. 8.20 Example 8.7: (a) load diagram; (b) SFD; (c) BMD

(a)

(b)

(c)

The shear force and bending moment diagrams are given in Fig. 8.20(b) and (c). Check that the reactions are 96 kN and 144 kN respectively. The maximum positive bending moment occurs at 1.6 m from the left end of the beam and is

$$M_{max} = \tfrac{1}{2}(66 \times 1.1 - 30 \times 0.5)$$

$$= \tfrac{1}{2}(72.6 - 15.0)$$

$$= 28.8 \text{ kN m}$$

The maximum negative bending moment occurs over the right-hand support and is $60 \times 0.5 = 30$ kN m.

By calculating several other bending moment values the diagram can be constructed as shown in Fig. 8.20(c).

Bending moment at point of contraflexure is

$$96(x - 0.5) - 60 \times x \times \tfrac{1}{2}x = 0$$

$$5x^2 - 16x + 8 = 0$$

$$x = \frac{16 \pm \sqrt{(256 - 160)}}{10}$$

$$x_1 = 0.62 \text{ m}$$

$$x_2 = 2.58 \text{ m}$$

Summary

Shear force At a point in the span of a beam, shear force is defined as the algebraic sum of the loads to the left or to the right of the point.

Bending moment At a point in the span of the beam, bending moment is defined as the algebraic sum of all the moments caused by the loads acting to the left or to the right of that point.

Maximum bending moment (M_{max}) The algebraic sum of the moments of the loads and reaction acting to one side of the point of maximum bending moment.

To determine the position of the maximum bending moment in a beam simply supported at its two ends, add together the downward loads starting from one reaction to the point where they equal (or suddenly become greater than) that reaction. This is the point of zero shear and the point of maximum bending moment.

The maximum bending moment in cantilevers will always occur at the fixed end and equals the sum of the moments of all the loads about the fixed end.

Point of contraflexure This occurs where the bending moments change sign and their value is zero.

Exercises

1–14 Calculate the reactions, determine the position and amount of the maximum bending moment for the beams shown in Figs. 8.Q1 to 8.Q14.

Fig. 8.Q3

Fig. 8.Q1

Fig. 8.Q4

Fig. 8.Q2

Fig. 8.Q5

Fig. 8.Q6

Fig. 8.Q11

Fig. 8.Q7

Fig. 8.Q12

Fig. 8.Q8

Fig. 8.Q13

Fig. 8.Q9

Fig. 8.Q14

Fig. 8.Q10

15 Fig. 8.Q15 shows the shear force diagram for a loaded beam. Sketch the beam, showing the loading conditions, and calculate the maximum positive and negative bending moments.

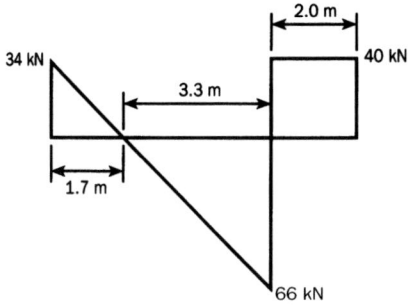

Fig. 8.Q15

19 Referring to Fig. 8.Q19, calculate (a) end reactions; (b) position and amount of M_{max}.

Fig. 8.Q19

16 A steel beam spans 4.8 m and carries on its whole length a brick wall 220 mm thick and 2.7 m high. The brickwork weighs 20 kN/m³ and the self-weight of beam and casing is estimated as being 5.7 kN. What is the maximum bending moment on the beam?

17 A steel beam is as shown in Fig. 8.Q17. The portion between supports A and B carries a uniform load of 30 kN/m and there are point loads at the free ends as shown. What is the length l in metres between A and B if the bending moment at a point C midway between these supports is just zero?

20 Calculate the maximum bending moment in Fig. 8.Q20.

Fig. 8.Q20

21 Determine the position and amount of the maximum shear force and bending moment in Fig. 8.Q21.

Fig. 8.Q17

Fig. 8.Q21

18 For the beam loaded as shown in Fig. 8.Q18, (a) calculate the reactions; (b) determine the position and amount of the maximum positive and maximum negative bending moments.

22 Referring to Fig. 8.Q22, (a) calculate the end reactions; (b) determine the position and amount of the maximum bending moment, M_{max}.

Fig. 8.Q18

Fig. 8.Q22

23 For the cantilever loaded as shown in Fig. 8.Q23, calculate (a) the bending moment at the 40 kN load; (b) the bending moment at the point D; (c) the M_{max}.

Fig. 8.Q23

24 Calculate the maximum bending moment for the cantilever shown in Fig. 8.Q24.

Fig. 8.Q24

25 A steel beam simply supported at its ends carries a load of varying intensity as shown (Fig. 8.Q25). Determine (a) the end reactions R_L and R_R; (b) the M_{max}; (c) the bending moment at point C.

Fig. 8.Q25

26 A steel post cantilevers vertically carrying two point loads as shown in Fig. 8.Q26. Calculate the bending moments at (a) the 35 kN load; (b) the base; (c) 1 m from the base.

Fig. 8.Q26

27 A steel beam loaded as shown in Fig. 8.Q27 has a maximum bending moment (occurring at the point load) of 135 kN m. What is the value W kN of the point load?

Fig. 8.Q27

28 In the beam shown in Fig. 8.Q28, the maximum bending moment occurs at the supports R_L and R_R and the bending moment at the central 20 kN load is zero. What is the length in metres of span l?

Fig. 8.Q28

29 In the beam shown in Fig. 8.Q29, the maximum negative bending moment is twice the amount of the maximum positive bending moment. What is the value in kN of the central load W?

Fig. 8.Q29

30 Derive an expression for the beam as shown in Fig. 8.Q30 for (a) the maximum bending moment; (b) the bending moment at C.

Fig. 8.Q30

This chapter considers the effect of the shape or profile of a beam's section on the beam's resistance to the punishing forces and moments induced by the loading. The beam itself must, of course, be made just strong enough to withstand these punishing effects with a reasonable factor of safety, and the strength of the beam or its degree of resistance to bending moment and shear force is built up in terms of:

- the shape and size of the beam's section
- the strength of the particular material of which the beam is made.

The final degree of 'defence' or resistance will be measured in units which take into account both of these two factors, but for a clearer understanding they will be treated separately to begin with. The present chapter will show how the shape or profile of a beam's section affects its strength.

The properties which various sections have by virtue of their shape alone are:

- cross-sectional area
- position of centre of gravity or area (centroid)
- moment of inertia or the second moment of area
- section modulus or modulus of section
- radius of gyration.

Section modulus and radius of gyration will be considered in Chapters 11 and 14 respectively.

The cross-sectional area should need no description and may be calculated with ease for most structural members.

The centre of gravity or centroid

The **centre of gravity** of a body is a point in or near the body through which the resultant attraction of the earth, i.e. the weight of the body, acts for all positions of the body.

It should be noted, however, that the section of a beam is a plane figure without weight, and therefore the term **centre of area** or **centroid** is more appropriate and is frequently used in this case. The determination of the position of the centre of gravity of a body or centroid of a section is equivalent to determining the resultant of a number of like, parallel forces.

Figure 9.1(a) shows a thin sheet of tinplate with several small holes drilled in it. To one of these holes (hole A) is attached a string. It should be obvious that the position shown for the sheet in Fig. 9.1(a) is an impossible one. The

Fig. 9.1 Determining the centre of gravity of a metal sheet

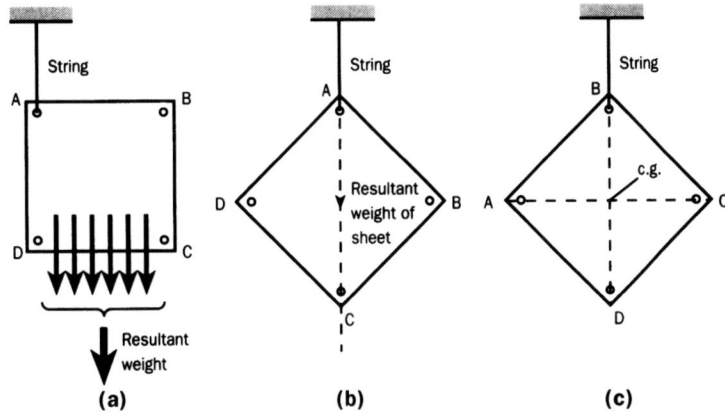

(a)   (b)   (c)

sheet will swing round in a clockwise direction and come to rest as indicated in Fig. 9.1(b). Each particle of the sheet in Fig. 9.1(a) is attracted vertically downwards by the force of gravity and the parallel lines indicate the direction of the gravity forces. The resultant of these parallel forces is the total weight of the sheet. The sheet comes to rest in such a position that the line of the resultant weight and the line of the vertical reaction in the string form one continuous line. When the string is attached to point B the sheet will hang as in Fig. 9.1(c) and the intersection of the two lines AC and BD is called the centre of gravity of the body. The actual position of the centre of gravity is in the middle of the thickness of the metal immediately behind the intersection of the two lines AC and BD. If the thickness is infinitely reduced, as in the case of a beam section, the position of the centre of gravity will coincide with that of the centroid (centre of area).

The position of the centre of gravity of sheets of metal of various shapes can be obtained by the method shown in Fig. 9.2. The sheet is suspended from a pin and from the same pin is suspended a plumb-line. The line of the string forming the plumb-line can be marked on the sheet behind it with pencil or chalk. The sheet can now be suspended in a different position and

Fig. 9.2 Experimental determination of the centre of gravity of an irregular shape: (a) front view; (b) side view

(a)   (b)

Fig. 9.3 The centre of gravity of simple shapes

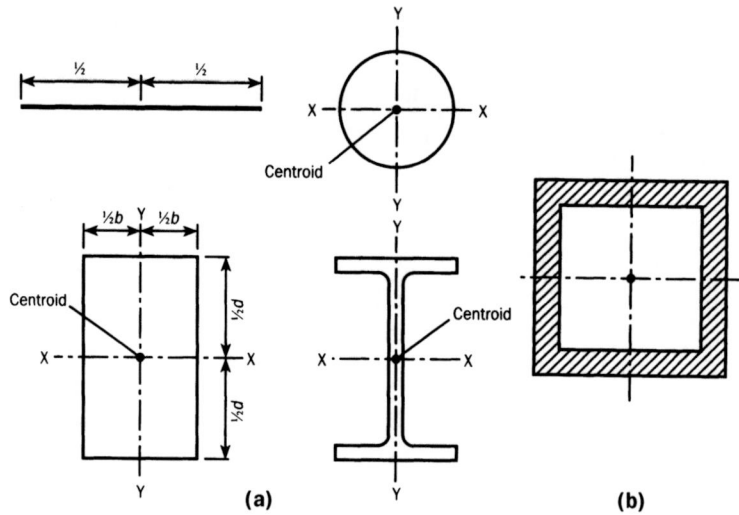

another line marked. The intersection of these two lines gives the position of the centre of gravity of the sheet.

The position of the centre of gravity of certain simple shapes is obvious by inspection (Fig. 9.3(a)), e.g. the centre of gravity of a line or uniform rod is halfway along its length and the centre of gravity of a circle is at its centre.

If it were required to balance any of these shapes in a horizontal position by placing a pencil underneath, the point of application of the pencil would be the centre of gravity of the sheet, and the reaction of the pencil would be equal to the weight of the sheet. Each of the shapes shown in Fig. 9.3 has at least two axes of symmetry and whenever a body has two axes of symmetry the centre of gravity is at the intersection of the axes.

The centre of gravity of a body need not necessarily be in the material of the body (see Fig. 9.3(b)). Note that it is impossible to balance this shape on one point so that the sheet lies in a horizontal plane.

To determine the position of the centre of gravity of a compound body or the centroid of a compound section which can be divided into several parts, such that the centres of gravity and weights of the individual parts are known, the following method applies:

1 Divide the body into its several parts.
2 Determine the area (or volume or weight) of each part.
3 Assume the area (or volume or weight) of each part to act at its centre of gravity.
4 Take moments about a convenient point or axis to determine the centre of gravity of the whole body. The method is identical with that of determining the resultant of a number of forces and is explained in the following example.

Example 9.1

A thin uniform sheet of material weighs w newtons for each mm^2 of its surface (Fig. 9.4). Determine the position of its centre of gravity.

Solution

Since the figure is symmetrical about line AB, its centre of gravity must lie on this line. The figure can be divided into three rectangles.

Fig. 9.4 Example 9.1

$$\text{Area (1)} = 60 \times 150 = 9000 \text{ mm}^2 \qquad \text{Weight} = 9w \text{ kN}$$

$$\text{Area (2)} = 200 \times 20 = 4000 \text{ mm}^2 \qquad \text{Weight} = 4w \text{ kN}$$

$$\text{Area (3)} = 20 \times 100 = \underline{2000 \text{ mm}^2} \qquad \text{Weight} = \underline{2w \text{ kN}}$$

$$\text{Total area} = 15\,000 \text{ mm}^2 \qquad \text{Total weight} = 15w \text{ kN}$$

Let $\bar{x}$ be the distance of the centre of gravity of the whole figure from O. Take moments about this point.

$$15w\bar{x} = 9w \times 30 + 4w \times 160 + 2w \times 270$$

$$= 270w + 640w + 540w$$

$$= 1450w$$

$$\bar{x} = 1450w/15w = 97 \text{ mm}$$

The centre of gravity is therefore on the line AB at 97 mm from O at the extreme left edge of the figure.

Note that the centre of gravity has been determined without knowing the actual weight of the material, and when a body is of uniform density throughout, its weight may be ignored and moments of areas or moments of volumes can be taken. The position of the centroid of a section is of great importance in beam design for, as will be seen later, the portion of section above this centroid performs a different function from that below the centroid.

Example 9.2

Determine the position of the centre of gravity of the body shown in Fig. 9.5(a). The body has a uniform thickness of 100 mm and weighs 10 N/m³.

Solution

Since the body is homogeneous (i.e. of uniform density) and is of uniform thickness throughout, its weight and thickness may be ignored and moments taken of areas.

$$\text{Area (1)} = \tfrac{1}{2}(3.0 \times 1.5) = \quad 2.25 \text{ m}^2$$

$$\text{Area (2)} = 4.0 \times 1.5 \quad = \quad 6.00 \text{ m}^2$$

$$\text{Area (3)} = 1.0 \times 3.0 \quad = \quad \underline{3.00 \text{ m}^2}$$

$$\text{Total area} \qquad\qquad = 11.25 \text{ m}^2$$

In the centre of gravity problems it is usually convenient to choose two axes A–A and B–B at one extreme edge of the figure.

Let $\bar{x}$ be the horizontal distance of the centre of gravity of the whole figure from A–A and $\bar{y}$ be the vertical distance of the centre of gravity from axis B–B. The positions of the centre of gravity of the three separate parts of the figure are shown in Fig. 9.5(a).

Taking moments about axis A–A:

$$11.25\,\bar{x} = 3.00 \times 1.5 + 6.00 \times 2.25 + 2.25 \times 2.5$$

$$= 4.5 + 13.5 + 5.6 = 23.6$$

$$\bar{x} = 23.6/11.25 = 2.1 \text{ m}$$

Taking moments about axis B–B:

$$11.25\,\bar{y} = 3.00 \times 0.5 + 6.00 + 3.0 + 2.25 \times 6.0$$

$$= 1.5 + 18.0 + 13.5 = 33.0$$

$$\bar{y} = 33.0/11.25 = 2.9 \text{ m}$$

Fig. 9.5 Example 9.2

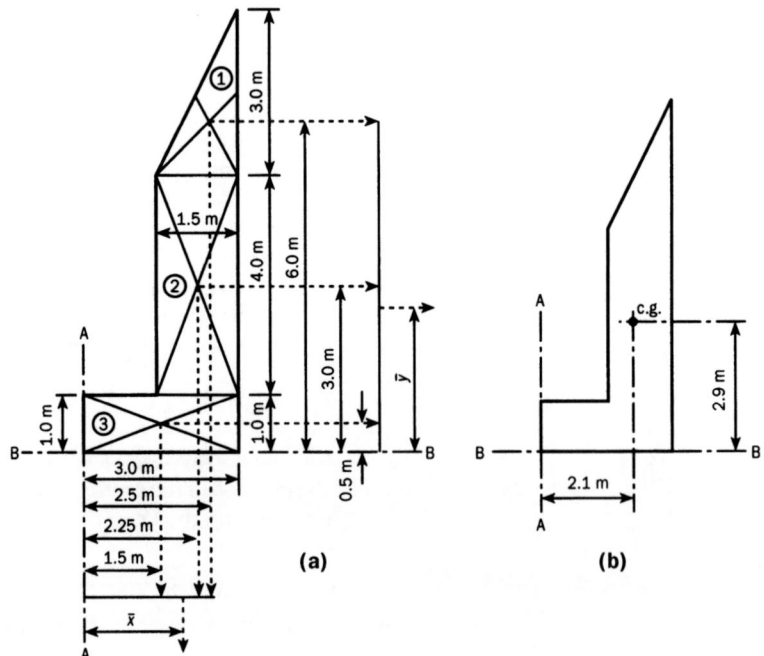

The centre of gravity is in the position indicated by Fig. 9.5(b) and is within the thickness of the body halfway between the front and back faces.

Use of the link polygon

The above problem may also be solved graphically by means of the principle of the link polygon as shown in Fig. 9.6, where the body has to be drawn to scale.

Fig. 9.6 Solving Example 9.2 using the link polygon method: (a) free-body diagram with link polygon; (b) force and polar diagrams (horizontal); (c) force and polar diagrams (vertical)

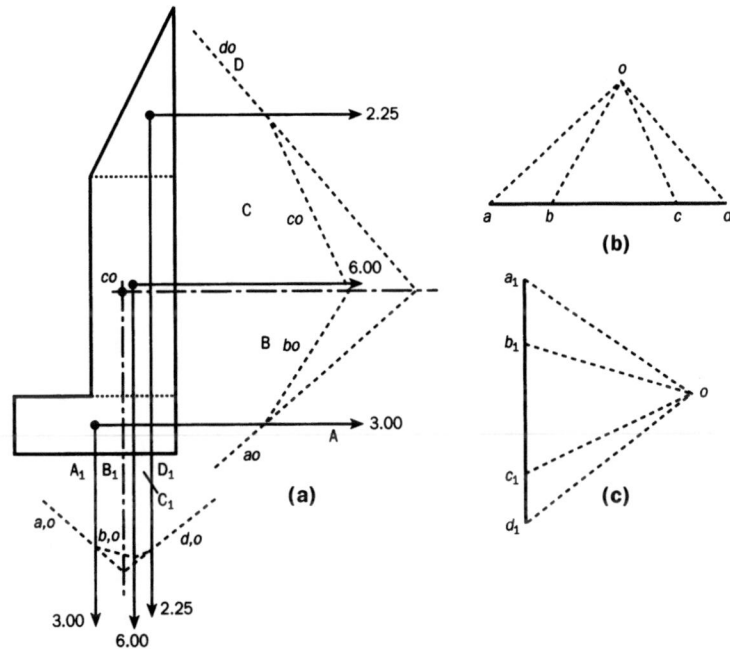

Example 9.3

A compound girder is built up of a 254 × 146 UB37 steel beam (i.e. a universal beam of 254 mm × 146 mm at 37 kg/m) with one 250 mm × 24 mm plate on the top flange only. The area of the steel beam alone is 4720 mm². Determine the position of the centroid of the compound girder (Fig. 9.7).

Solution

- The compound section is symmetrical about the vertical axis Y–Y, so the centroid must lie on this line.
- The addition of a plate to the top flange has the effect of moving the centroid (the X–X axis) towards that plate, and taking moments about line B–B at the lower edge of the section,

$$\text{Total area of section} \times \bar{y} = (\text{area of UB} \times 128 \text{ mm})$$
$$+ (\text{area of plate} \times 268 \text{ mm})$$

$$(4720 + 6000)\bar{y} = 4720 \times 128 + 6000 \times 268$$

Fig. 9.7 Example 9.4

$$10\,720\bar{y} = 604\,160 + 1\,608\,000$$
$$= 2\,212\,160$$
$$\bar{y} = 2\,212\,160/10\,720 = 206 \text{ mm}$$

Moment of inertia

The **moment of inertia** or, more appropriately in the case of a beam section (which, as stated earlier, is a plane figure without weight), the **second moment of area** of a shape, is a property which measures the *efficiency* of that shape in its resistance to bending.

Other factors besides shape enter into the building up of a beam's resistance to bending moment; the material of which a beam is made has a very obvious effect on its strength, but this is allowed for in other ways. The moment of inertia takes no regard of the strength of the material; it measures only the manner in which the geometric properties or shape of a section affect its value as a beam.

A beam such as the one shown in Fig. 9.8 may, in theory, be used with the web vertical or with the web horizontal, and it will offer much more resistance to bending when fixed as in (a) than when as in (b). This is because

Fig. 9.8 The universal beam (UB) section.

(a)

(b)

the moment of inertia about the X–X axis is larger than the moment of inertia about the Y–Y axis.

These axes of symmetry X–X and Y–Y are termed the **principal axes** and they are in fact axes which intersect at the centroid of the section concerned.

It will normally be necessary to calculate the moments of inertia about both these principal axes, and these are usually described as I_{xx} and I_{yy}, the moments of inertia about the X–X and Y–Y axes respectively.

The manner in which the 'build-up' of a shape affects its strength against bending must – to be understood completely – involve the use of calculus, but it may still be made reasonably clear from fairly simple considerations.

The term *moment of inertia* is itself responsible for a certain amount of confusion. Inertia suggests laziness in some ways, whereas in fact the true meaning of inertia may be described as the resistance which a body makes to any forces or moments which attempt to change its shape (or its motion in the case of a moving body). A beam tends to change its shape when loaded, and inertia is the internal resistance with which the beam opposes this change of shape. The moment of inertia is a measure of the resistance which the section can supply in terms of its shape alone.

Good and bad beam shapes

In order to make the best use of the beam material, the 'shape' of the section has to be chosen with care. Certain shapes are better able to resist bending than others, and in general it may be stated that a shape will be more efficient when the greater part of its area is as far away as possible from its centroid.

A universal beam (UB) section (Fig. 9.8(a)), for example, has its flanges (which comprise the greater part of its area) well away from the centroid and the X–X axis, and is in consequence an excellent shape for resisting bending.

Figure 9.9(a) shows a shape built up by riveting together four angles. The bulk of its area (shown shaded) is situated *near to* the centroid, and the section is not a good one from the point of view of resistance to bending about the X–X axis.

If the same four angles are arranged as shown in Fig. 9.9(b), however, then the bulk of the area has been moved away from the X–X axis, and the section – which now resembles roughly a UB form – is a good one, with a high resistance to bending.

Fig. 9.9 Good and bad beam shapes

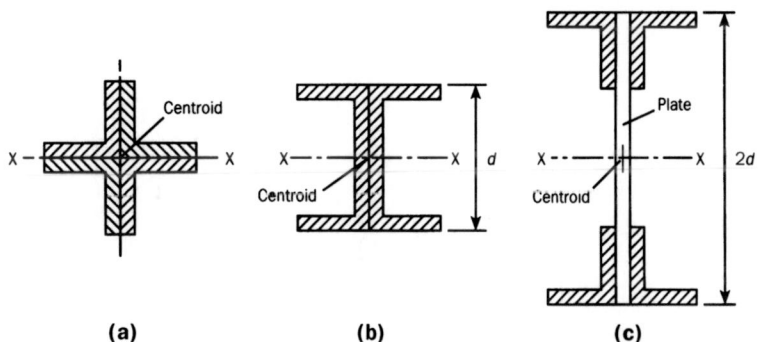

(a)   (b)   (c)

When the same four angles are used with a plate placed between them as in Fig. 9.9(c), the flanges are moved even further from the axis which passes through the centroid and is called the **neutral axis** or the axis of bending, and the efficiency of the shape is much greater. Large deep girders are built up in this way when very heavy loads have to be supported.

When a shape such as that shown in Fig. 9.9(b) is being designed, it will be found that doubling the area of the *flange* will approximately double the flange's efficiency, but doubling the depth d as in Fig. 9.9(c) will increase the efficiency by 4, i.e. 2^2. The efficiency of the flange, then, varies directly as its area and as the square of its distance from the neutral axis.

Calculation of the moment of inertia

In order to measure the increase in efficiency of a section as its area and depth increase, the moment of inertia (second moment of area) is calculated, and this property does in fact measure both the direct increase in area and the square of the increase in depth.

To determine the moment of inertia of the rectangle shown in Fig. 9.10(a), it will be necessary to divide the shape into a number of strips of equal area as shown. The area of each strip will be multiplied by the square of the distance of its centroid from the centroid of the whole section. The sum of all such products, $a \times y^2$, will be the moment of inertia (second moment of area) of the whole shape about the X–X axis, i.e. the total I_{xx} of section.

Fig. 9.10 Calculating the moment of inertia of a rectangle by division into a number of strips

Assume a rectangle to be as shown in Fig. 9.10(b), 180 mm wide and 320 mm in depth, divided into 8 strips each 40 mm deep, each strip having an area of 7200 mm².

The sum of all the products

$$\sum ay^2 = \sum 2 \times a(y_1^2 + y_2^2 + y_3^2 + \cdots)$$

$$= 2 \times 7200(20^2 + 60^2 + 100^2 + 140^2)$$

$$= 14440 \times 33600$$

$$= 483.84 \times 10^6 \text{ mm}^4$$

This is an approximate value of the I_{xx}, or moment of inertia about the X–X axis, but the exact value of this factor will, of course, depend upon the number of strips into which the shape is divided. It can be shown that if b is the width of the rectangle and d is the depth, then the exact value of I_{xx} is given by

$$I_{xx} = \tfrac{1}{12} bd^3$$

In the case above this is

$$\tfrac{1}{12} \times 180 \times 320^3 \quad \text{or} \quad 491.52 \times 10^6 \text{ mm}^4$$

The units of the answer are important, and it should be appreciated that, as an area (mm²) has been multiplied by a distance squared (y^2), the answer is the second moment of area, or more simply the moment of inertia of the shape, and is measured in mm⁴.

For those who have an elementary knowledge of calculus, the foregoing approximate derivation of $\tfrac{1}{12} bd^3$ will appear somewhat lengthy, and the exact value is obtained by integrating as follows.

Consider a small strip of area of breadth b and depth dy at a distance of y from the neutral axis as shown in Fig. 9.10(c). The moment of inertia of this strip (shown shaded) is

$$(\text{its area}) \times (y)^2 = b \times dy \times y^2 = b \times y^2 \times dy$$

The second moment of half of the rectangle is the sum of all such quantities $by^2\, dy$ between the limits of $y = 0$ and $y = \tfrac{1}{2} d$

$$I_{xx} \text{ of half rectangle} = \int_0^{d/2} by^2\, dy = \left[\frac{by^3}{3}\right]_0^{d/2} = \frac{bd^3}{24}$$

Thus,

$$I_{xx} \text{ of the complete rectangle} = \frac{bd^3}{24} \times 2 = \frac{bd^3}{12}$$

Similarly, I_{yy} of the rectangle $= db^3/12$.

The values of the moments of inertia of a number of common shapes are listed below for reference (Fig. 9.11).

Fig. 9.11 Moments of inertia of
common shapes

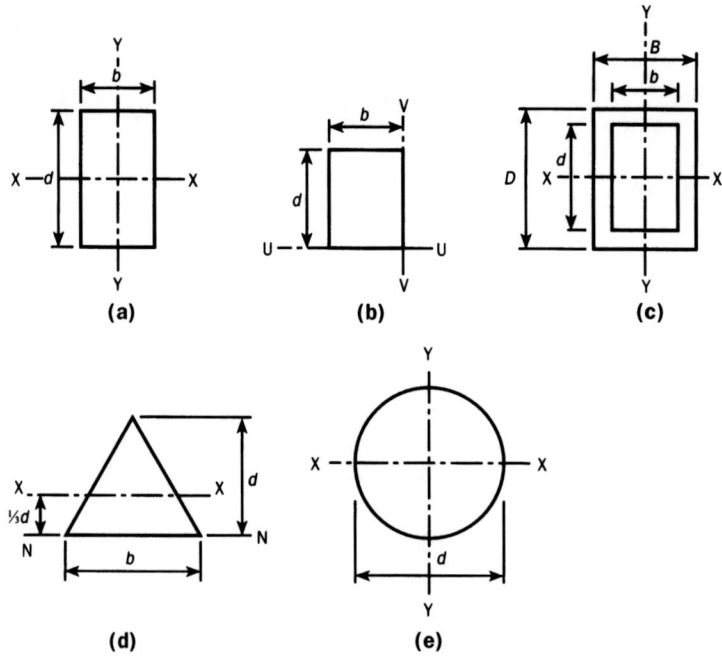

(a)　　　　　　(b)　　　　　　(c)

(d)　　　　　　(e)

Rectangle, about neutral axes (Fig. 9.11(a)):

$$I_{xx} = \tfrac{1}{12}bd^3$$

$$I_{yy} = \tfrac{1}{12}db^3$$

Rectangle, about one edge (Fig. 9.11(b)):

$$I_{uu} = \tfrac{1}{3}bd^3$$

$$I_{vv} = \tfrac{1}{3}db^3$$

Hollow rectangular shape (Fig. 9.11(c)):

$$I_{xx} = \tfrac{1}{12}(BD^3 - bd^3)$$

$$I_{yy} = \tfrac{1}{12}(DB^3 - db^3)$$

Triangle (Fig. 9.11(d)):

$$I_{xx} \text{ about neutral axis} = bd^3/36$$

$$I_{nn} \text{ about base} = bd^3/12$$

Circle (Fig. 9.11(e)):

$$I_{xx} = I_{yy} = \pi d^4/64$$

Principle of parallel axes

Figure 9.12(a) shows a simple rectangular section of size $b \times d$. The I_{xx} of the rectangle is $\frac{1}{12}bd^3$. It will be seen, however, that there are times when the moment of inertia of the rectangle about some other parallel axis such as Z–Z is required, and the I_{zz} will obviously be greater than the I_{xx}, since larger distances are involved in the summation AH^2.

The rule for use in these cases may be stated as follows: To find the moment of inertia of any shape about an axis Z–Z, parallel to the neutral axis (X–X) and at a perpendicular distance of H away from the neutral axis, the amount AH^2 (area of shape $\times$ distance H squared) must be added to I_{xx}.

For example, in the case of the rectangle shown in Fig. 9.12(b),

$$I_{xx} = \tfrac{1}{12}bd^3 = \frac{150 \times 100^3}{12} = 12.5 \times 10^6 \, \text{mm}^4$$

The I_{zz} about the base (where $H = 50$ mm) is

$$I_{zz} = I_{xx} + AH^2 = 12.5 \times 10^6 + 15\,000 \times 50^2$$

$$= (12.5 + 37.5) \times 10^6$$

$$= 50 \times 10^6 \, \text{mm}^4$$

Note: This particular case could have been derived directly from the formula of $\frac{1}{3}bd^3$ given in Fig. 9.11(b).

$\frac{1}{3}bd^3$ in this example is $\frac{1}{3} \times 150 \times 100^3 = 50 \times 10^6$ mm^4

Fig. 9.12 Principle of parallel axes

(a)   (b)

The principle of parallel axes may be used to calculate the values of the moments of inertia of structural sections like the I-beam shown in Fig. 9.13(a).

The web has its centroid on the X–X axis of the beam and the I_{xx} of the web thus equals

$$\tfrac{1}{12} \times 12 \times 400^3 = 64 \times 10^6 \, \text{mm}^4$$

The moment of inertia of one flange about *its own axis* (F–F) is

$$\tfrac{1}{12} \times 200 \times 24^3 = 0.23 \times 10^6 \, \text{mm}^4$$

and from the principle of parallel axes, the I_{xx} of the one flange is

$$I_{xx} = 0.23 \times 10^6 + 200 \times 24 \times 212^2$$

$$= 215.96 \times 10^6 \, \text{mm}^4$$

Fig. 9.13 Example 9.4

(a)   (b)

(c)

The total I_{xx} of the two flanges plus the web is

$$\text{Total } I_{xx} = (64 + 2 \times 216) \times 10^6 \text{ mm}^4$$
$$= 496 \times 10^6 \text{ mm}^4$$

An alternative method of calculating the moment of inertia about X–X is to calculate the I_{xx} of rectangle ABCD and to subtract the I_{xx} of the two rectangles EFGH (Fig. 9.13(b)). Thus

$$\text{Total } I_{xx} = \tfrac{1}{12} \times 200 \times 448^3 - \tfrac{1}{12} \times 2(94 \times 400^3)$$
$$= (1498.59 - 1002.66) \times 10^6$$
$$= 496 \times 10^6 \text{ mm}^4$$

Note: Particular care should be taken in using this method of the subtraction of moments of inertia to see that all the rectangles concerned have axis X–X as their common neutral axis.

The I_{yy} of the above beam section may most easily be calculated by adding the I_{yy} of the three rectangles of which the joist consists, as shown in Fig. 9.13(c), because axis Y–Y is their common neutral axis.

$$I_{yy} = 2 \times (\tfrac{1}{12} \times 24 \times 200^3) + \tfrac{1}{12} \times 400 \times 12^3$$
$$= (32.00 + 0.06) \times 10^6$$
$$= 32.06 \times 10^6 \text{ mm}^4$$

The method shown above is accurate and can be used for steel girders built up by welding together plates of rectangular cross-section. It should be noted, however, that for structural rolled steel sections the moments of inertia can be found tabulated in handbooks. An example of such a table is given on pages 260–3 and the given moments of inertia take into account the root radius, fillets, etc.

Example 9.5

A T-section measures 140 mm $\times$ 140 mm $\times$ 20 mm as shown in Fig. 9.14. Calculate the I_{xx}.

Solution

Taking moments of areas about the base to determine the position of the neutral axis X–X:

$$(2400 + 2800)\bar{x} = 2400 \times 80 + 2800 \times 10$$

$$\bar{x} = \frac{(192 + 28) \times 10^3}{5.2 \times 10^3} = 42.3 \text{ mm}$$

I_{xx} of vertical rectangle:

$$\tfrac{1}{12} \times 20 \times 120^3 + 2400 \times 37.7^2$$

$$= (2.88 + 3.41) \times 10^6$$

$$= 6.29 \times 10^6 \text{ mm}^4$$

I_{xx} of horizontal rectangle:

$$\tfrac{1}{12} \times 140 \times 20^3 + 2800 \times 32.2^2$$

$$= (0.09 + 2.92) \times 10^6$$

$$= 3.01 \times 10^6 \text{ mm}^4$$

Fig. 9.14 Example 9.5

Total I_{xx}:

$$(6.29 + 3.01) \times 10^6 = 9.30 \times 10^6 \, \text{mm}^4$$

Calculate the I_{xx} and I_{yy} of the section shown in Fig. 9.15.

Taking moments of area about the base to find the distance $\bar{x}$ to the neutral axis X–X:

$$9600\bar{x} = 4800 \times 12 + 2400 \times 124 + 2400 \times 236$$
$$= 57\,600 + 297\,600 + 566\,400$$
$$\bar{x} = 921\,600/9600 = 96 \, \text{mm}$$

The figure is divided into three rectangles as shown in Fig. 9.15 and the distances of the centroids of each from the centroid of the whole section are also given.

$$I_{xx}\,(\text{top flange}) = \tfrac{1}{12} \times 100 \times 24^3 + 2400 \times 140^2$$
$$= (0.11 + 47.04) \times 10^6$$
$$= 47.15 \times 10^6 \, \text{mm}^4$$

$$I_{xx}\,(\text{web}) = \tfrac{1}{12} \times 12 \times 200^3 + 2400 \times 28^2$$
$$= (8.00 + 1.88) \times 10^6$$
$$= 9.88 \times 10^6 \, \text{mm}^4$$

Fig. 9.15 Example 9.6

$A_1 = 2400 \, \text{mm}^2$
$A_2 = 2400 \, \text{mm}^2$
$A_3 = 4800 \, \text{mm}^2$
Total $A = 9600 \, \text{mm}^2$

$$I_{xx} \text{ (bottom flange)} = \tfrac{1}{12} \times 200 \times 24^3 + 4800 \times 84^2$$

$$= (0.23 + 53.87) \times 10^6$$

$$= 34.10 \times 10^6 \, \text{mm}^4$$

Total I_{xx} of the whole section

$$= (47.15 + 9.88 + 34.10) \times 10^6$$

$$= 91.13 \times 10^6 \, \text{mm}^4$$

$$\text{Total } I_{yy} = \tfrac{1}{12} \times 24 \times 100^3 + \tfrac{1}{12} \times 24 \times 200^3 + \tfrac{1}{12} \times 200 \times 12^3$$

$$= (2.00 + 16.00 + 0.03) \times 10^6$$

$$= 18.03 \times 10^6 \, \text{mm}^4$$

Example 9.7   Calculate the I_{xx} and I_{yy} of the channel section shown in Fig. 9.16.

Solution   X–X axis:

$$I_{xx} = \tfrac{1}{2} \times 100 \times 300^3 - \tfrac{1}{12} \times 88 \times 252^3$$

$$= (225.00 - 117.36) \times 10^6$$

$$= 107.64 \times 10^6 \, \text{mm}^4$$

Check by addition:

$$I_{xx} = \tfrac{1}{12} \times 12 \times 300^3 + 2 \times (\tfrac{1}{12} \times 88 \times 24^3 + 88 \times 24 \times 138^2)$$

$$= 27 \times 10^6 + 2(0.10 + 40.22) \times 10^6$$

$$= 107.64 \times 10^6 \, \text{mm}^4 \, \text{(as before)}$$

Fig. 9.16 Example 9.7

Y–Y axis:
Taking moments of areas about back of channel:

$$\text{Area} \times \text{distance } \bar{x} = 300 \times 12 \times 6 + 2(24 \times 88 \times 56)$$
$$= 21\,600 + 236\,544$$
$$= 258\,144 \text{ mm}^3$$

$$\text{Distance } \bar{x} = \frac{258\,144}{3600 + 2 \times 2112} = 33 \text{ mm}$$

$$I_{yy} = \tfrac{1}{12} \times 300 \times 12^3 + 3600 \times 27^2$$
$$+ 2(\tfrac{1}{12} \times 24 \times 88^3 + 2112 \times 23^2)$$
$$= (0.04 + 2.63 + 2(1.36 + 1.12)) \times 10^6$$
$$= 7.63 \times 10^6 \text{ mm}^4$$

Check by subtraction:

$$I_{yy} = (\tfrac{1}{12} \times 300 \times 100^3 + 30\,000 \times 17^2)$$
$$- (\tfrac{1}{12} \times 252 \times 88^3 + 22\,176 \times 23^2)$$
$$= (25.00 + 8.67 - 14.31 - 11.73) \times 10^6$$
$$= 7.63 \times 10^6 \text{ mm}^4 \text{ (as before)}$$

Example 9.8 Calculate the I_{xx} and I_{yy} of the compound girder shown in Fig. 9.17. The properties of the UB alone are:

$$\text{Area} = 2800 \text{ mm}^2$$
$$I_{xx} = 28.41 \times 10^6 \text{ mm}^4$$
$$I_{yy} = 1.19 \times 10^6 \text{ mm}^4$$

Fig. 9.17 Example 9.8

Solution   *Note*: The moment of inertia given above for the UB (without the plate) is of course about the X–X axis of the UB.

The addition of a single plate renders the compound section unsymmetrical about the X–X axis of the compound, and the AH^2 of the UB must be added to its own I_{xx}.

Taking moments about the line A–A:

$$\text{Distance } \bar{x} = \frac{2800 \times 145 + 2700 \times 9}{2800 + 2700}$$

$$= 430\,300/5500$$

$$= 78 \text{ mm}$$

$$I_{xx} = 28.41 \times 10^6 + 2800 \times 66^2$$

$$+ \tfrac{1}{12} \times 150 \times 18^3 + 2700 \times 69^2$$

$$= (28.41 + 12.20 + 0.07 + 12.85) \times 10^6$$

$$= 53.53 \times 10^6 \text{ mm}^4$$

$$I_{yy} = 1.19 \times 10^6 + \tfrac{1}{12} \times 18 \times 150^3$$

$$= (1.19 + 5.06) \times 10^6$$

$$= 6.25 \times 10^6 \text{ mm}^4$$

Example 9.9   Calculate the I_{xx} and I_{yy} of the compound girder shown in Fig. 9.18. The properties of the UB alone are:

$$\text{Area} = 2800 \text{ mm}^2$$

$$I_{xx} = 28.41 \times 10^6 \text{ mm}^4$$

$$I_{yy} = 1.19 \times 10^6 \text{ mm}^4$$

Fig. 9.18 Example 9.9

Note: The addition of a 150 mm $\times$ 12 mm plate to each flange does not move the neutral axis of the UB from its original position, so that

$$I_{xx} = 28.41 \times 10^6 + \tfrac{1}{12} \times 150 \times 278^3 - \tfrac{1}{12} \times 150 \times 254^3$$

$$= (28.41 + 268.56 - 204.84) \times 10^6$$

$$= 92.13 \times 10^6 \text{ mm}^4$$

Check I_{xx} by addition of the I_{xx} of plates:

$$I_{xx} = 28.41 \times 10^6 + 2(\tfrac{1}{12} \times 150 \times 12^3 + 150 \times 12 \times 133^2)$$

$$= (28.41 + 2 \times 31.86) \times 10^6$$

$$= 92.13 \times 10^6 \text{ mm}^4 \text{ (as before)}$$

$$I_{yy} = 1.19 \times 10^6 + 2(\tfrac{1}{12} \times 12 \times 150^3)$$

$$= (1.19 + 6.75) \times 10^6$$

$$= 7.94 \times 10^6 \text{ mm}^4$$

Summary

The *centre of gravity* of a body is a point in or near the body through which the resultant weight of the body acts. When dealing with areas, the terms *centroid*, *centre of area* and *neutral axis* are frequently used.

With respect to beam sections, which are plane figures without weight, the *moment of inertia* about an axis is the sum of the *second moments of area* about that axis, i.e.

$$I = \sum ay^2$$

If a section is divided into an infinite number of strips parallel to the axis in question, and the area of each strip is multiplied by the square of its distance from the axis, and then all these quantities are added together, the result is the moment of inertia of the section.

For geometrical shapes, formulae for the moments of inertia can be obtained with the aid of calculus.

The *principle of parallel axes* is used to determine the moment of inertia of any shape about an axis Z–Z parallel to another axis X–X at a perpendicular distance of H; the amount AH^2 (i.e. area of shape multiplied by the square of the distance H) must be added to the moments of inertia about X–X.

Exercises

1 Fig. 9.Q1 shows a system of three weights connected together by rigid bars. Determine the position of the centre of gravity of the system with respect to point A, ignoring the weight of the bars.

Fig. 9.Q1

2 Each of the shapes shown in Fig. 9.Q2(a), (b), (c), (d) is symmetrical about a vertical axis. Calculate the distance of the centre of gravity from the base. (All dimensions are in millimetres.)

Fig. 9.Q2

3 In Fig. 9.Q3(a) to (e) take point P as the intersection of the A–A and B–B axes and calculate the position of the centre of gravity with respect to these axes. ($\bar{x}$ is the distance of the c.g. from the vertical axis A–A and $\bar{y}$ is the distance of the c.g. from the horizontal axis B–B. All dimensions are in millimetres.)

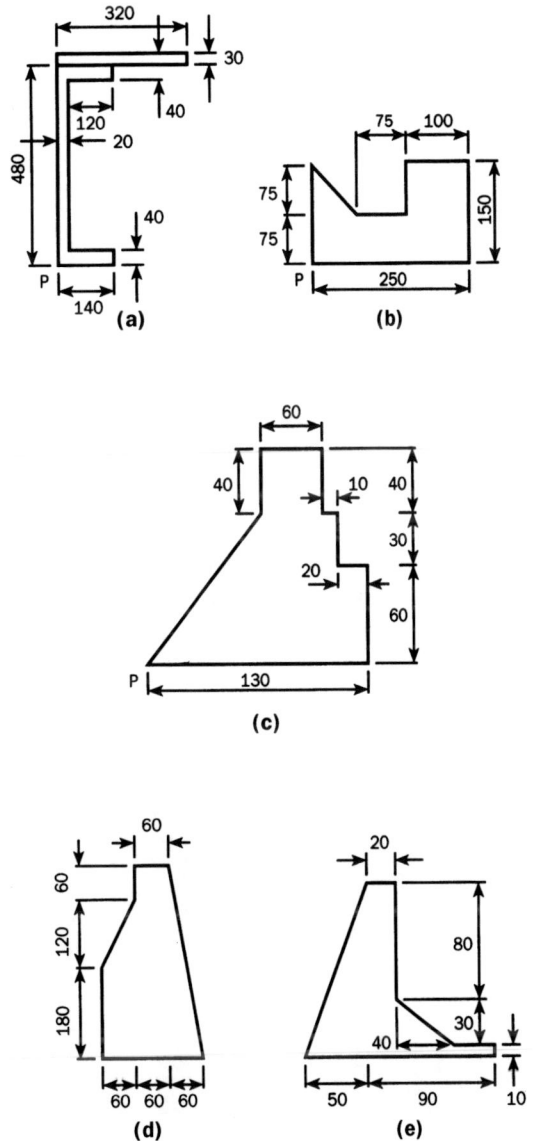

Fig. 9.Q3

4–9 Calculate the I_{xx} and the I_{yy} of the shapes shown in Figs. 9.Q4–9.Q9.

Fig. 9.Q4

Fig. 9.Q6

Fig. 9.Q7

Fig. 9.Q5

Fig. 9.Q8

250 mm x 40 mm plate

533 x 210 UB92
A = 11 700 mm²

I_{xx} of UB alone =
552.30 × 10⁶ mm⁴
I_{yy} of UB alone =
23.89 × 10⁶ mm⁴

Fig. 9.Q9

10 Two steel channels, 229 mm × 76 mm, are to be arranged as shown in Fig. 9.Q10, so that the I_{xx} and the I_{yy} of the compound section are equal.

The properties of one single channel are:

Area $= 3320$ mm²

$I_{xx} = 26.15 \times 10^6$ mm⁴

Distance $b = 20$ mm

$I_{yy} = 15.90 \times 10^6$ mm⁴

(about axis shown dotted)

What should be the distance a?

Fig. 9.Q10

11 The properties of a single 762×267 UB173 are

$$\text{Area} = 22\,000 \text{ mm}^2$$
$$I_{xx} = 2053.0 \times 10^6 \text{ mm}^4$$
$$I_{yy} = 68.5 \times 10^6 \text{ mm}^4$$

Calculate the I_{xx} and I_{yy} of a compound girder which consists of two such beams at 300 mm centres and two 700 mm × 36 mm steel plates attached to the flanges of the beams as shown in Fig. 9.Q11.

300 mm

Fig. 9.Q11

12–14 Determine the position of the centre of area of the shapes shown in Figs. 9.Q12–9.Q14 and calculate the values of their I_{xx}.

108 mm

36 mm

24 mm

300 mm

x mm

150 mm

48 mm

Fig. 9.Q12

Fig. 9.Q13

Fig. 9.Q14

15 A strut is made up by inserting a 178 mm × 24 mm steel plate between two channels as shown in Fig. 9.Q15. The properties of a single 178 mm × 76 mm steel channel are

Fig. 9.Q15

Area = 2660 mm^2

$I_{yy} = 13.38 \times 10^6$ mm^4

$I_{yy} = 1.34 \times 10^6$ mm^4

Calculate the values of I_{xx} and I_{yy} for the strut.

16 Calculate the I_{xx} and I_{yy} of the square section shown in Fig. 9.Q16.

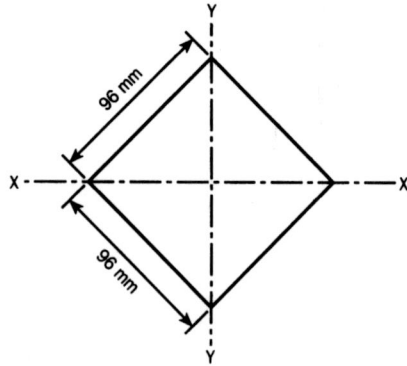

Fig. 9.Q16

17 A special stanchion section is built up using two UBs fixed together as shown in Fig. 9.Q17. The properties of each individual UB are

356 × 171 UB57	254 × 102 UB22
Area 7260 mm^2	2800 mm^2
I_{xx} 160.40 × 10^6 mm^4	28.41 × 10^6 mm^4
I_{yy} 11.08 × 10^6 mm^4	1.19 × 10^6 mm^4

Calculate the dimension x to the centroid of the compound section and the values of I_{xx} and I_{yy}.

Fig. 9.Q17

18 A timber I-beam consists of two 120 mm $\times$ 36 mm flanges and a 48 mm thick web. The overall depth of the beam is 276 mm. Determine its I_{xx} and I_{yy}.

19 A hollow circular section has an external diameter of 200 mm. The I_{xx} of the section is 52.34×10^6 mm^4. What is the thickness of the material?

20 The overall depth of a hollow rectangular section is 300 mm and the thickness of the material is 20 mm throughout. The I_{xx} about the horizontal axis is 184.24×10^6 mm^4. What is the overall width of the section?

21 The I_{xx} of a 352 mm deep UB is 121×10^6 mm^4. The beam has to be increased in strength by the addition of a 220 mm wide plate to each flange so that the total I_{xx} of the compound girder is brought up to 495×10^6 mm^4. What thickness plate will be required? Bolt or rivet holes need not be deducted.

22 The UB mentioned in question 21 ($I_{xx} = 121 \times 10^6$ mm^4) is to be strengthened by the addition of 30 mm thick plate to each flange so that the I_{xx} is increased to 605×10^6 mm^4. What is the required width of the plates? Bolt or rivet holes may be ignored.

23 Calculate the second moment of area about the X–X (horizontal) axis of the crane gantry girder shown in Fig. 9.Q23.

The properties of the individual components are

	610 $\times$ 305 UB238	432 $\times$ 102 [
Area	30 300 mm^2	8340 mm^2
I_{xx}	2095.0×10^6 mm^4	213.7×10^4 mm^4
I_{yy}	158.4×10^6 mm^4	6.27×10^6 mm^4
Web thickness	18.4 mm	12.2 mm

Fig. 9.Q23

Chapter eleven Simple beam design to BS 5950, BS 5268, EC3 and EC5

In the previous two chapters it has been shown that

- When a beam is loaded, the beam has a bending tendency which is measured in newton millimetres (N mm), etc., and is known as the *bending moment* on the beam. There is, for every loaded beam, a certain critical point at which this bending moment has a maximum value (M_{max}).
- The shape of the beam's cross-section has an effect upon its strength and this shape effect is measured in mm⁴ units and is called the *moment of inertia* (second moment of area).
- The material of which the beam is constructed also affects the beam's strength and this factor is measured in terms of the material's *safe allowable stress* (in tension or compression) and is measured in newtons per square millimetre (N/mm²), etc.

The maximum bending moment, M_{max}, depends on the length of the beam and on the nature and disposition of the applied loads.

The factor measuring the strength of the section by virtue of its shape may be varied by the designer so that, when the strength of the material is also taken into account, a beam may be designed of just sufficient strength to take the calculated bending moment.

The bending moment may be thought of as the *punishment factor*.

A suitable combination of the moment of inertia and the safe allowable stress may be described as the beam's *resistance factor* and, indeed, this factor is termed the *moment of resistance* M_r of the beam.

The general theory of bending

It has been seen that, in general, most beams tend to bend in the form shown in Fig. 11.1(a), and if X–X is the neutral axis of such a beam, the fibres above X–X are stressed in compression and those below X–X in tension.

Furthermore, fibres far away from the neutral axis are stressed more heavily than those near to the neutral axis. Fibres lying on the neutral axis are neither in tension nor in compression, and are, in fact, quite unstressed.

The distribution of stress across a plane section such as A–A in Fig. 11.1(a) may thus be seen to vary from zero at the neutral axis to maximum tension and maximum compression at the extreme fibres, as shown in the stress distribution diagram (Fig. 11.1(b)).

The stress varies directly as the distance from the neutral axis, i.e. the stress at C is twice that at B.

It should be appreciated by now that material far from the neutral axis is more useful than material near the neutral axis. This is why the universal beam (UB) is such a popular beam section; the mass of its material (i.e. the

Fig. 11.1 General theory
of bending

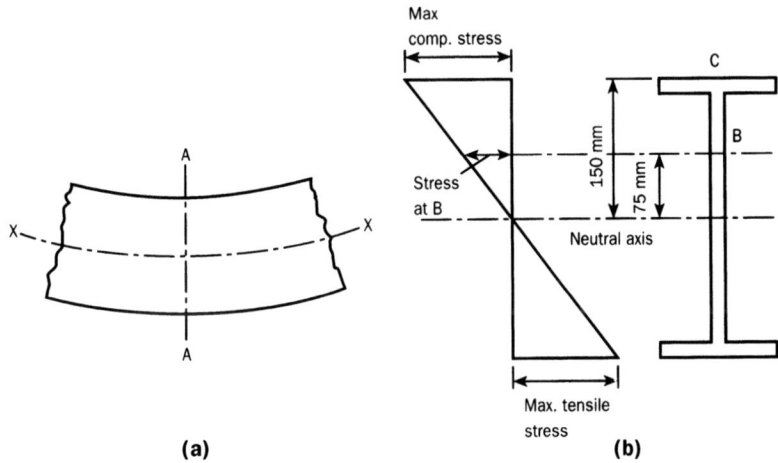

(a)

(b)

two flanges) is positioned as far as possible from the centroid, that is, from
the neutral axis (NA).

A simple analogy will help to show how the compression and tension generated within the beam combine to resist the external bending moment.

Consider, for example, the cantilever shown in Fig. 11.2(a), and let a load
of W kN be suspended from the free end B, the self-weight of the beam being
neglected. If the beam were to be sawn through at section C–C then the portion to the right of the cut would fall, but it could be prevented from falling
by an arrangement as shown in Fig. 11.2(b).

A load of W kN, represented by the weight W, is attached to a wire
which, in turn, passes over a pulley P and is connected to the small portion

Fig. 11.2 Bending of a cantilever:
(a) load diagram; (b) theoretical
representation at section C–C;
(c) representation preventing
rotation

(a)

(b)

(c)

of cantilever. (The weight of the cantilever itself is ignored for the purpose of this discussion.)

However, although this arrangement would prevent the small portion from falling, the portion would still not be in equilibrium, for it would now twist or rotate as shown by the broken lines. This rotation could also be prevented by a small length of chain D–D and a steel block at S–S, as shown in Fig. 11.2(c).

This is because the chain exerts a pull (tension) on the portion of cantilever to the right, and the steel block exerts a push (compression) on the portion.

These forces T and C are equal to each other, and they form an *internal couple* whose moment is equal to and resists the bending moment Wx. This couple provides the moment of resistance of the section which equals $T \times$ lever arm or $C \times$ lever arm. In a real beam these forces T and C are, of course, provided by the actual tension and compression in the many fibres of the cross-section.

Similarly, in a real beam, the force W which prevents the portion from falling is provided by the shear stress generated within the beam itself.

A cantilever has been chosen to illustrate the nature of these internal forces and moments, but the principle remains the same in the case of the simply supported beam, except that the tension will now occur in the layers below the NA and compression in those above the NA.

Figure 11.3(a) shows a short portion of beam (of any shape) before loading, with two plane sections A–B and C–D taken very close together. The layer E–F lies on the neutral axis (NA) and layer G–H is at a distance of y below the NA and has a small cross-sectional area of a.

Fig. 11.3 Bending of a simple beam: (a) cross-section and longitudinal section; (b) the beam after bending

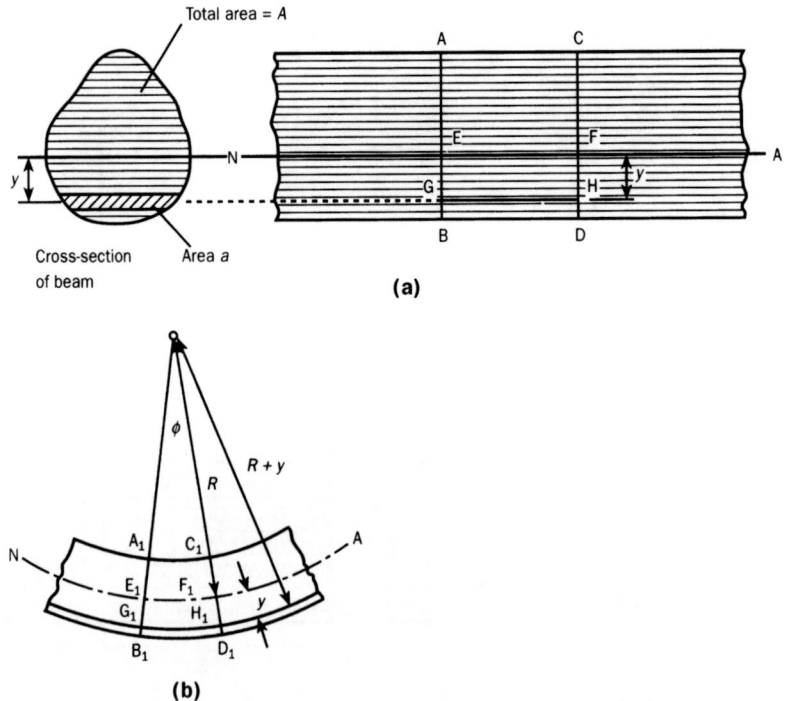

Figure 11.3(b) shows the same length of beam after bending. The sections A–B and C–D remain straight but are rotated to the positions shown, A_1–B_1 and C_1–D_1. The small portion has bent through an angle of ϕ radians, at a radius of curvature (measured to the NA) of R.

The fibre AC has decreased in length to A_1–C_1, while the fibre BD has increased in length to B_1–D_1. G–H has also increased to G_1–H_1 but the increase is less than in the case of the fibre B–D. The fibre E–F, being on the NA, neither increases nor decreases and E–$F = E_1$–F_1.

This straining (alteration in length) of the various fibres in the depth of the section is shown in Fig. 11.4(b), and as stress and strain are proportional to each other (stress/strain $= E$, see Chapter 7) a similar diagram, Fig. 11.4(c), shows the distribution of stress over the depth of the section.

Referring again to Fig. 11.3(b), the fibre G–H increases in length to G_1–H_1. Therefore

$$\text{Strain in fibre G–H} = \frac{\text{increase in length}}{\text{original length}}$$

$$= \frac{(G_1\text{–}H_1) - (G\text{–}H)}{G\text{–}H}$$

But length of arc = radius × angle in radians, therefore

$$G_1\text{–}H_1 = (R + y)\,\phi$$

Now E_1–F_1 remains the same length and thus E_1–$F_1 = $ G–H. Also E_1–$F_1 = R\phi$.

Thus

$$\frac{(G_1\text{–}H_1) - (G\text{–}H)}{G\text{–}H} = \text{strain in fibres G–H} = \frac{(R + y)\phi - R\phi}{R\phi}$$

$$= \frac{R\phi + y\phi - R\phi}{R\phi} = \frac{y}{R} \tag{1}$$

and, since stress/strain $= E$, then stress $=$ strain $\times E$, therefore,

$$\text{Stress in fibres G–H} = f = \frac{y}{R} \times E = \frac{Ey}{R} \tag{2}$$

Fig. 11.4 Stress and strain within the beam: (a) cross-section; (b) strain profile; (c) stress profile

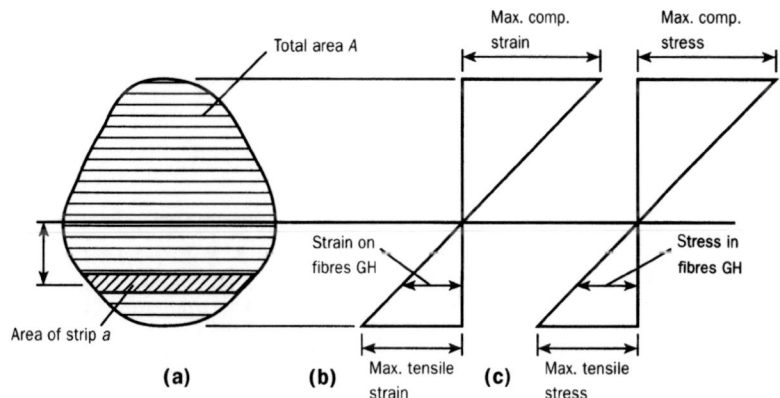

i.e.

$$\frac{f}{y} = \frac{E}{R} \tag{3}$$

The total load over the area a = stress on the area $\times$ the area

$$= \frac{Ey}{R} \times a = \frac{Eay}{R}$$

The first moment of the load about the NA is

$$\text{Load} \times y = \frac{Eay^2}{R}$$

The summation of all such moments over the total area A (i.e. the sum of the moments of all such areas as a), including areas above the neutral axis as well as below, is

$$\sum \frac{Eay^2}{R}$$

and this is the total moment of resistance of the section.

But E and R are constants (i.e. only a and y^2 vary) and, since in design the moment of resistance is made equal to the bending moment (usually the maximum bending moment, $M_{\max}$),

$$M_{\max} = M_r = \frac{E}{R} \sum ay^2$$

i.e.

$$\text{Safe bending moment} = \frac{E}{R} \times \text{the sum of all the } ay^2$$

But as was already stated in Chapter 9, the sum of all the ay^2, i.e. $\sum ay^2$, is the moment of inertia or second moment of area of the shape, I. So it may now be written

$$M_r = \frac{EI}{R} \tag{4}$$

Referring again to equation (3), $f/y = E/R$ and substituting f/y for E/R in equation (4),

$$M_r = \frac{fI}{y} = f\left(\frac{I}{y}\right) \tag{5}$$

Finally, the main formulae arising from this theory may be stated as follows:

$$\frac{M_r}{I} = \frac{f}{y} = \frac{E}{R} \tag{6}$$

and the most important portion consists of the first two terms

$$\frac{M_r}{I} = \frac{f}{y} \quad \text{or} \quad M_r = f\left(\frac{I}{y}\right) \quad \text{i.e. equation (5)}$$

In the above formula f is the permissible bending stress for the material of the beam. For the most commonly used steel (Grade S275), f may be taken as 165 N/mm^2, whereas the value of f for timber ranges between 3 N/mm^2 and 12 N/mm^2 depending on the species.

These values, however, apply only in those cases where the compression flange of the beam is adequately restrained laterally to prevent sideways buckling. For beams which are not restrained laterally, the above values have to be appropriately reduced. This is outside the scope of this textbook and it can be assumed that all the beams dealt with in this chapter are adequately supported laterally.

Elastic section modulus – symmetrical sections

In equation (5) the factor I/y is called the **section modulus** (or modulus of section) and is usually denoted by the letter Z,

$$\frac{I}{y} = Z$$

Where a beam is symmetrical about its X–X axis, as in the case of those shown in Fig. 11.5, the X–X axis is also the neutral axis (NA) of the beam section, and so the distance y to the top flange is the same as that to the bottom flange, hence

$$Z = \frac{I_{xx}}{y} = \frac{I_{xx}}{\frac{1}{2}d}$$

Fig. 11.5 Beams with symmetrical sections about the X–X axis

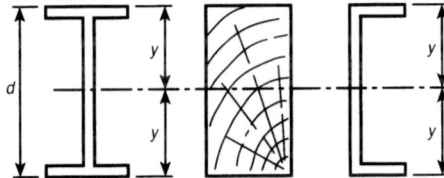

Now, for a rectangular section, $I_{xx} = \frac{1}{12}bd^3$, and so

$$Z = \frac{I}{y} = \frac{bd^3}{12} \div \frac{d}{2} = \frac{bd^2}{6}$$

In the case of rolled steel sections the values of Z (i.e. I/y) are normally taken directly from tables similar to those on pages 260–3 (elastic modulus column) but the following examples include some in which the values are calculated.

Example 11.1

A timber beam of rectangular cross-section is 150 mm wide and 300 mm deep. The maximum allowable bending stress in tension and compression must not exceed 6 N/mm^2. What maximum bending moment in N mm can the beam safely carry?

Solution

$$\text{Section modulus } Z = \tfrac{1}{6}bd^2 = \tfrac{1}{6} \times 150 \times 300^2$$
$$= 2.25 \times 10^6 \text{ mm}^3 \text{ units}$$

$$\text{Safe allowable bending moment } M_{max} = fZ = 6 \times 2.25 \times 10^6$$
$$= 13.5 \times 10^6 \text{ N mm}$$

Example 11.2

A timber beam has to support loading which will cause a maximum bending moment of 25×10^6 N mm. The safe bending stress must not exceed 7 N/mm^2. What section modulus will be required in choosing a suitable size section?

Solution

$M_r = fZ$ and, therefore, the required $Z = M_r/f$, i.e.

$$Z = \frac{25 \times 10^6}{7} = 3.57 \times 10^6 \text{ mm}^3$$

Example 11.3

A timber beam is required to span 4 m carrying a total uniform load (inclusive of the beam's self-weight) of 40 kN. The safe allowable bending stress is 8 N/mm^2. Choose a suitable depth for the beam if the width is to be 120 mm.

Solution

$$M_{max} = \tfrac{1}{8}Wl = \tfrac{1}{8} \times 40 \times 4 \times 10^6 = 20 \times 10^6 \text{ N mm}$$

but $M_{max} = M_r = f \times Z$, and it follows that

$$\text{required } Z = \frac{M_{max}}{f} = \frac{20 \times 10^6}{8} = 2.5 \times 10^6 \text{ mm}^3$$

The Z of the section is $\tfrac{1}{6}bd^2$, where b is given as 120 mm, therefore

$$\tfrac{1}{6} \times 120 \times d^2 = 2.5 \times 10^6 \text{ mm}^3$$

$$d^2 = \frac{25 \times 10^6 \times 6}{120}$$

$$d = \sqrt{125\,000} = 353 \text{ mm, say 360 mm}$$

Example 11.4

The section of floor shown in Fig. 11.6 is to be carried by 125 mm × 75 mm timber joists spanning the 3 m length. The bending stress must not exceed 4.6 N/mm^2 and the total inclusive load per m^2 of floor is estimated to be 2.0 kN. At what cross-centres x in mm must the timber beams be fixed?

Solution

Total load carried by *one* timber joist is

$$3 \times x \times 2.0 = 6x \text{ kN}$$

$$Z \text{ of joist} = \tfrac{1}{6}bd^2 = \tfrac{1}{6} \times 75 \times 125^2 = 195 \times 10^3 \text{ mm}^3$$

Moment of resistance of one joist = bending moment on one joist

$$M_r = fZ = 4.6 \times 195 \times 10^3 = 0.9 \times 10^6 \text{ N mm}$$

Fig. 11.6 Example 11.4

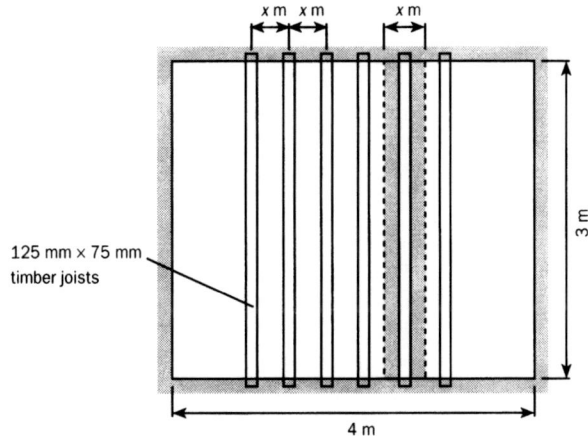

Thus

$$M_{max} = \tfrac{1}{8}Wl = \tfrac{1}{8} \times 6x \times 3 \times 10^6 = 0.9 \times 10^6 \, \text{N mm}$$

and

$$x = \frac{0.9 \times 10^6 \times 8}{6 \times 3 \times 10^6} = 0.4 \, \text{m}$$

Example 11.5

If the floor mentioned in Example 11.4 has its 125 mm × 75 mm timber joists at 450 mm centres and the span of the timber joists is halved by the introduction of a main timber beam 150 mm wide, as shown in Fig. 11.7, what load in kN/m² will the floor now safely carry? And what will be the required depth of the 150 mm wide main timber beam if $f = 5.25 \, \text{N/mm}^2$?

Fig. 11.7 Example 11.5

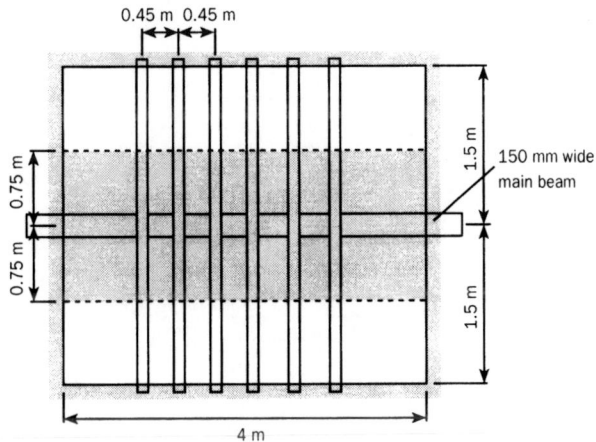

Solution

Let w be the safe load in kN/m². Then load carried by one secondary timber joist is

$$1.5 \times 0.45 \times w = 0.675w \, \text{kN}$$

M_r of the joists is unchanged at 0.9×10^6 N mm, therefore

$$M_{max} = \tfrac{1}{8} \times 0.675w \times 1.5 \times 10^6 = 0.9 \times 10^6 \text{ N mm}$$

and

$$w = \frac{0.9 \times 10^6 \times 8}{0.675 \times 1.5 \times 10^6} = 7 \text{ kN/m}^2$$

Total load on the main beam
Each secondary timber joist transfers half of its load to the main beam in the form of an end reaction, and the other half to the wall.

Thus, the total area of floor load carried by the main beam is the area shown shaded in Fig. 11.7.

The total load carried by the main beam is thus $4.0 \times 1.5 \times 7 = 42$ kN and, although this in fact consists of a large number of small point loads from the secondary beams, it is normal practice to treat this in design as a uniformly distributed load. Therefore

$$M_{max} \text{ on main beam} = \tfrac{1}{8} \times 42 \times 4 \times 10^6$$

$$= 21 \times 10^6 \text{ N mm}$$

and

$$\text{required } Z = \frac{M_r}{f} = \frac{21 \times 10^6}{5.25} = 4 \times 10^6 \text{ mm}^3$$

but for a rectangular section, $Z = \tfrac{1}{6}bd^2$, so,

$$d = \sqrt{\left(\frac{4 \times 10^6 \times 6}{150}\right)} = 400 \text{ mm}$$

Example 11.6

A welded steel girder is made up of plates as shown in Fig. 11.8.

Fig. 11.8 Example 11.6

What safe, uniformly distributed load can this girder carry on a simply supported span of 4.0 m if the permissible bending stress is limited to 165 N/mm²?

Solution

$$I_{xx} \text{ of section} = \tfrac{1}{12} \times 120 \times 300^3 - \tfrac{1}{12} \times 108 \times 250^3$$

$$= 270 \times 10^6 - 140.625 \times 10^6$$

$$= 129 \times 10^6 \text{ mm}^4$$

$$Z_{xx} \text{ of section} = \frac{I}{y} = \frac{129 \times 10^6}{150} = 0.86 \times 10^6 \text{ mm}^3$$

Hence

$$M_r = 165 \times 0.86 \times 10^6 = 142 \times 10^6 \text{ N mm}$$

Let W be the total safe, uniformly distributed load the girder can carry (in kN), then

$$\tfrac{1}{8}W \times 4 \times 10^6 = 142 \times 10^6 \text{ N mm}$$

$$W = \frac{142 \times 8}{4} = 284 \text{ kN}$$

Example 11.7

A steel beam is required to span 5.5 m between centres of simple supports carrying a 220 mm thick brick wall as detailed in Fig. 11.9.

Choose from the table of properties (pages 260–3) a suitable beam section given that the permissible stress in bending is 165 mm².

Fig. 11.9 Example 11.7

Brickwork at 20 kN/m³
= 0.22 × 2.6 × 5.5 × 20 = 63 kN

2.6 m

5.5 m

Beam, say, 2 kN self-weight

Solution

Total uniformly distributed load $W = 63 + 2 = 65$ kN.
Therefore,

$$M_{max} = \tfrac{1}{8} \times 65 \times 5.5 \times 10^6 = 44.69 \times 10^6 \text{ N mm}$$

and

$$\text{required } Z = 44.69 \times 10^6/165 = 270\,800 \text{ mm}^3$$

$$= 270.8 \text{ cm}^3 \text{ (as shown in tables)}$$

A suitable section would be the 305 × 102 UB25 (i.e. 305 mm × 102 mm at 25 kg/m universal beam) with an actual value of Z 292 cm³.

The 203 × 133 UB30 with a Z value of 280 cm³ is nearer to the required 270.5 cm³, but the former section was chosen because of its smaller weight.

Example 11.8

Figure 11.10 shows a portion of floor of a steel-framed building. The floor slab, which weighs 3 kN/m², spans in the direction of the arrows, carrying a super (live) load of 5 kN/m² and transferring it to the secondary beams marked A. These in turn pass the loads to the main beams marked B and to the columns.

Fig. 11.10 Example 11.8

Fig. 11.10 Example 11.8

Choose suitable sizes for beams A and B, using a permissible bending stress of 165 N/mm².

Solution

Secondary beam, A

$$\text{Total load } W = 3.8 \times 7.5 \times (3 + 5) = 228 \text{ kN}$$

$$M_{max} = \tfrac{1}{8} \times 228 \times 7.5 \times 10^6 = 213.75 \times 10^6 \text{ N mm}$$

and

$$\text{required } Z = \frac{213.75 \times 10^6}{165} = 1.295 \times 10^6 \text{ mm}^3$$

$$= 1295 \text{ cm}^3$$

Use 457 × 191 UB67 with a *Z* value of 1296 cm³.

Main beam, B

Reaction from beams A at midspan = 228 kN (point load). Assumed weight of beam (UDL), say, 3 kN/m

$$M_{max} = \left(\tfrac{1}{4} \times 228 + \tfrac{1}{8} \times 3 \times 7.6\right) \times 7.6 \times 10^6$$

$$= (57 + 2.85) \times 7.6 \times 10^6$$

$$= 454.86 \times 10^6 \text{ N mm}$$

and

$$\text{required } Z = \frac{454.86 \times 10^6}{165} = 2.757 \times 10^6 \text{ mm}^3$$

$$= 2757 \text{ cm}^3$$

Use 610 × 229 UB113 with a *Z* value of 2874 cm³.

Example 11.9

The timber box beam shown in Fig. 11.11 spans 6 m and carries a uniformly distributed load of 2 kN/m and a centrally placed point load of 3 kN. Determine the maximum stresses due to bending.

Fig. 11.11 Example 11.9

Solution

Because of the symmetry of the loading, the maximum bending moment due to the combined action of the two loads will occur at midspan.

$$M_{max} = \left(\tfrac{1}{8} \times 2 \times 6 + \tfrac{1}{4} \times 3 \right) \times 6 \times 10^6$$

$$= 13.5 \times 10^6 \, \text{N mm}$$

$$I_{xx} = \tfrac{1}{12} \times 120 \times 450^3 - \tfrac{1}{12} \times 96 \times 350^3$$

$$= (911.25 - 343.00) \times 10^6 = 568.25 \times 10^6 \, \text{mm}^4$$

$$Z_{xx} = \frac{568.25 \times 10^6}{225} = 2.525 \times 10^6 \, \text{mm}^3$$

Now, from $M = f \times Z, f = M/Z$, therefore

$$f = \frac{13.5 \times 10^6}{2.525 \times 10^6} = 5.35 \, \text{N/mm}^2$$

Elastic section modulus – non-symmetrical sections

Figure 11.12 shows two examples of beam sections which are not symmetrical about the X–X axis. In such cases the distance y between the neutral axis and

Fig. 11.12 Beams with non-symmetrical sections about the X–X axis

the top and bottom fibres will have two values, y_1 and y_2, and, consequently, there will also be two values of Z_{xx} – one obtained by dividing I_{xx} by the distance y_1, and the other obtained by dividing I_{xx} by the value of y_2.

If in these unsymmetrical shapes the permissible stress is the same for both top and bottom flanges, as it is, for example, in the case of steel, then

Safe bending moment $= f \times$ least Z

If, as in the case of the now obsolete cast iron joist shown in Fig. 11.12, the permissible stresses in tension and compression are not the same, then the safe bending moment is the lesser of the following:

$$M_{\text{rc}} = \frac{I}{y_1} \times \text{compression stress}$$

$$M_{\text{rt}} = \frac{I}{y_2} \times \text{tension stress}$$

Example 11.10

A 254×102 UB22 has one 200 mm $\times$ 12 mm steel plate welded to the top flange only, as shown in Fig. 11.13. The area of the universal beam alone is 2800 mm^2 and $I_{xx} = 28.41 \times 10^6$ mm^4. What safe uniform load can such a beam carry on a 5.0 m simply supported span if $f = 165$ N/mm^2 in tension or compression?

Fig. 11.13 Example 11.10

Solution

Taking moments about line A–A to find the neutral axis which passes through the centroid of the section:

$$(2800 + 2400)x = 2800 \times 127 + 2400 \times 260 = 979\,600$$
$$x = 979\,600/5200 = 188 \text{ mm}$$

Applying the principle of parallel axes (Chapter 9) to determine the second moment of area of the section about NA:

$$I_{\text{NA}} = 28.41 \times 10^6 + 2800 \times 61^2$$
$$+ \tfrac{1}{12} \times 200 \times 12^3 + 2400 \times 72^2$$
$$= (28.41 + 10.45 + 0.03 + 12.44) \times 10^6$$
$$= 51.30 \times 10^6 \text{ mm}^4$$

$$Z_{top} = (51.30 \times 10^6)/78 = 657\,700 \text{ mm}^3$$

$$Z_{bot} = (51.30 \times 10^6)/188 = 272\,800 \text{ mm}^3$$

Therefore

$$\text{Critical } M_r = 165 \times 272\,800 = 45.01 \times 10^6 \text{ N mm}$$

For a UDL, $M_{max} = \frac{1}{8}Wl$

$$W = 45.01 \times 8/5 = 72.0 \text{ kN}$$

This load will cause the bottom fibres of the beam to be stressed in tension at 165 N/mm^2, while the maximum compressive stress in the top fibres will be much less, namely

$$165 \times \frac{272\,800}{657\,700} \quad \text{or, more simply,}$$

$$165 \times \frac{78}{188} = 68.5 \text{ N/mm}^2$$

Example 11.11

Figure 11.14 shows an old-type cast iron joist (dimensions in mm) with a tension flange of 9600 mm^2, a compression flange of 2880 mm^2 and a web of 7200 mm^2.

The safe stress in compression is 5 N/mm^2, and in tension 2.5 N/mm^2. What is the safe bending moment for the section? What safe uniform load will the beam carry on a 4.8 m span?

Fig. 11.14 Example 11.11

Solution

Taking moments about the lower edge A–A to find the neutral axis,

$$2880 \times 360 = 1\,036\,800$$
$$7200 \times 198 = 1\,425\,600$$
$$\underline{9600 \times \quad 24 = \quad 230\,400}$$
$$\overline{19\,680 \qquad\qquad 2\,692\,800}$$

Therefore $x = 2\,692\,800/19\,680 = 137$ mm

Total I_{NA} is

$$\tfrac{1}{12} \times 120 \times 24^3 + 2880 \times 223^2 = 143.36 \times 10^6$$

$$\tfrac{1}{12} \times 24 \times 300^3 + 7200 \times 61^2 = 80.79 \times 10^6$$

$$\tfrac{1}{12} \times 200 \times 48^3 + 960 \times 113^2 = \underline{124.42 \times 10^6}$$

$$348.57 \times 10^6 \text{ mm}^4$$

Safe bending moment in tension $=$ tension $f \times$ tension Z

$$= 2.5 \times \frac{348.57 \times 10^6}{137}$$

$$= 6.36 \times 10^6 \text{ N mm}$$

Safe bending moment in compression $=$ compression $f \times$ compression Z

$$= 5.0 \times \frac{348.57 \times 10^6}{235}$$

$$= 7.42 \times 10^6 \text{ N mm}$$

- Thus tension is the critical stress, and safe bending moment $= 6.36 \times 10^6$ N mm.
- Therefore, since $\frac{1}{8}Wl = 6.36 \times 10^6$ N mm the safe uniformly distributed load $W = (6.36 \times 8)/4.8 = 10.6$ kN.

Example 11.12   A timber joist has a 48 mm thick flange of the same timber fixed to it as shown below in Fig. 11.15, so that the resulting section may be considered to act as a tee beam.

Fig. 11.15 Example 11.12

Calculate the safe distributed load on a span of 3.6 m with an extreme fibre stress of 7 N/mm^2.

Solution   Taking moments about line A–A to find the NA:

$$8640 \times 24 = 207\,360$$

$$\frac{11\,664}{20\,304} \times (48 + \tfrac{1}{2} \times 162) = \frac{1\,504\,656}{1\,712\,016}$$

Therefore $x = 1\,172\,016/20\,304 = 84$ mm.

Total I_{NA} is

$$\tfrac{1}{12} \times 180 \times 48^3 + 8640 \times 60^2$$

$$+ \tfrac{1}{12} \times 72 \times 162^3 + 11\,664 \times 45^2$$

$$= (1.66 + 31.10 + 25.51 + 23.63) \times 10^6$$

$$= 81.9 \times 10^6 \text{ mm}^4$$

$$\text{Least } Z_{xx} = \frac{I_{xx}}{y} = \frac{81.9 \times 10^6}{210 - 84} = 650\,000 \text{ mm}^3$$

Therefore

$$M_r = fZ = 7 \times 650\,000 = 4.55 \times 10^6 \text{ N mm}$$

If W = safe distributed load in kN, then

$$\tfrac{1}{8}Wl = 4.55 \times 10^6 \text{ N mm}$$

$$W = \frac{4.55 \times 10^6 \times 8}{3600} = 10\,000 \text{ N} = 10 \text{ kN}$$

Example 11.13   A timber cantilever beam projects 2 m and carries a 6 kN point load at the free end. The beam is 150 mm wide throughout, but varies in depth from 150 mm to 250 mm, as shown in Fig. 11.16. Calculate the stress in the extreme fibres at the support and at a point 1 m from the support. Ignore the weight of the beam.

Fig. 11.16 Example 11.13

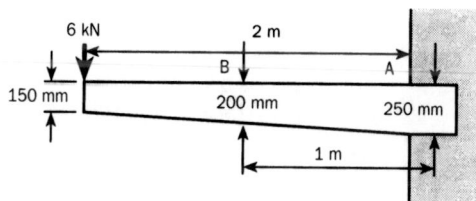

To find stress at the support (point A):

$$M_{max} = 6 \times 2 \times 10^6 = 12 \times 10^6 \, \text{N mm}$$

$$Z \text{ at point } A = \tfrac{1}{6}bd^2 = \tfrac{1}{6} \times 150 \times 250^2 = 1.56 \times 10^6 \, \text{mm}^3$$

$$\text{Stress } f \text{ at } A = \frac{M}{Z} = \frac{12 \times 10^6}{1.56 \times 10^6} = 7.68 \, \text{N/mm}^2$$

To find stress at point B:

$$M_B = 6 \times 1 \times 10^6 = 6 \times 10^6 \, \text{N mm}$$

$$Z \text{ at point } B = \tfrac{1}{6}bd^2 = \tfrac{1}{6} \times 150 \times 200^2 = 1.0 \times 10^6 \, \text{mm}^3$$

$$\text{Stress } f \text{ at } B = \frac{M}{Z} = \frac{6 \times 10^6}{1 \times 10^6} = 6.0 \, \text{N/mm}^2$$

Example 11.14

A hollow steel pipe of 150 mm external and 100 mm internal diameter, as shown in Fig. 11.17, is to span between two buildings. What is the greatest permissible span in metres if the stresses in tension and compression must not exceed 150 N/mm²?

Fig. 11.17 Example 11.14

Solution *Note*: The unit weight of steel is 78 kN/m³.

$$\text{Area} = \tfrac{1}{4}\pi(150^2 - 100^2) = 0.7854 \times (22\,500 - 10\,000)$$
$$= 9.8 \times 10^3 \, \text{mm}^2$$

If l = length of span in millimetres, then

$$\text{Total volume of pipe} = l \times 9800 \, \text{mm}^3$$

$$\text{Total weight of pipe} = \frac{l \times 9800 \times 78\,000}{1\,000\,000\,000} = 0.77 \times l \, \text{N}$$

But I_{xx} of pipe $= \tfrac{1}{64}\pi(150^4 - 100^4) = \tfrac{1}{64}\pi(406.25 \times 10^6) \, \text{mm}^4 = 19.94 \times 10^6 \, \text{mm}^4$, therefore

$$Z_{xx} \text{ of pipe} = \frac{I}{y} = \frac{19.94 \times 10^6}{75} = 0.27 \times 10^6 \, \text{mm}^3$$

$$\text{Permissible } M_{\max} = M_r = \tfrac{1}{8}Wl = fZ = 150 \times 0.27 \times 10^6$$
$$= 40.5 \times 10^6 \, \text{N mm}$$

therefore

$$\tfrac{1}{8} \times 0.77l \times l = 40.5 \times 10^6 \, \text{N mm}$$

$$l = \sqrt{\left(\frac{40.5 \times 10^6 \times 8}{0.77 \times 10^6}\right)} = 20.5 \, \text{m}$$

Limit state design

A limit state may be defined as that state of a structure at which it becomes unfit for the use for which it was designed.

To satisfy the object of this method of design, all relevant limit states should be considered in order to ensure an adequate degree of safety and serviceability. The codes therefore distinguish between the **ultimate limit states**, which apply to the safety of the structure, and the **serviceability limit states**, which deal with factors such as deflection, vibration, local damage and cracking of concrete.

Whereas the permissible stress design methods relied on a single factor of safety (or load factor), the limit state design codes introduce two partial safety factors, one applying to the strength of the materials, γ_m, and the other to loads, γ_f. This method, therefore, enables the designer to vary the degree of risk by choosing different partial safety factors. In this way the limit state design ensures an acceptable probability that the limit states will not be reached, and so provides a safe and serviceable structure economically.

Part 1 of BS 5950 *Structural use of steelwork in building, Code of practice for design in simple and continuous construction: hot rolled sections*, first published in 1985, current publication dated 2000, gives some examples of limit states. These are listed in Table 11.1.

Table 11.1 Limit states

Ultimate	Serviceability
1 Strength (including general yielding, rupture, buckling and forming a mechanism)	5 Deflection
2 Stability against overturning and sway	6 Vibration
3 Fracture due to failure	7 Wind-induced oscillation
4 Brittle fracture	8 Durability

Steel beam, joist or lintels: design to BS 5950: Part 1: 2000

In the design of a steel beam, steel joist or a steel lintel for the ultimate limit state of strength, the following points should be considered.

Loads

For the purpose of checking the strength and stability of a structure the specified loads, which are based on the values given in BS 6399: Part 1: 1996 for dead and imposed loads and in BS 399–2: 1997 for wind loads, have to be multiplied by the partial factor γ_f. The value of γ_f depends on the combination of loads: for dead loads only it is 1.4, for imposed (or live) loads it is 1.6 and for wind loads it is 1.4. However, for dead loads combined with wind and live loads it is 1.2.

So, the factored load, also called the design load, for a combination of dead and live loads will be $1.4 \times$ dead loads $+ 1.6 \times$ live loads and for the combination of dead, live and wind loads it will be $1.2 \times$ (dead + live + wind load).

Strength of steel

The design strength, ρ_y, is based on the minimum yield strength as specified in BS 4360: 1990 *Specifications for weldable steels* (see Table 11.2). The material factor, γ_m for steel is 1.0 and the modulus of elasticity, E, is 205 000 N/mm².

Table 11.2 Design strength, ρ_y, for sections, plates and hollow sections

Thickness (mm)	Design strength (N/mm²) for BS 5950–2		
	S275	S355	S460
16	275	355	460
40	265	345	440
63	255	335	430
80	245	325	410
100	235	315	400
150	225	295	

(*Source*: Adapted from Table 9, BS 5950–1: 2000)
Note: For rolled sections, the thickness is that specified for the thickest element of the cross-section.

Strength classification

According to Table 11.3 which is based on Table 11 of BS 5950: 2000, there are four classes of rolled steel sections. Plastic section must be used if plastic design method is adopted in the structural analysis.

Moment capacity

The **moment capacity** (or moment of resistance), M_c, of a steel section depends on lateral restraint and the cross-section of the beam. Clause 3.5.2 of BS 5950: Part 1: 2000 distinguishes four classes of cross-section, according to their width-to-thickness ratio, see Table 11.3. The universal beam sections are Class 1 or plastic cross-sections, and as such may be used for plastic (limit state) design.

For these sections the moment capacity should be taken as follows (see Clause 4.2.5 of BS 5950):

$$M_c = \rho_y S \le 1.2\rho_y Z \text{ (in the case of a simply supported beam or cantilever)}$$

$$\le 1.5\rho_y Z \text{ (generally)}$$

Table 11.3 Class of rolled steel sections

	Plastic	*Compact*	*Semi-compact*
Outstand element of compression flange	$\dfrac{b}{T} \le 9\,\varepsilon$	$\dfrac{b}{T} \le 10\,\varepsilon$	$\dfrac{b}{T} \le 15\,\varepsilon$
Web with neutral axis at mid-depth	$\dfrac{d}{t} \le 80\,\varepsilon$	$\dfrac{d}{t} \le 100\,\varepsilon$	$\dfrac{d}{t} \le 120\,\varepsilon$

where

$$\varepsilon = \sqrt{(275/\rho_y)}$$

and

ρ_y = design strength from Table 11.2

T, b, d and t are sectional dimensions as shown in the below figure

(*Source*: Adapted from Table 11, BS 5950–1: 2000)

provided that the shear force, F_v, does not exceed

$$0.36\rho_y tD$$

where

S is the plastic modulus of the section
t is the web thickness of the section
D is the depth of the section

Permissible deflection

BS 5950 limits the vertical deflecting of a steel beam to:

Span/360	For beams carrying plaster or other brittle finishes
Span/200	Others
	For purlins and sheeting rails, consult Table 8, BS 5950
Beam length/180	cantilever beam

Figure 11.18 below shows examples of beams and joists effectively laterally restrained and beams and/or joists without full lateral restraint.

A   No lateral movement due to the friction between the concrete and the surface of the compression flange

Reinforced concrete floor or roof

A   Lateral movement is prevented by the beams/joists

Screed on the top of the beam

Steel angle   Precast concrete/timber joist

A   Lateral movement is prevented by the beams/joists

Timber beam/steel beam bolted to the steel beam

B   Lateral movement is possible: movement of compression flange

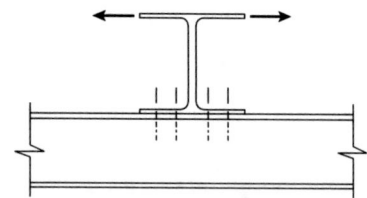

Brick, block or panel wall

B   Lateral movement is possible: movement of compression flange

B   Lateral movement is possible: timber beam is not connected via bolts or other suitable means to the steel compression flange

Timber joist or beam with no bolts to prevent lateral movemen

B   Lateral movement is possible: no suitable connection between the timber beam or joist and the steel beam

Timber beam or joist not bolted to the steel beam

Fig. 11.18 Beams A with full lateral restraints and B without full lateral restraints

Example 11.15

Using the data given in Example 11.8, choose suitable sections for beams A and B. Both beams are laterally restrained, given that $\rho_y = 275 \text{ N/mm}^2$ and the beams have full lateral restraint.

$E = 205\ 000 \text{ N/mm}^2$

Solution

Secondary beam, A

Selection of beam section

Loading $= 3.8 \times 7.5 \times (1.4 \times 3 + 1.6 \times 5) = 347.7 \text{ kN}$

Applied moment, $M_{max} = \frac{1}{8} \times 347.7 \times 7.5 \times 10^6 = 325.97 \times 10^6 \text{ N mm}$

$\therefore$ required $S = \dfrac{325.97 \times 10^6}{275} = 1.185 \times 10^6 \text{ mm}^3 = 1185 \text{ cm}^3$

Use a 457×152 UB60 $(S = 1287 \text{ cm}^3 \le 1.2 \times Z_x)$
$(1.2 \times 1122 \text{ cm}^3 = 1346.4 \text{ cm}^3)$

Strength classification

For this beam, $\rho_y = 275 \text{ N/mm}^2$ (as $T_{flange} = 13.3 \text{ mm}$, see Table 11.21 or Table 9, BS 5950).

Section classification

$\varepsilon = \sqrt{\dfrac{(275)}{\rho_y}} = \sqrt{\dfrac{275}{275}} = 1.0$

$b/T = 5.75$ (see Table 11.21) $< 9\varepsilon$

where $\varepsilon = 1.0$
$\therefore$ Flange is plastic

$d/t = 50.3 < 80\varepsilon$

$\therefore$ Web is plastic
$\therefore$ The section is plastic or Class 1

Check for shear capacity

$F_v = \dfrac{347.7 \text{ kN}}{2} < \dfrac{0.36 \times 275 \times 8.1 \times 454.6 \text{ kN}}{1000}$

Check for deflection

Check that actual (elastic) deflection $<$ permissible deflection.

Actual deflection $= \delta = \dfrac{5}{384} \dfrac{WL^3}{EI}$

where

$W = Q_k$, unfactored imposed loads for deflection due to imposed load or live load, or
$W =$ total unfactored loads $= Q_k + G_k$ for total deflection due to total unfactored loads

For $W = Q_k = 5 \times 3.8 \times 7.5 = 142.5$ kN

$$\delta = \frac{5 \times 142.5 \times 1000 \times (7500)^3}{384 \times 205\,000 \times 25\,500 \times 10^4} = 5.98 \text{ mm}$$

Permissible deflection $= \dfrac{\text{span}}{360}$ (for brittle finishes) $= \dfrac{7500}{360} = 20.83$ mm

Actual deflection $<$ permissible deflection
$\therefore$ The section is satisfactory.

If for practical application, W equals total unfactored load, i.e.

$W = G_k + Q_k = 3.8 \times 7.5\,(3 + 5) = 228$ kN

$\delta = 9.586$ mm $<$ permissible deflection

The section is satisfactory.

Therefore the chosen section is satisfactory in terms of bending, shear and deflection. Web bearing and web buckling capacities need to be checked too.

Main beam, B

Selection of beam section

Loading: own weight of beam, say: 3 kN/m UDL, point load at midspan from beam A $= 347.7$ kN.

$$\therefore M_{max} = \left(\tfrac{1}{4} \times 347.7 + \tfrac{1}{8} \times 1.4 \times 3 \times 7.6\right) \times 7.6 \times 10^6$$

$$= 690.95 \times 10^6 \text{ N mm}$$

Assume $\rho_y = 275$ N/mm^2

$$\therefore \text{ required } S = \frac{690.95 \times 10^6}{275} = 2\,512\,545 \text{ mm}^3 = 2512.545 \text{ cm}^3$$

Use a 533 $\times$ 210 UB101 ($S = 2612$ cm$^3 < 1.2 \times 2292$ cm^3)

Strength classification

For this beam, $\rho_y = 265$ N/mm^2 as $T_{flange} = 17.4$ mm.

Section classification

$b/T = 6.03 < 9\,\varepsilon$

where $\varepsilon = \dfrac{\sqrt{(275)}}{\rho_y} = \dfrac{\sqrt{275}}{265} = 1.02$

$< (9 \times 1.02 = 9.18)$
$\therefore$ Flange is plastic

$d/t = 44.1 < 80\,\varepsilon\,(80 \times 1.02 = 81.6)$
$\therefore$ Web is plastic
$\therefore$ The whole section is plastic

Check for deflection

Check that actual deflection < permissible deflection.

For unfactored imposed load $W = \dfrac{3.8 \times 7.5 \times 5 \times 2}{2} = 142.5\ \text{kN}$

$$\delta = \frac{WL^3}{48EI} = \frac{142.5 \times 1000 \times (7600)^3}{48 \times 205\,000 \times 61\,520 \times 10^4} = 10.333\ \text{mm}$$

$$< \frac{\text{span}}{360} < 7600/360 = 21.111\ \text{mm}$$

For unfactored loads $G_k + Q_k$

$$\delta = \frac{5 \times 22.8 \times 1000 \times (7600)^3}{384 \times 205\,000 \times 61\,520 \times 10^4} + \frac{142.5 \times 1000 \times (7600)^3}{48 \times 205\,000 \times 61\,520 \times 10^4}$$

$$= 1.033\ \text{mm} + 10.333$$

$$= 11.36\ \text{mm} < \text{span}/360 < 7600/360 = 21.11\ \text{mm}$$

Check for shear capacity

$$F_v = \frac{347.7 + 31.92}{2} < \frac{0.36 \times 265 \times 10.8 \times 536.7}{1000}$$

$$= 189.81\ \text{kN} < 552.972\ \text{kN}$$

$\therefore$ The chosen section is satisfactory in terms of bending, shear and deflection. Web bearing and web buckling capacities need to be checked too, see BS 5059: 2000.

It has to be pointed out that this very brief introduction to limit state design of steelwork treats the topic in an extremely simplified manner. For more detailed application of the principles it is imperative that specialist textbooks be consulted.

Design of steel beams, lintels and joists to Eurocode 3 (EC3)

In the design of a steel beam for ultimate limit state of strength, EC3 recommends that for a fully laterally restrained steel beam, the following strength and serviceability check should be satisfied, Clauses 6.2.5 to 6.2.8, Clause 7 and Clause 8, EC3. Also, see EN 1990. For the design of a laterally unrestrained beam see Clause 6.3.2 of EC3.

    (a) Resistance of cross-section to shear, Clause 6.2.6, EC3
    (b) Resistance of cross-section to bending moment, Clause 6.2.5, EC3
    (c) Resistance of cross-section to bending and shear, Clause 6.2.8, EC3
    (d) Shear buckling resistance of web, Clause 6.2.6, EC3
    (e) Flange-induced buckling, Clause 8, EC3–5
    (f) Resistance of web to transverse forces, Clause 6, EC3–5. This covers (a) web crushing and (b) web crippling and web buckling
    (g) Deflection, Clause 7, EC3.

Figure 11.19 shows examples of beams with and without full lateral restraint.

A   No lateral movement due to the friction between the concrete and the surface of the compression flange

Reinforced concrete floor or roof

A   Lateral movement is prevented by the beams/joists

Screed on the top of the beam

Steel angle   Precast concrete/timber joist

A   Lateral movement is prevented by the beams/joists

Timber beam/steel beam bolted to the steel beam

B   Lateral movement is possible: movement of compression flange

Brick, block or panel wall

B   Lateral movement is possible: movement of compression flange

B   Lateral movement is possible: timber beam is not connected via bolts to the steel compression flange

Timber joist or beam with no bolts to prevent lateral movement

B   Lateral movement is possible: no connection between the timber beam or joist and the steel beam

Timber beam or joist not bolted to the steel beam

Fig. 11.19 Beams: A with full lateral restraints and B without full lateral restraints.

(a) Check resistance of cross-section to shear (Clause 6.2.6)

Check that:

$V_{c,Rd} > V_{Ed}$

$V_{c,Rd}$ = design shear resistance

V_{Ed} = design value of shear force

- for plastic design $V_{c,Rd} = V_{pl,.Rd}$

$V_{pl,.Rd}$ = design plastic shear resistance

$\therefore V_{pl,.Rd} > V_{Ed}$ (for plastic design)

$$V_{pl,.Rd} = \frac{A_v(f_y\sqrt{3})}{\gamma_{M0}}$$

γ_{M0} = partial factor of safety = 1.00 for resistance of cross-section

$A_v = A - 2bt_f + (t_w + 2r)t_f \geq \eta h_w t_w$

$A_v = \eta h t_w$ (for conservative design use $\eta = 1.0$)

A = area of cross-section

b = overall width

r = root radius

t_f = flange thickness

t_w = web thickness

$\eta = 1.0$ (conservatively, for all steel up to S460)

Shear buckling resistance needs to be considered too when $h_w/t_w > 72\ \varepsilon/\eta$ for unstiffened webs.

For stiffened web see Clause 6.2.6, EC3.

f_y = yield strength, see Table 11.4.

Table 11.4 Nominal values of yield strength, f_y, and ultimate tensile strength, f_u, for hot rolled structural steel

	Nominal thickness of the element (mm)			
	≤ 16 mm		16 < t ≤ 40 mm	
Nominal steel grade	f_y (N/mm²)	f_u (N/mm²)	f_y (N/mm²)	f_u (N/mm²)
S235	235	360	235	360
S275	275	410	265	410
S355	355	470	345	470
S450	440	550	430	550

(*Source*: Adapted from various extracts, BS EN 10025–2: 2004 (British Standards Institute))

Use Table 11.5 for section classification.

Table 11.5 Maximum width to thickness ratios for compression elements

	Class 1 plastic	Class 2 compact slender	Class 3 semi-compact slender
Outstand element of compression flange	$\dfrac{c}{t_f} \leq 9\,\varepsilon$	$\dfrac{c}{t_f} \leq 10\,\varepsilon$	$\dfrac{c}{t_f} \leq 14\,\varepsilon$
Web with neutral axis at mid-depth	$\dfrac{d}{t_w} \leq 72\,\varepsilon$	$\dfrac{d}{t_w} \leq 83\,\varepsilon$	$\dfrac{d}{t_w} \leq 124\,\varepsilon$
Web subject to compression, rolled sections	$\dfrac{d}{t_w} \leq 33\,\varepsilon$	$\dfrac{d}{t_w} \leq 38\,\varepsilon$	$\dfrac{d}{t_w} \leq 42\,\varepsilon$
$c = (b - t_w - 2r)/2, r = $ root radius, $\varepsilon = (235/f_y)^{0.5}$			

(*Source*: Adapted from Table 5.2, EC3, Part 1–1, BS EN 1993–1–1)

(b) and (c) Check resistance of cross-section to bending moment (Clause 6.2.5, EC3) and bending and shear (Clause 6.2.8, EC3)

Check that:

1 $V_{Ed} \leq 0.5\, V_{pl.Rd}$

Then check that:

$M_{y,v,Rd} > M_{Ed}$
$M_{y,v,Rd} = f_y W_{pl,y}/\gamma_{M0}$
$W_{pl,y} = $ plastic modulus
$M_{Ed} = $ design bending moment

2 If $V_{Ed} > 0.5\, V_{pl.Rd}$

Then the design plastic resistance moment of the section should be calculated using a reduced yield strength calculated as follows:

$f_y(1 - \rho)$ for the shear area only
where

$$\rho = \left[\frac{2V_{Ed}}{V_{pl,Rd}} - 1 \right]^2$$

Therefore for rolled I- and H-sections the reduced design resistance moment about the major axis is:

$M_{y,v,Rd} = f_y(W_{pl,y} - \rho\, A_v^2/4t_w)/\gamma_{M0} \leq M_{y,c,Rd}$
$M_{y,c,Rd} = f_y W_{pl,y}/\gamma_{M0}$
$W_{pl,y} = $ plastic modulus

A beam is said to be fully laterally restrained when the beam supports a floor or a roof construction which is capable of resisting a lateral force of not less than 1 per cent of the maximum factored force in the compression flange of the beam. This is only true if the dead and imposed load of the roof or the floor constitutes a uniformly distributed dominant loading on the beam.

Section moment capacity

Using the limit state design method the section moment capacity is defined as follows:

Where $V_{Ed} \leq 0.5 \ V_{pl.Rd}$ the moment capacity for plastic or compact section should be calculated as:

$$M_{y,v,Rd} = f_y W_{pl}$$

where

$M_{y,v,Rd}$ = ultimate moment capacity of the section

f_y = the yield strength

W_{pl} = the plastic modulus about the relevant axis = first moment of area about the neutral axis

(d) Shear buckling resistance of web (Clause 6.2.6, EC3)

If $h_w/t_w > 72 \ \varepsilon/\eta$ for unstiffened webs, shear buckling resistance needs to be checked, see Clause 6.2.6.

(e) Flange-induced buckling (Clause 8, EC3−5)

To prevent the compression flange buckling in the plane of the web check that:

$$h_w/t_w < k(E/f_{yf})(A_w/A_{fc})^{1/2}$$

where

A_w = area of web = $(h_w - 2t_f)t_w$

A_{fc} = area of compression flange = bt_f

f_{yf} = yield strength of compression flange

E = elastic modulus = 210×10^3 N mm^2

k, see Table 11.6

Table 11.6 K values, Clause 8, EC3–5

$K = 0.3$	For Class 1, where plastic rotation utilized
$K = 0.4$	For Class 2, where moment resistance utilized
$K = 0.55$	For Classes 3 and 4, where elastic moment resistance utilized

(f) Resistance of web to transverse forces (Clause 6, EC3−5)

This covers (a) web crushing and (b) web crippling and web buckling (Fig. 11.20).

Fig. 11.20 Web crushing, buckling and crippling

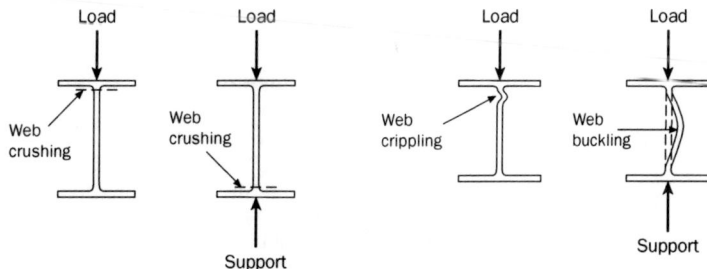

For rolled steel sections, if the compression flange is adequately restrained to lateral buckling, the design resistance of web to transverse forces can be checked as follows:

$$F_{Rd} = f_{yw}\, L_{eff}\, t_w / \gamma_{M1} \text{ (for I- and H-sections)}$$

f_{yw} = yield strength of the web

F_{Rd} = design resistance of web to local buckling

t_w = web thickness

γ_{M1} = resistance of member to instability = 1.0   (see Clause 6.1, EC3)

$L_{eff} = \chi_F\, l_y$

$\chi_F = 0.15/\overline{\lambda}_F \le 1.0$ (χ_F = reduction factor)

$\overline{\lambda}_F = \sqrt{(l_y t_w f_{yw}/F_{cr})}$

$F_{cr} = 0.9\, k_f\, E\, t_w^3 / h_w$

$k_f = 2 + 6\dfrac{(S_s + c)}{h_w} \le 6.0$ (at unstiffened end support)

S_s, see Figure 6.1, EC3–5 (reproduced below)

(Figure 6.1 EC3–5)

l_y is the effective loaded length of the stiff bearing $S_s \cdot S_s$ = the distance over which the applied load is effectively distributed at a slop of 1:1 as shown in the figure below.

(Figure 6.2 EC3–5)

For the loading of a beam without stiffeners, see Figure 6.1, EC3–5 above. l_y is the smaller of:

(i) $l_y = l_e + t_f\sqrt{[m_1/2 + (l_e/t_f)^2 + m_2]}$

(ii) $l_y = l_e + t_f\left[\sqrt{(m_1 + m_2)}\right]$

$\quad m_1 = f_{yf}\, b_f / f_{yw} t_w$

For $\overline{\lambda}_F > 0.5$

$\qquad m_2 = 0.02(h_w/t_f)^2$

For $\overline{\lambda}_F \le 0.5\ m_2 = 0.0$

$l_e = k_F\, E t_w^2 / 2 f_{yw} h_w \le (S_s + c)$

See Clause 7 of EC3 for web with stiffeners and subjected to a combination of load and bending.

(g) Deflection (Clause 7, EC3)

Deflection of beams should be checked under the most realistic combination and arrangements of serviceability loads. The structural element behaviour may be assumed elastic for the calculation of deflection. The recommended deflection limits are given in Clause 2.24, of NA to EC3. For example, the elastic deflection of a beam caused by the unfactored variable action (imposed load) should not exceed:

1 Span/360 for beams carrying brittle finishes such as plaster, or
2 Span/200 for all other beams (not including purlins and sheeting rails),
3 Length/180 for cantilevers.

In the following example, the main steps for designing a fully laterally restrained beam to EC3 are detailed.

Example 11.16

The figure below shows a portion of floor of a steel-framed building. The floor slab, which weighs 3 kN/m², spans in the direction of the arrows, carrying a variable action (live load) of 5 kN/m² and transferring it to the secondary beams marked A. These in turn pass the loads to the main beams marked B and the columns. Select a suitable section for beam A, given steel S275 with $f_y = 275$ N/mm². The beam is fully laterally restrained and is supported by 120 mm bearing at its ends.

To calculate the load acting on the steel beam A the following design comments are important.

1 A roof or a floor is considered spanning in one way when the following are satisfied:
   - Where the ratio $L_1/L_2 \geq 2$ (see Fig. 11.21). The load on the roof ABCD can be assumed to be carried equally between purlins AB and DC.
   - When the roof is constructed of precast concrete units with the ratio $L_1/L_2 \geq 2$ (see Fig. 11.21). The load on the roof ABCD may be assumed to be carried equally between purlins AB and DC.

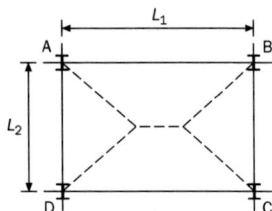

Fig. 11.22

Fig. 11.21

2   When the above rules are not satisfied then the loads on the roof or the floor can be distributed as shown in Fig. 11.22.

1   **Section selection and strength classification**

1.1 Calculate design action F_{Ed}

$$F_d = \gamma_G \, g_k + \gamma_Q \, q_k = 3.8 \times 7.5 \,(1.35 \times 3 + 1.5 \times 5) = 329.175 \text{ kN}$$

1.2 Calculate design bending moment M_{Ed}

$$M_{Ed} = \frac{F_{Ed}L}{8} = \frac{329.175 \times 7.5 \times 10^6}{8} = 308.602 \times 10^6 \text{ N mm}$$

1.3 Calculate W_{pl} (required)

$$W_{pl,y}(\text{required}) = \frac{M_{Ed}}{f_y} = \frac{308.602 \times 10^6}{275} = 1.122 \times 10^6 \text{ mm}^3 = \frac{1.122 \times 10^6}{1000}$$

$$= 1122 \text{ cm}^3$$

1.4 Select 457 × 152 × 60 with

$$W_{pl,y} = 1287 \text{ cm}^3 \qquad I_x = 25\,500 \text{ cm}^4$$

$$t_f = 13.3 \text{ mm} \qquad f_y = 275 \text{ N/mm}^2 \text{ (Table 3.1, EC3)}$$

Table 11.7 Maximum width to thickness ratios for compression elements

	Class 1 plastic	Class 2 compact	Class 3 semi-compact
Outstand element of compression flange	$\dfrac{c}{t_f} \le 9\varepsilon$	$\dfrac{c}{t_f} \le 10\varepsilon$	$\dfrac{c}{t_f} \le 14\varepsilon$
Web with neutral axis at mid-depth	$\dfrac{d}{t_w} \le 72\varepsilon$	$\dfrac{d}{t_w} \le 83\varepsilon$	$\dfrac{d}{t_w} \le 124\varepsilon$
where $c = (b - t_w - 2r)/2$, r = root radius			

(*Source*: Adapted from Table 5.2, BS EN 1993–1–1: 2005 (British Standards Institute))

1.5 Strength classification

$$\varepsilon = \frac{[\sqrt{235}]}{f_y} = 0.924$$

$$\frac{c}{t_f} = 62.25/13.3 = 4.68 < 9\varepsilon = 9 \times 0.924$$

$$= 9.24$$

$$c = (b - t_w - 2r)/2 = (152.9 - 8.1 - 2 \times 10.2)/2$$

$$= 62.25 \text{ mm}$$

∴ 4.68 < 9.24, flange is Class 1, plastic

$$\frac{d}{t_w} = 407.7/8.1 = 51 < 72\ \varepsilon = 72 \times 0.924$$

$$= 66.5$$

∴ 51 < 66.5, web is Class 1, plastic

∴ 457 × 152 × 60 section is classified as Class 1

2 Check resistance of cross-section to bending moment

Check that:

$$M_{\text{pl..Rd}} > M_{\text{Ed}}$$

$$M_{\text{pl..Rd}} = \frac{W_{\text{pl,Y}}\, f_y}{\gamma_{\text{MO}}} = \frac{1287 \times 10^3 \times 275}{1.0}$$

$$= 353.924 \times 10^6 \text{ N mm}$$

$$= 353.924 \text{ kN m}$$

∴ $M_{\text{pl..Rd}}$ (353.924 kN m) > M_{Ed} (308.602 kN m)

∴ Satisfactory

3 Check resistance of cross-section to shear

Check that:

$$V_{\text{pl,.Rd}} > V_{\text{Ed}}$$

$$V_{\text{pl,.Rd}} = \frac{A_v(f_y\sqrt{3})}{\gamma_{\text{MO}}}$$

γ_{MO} = partial factor of safety = 1.00 for resistance of cross-section

$$A_v = \eta\, h\, t_w \text{ (for conservative design use } \eta = 1.0)$$

$$= 1.0 \times 454.6 \times 8.1$$

$$= 3637.6 \text{ mm}^2$$

$$\eta = 1.0 \text{ for all steel up to S460}$$

$$V_{\text{pl.Rd}} = \frac{3637.6\,(275 \times \sqrt{3})}{1.0}$$

$$= 1\,732\,639 \text{ N}$$

$$= 1732.639 \text{ kN}$$

$$V_{Ed} = \frac{F_{Ed}}{2}$$

$$= \frac{329.175}{2}$$

$$= 164.587 \text{ kN}$$

$\therefore V_{pl.Rd} > V_{Ed}$

$\therefore$ Satisfactory

4 Check resistance of cross-section to bending and shear

Check that:

$V_{Ed} > 0.5\ V_{pl.Rd}$ (then reduce the theoretical plastic resistance moment of the section)

$V_{Ed} = 0.0$ (at midspan where the moment is maximum)

$\therefore V_{Ed} < 0.5\ V_{pl.Rd}$

$\therefore$ No need to reduce the theoretical plastic resistance moment of the steel beam section.

5 Check shear buckling resistance of web (Clause 6.2.6, EC3)

Check that:

$\dfrac{h_w}{t_w} < 72\varepsilon/\eta$ (for unstiffened beam web; for a stiffened web see Clause 5.1, EC3–5)

$\eta = 1.0$ for steel grade up to S460

$h_w = 454.7 - 2t_f = 454.7 - 2 \times 13.3 = 428.1$ mm

$53.51 < 72 \times 0.924/1.0$

$53.51 < 66.528$

$\therefore$ No need to check shear buckling.

6 Check resistance to flange-induced buckling

Check that:

$h_w/t_w < k\ (E/f_{yf})\ (A_w/A_{fc})^{1/2}$

$A_w = (h - 2t_f)t_w = (454.7 - 2 \times 13.3) \times 8.0$

$\qquad = 3424.8$ mm^2

$A_{fc} = bt_f = 152.9 \times 13.3$

$\qquad = 2{,}033.57$ mm^2

$K = 0.3$, see Table 11.8

Table 11.8 K values, Clause 8, EC3–5

$K = 0.3$	For Class 1, where plastic rotation utilized
$K = 0.4$	For Class 2, where moment resistance utilized
$K = 0.55$	For Classes 3 and 4, where elastic moment resistance utilized

$\therefore k\,(E/f_{\text{yf}})\,(A_{\text{w}}/A_{\text{fc}})^{1/2} = 0.3\,(210 \times 10^3/275)(3424.8/2{,}033.57)^{1/2} = 299.11$

$\therefore 299.1 > h_{\text{w}}/t_{\text{w}}\,(53.51)$.

$\therefore$ No check is required

$\therefore$ Satisfactory

7 Check resistance of web to transverse forces (Clause 6, EC3–5)

For rolled steel sections, if the compression flange is adequately restrained to lateral buckling, the design resistance of web under transverse forces can be checked as follows:

$F_{\text{Rd}} > V_{\text{Ed}}$

$F_{\text{Rd}} =$ design resistance of web to local buckling

$F_{\text{Rd}} = f_{\text{yw}}\,L_{\text{eff}}\,t_{\text{w}}/\gamma_{\text{M1}}$ (for I- and H-sections)

$f_{\text{yw}} = 275\ \text{N/mm}^2$ as $t_{\text{w}} = 8.1$ mm

$\gamma_{\text{M1}} =$ resistance of member to instability $= 1.0$ (see Clause 6.1, EC3)

$L_{\text{eff}} = \chi_{\text{F}}\,l_{\text{y}}$

$\chi_{\text{F}} = 0.5/\overline{\lambda}_{\text{F}} \leq 1.0$ ($\chi_{\text{F}} =$ reduction factor)

$\overline{\lambda}_{\text{F}} = \sqrt{(l_{\text{y}}\,t_{\text{w}}\,f_{\text{yw}}/F_{\text{cr}})}$

$F_{\text{cr}} = 0.9\,k_{\text{F}}\,E\,t_{\text{w}}^3/h_{\text{w}}$

$k_{\text{F}} = 2 + 6\dfrac{(S_{\text{s}} + c)}{h_{\text{w}}} \leq 6.0$ (at unstiffened end support)

$S_{\text{s}} = 120$ mm

$c = 0.0 =$ distance from end of bearing to the end of the beam, see Figure 11.23.

Fig. 11.23 Distance c and S_{s} for calculating k_{F}

(Figure 6.1, EC3–5)

$k_{\text{F}} = 2 + 6(120 + 0.0/428.1) = 3.681$

For web with stiffeners, see Clause 6.1, EC3–5

$F_{\text{cr}} = 0.9\,k_{\text{f}}\,E\,t_{\text{w}}^3/h_{\text{w}} = 0.9 \times 3.681 \times 210 \times 10^3 \times 8.1^3/428.1$
$\qquad = 832.0556$ kN

l_{y} is the smaller of:

(i) $l_{\text{y}} = l_{\text{e}} + t_{\text{f}}\sqrt{[m_1/2 + (l_{\text{e}}/t_{\text{f}})^2 + m_2]}$

(ii) $l_{\text{y}} = l_{\text{e}} + t_{\text{f}}[\sqrt{(m_1 + m_2)}]$

$m_1 = f_{\text{yf}}\,b_{\text{f}}/f_{\text{yw}}t_{\text{w}}$
$m_1 = 275 \times 152.9/(275 \times 8.1) = 19.112$
$m_2 = 0.02(h_{\text{w}}/t_{\text{f}})^2 = 0.02 \times (428.1/13.3)^2 = 20.721$
$l_{\text{e}} = k_{\text{F}}\,Et_{\text{w}}^2/2f_{\text{yw}}h_{\text{w}} \leq (S_{\text{s}} + c = 120 + 0.0 = 120$ mm)

$$l_e = 3.681 \times 210 \times 10^3 \times 8.1^2/(2 \times 275 \times 428.1)$$
$$= 210.115 \text{ mm}$$
$$\therefore l_e = 120 \text{ mm}$$
$$\therefore l_y \text{ is the smaller of:}$$

(iii) $$l_y = l_e + t_f\left[\sqrt{(m_1/2 + (l_e/t_f)^2 + m_2)}\right]$$
$$= 120 + 13.3\left[\sqrt{(19.112/2 + (120/13.3)^2 + 20.721)}\right]$$
$$= 260.554 \text{ mm}$$

(iv) $$l_y = l_e + t_f\left[\sqrt{(m_1 + m_2)}\right]$$
$$= 120 + 13.3\left(\sqrt{(19.112 + 20.721)}\right)$$
$$= 203.940 \text{ mm}$$

$$\therefore l_y = 203.940 \text{ mm}$$
$$\overline{\lambda}_F = \sqrt{(l_y\, t_w\, f_{yw}/F_{cr})}$$
$$= \sqrt{(203.940 \times 8.1 \times 275/832.055 \times 10^3)} = 0.734 > 0.5$$
$$\text{(satisfactory)}$$

$$\chi_F = 0.5/\overline{\lambda}_F \leq 1.0$$
$$= 0.5/0.734 = 0.681 < 1.0 \quad \text{(satisfactory)}$$

$$L_{eff} = \chi_F\, l_y = 0.681 \times 203.940 = 138.883 \text{ mm}$$
$$\therefore F_{RD} = f_{yw}L_{eff}\, t_w/\gamma_{M1}$$
$$= 275 \times 138.883 \times 8/1.0 = 305.5554 \text{ kN} > V_{ED} \text{ (164.587 kN)}$$
$$\therefore \text{ Satisfactory}$$

8 Check deflection

Check that deflection can be calculated elastically, i.e. check that:

$$M_{max} < M \text{ (elastic moment resistance)}$$
$$M_{max} = \frac{WL}{8}$$
$$W = 3.8 \times 7.5\ (3 + 5)$$
$$= 228 \text{ kN}$$
$$M_{max} = \frac{228 \times 7.5}{8} = 213.75 \text{ kN m}$$

$$\frac{W_{el,}f_y}{\gamma_{M0}} = \frac{1122 \times 275}{1.0} = 293.857 \text{ kN m} = M_{max} \text{ (elastic moment resistance)}$$

$$\therefore M_{max} \text{ (213.75 kN m)} < M_{elastic} \text{ (293.857 kN m)}$$

$$\therefore \text{ Deflection can be calculated elastically}$$

Check deflection due to variable loading (q_k)

Check that:

$$\frac{5\,q_kL^3}{384EI} < \frac{\text{span}}{360} \text{ (for brittle finishes for other beams } < \text{span}/200\text{)}$$

$$q_k = 3.8 \times 7.5 \times 5$$
$$= 142.5 \text{ kN}$$

$$\frac{5 \times 142.5 \times 10^3 \times (7500)^3}{384 \times 210 \times 10^3 \times 25\,500 \times 10\,000} < \frac{7500}{360}$$

$$14.618 \text{ mm} < 20.833 \text{ mm} \quad \text{(satisfactory)}$$

Coursework

Using the design summary main steps given in the example above choose suitable sections for beams B. The beam is laterally restrained, given that

$$\rho_y = 275 \text{ N/mm}^2 \quad \text{and} \quad E = 210 \times 10^3 \text{ N/mm}^2$$

For more detailed application of the EC3 design and analysis principles it is imperative that specialist textbooks and EC3 are consulted.

Timber beam, joist or lintels: design to BS 5268: Part 2: 2002

In the design of a timber beam, joist or lintels which is based on the permissible stress philosophy, the following should be considered.

Design loading

Calculate the design loads which are based on the values given in BS 6399: Part 1: 1996 for dead loads and imposed loads and in BS 399-2: 1997 for wind loads.

Permissible stress and modulus of elasticity

Permissible stress = grade stress × modification factors

Grade stress is normally taken from Tables 8 and 10 of BS 5268 for service classes 1 and 2. See Tables 11.9, 11.10, 11.11.

Grade stress values for service class 3 obtained by multiplying the values in Tables 8 and 10 of BS 5268 including moduli by K_2 from Table 16 of BS 5268.

- *Service class 1*: refers to timber with a moisture content $\leq$ 12 per cent. Timber used internally in a continuously heated building experiencing a temperature of 20°C and relative humidity of surrounding air exceeding 65 per cent for only a few weeks.
- *Service class 2*: refers to timber with a moisture content of $\leq$ 20 per cent. Corresponds to a temperature of 20°C and air relative humidity only exceeds 85 per cent for only a few weeks. This condition applies for covered buildings.
- *Service class 3*: used for timber externally used and fully exposed. Moisture content of the timber is $>$ 20 per cent.

Table 11.9 Grade stress for services classes 1 and 2, softwoods, according to BS 4978

Standard name	Grade	Bending parallel to grain[a] N/mm²	Tension parallel to grain[a] N/mm²	Compression Parallel to grain N/mm²	Perpendicular to grain[b] N/mm²	Shear parallel to grain N/mm²	Modulus of elasticity Mean N/mm²	Minimum N/mm²
Redwood/white	SS	7.5	4.5	7.9	2.1	0.82	10500	7000
Wood (imported)	GS	5.3	3.2	6.8	1.8	0.82	9000	6000
British larch	SS	7.5	4.5	7.9	2.1	0.82	10500	7000
	GS	5.3	3.2	6.8	1.8	0.82	9000	6000
British pine	SS	6.8	4.1	7.5	2.1	0.82	10500	7000
	GS	4.7	2.9	6.1	1.8	0.82	9000	6000
British spruce	SS	5.7	3.4	6.1	1.6	0.64	8000	5000
	GS	4.1	2.5	5.2	1.4	0.64	6500	4500
Douglas fir	SS	6.2	3.7	6.6	2.4	0.88	11000	7000
(British grown)	GS	4.4	2.6	5.2	2.1	0.88	9500	6000
Parana pine	SS	9.0	5.4	9.5	2.4	1.03	11000	7500
(imported)	GS	6.4	3.8	8.1	2.2	1.03	9500	6000
Pitch pine	SS	10.5	6.3	11.0	3.2	1.16	13500	9000
Caribbean)	GS	7.4	4.4	9.4	2.8	1.16	11000	7500
Western red cedar	SS	5.7	3.4	6.1	1.7	0.63	8500	5500
(imported)	GS	4.1	2.5	5.2	1.6	0.63	7000	4500
Douglas fir–larch	SS	7.5	4.5	7.9	2.4	0.85	11000	7500
(Canada and USA)	GS	5.3	3.2	6.8	2.2	0.85	10000	6500
Hem–fir (Canada	SS	7.5	4.5	7.9	1.9	0.68	11000	7500
and USA)	GS	5.3	3.2	6.8	1.7	0.68	9000	6000
Spruce–pine–fir	SS	7.5	4.5	7.9	1.8	0.68	10000	6500
(Canada and USA)	GS	5.3	3.2	6.8	1.6	0.68	8500	5500
Sitka spruce	SS	6.6	4.0	7.0	1.7	0.66	10000	6500
(Canada)	GS	4.7	2.8	6.0	1.5	0.66	8000	5500
Western	SS	6.6	4.0	7.0	1.7	0.66	9000	6000
whitewoods (USA)	GS	4.7	2.8	6.0	1.5	0.66	7500	5000
Southern pine	SS	9.6	5.8	10.2	2.5	0.98	12500	8500
(USA)	GS	6.8	4.1	8.7	2.2	0.98	10500	7000

(*Source*: Table 10, BS 5268–2: 1996 (British Standards Institute))
[a] Stresses applicable to timber 300 mm deep (or wide): for other section sizes see 2.10.6 and 2.12.2 of BS 5268.
[b] When specifically prohibiting wane at bearing areas, the SS grade compression perpendicular to grain stress may be multiplied by 1.33 and used for all grades.

Permissible bending stress

Permissible bending stress, $\sigma_{m,adm,\parallel} = \sigma_{m,g,\parallel} K_2 K_3 K_7 K_8$

where K_2, K_3, K_7, and K_8 are defined as follows.

K_2, moisture content (Clause 2.6.1, BS 5268)

- For service grades 1 and 2: $K_2 = 1.0$
- For service grade 3: K_2 from Table 11.12 below or Table 16 of BS 5268.

Table 11.10 Stress classes of softwood, visual grades

Standard name	Strength classes			
	C14	C16	C18	C24
Imported				
Redwood		GS		SS
Whitewood		GS		SS
Western red cedar	GS		SS	
Douglas fir–larch (Canada and USA)		GS		SS
Parana pine		GS		SS
Spruce–pine–fir (Canada and USA)		GS		SS
Western whitewoods (USA)	GS		SS	
Southern pine (USA)			GS	SS
British grown				
British larch			GS	SS
British pine			GS	
British spruce	GS		SS	
Douglas fir	GS		SS	
(British grown)				

Table 11.11 Grade stress and properties for C14 to C30, services 1 and 2

Strength class	Bending parallel to grain (N/mm²) $\sigma_{m,g,\parallel}$	Tension parallel to grain (N/mm²)	Compression			Shear parallel to grain (N/mm²) τ_g	Modulus of elasticity		Characteristic density^b (kg/m³) ρ_k	Average density^b (kg/m³) ρ_{mean}
			Parallel to grain (N/mm²) $\sigma_{c,g,\parallel}$	Perpendicular to grain^a (N/mm²) $\sigma_{c,g,\perp}$	$\tau_c \cdot gf$		Mean (N/mm²) E_{mean}	Minimum (N/mm²) E_{min}		
C14	4.1	2.5	5.2	2.1	1.6	0.6	6800	4600	290	350
C16	5.3	3.2	6.8	2.2	1.7	0.67	8800	5800	310	370
C18	5.8	3.5	7.1	2.2	1.7	0.67	9100	6000	320	380
C24	7.5	4.5	7.9	2.4	1.9	0.71	10800	7200	350	420
C30	11.0	6.6	8.6	2.7	2.2	1.2	12300	8200	380	460

(*Source*: Based on Tables 8 and 9, BS 5268: 2002)

^{a} The higher value may be used when the specification specifically prohibits wane at bearing areas.
^{b} Use the average density when calculating the wood dead loads.

K_3, duration of loading (Table 17, BS 5268)
For various duration of loading, K_3 is given in Table 17 of BS 5268. K_3 for the following loading duration is given as shown in Table 11.13.

K_7, depth factor (Clause 2.10.6, BS 5268)
Grade stress in bending should be multiplied by K_7. For solid section with a given h (depth) K_7 can be taken/calculated from Table 11.14.

Table 11.12 Modification factor K_2

Basic properties	K_2
Bending parallel to grain	0.8
Compression parallel to grain	0.6
Compression perpendicular to grain	0.6
Shear parallel to grain	0.9
Mean and minimum modulus of elasticity	0.8

(*Source*: Based on Table 16, BS 5268: 2002)

Table 11.13 K_3 values

1	Long-term loading (e.g. dead + permanent imposed). Example: Floors in a building.
1.25	Medium-term (e.g. dead + snow, dead + temporary imposed). Example: a roof for a garage or a roof for a building.
1.5 and 1.75	For short- and very short-term loadings respectively, see Table 17, BS 5268

(*Source*: Based on Table 17, BS 5268)

Table 11.14 K_7 values

K_7	h
1.0	$h = 300$ mm
1.17	$h \leq 72$ mm
$K_7 = \left(\dfrac{300}{h}\right)^{0.11}$	72 mm $< h < 300$ mm
$K_7 = \dfrac{0.81(h^2 + 92\,300)}{(h^2 + 56\,800)}$	$h > 300$ mm

K_8, load sharing factor (Clause 2.9, BS 5268)
$k_8 = 1.1$ when four or more members such as beams or joists are spaced 610 mm centre to centre and act together to resist the applied loads.

Permissible shear stress for beams or joists

Permissible shear stress for beams or joists, $\tau_{adm} = \tau_g\, k_2 k_3 k_5 k_8$

where τ_g = grade shear stress parallel to grain (see Tables 11.9–11.11 above or Tables 8 and 10 of BS 5268).

Table 11.15 K_{12} values for compression members

K_{12}																				
Slenderness ratio, $\lambda = l_e/i$																				
	<5	5	10	20	30	40	50	60	70	80	90	100	120	140	160	180	200	220	240	250
L_e/b for rectangular sections																				
$E/\sigma_{c,\parallel}$	<1.4	1.4	2.9	5.8	8.7	11.6	14.5	17.3	20.2	23.1	26	28.9	34.7	40.5	46.2	52	57.8	63.6	69.4	72.3
400	1	0.975	0.951	0.896	0.827	0.735	0.621	0.506	0.408	0.33	0.271	0.225	0.162	0.121	0.094	0.075	0.061	0.051	0.043	0.04
500	1	0.975	0.951	0.899	0.837	0.759	0.664	0.562	0.466	0.385	0.32	0.269	0.195	0.148	0.115	0.092	0.076	0.063	0.053	0.049
600	1	0.975	0.951	0.901	0.843	0.774	0.692	0.601	0.511	0.43	0.363	0.307	0.226	0.172	0.135	0.109	0.089	0.074	0.063	0.058
700	1	0.975	0.951	0.902	0.848	0.784	0.711	0.629	0.545	0.467	0.399	0.341	0.254	0.195	0.154	0.124	0.102	0.085	0.072	0.067
800	1	0.975	0.952	0.903	0.851	0.792	0.724	0.649	0.572	0.497	0.43	0.371	0.28	0.217	0.172	0.139	0.115	0.096	0.082	0.076
900	1	0.976	0.952	0.904	0.853	0.797	0.734	0.665	0.593	0.522	0.456	0.397	0.304	0.237	0.188	0.153	0.127	0.106	0.091	0.084
1000	1	0.976	0.952	0.904	0.855	0.801	0.742	0.677	0.609	0.542	0.478	0.42	0.325	0.255	0.204	0.167	0.138	0.116	0.099	0.092
1100	1	0.976	0.952	0.905	0.856	0.804	0.748	0.687	0.623	0.559	0.497	0.44	0.344	0.272	0.219	0.179	0.149	0.126	0.107	0.1
1200	1	0.976	0.952	0.905	0.857	0.807	0.753	0.695	0.634	0.573	0.513	0.457	0.362	0.288	0.233	0.192	0.16	0.135	0.116	0.107
1300	1	0.976	0.952	0.905	0.858	0.809	0.757	0.701	0.643	0.584	0.527	0.472	0.378	0.303	0.247	0.203	0.17	0.144	0.123	0.115
1400	1	0.976	0.952	0.906	0.859	0.811	0.76	0.707	0.651	0.595	0.539	0.486	0.392	0.317	0.259	0.214	0.18	0.153	0.131	0.122
1500	1	0.976	0.952	0.906	0.86	0.813	0.763	0.712	0.658	0.603	0.55	0.498	0.405	0.33	0.271	0.225	0.189	0.161	0.138	0.129
1600	1	0.976	0.952	0.906	0.861	0.814	0.766	0.716	0.664	0.611	0.559	0.508	0.417	0.342	0.282	0.235	0.198	0.169	0.145	0.135
1700	1	0.976	0.952	0.906	0.861	0.815	0.768	0.719	0.669	0.618	0.567	0.518	0.428	0.353	0.292	0.245	0.207	0.177	0.152	0.142
1800	1	0.976	0.952	0.906	0.862	0.816	0.77	0.722	0.673	0.624	0.574	0.526	0.438	0.363	0.302	0.254	0.215	0.184	0.159	0.148
1900	1	0.976	0.952	0.907	0.862	0.817	0.772	0.725	0.677	0.629	0.581	0.534	0.447	0.373	0.312	0.262	0.223	0.191	0.165	0.154
2000	1	0.976	0.952	0.907	0.863	0.818	0.773	0.728	0.681	0.634	0.587	0.541	0.455	0.382	0.32	0.271	0.23	0.198	0.172	0.16

(*Source:* Based on Table 22, BS 5268: 2002)

Permissible compression stress

Permissible compression stress perpendicular to grain, $\sigma_{c,adm,\perp}$

Mainly applied to avoid bearing failure of flexural members supported at their ends.

$$\sigma_{c,a,\perp} \leq \sigma_{c,adm,\perp}$$

where

$\sigma_{c,a,\perp}$ = bearing force$/bl_b$

b = width or breath of section

l_b = bearing length

$\sigma_{c,adm,\perp} = \sigma_{c,g,\perp}\, k_2\, k_3\, k_8$

Permissible compression stress parallel to grain, $\sigma_{c,\parallel}$

$$\sigma_{c,\parallel} = \sigma_{c,g,\parallel}\, k_2\, k_3\, k_8\, k_{12}$$

where

$\sigma_{c,g,\parallel}$ = compression stress parallel to grain

K_{12} is a factor based on the minimum modulus of elasticity, E_{min} (see Table 11.15 above or Table 22, BS 5268).

K_5, notched ends factor (Clause 2.10.4, BS 5268)

Fig. 11.24 (Fig. 2 of BS 5268) shows:

1 Beam with notch on top edge, and
2 Beam with notch on underside.

In these cases, the shear stress parallel to grain should be multiplied by k_5 taken from Table 11.16.

Note: BS 5268 recommends that $h_e \geq 0.5\, h$.

Table 11.16 K_5 values

Notch on top edge		Notch on underside
$a > h_e$	$k_5 = 1.0$	$k_5 = \dfrac{h_e}{h}$
$a \leq h_e$	$k_5 = \dfrac{h\,(h_e - a) + a\,h_e}{h_e^2}$	

Fig. 11.24 Notched beams (*Source*: From Fig. 2, BS 5268–2: 1996 (British Standards Institute))

(1) Notch on top edge

(2) Notch on underside

Design of timber beams and joists: design to BS 5268

In the design and analysis of effectively laterally restrained timber flexural members such as beams, joists and rafters, the following capacity checks need to be covered:

- Bending capacity
- Shear capacity
- Deflection
- Lateral buckling
- Bearing capacity.

Effectively laterally restrained beams and joists can be achieved by providing flexural members with depth to breadth ratios within the limits given in Table 11.17 (Table 19 of BS 5268).

Table 11.17 Maximum depth to breadth ratio

Degree of lateral supports	Maximum depth to breadth ratio
No lateral supports	2
Ends held in position	3
Ends held in position and compression edge held in line, as by direct connection of sheeting, deck or joists	5
For other degree of lateral supports	See Table 19, BS 5268

(*Source*: From Table 19, BS 5268–2: 1996 (British Standards Institute))

Example 11.17

Design of a timber beam and joists to BS 5268
Figure 11.25 shows a plan and the second floor details of an extension to a domestic dwelling house. Provide structural calculations to arrive at a suitable size of the timber floor joists and the beam using timber strength C16 under service 1. Spacing between the joists = 600 mm centre to centre. The floor has an effective span of 3 m.

Fig. 11.25 Example 11.17

Given:

1 The timber beam span on a 150 mm bearing length and its ends are held in position and the compression edge held in line by direct connection to the joists.

2 The floor joists span onto 100 mm wide wall plates.

Design loading as follows:

Imposed loads (assume the floor carries bedrooms), $Q_k = 1.5 \, \text{kN/m}^2$

See Table 5, BS 6399.

$$\text{Tongue and groove boarding (T\&G)} = 0.1 \, \text{kN/m}^2$$
$$\text{Joists} = 0.12 \, \text{kN/m}^2$$
$$\text{Plasterboard} = 0.11 \, \text{kN/m}^2$$
$$\text{Skims} = 0.1 \, \text{kN/m}^2$$
$$\text{Total } G_k = 0.43 \, \text{kN/m}^2$$

Design and capacity checks for timber joists

1 Total uniformly distributed loads $= G_k + Q_k$
$$= 0.43 + 1.5$$
$$= 1.93 \, \text{kN/m}^2$$

2 Area carried by one joist $= 0.6 \times 3 = 1.8 \, \text{m}^2$

3 Loads on one joist, $W = \text{area} \times 1.93 = 3.474 \, \text{kN}$

4 $Z_{xx} \text{(required)} \geq \dfrac{M_{max}}{\sigma_{m,adm,\|}}$

5 $M_{max} = \dfrac{WL}{8} = \dfrac{3.474 \times 3}{8} = 1.303 \, \text{kN m}$

6 $\sigma_{m,adm,\|} = \sigma_{m,g,\|} \, K_2 \, K_3 \, K_7 \, K_8$

$\sigma_{m,g,\|} = 5.3 \, \text{N/mm}^2$ (Tables 11.10–11.12 above or Table 8, BS 5268)

$K_2 = 1.0$, service class 1

$K_3 = 1.0$, long-term duration of loading (Table 11.13 above or Table 17, BS 5268)

$K_7 = 1.0$ (assume $k_7 = 1.0$ until you decide the depth h of the joist)

$K_8 = 1.1$, more than 4 joists at 600 mm centre to centre

$\sigma_{m,adm,\|} = 5.3 \times 1 \times 1 \times 1.1 = 5.83 \, \text{N/mm}^2$

$$Z_x \text{(required)} = \frac{M_{max}}{\sigma_{m,adm,\|}} = \frac{1.303 \times 1000 \times 1000}{5.83} = 223.45 \times 10^3 \, \text{mm}^3$$

From Table 11.18 below, 44×175 mm joists can be selected with Z_{xx} (provided) (225×10^3 mm^3 > 223.45×10^3 mm^3)

$A = 7.70 \times 10^3$ mm^2, $I_{xx} = 19.7 \times 10^6$ mm^4

7   $K_7 = \left(\dfrac{300}{h}\right)^{1.1} = \left(\dfrac{300}{175}\right)^{0.11} = 1.061$

8   Z_{xx} (required) $= \dfrac{1.303 \times 1000 \times 1000}{5.3 \times 1 \times 1 \times 1.061 \times 1.1} = 210.65 \times 10^3$ mm^3

Z_{xx} (provided) $> Z_{xx}$ (required)

9   Check joist deflection

Check that permissible deflection > total deflection

(a) Permissible deflection (δ_p) $= 0.003 \times$ span

span $= 3000$ mm

permissible deflection $= 0.003 \times 3000 = 9$ mm

(b) Total deflection $\delta_t =$ bending deflection (δ_m) + shear deflection (δ_v)

$$= \frac{5WL^3}{384EI} + \frac{12WL}{5EA} \quad \text{(see Table 13.1; add shear values of } c)$$

$E = E_{\text{mean}}$, as load shearing factor does apply (Table 11.11 above or Tables 8 and 10, BS 5268)

$I = I_{xx}$

$$\delta_t = \frac{5 \times 3.474 \times 1000 \times (3000)^3}{384 \times 8800 \times 19.7 \times 10^6} + \frac{12 \times 3.474 \times 1000 \times 3000}{5 \times 8800 \times 7.7 \times 10^3}$$

$$= 7.045 + 0.369$$

$$= 7.414 \text{ mm}$$

Permissible deflection (9 mm) > total deflection (7.414 mm) (satisfactory)

10   Check lateral buckling

Check $\dfrac{h}{b} <$ max $\left(\dfrac{h}{b}\right)$ (Table 11.17 above or Table 19, BS 5268)

$\dfrac{h}{b} = \dfrac{175}{44} = 3.97 < 5$

The joist sections are satisfactory for lateral buckling.

11   Check shear capacity

Check that $\tau_{\text{adm}} > \tau_a$

$$\tau_{\text{adm}} = \tau_g K_3 K_8$$

$$= 0.67 \times 1 \times 1.1$$

$$= 0.737 \text{ N/mm}^2$$

$$\tau_a = \frac{3}{2}\frac{F_v}{A}$$

Table 11.18 Geometric properties of sawn softwoods

Basic size[a] (mm)	Area (10³ mm²)	Section modulus (10³ mm³)		Second moment of area (10⁶ mm⁴)		Radius of gyration (mm)	
		About x–x	About y–y	About x–x	About y–y	About x–x	About y–y
36 × 75	2.70	~3.8	16.2	1.27	0.292	21.7	10.4
36 × 100	3.60	60.0	21.6	3.00	0.389	28.9	10.4
36 × 125	4.50	93.8	27.0	5.86	0.486	36.1	10.4
36 × 150	5.40	135	32.4	10.1	0.583	43.3	10.4
38 × 75	2.85	35.6	18.1	1.34	0.343	21.7	11.0
38 × 100	3.80	63.3	24.1	3.17	0.457	28.9	11.0
38 × 125	4.75	99.0	30.1	6.86	0.572	36.1	11.0
38 × 150	5.70	143	36.1	10.7	0.686	43.3	11.0
38 × 175	6.54	194	42.1	17.0	0.800	50.5	11.0
38 × 200	7.60	253	48.1	25.3	0.915	57.7	11.0
38 × 225	8.55	321	54.2	36.1	1.03	65.0	11.0
44 × 75	3.30	41.3	24.2	1.55	0.532	21.7	12.7
44 × 100	4.40	73.3	32.3	3.67	0.71	28.9	12.7
44 × 125	5.40	115	7.16	7.16	0.887	36.1	12.7
44 × 150	6.60	165	48.4	12.4	1.06	43.3	12.7
44 × 175	7.70	225	56.5	19.7	1.24	50.5	12.7
44 × 200	8.80	293	64.5	29.3	1.42	57.7	12.7
44 × 225	9.90	371	72.6	41.8	1.60	65.0	12.7
44 × 250	11.0	458	80.7	57.3	1.77	72.2	12.7
44 × 300	13.2	660	96.8	99.0	2.13	86.6	13.6
47 × 75	3.53	44.1	27.6	1.65	0.649	21.7	13.6
47 × 100	4.70	78.3	36.8	3.92	0.865	28.9	13.6
47 × 125	5.88	122	46.0	7.65	1.08	36.1	13.6
47 × 150	7.05	176	55.2	13.2	1.30	43.3	13.6
47 × 175	8.23	240	64.4	21.0	1.51	50.5	13.6
47 × 200	9.40	313	73.6	31.3	1.73	57.7	13.6
47 × 225	10.6	397	82.8	44.6	1.95	65.0	13.6
47 × 250	11.8	490	92.0	61.2	2.16	72.2	13.6
47 × 300	14.1	705	110	106	2.60	86.6	13.6
50 × 75	3.75	46.9	31.3	1.76	0.781	21.7	14.4
50 × 100	5.00	83.3	41.7	4.17	1.04	28.9	14.4
50 × 125	6.25	130	52.1	8.14	1.30	36.1	14.4
50 × 150	7.50	188	62.5	14.1	1.56	43.3	14.4
50 × 175	8.75	255	72.9	22.3	1.82	50.5	14.4
50 × 200	10.0	333	83.3	33.3	2.08	57.7	14.4
50 × 225	11.3	422	93.8	47.5	2.34	65.0	14.4
50 × 250	12.5	521	104	65.1	2.60	72.2	14.4
50 × 300	15.0	750	125	113	3.13	86.6	14.4
63 × 100	6.30	105	66.2	5.25	2.08	28.9	18.2
63 × 125	7.88	164	82.7	10.3	2.60	36.1	18.2
63 × 150	9.45	236	99.2	17.7	3.13	43.3	18.2
63 × 175	11.0	322	116	28.1	3.65	50.5	18.2
63 × 200	12.6	420	132	42.0	4.17	57.7	18.2
63 × 225	14.2	532	149	59.8	4.69	65.0	18.2
75 × 100	7.50	125	93.8	6.25	3.52	28.9	21.7

Table 11.18 (*Continued*)

Basic size[a] (mm)	Area (10³ mm²)	Section modulus (10³ mm³)		Second moment of area (10⁶ mm⁴)		Radius of gyration (mm)	
		About x–x	About y–y	About x–x	About y–y	About x–x	About y–y
75 × 125	9.38	195	117	12.2	4.39	36.1	21.7
75 × 150	11.3	281	141	21.1	527	~43.3	21.7
75 × 175	13.1	383	164	33.5	6.15	50.5	21.7
75 × 200	15.0	500	188	50.0	7.03	57.7	21.7
75 × 225	16.9	633	211	71.2	7.91	65.0	21.7
75 × 250	18.8	781	234	97.7	8.79	72.2	21.7
75 × 300	22.5	1130	281	169	10.5	86.6	21.7
100 × 100	10.0	167	167	8.33	8.33	28.9	28.9
100 × 150	15.0	375	250	28.1	12.5	43.3	28.9
100 × 200	20	667	333	66.7	16.7	57.7	28.9
100 × 250	25	1040	417	130	20.8	72.2	28.9
100 × 300	30	1500	500	225	25.0	86.6	28.9
150 × 150	20.0	563	563	42.2	42.2	43.3	43.3
150 × 200	25.5	1000	750	100	56.3	57.7	43.3
150 × 300	45.0	2250	1130	338	84.4	86.6	43.3
200 × 200	40.0	1330	1330	133	133	57.7	57.7
250 × 250	62.5	2600	2600	326	326	72.2	72.2
300 × 300	90.0	4500	4500	675	675	86.6	86.6

(*Source*: Table 98, BS 5268–2: 1996 (British Standards Institute))
[a] Basic size measured at 20 per cent moisture content.

$$F_{\mathrm{v}} = \text{Maximum shear force} = \frac{W}{2}$$

$$= \frac{3.474}{2} = 1.737 \text{ kN}$$

$$\tau_{\mathrm{a}} = \frac{3}{2} \times \frac{1.737 \times 1000}{7.7 \times 10^3} = 0.338 \text{ N/mm}^2$$

$$\tau_{\mathrm{adm}} > \tau_{\mathrm{a}}$$

$\therefore$ Shear capacity is satisfactory.

12 Check bearing capacity

Check that $\sigma_{\mathrm{c,adm},\perp} > \sigma_{\mathrm{c,a},\perp}$

$$\sigma_{\mathrm{c,adm}} = \sigma_{\mathrm{c,g},\perp}\, K_3\, K_8 = 1.7^* \times 1 \times 1.1 = 1.87 \text{ N/mm}^2$$

*No specification specifically prohibits wane at the bearing area.

$$\sigma_{\mathrm{c,a},\perp} = \frac{\text{maximum end reaction}}{b l_{\mathrm{b}}}$$

$$\text{Maximum end reaction} = \frac{W}{2} = \frac{3.474}{2} = 1.737 \text{ kN}$$

$$b = 44 \text{ mm}$$
$$l_{\mathrm{b}} = \text{width of wall plates} = 100 \text{ mm}$$

$$\sigma_{c,a,\perp} = \frac{1.737}{44 \times 100} = 0.395 \text{ N/mm}^2$$

$$\sigma_{c,adm} (1.87 \text{ N/mm}^2) > \sigma_{c,a,\perp} (0.395 \text{ N/mm}^2)$$

∴ Joists' bearing capacity is satisfactory

Use 44 × 175 mm sawn C16 timber joists.

Example 11.18

Selection and checking of a timber beam

Select beam section

1　Total loads on beam $= G_k + Q_k$

2　Area carried by the beam $= 3 \times 3.2 = 9.6 \text{ m}^2$

3　Loads on the beam, $W = 0.43 \times (3 \times 3.2) + 1.5 \times (3 \times 3.2)$

$$= 4.128 + 14.4$$
$$= 18.528 \text{ kN}$$

4　Z_{xx} (required) $= \dfrac{M_{max}}{\sigma_{m,adm,\parallel}}$

5　$M_{max} = \dfrac{WL}{8}$　(for UDL and W in kN)

$$= \frac{18.528 \times 3.2}{8} = 7.411 \text{ kN m}$$

6　$\sigma_{m,adm,\parallel} = \sigma_{m,g,\parallel} K_2 K_3 K_7 K_8$

$\sigma_{m,g,\parallel} = 5.3 \text{ N/mm}^2$　(Table 11.11 above or Table 8, BS 5268)

$K_2 = 1.0$, service class 1

$K_3 = 1.0$, loads on floor, i.e. long-term duration of loading (Table 11.13 above or Table 17, BS 5268)

K_7 (assumed) $= 1.0$ at this stage until you select the beam size

$K_8 = 1.0$, one beam, no load-shearing factor does apply

$\sigma_{m,adm,\parallel} = 5.3 \times 1 \times 1 \times 1 \times 1 = 5.3 \text{ N/mm}^2$

$$Z_{xx} \text{ (required)} = \frac{M_{max}}{\sigma_{m,adm,\parallel}} = \frac{7.411 \times 1000 \times 1000}{5.3} = 1398.3 \times 10^3 \text{ mm}^3$$

Try 150 × 300 mm beam with:

Z_{xx} (provided) $= 2250 \times 10^3 \text{ mm}^3 > 1398.3 \times 10^3 \text{ mm}^3$

$A = 45.0 \times 10^3 \text{ mm}^2$

$I_{xx} = 338 \times 10^6 \text{ mm}^4$

7　Calculate K_7, $K_7 = \left(\dfrac{300}{h}\right)^{0.11} = \left(\dfrac{300}{300}\right)^{0.11} = 1.0$

8　$\sigma_{m,adm,\parallel} = 5.3 \text{ N/mm}^2$ and no change in Z_{xx} (required) value.

Check beam deflection

Check that $\delta_{\text{permissible}} \geq \delta_t$

$\delta_p = 0.003 \times \text{span} = 0.003 \times 3200 = 9.6 \text{ mm}$

$$\delta_t = \frac{5WL^3}{384E_{\min}I_{xx}} + \frac{12WL}{5E_{\min}A} \quad \text{(see Table 13.1)}$$

Hint: Use $E_{\min}$ as load shearing factor does not apply, one beam only

$$\delta_t = \frac{5 \times 18.528 \times 1000 \times (3200)^3}{384 \times 5800 \times 338 \times 10^6} + \frac{12 \times 18.528 \times 1000 \times (3200)}{5 \times 5800 \times 45 \times 10^3}$$

$\quad = 4.032 + 0.544$

$\delta_t = 4.576 \text{ mm}$

$\delta_p \ (9.6 \text{ mm}) > \delta_t \ (4.576 \text{ mm})$

Beam deflection is satisfactory.

Check lateral buckling capacity

$$\frac{h}{b} < \max\left(\frac{h}{b}\right) \qquad \text{(Table 11.17 above or Table 19, BS 5268)}$$

$$\frac{300}{150} = 2.0 < 5 \qquad \text{(Table 19, BS 5268)}$$

Lateral buckling capacity is satisfactory.

Check shear capacity

Check that $\tau_{\text{adm}} > \tau_a$

$\tau_{\text{adm}} = \tau_g \, K_2 \, K_3 \, K_8$

$K_2 = 1.0$, service class 1 (Table 11.12 above or Table 8, BS 5268)

$K_3 = 1.0$, long-term loading, floor

$K_8 = 1.0$, isolated one beam

$\tau_g = 0.67 \text{ N/mm}^2$ (Table 11.11 above or Table 8, BS 5268)

$$\tau_a = \frac{2F_v}{3A}, \qquad F_v = \frac{W}{2} = \frac{18.528}{2} = 9.269 \text{ kN}$$

$$\tau_a = \frac{2 \times 9.264 \times 1000}{3 \times 30 \times 1000} = 0.206 \text{ N/mm}^2$$

$\tau_{\text{adm}} \ (0.67 \text{ N/mm}^2) > \tau_a \ (0.206 \text{ N/mm}^2)$

Shear capacity is satisfactory.

Check bearing capacity

Check that $\sigma_{c,\text{adm},\perp} > \sigma_{c,a,\perp}$

$\sigma_{c,\text{adm},\perp} = \sigma_{c,g,\perp} K_2 \, K_3 \, K_8 = 1.7 \times 1 \times 1 \times 1 = 1.7 \text{ N/mm}^2$

$$\sigma_{c,a,\perp} = \frac{\text{end reaction (max)}}{bl_b}$$

$$\text{Max end reaction} = \frac{W}{2}$$

$$= \frac{18.528}{2}$$

$$= 9.264 \text{ kN}$$

$$\sigma_{c,a,\perp} = \frac{9.264 \times 1000}{150 \times 150} = 0.4117 \text{ N/mm}^2 < 1.7 \text{ N/mm}^2$$

The beam bearing capacity is satisfactory.

Use 150×300 mm sawn C16 beam.

Example 11.19

Repeat the design of the beam in Example 11.17, using a beam with a notched edge at the bearing with a 110 mm deep notch as shown in Fig. 11.26.

Fig. 11.26 Notched beams

(a) Notch on top edge   (b) Notch on underside

For both (a) and (b) in Fig. 11.26, notches affect only shear stress and

$$\tau_{adm} > \tau_a$$

For:

(a) $\tau_{adm} = \tau_g K_2 K_3 K_5 K_8$

$\tau_{adm} = 0.67 \times 1 \times 1 \times K_5 \times 1$

Calculate K_5:

$a < h_e$ where $a = 100$ mm and $h_e = 190$ mm

$$K_5 = \frac{h(h_e - a) + a h_e}{h_e^2}$$

$$= \frac{300(190 - 100) + 100 \times 190}{190^2}$$

$$= 1.274$$

$K_5 > 0.5$ (satisfactory; Clause 2.10.4, BS 5268)

$\tau_{adm} = 0.67 \times 1 \times 1 \times 1.274 \times 1 = 0.853 \text{ N/mm}^2$

$\tau_a = 0.206 \text{ N/mm}^2$ (see Example 11.18)

$\therefore \tau_{adm} (0.853 \text{ N/mm}^2) > \tau_a (0.206 \text{ N/mm}^2)$

The beam is adequate when notched with a 110 mm deep top edge notch at the bearings.

(b) $\tau_{adm} = \tau_g K_2 K_3 K_5 K_8$

$K_2 = 1, K_3 = 1, K_8 = 1$ (see Example 11.18)

Calculate K_5:

$$K_5 = \frac{h_e}{h}$$

$$= \frac{190}{300} = 0.633 > 0.5 \text{ (min) (satisfactory; Clause 2.10.4, BS 5268)}$$

$$\tau_{adm} = 0.67 \times 1 \times 1 \times 0.633 \times 1 = 0.424 \text{ N/mm}^2 > 0.206 \text{ N/mm}^2$$

The beam is adequate when notched with 110 mm deep notch on its underside at the bearings.

| **Design of timber beams and joists: design to EC5** | Design and check timber beams and joists to EC5 (Eurocode 5: *Design of timber structures*). |

Design summary

1 Calculate the design load, W

    W = design load $= \gamma_G\, G_k + \gamma_Q\, Q_k = 1.35\, G_k + 1.5\, Q_k$

    γ_G = partial coefficient for permanent actions $= 1.35$

    γ_Q = partial coefficient for variable actions $= 1.5$

2 Calculate bending moment (M_{max})

    For UDL (in KN) $M_{max} = \dfrac{F_d L}{8}$

    L = beam or joist span

    F_d = design load

3 Calculate $f_{m,y,d}$

    $f_{m,y,d} = K_h\, K_{sys}\, K_{mod}\, f_{m,k} / \gamma_m$

    $f_{m,y,d}$ = design bending strength

    K_h = the smaller of $\dfrac{(150)^{0.2}}{h}$ or 1.3

K_{sys} = load sharing factor $= 1.1$ from several equally spaced similar members are able to resist common load, member length ≤ 6 m, see Clause 6.6, EC5

K_{mod} = modification factor for strength values, see Table 11.19 (Table 3.1, EC5)

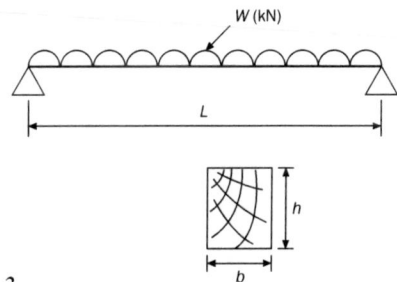

Table 11.19 k_{mod} for solid timber members

Duration of load	Service class		
	1	*2*	*3*
Permanent lodgings	0.60	0.60	0.50
Long-term lodgings	0.70	0.70	0.55
Medium-term	0.80	0.80	0.65
Short-term	0.90	0.90	0.70
Instantaneous	1.10	1.10	0.90

(*Source*: Based on Table 3.1, EC5, BS EN 1995)

Table 11.20 Strength classes

Species type Deciduous species		Poplar and conifer species														
		C14	C16	C18	C22	C24	C27	C30	C35	C40	D30	D35	D40	D50	D60	D70
		Strength properties (N/mm)														
Bending	$f_{m,k}$	14	16	18	22	24	27	30	35	40	30	35	40	50	60	70
Tension parallel	$f_{t,0,k}$	8	10	11	13	14	16	18	21	24	18	21	24	30	36	42
Tension perpendicular	$f_{t,90,k}$	0.3	0.3	0.3	0.3	0.4	0.4	0.4	0.4	0.4	0.6	0.6	0.6	0.6	0.7	0.9
Compression parallel	$f_{c,0,k}$	16	17	18	20	21	22	23	25	26	23	25	26	29	32	34
Compression perpendicular	$F_{c,90,k}$	4.3	4.6	4.8	5.1	5.3	5.6	5.7	6.0	6.3	8.0	8.4	8.8	9.7	10.5	13.5
Shear	f_{vk}	1.7	1.8	2.0	2.4	2.5	2.8	3.0	3.4	3.8	3.0	3.4	3.8	4.6	5.3	6.0
		Stiffness properties (kN/mm²)														
Mean modulus of elasticity parallel	$E_{0,mean}$	7	8	9	10	11	12	12	13	14	10	10	11	14	17	20
5% modulus of elasticity parallel	$E_{0,05}$	4.7	5.4	6.0	6.7	7.4	8.0	8.0	8.7	9.4	8.0	8.7	9.4	11.8	14.3	6.8
Mean modulus of elasticity perpendicular	$E_{90,mean}$	0.23	0.27	0.30	0.33	0.37	0.40	0.40	0.43	0.47	0.64	0.69	0.75	0.93	1.13	1.33
Mean shear modulus	G_{mean}	0.44	0.50	0.56	0.63	0.69	0.75	0.75	0.81	0.88	0.60	0.65	0.70	0.88	1.06	1.25
		Density (kg/m³)														
Density	ρ_k	290	310	320	340	350	370	380	400	420	530	560	590	650	700	900
Average density	ρ_{mean}	350	370	380	410	420	450	460	480	500	640	670	700	780	840	1080

(*Source*: Table 1, BS EN 338: 1995 (British Standards Institute))

$f_{m,k}$ = characteristic bending strength (Table 11.20 above or Table 1, EN 338)

γ_m = partial coefficient for material properties (Table 2.3, EC5)

γ_m = 1.3 fundamental combinations for solid timber, and γ_m = 1.0 for other design situations.

4 Calculate $\sigma_{m,y,d}$

From

$$\frac{\sigma_{m,y,d}}{f_{m,y,d}} + K_m \frac{\sigma_{m,z,d}}{f_{m,z,d}}$$

$\sigma_{m,y,d}$ = design normal bending stress about y–y axis

$\sigma_{m,y,d}$ = design normal bending stress about z–z axis

K_m = factor allows for redistribution of secondary bending stress

K_m = 0.7 for rectangular or square cross-section

K_m = 1.0 for other cross-sections

$f_{m,y,d}$ and $f_{m,z,d}$ are corresponding design strengths about the y–y and z–z axes respectively

5 Calculate $W_{y(required)}$ or $_{z(required)} = \dfrac{M_{d,y(max)}}{\sigma_{m,y,d}}$

W_y = section modulus

6 Select from Table 11.18 a beam or a joist with $W_{y(provided)} > W_{y(required)}$

7 Check joist or beam deflection

Check that 7.1 to 7.3 below are all satisfactory.

7.1 (a) Instantaneous deflections due to permanent actions, U_{instG}

U_{instG} = deflection due to bending + deflection due to shear

Example, for a UDL (KN) on a simply supported joist or beam with square or rectangular cross-section:

$$U_{instG} = \frac{5}{384}\frac{F_{d,G}L^3}{EI} + \frac{12}{5}\frac{F_{d,G}L}{EA}$$

$F_{d,G} = \gamma_G G_k$

$\gamma_G = 1.0$ for servicebility limit states (Table 2.3, EC5)

7.1 (b) Final deflection due to permanent actions

$U_{fin,G} = U_{instG}(1 + k_{def})$

For solid square or rectangular section, K_{def} for medium-term loading is given by:

$K_{def} = 0.6, 0.8, 2.0$ for solid timber, service classes 1, 2 and 3 respectively (see Table 3.2, EC5)

7.2 (a) Instantaneous deflections due to Q_k, U_{instQ}

Example, for a UDL (KN) on a simply supported joist or beam with square or rectangular cross-section:

U_{instQ} = deflection due to bending + deflection due to shear

$$U_{instQ} = \frac{5}{384}\frac{F_{d,Q}L^3}{EI} + \frac{12}{5}\frac{F_{d,Q}L}{EA}$$

A = area of cross-section

$F_{d,Q} = \gamma_Q Q_k$

$\gamma_{Q1} = 1.0$ for servicebility limit states (Table 2.3, EC5)

7.2 (b) Final deflection due to variable load Q_k

$U_{fin,Q1} = U_{instQ1}(1 + \psi_2 K_{def})$

ψ_2 = factor for quasi-permanent value of permanent actions, used to determine values of accidental action such as impact and explosion (Clause 2.4.1, EC2 and Clause 6, EN 1990)

$\psi_2 = 0.3$ for dwellings and offices

K_{def} = deformation factor; Table 3.2, EC5 takes into account the combined effect of moisture and creep on the deformation of beam or joists. For solid square or rectangular section, K_{def} for medium-term loading is given by:

$K_{def} = 0.6, 0.8, 2.0$ for solid timber, service classes 1, 2 and 3 respectively

7.3 Check final deflection

$U_{\text{fin}} \leq$ permissible def

$U_{\text{fin}} = U_{\text{finG}} + U_{\text{finQl}}$

Permissible deflection is given by:

For roofs and floors – member of span of l between two supports and with brittle finishes (plastered or plasterboard ceilings):

$$U_{\text{fin}} \leq \frac{\text{span}}{250}$$

$$U_{\text{fin}} \leq \frac{\text{span}}{125} \text{ (for cantilever)}$$

For roofs and floors – member with span of l between two supports and without brittle finishes:

$$U_{\text{fin}} \leq \frac{\text{span}}{150}$$

$$U_{\text{fin}} \leq \frac{\text{span}}{75} \text{ (for cantilevers)}$$

8 If the following are prevented, lateral buckling should not occur.

8.1 Twisting of the beam or joist at their support is prevented, and

8.2 The lateral displacement of the compression edge throughout the length of the beam or the joist is prevented (see Clause 6.3.3, EC5).

9 Check shear

(a) For joist or beam without notch, check that:

$\tau_d < f_{v,d}$

$\tau_d =$ design shear stress

$$= \frac{1.5 \ V_{Ed}}{A}$$

$V_{Ed} =$ maximum shear force

$f_{v,d} = k_{\text{sys}} \, k_{\text{mod}} f_{v,k} / \gamma_M$

(b) For joist or notched beam, check that:

$\tau_d < f_{v,d}$ (Clause 6.1.7, EC5)

$$\tau_d = \frac{1.5 \ V_{Ed}}{bh_{\text{ef}}}$$

$f_{v,k} =$ characteristic shear stress (Table 11.20 above or Table 1, BS EN 338)

(a) Check bearing

Check that:

$\sigma_{c,90,d} < k_{c,90} f_{c,90,d}$

$$\sigma_{c,90,d} = \frac{F_{c,90,d}}{A_{\text{ef}}}$$

where $F_{c,90,d} =$ maximum design bearing force

A_{cf} = effective contact area in compression perpendicular to the grain = L_b (for beam or joist of rectangular section) (Clause 6.1.5 and Fig. 6.2, EC5)

b = width of the joist or the beam

L = bearing length

$f_{c,90,d} = k_{sys}k_{mod}f_{c,90k}/\gamma_M$ = design compressive strength perpendicular to grain

$K_{c,90k}$ = compressive strength factor, takes the effect of support position and bearing length on member bearing strength (Clause 6.1.5, EC5)

$K_{c,90}$ for a beam or a joist supported at its end and internal supports with sectional dimensions b = width, h = depth and with bearing length = L and overhang $\leq h/3$ is given by:

$$k_{c,90k} = (2.38 - L/250)(1+h/12L) \leq 4.0$$

For more details, see Clause 6.5.1, EC5 and the corresponding figures.

Example 11.20

Design of timber joists to EC5

Figure 11.27 shows a plan and second floor details of an extension to a domestic dwelling house. Provide structural calculations to arrive at a suitable

Fig. 11.27 Example 11.20

size for the timber floor joists and the beam using timber strength C16 under service 1. Spacing between the joists = 600 mm centre to centre. The floor has an effective span of 3 m.

Given:

1 The timber beam span on a 150 mm bearing length and its ends are held in position and compression edge held in line by direct connection to the joists.
2 The floor joists span onto 100 mm wide wall plates.

Design loading is as follows:

Imposed loads (assume the floor carries bedrooms), Q_k = 1.5 kN/m²

Tongue and groove boarding (T&G)	− 0.1 kN/m²
Joists	= 0.12 kN/m²
Plasterboard	= 0.11 kN/m²
Skims	= 0.1 kN/m²
Total G_k	= 0.43 kN/m²

1   Design loads

Total characteristics $\quad = G_k = 0.43 \text{ kN/m}^2$
permanent load
Variable action $\qquad\qquad = Q_k = 1.5 \text{ kN/m}^2$ (Table 3 of UK NA to
EN 1991-1-1)
Design loads $\qquad\qquad = \gamma_G\, G_k + \gamma_Q\, Q_k = 1.35 \times 0.43 + 1.5 \times 1.5$
$\qquad\qquad\qquad\qquad = 2.83 \text{ kN/m}^2$
Design load on one joist, $F_d = 2.83 \times 0.6 \times 3$
$\qquad\qquad\qquad\qquad = 5.094 \text{ kN}$

2   Calculate bending moment
$$M_{d,y} = \frac{F_d L}{8} = \frac{5.094 \times 3}{8} = 1.91 \text{ kN m}$$

3   Calculate $f_{m,y,d} = K_h\, K_{sys}\, K_{mod}\, f_{m,k}/\gamma_m$

Assume $k_h = 1.0$, i.e. $h \geq 150$ mm
$K_{sys} = 1.1$
$K_{mod} = 0.8$ $\qquad$ (service class 1, medium term of loading; Table 3.1, EC5)
$f_{m,k} = 16 \text{ N/mm}^2$ $\qquad$ (Table 11.20 above or Table 3.1, EC5)
$\gamma_m = 1.3$ $\qquad$ (Table 2.3, EC5)
$\qquad \therefore \quad f_{m,y,d} = 1 \times 1.1 \times 0.8 \times 16/1.3$

$\qquad\qquad\qquad = 10.83 \text{ N/mm}^2$

4   Calculate $\sigma_{m,y,d}$

$$\frac{\sigma_{m,y,d}}{f_{m,y,d}} + K_m \frac{\sigma_{m,z,d}}{f_{m,z,d}} \leq 1$$

$$\frac{\sigma_{m,y,d}}{10.83} + 0.7 \frac{0.0}{f_{m,z,d}} \leq 1$$

$$\therefore \sigma_{m,y,d} = 10.83 \text{ N/mm}^2$$

5   Calculate $W_{y \text{ (required)}}$:

$$W_{y \text{ (required)}} = \frac{M_{d,y}}{\sigma_{m,y,d}} = \frac{1.91 \times 10^6}{10.83} = 176.36 \times 10^3 \text{ mm}^3$$

6   $\therefore$ use 47×150 mm or 63×150 mm. Let us try the 63×150 mm,
with $W_{y \text{ (provided)}} = 236 \times 10^3 \text{ mm}^3$ (Table 11.18)
since $h = 150$ mm then $k_h = 1.0$ as assumed

7   Check deflection

(a) U_{instG}, instantaneous deflection due to permanent action
U_{instG} = deflection due to bending + deflection due to shear
for a UDL (KN) on a simply supported joist or beam with square or
rectangular cross-section (Table 13.1):

$$U_{instG} = \frac{5}{384} \frac{F_{d,G} L^3}{EI} + \frac{12}{5} \frac{F_{d,G} L}{EA}$$

$$F_{d,G} = \gamma_G G_k \times 0.6 \times L = 1.0 \times 0.43 \times 0.6 \times 3 = 0.774 \, \text{kN}$$

$\gamma_G = 1.0$ for serviceability limit states (Table 2.3, EC5)

$$U_{instG} = \frac{5}{384} \frac{F_{d,G} L^3}{EI} + \frac{12}{5} \frac{F_{d,G} L}{EA}$$

$$= \frac{5}{384} \frac{0.774 \times 1000 \times 3000^3}{8000 \times 17.7 \times 10^6} + \frac{12}{5} \frac{0.774 \times 1000 \times 3000}{8000 \times 63 \times 150}$$

$U_{instG} = 1.921 + 0.073 = 1.994 \, \text{mm}$

$U_{fin,G} = U_{instG}(1 + K_{def}) = 1.994(1 + 0.8) = 3.589 \, \text{mm}$

(b) U_{instQ}, instantaneous deflection due to variable action

$$U_{instQ} = \frac{5}{384} \frac{F_{d,Q} L^3}{EI} + \frac{12}{5} \frac{F_{d,Q} L}{EA}$$

$F_{d,Q} = \gamma_Q Q_k \times$ area carried by the joist $= 1.0 \times 1.5 \times 0.6 \times 3 = 2.70 \, \text{kN}$

$$U_{instQ} = \frac{5}{384} \frac{2.7 \times 1000 \times 3000^3}{8000 \times 17.7 \times 10^6} + \frac{12}{5} \frac{2.7 \times 1000 \times 3000}{8000 \times 150 \times 63}$$

$$6.703 + 0.257 = 6.81 \, \text{mm}$$

$U_{fin,Q} = U_{instQ}(1 + \psi_2 K_{def}) = 6.81(1 + 0.3 \times 0.8) = 8.444 \, \text{mm}$

Total deflection or final deflection, $U_{fin} = U_{instQ} + U_{fin,Q}$

$$= 3.589 + 8.444 = 12.033 \, \text{mm}$$

Permissible deflection $=$ span/250 for brittle finishes
$= 3000/250 = 12.00 \, \text{mm}$. The joist is just
satisfactory in deflection

8 Lateral buckling

No need for this check as the compressive edge of the joist is restrained by the tongue and groove boarding.

9 Shear strength

Check that $\tau_d < f_{v,d}$

$\tau_d =$ design shear stress

$$\tau_d = \frac{1.5 \, V_{Ed}}{A}$$

$V_{Ed} =$ maximum shear force

$V_{Ed} = F_d/2 = 5.094/2 = 2.547 \, \text{kN}$

$$\tau_d = \frac{1.5 \, V_{Ed}}{A} = 1.5 \times 2.547 \times 1000/63 \times 150 = 0.134 \, \text{N/mm}^2$$

$f_{v,d} = K_{sys} K_{mod} f_{v,k}/\gamma_M = 1.1 \times 0.8 \times 1.8/1.3 = 1.218 \, \text{N/mm}^2 > 0.134$

Therefore satisfactory.

10 Bearing capacity

Check that $\sigma_{c,90,d} < k_{c,90} f_{c,90,d}$

$F_{90,d} = F_d/2 = 5.094/2 = 2.547 \, \text{kN}$

$$\sigma_{c,90,d} = \frac{F_{90,d}}{bl} = 2.547 \times 1000/63 \times 100 = 0.404 \, \text{N/mm}^2$$

$$f_{c,90,d} = k_{sys}k_{mod}f_{c,90k}/\gamma_M = 1.1 \times 0.8 \times 4.6/1.3 = 3.113 \text{ N/mm}^2$$

$$k_{c,90} = [2.38 - L/250][1 + h/12L] \le 4.0$$

$$k_{c,90} = [2.38 - 100/250][1 + 150/12 \times 100] = 2.23 < 4$$

$$k_{c,90}f_{c,90,d} = 2.23 \times 3.113 = 6.942 \text{ N/mm}^2 > \sigma_{c,90,d} \ (0.404 \text{ N/mm}^2)$$

Therefore satisfactory.

Coursework

Use the EC5, repeat the design of the example above with the joist to be notched at the end bearing with a 65 mm deep notch. Bearing is still $= 100$ mm and $i = 2$ (see Fig. 6.11 of the EC5).

Summary

The following variables are used in the design of timber and steel beams by the *elastic method*:

$$M_r = f \times \frac{I}{y} = fZ$$

$$= \text{moment of resistance}$$

$$= \text{maximum bending moment, } M_{max} \text{ in N mm, kN m, etc.}$$

$f = $ maximum permissible bending stress in N/mm^2

$I = $ moment of inertia about the axis of bending (mm^4)

$y = $ the distance from the neutral axis to the extreme beam fibres

$Z = $ elastic section modulus (mm^3) $= \dfrac{I}{y}$

For rectangular cross-section beams, $Z = bd^2/6$

For circular cross-section beams, $Z = \pi D^3/32$

For rolled steel sections, values of Z can be found from Table 11.21 (pages 260–3) under the heading 'Elastic modulus'

For sections built up with rectangular plates, values of Z can be calculated from first principles, having first obtained the moments of inertia (see Chapter 9)

For limit state design of steel beams see BS 5950: Part 1: 2000

The code for the limit state design in timber is BS 5268: Part 1: 1996

Exercises

1 A 250 mm × 75 mm timber beam with its longer edge vertical spans 2 m between simple supports. What safe uniformly distributed load W can the beam carry if the permissible bending stress is 8 N/mm^2?

2 A timber joist 75 mm wide has to carry a uniform load of 10 kN on a span of 4 m. The bending stress is to be 6 N/mm^2. What depth should the joist be?

3 A girder shaped as shown in Fig. 11.Q3 spans 3 m carrying a uniform load over the entire span. The bending stress is to be 150 N/mm^2. What may be the value of the uniform load?

Fig. 11.Q3

4 The properties of a 356 × 171 UB45 are as follows:

$$I_{xx} = 120.7 \times 10^6 \text{ mm}^4$$
$$I_{yy} = 8.11 \times 10^6 \text{ mm}^4$$

What safe uniform load will the beam carry on a span of 4 m, if the stress is to be 125 N/mm²?

5 The universal beam used in question 4 now spans 4.8 m carrying a uniform load of 170 kN. What is the maximum bending stress in N/mm²?

6 Two 254 mm × 89 mm steel channels, arranged back to back with 20 mm space between them, act as a beam on a span of 4.8 m. Each channel has a section modulus (Z) about axis X–X of 350 000 mm³. Calculate the maximum point load that the beam can carry at midspan if the safe stress is 165 N/mm² and the beam's self-weight is ignored.

7 A timber T-beam is formed by rigidly fixing together two joists, as shown in Fig. 11.Q7. The resulting section

Fig. 11.Q7

is used (with the 216 mm rectangle placed vertically) as a beam spanning 3.6 m between simple supports. Calculate the safe uniformly distributed load if the permissible fibre stress is 5.6 N/mm².

8 A 152 mm × 76 mm @ 19 kg/m steel tee section, as shown in Fig. 11.Q8, may be stressed to not more than 155 N/mm². What safe inclusive uniform load can the section carry as a beam spanning 2.0 m between simple supports?

Fig. 11.Q8

9 Timber floor joists 200 mm × 75 mm at 300 mm centres span 3 m between centres of simple supports (Fig. 11.Q9). What safe inclusive load, in kN/mm², may the floor carry if the timber stress is not to exceed 6.0 N/mm²?

Fig. 11.Q9

10 A small floor 4.8 m × 4.2 m is to be supported by one main beam and 150 mm × 48 mm joists spanning

Table 11.21 Dimensions and properties of universal beams

Designation	Area of section (cm²)	Mass per metre (kg/m)	Dimensions (mm)						Ratios for local buckling	
			D Section depth	b Section width	t Web thickness	T Flange thickness	r Root radius	d Depth between fillets	b/T Flange	d/t Web
1016 × 305 × 487	619	487.0	1036.1	308.5	30.0	54.1	30.0	867.8	2.85	29.0
1016 × 305 × 438	556	438.0	1025.9	305.4	26.9	49.0	30.0	868.0	3.12	32.3
1016 × 305 × 393	500	393.0	1016.0	303.0	24.4	43.9	30.0	868.2	3.45	35.7
1016 × 305 × 349	445	349.0	1008.1	302.0	21.1	40.0	30.0	868.0	3.78	41.2
1016 × 305 × 314	400	314.0	1000.0	300.0	19.1	35.9	30.0	868.2	4.18	45.6
1016 × 305 × 272	346	272.0	990.1	300.0	16.5	31.0	30.0	868.0	4.84	52.7
1016 × 305 × 249	316	249.0	980.2	300.0	16.5	26.0	30.0	868.0	5.77	52.7
1016 × 305 × 222	282	222.0	970.3	300.0	16.0	21.1	30.0	867.8	7.11	54.4
914 × 419 × 388	494	388.0	921.0	420.5	21.4	36.6	24.1	799.6	5.74	37.4
914 × 419 × 343	437	343.3	911.8	418.5	19.4	32.0	24.1	799.6	6.54	41.2
914 × 305 × 289	368	289.1	926.6	307.7	19.5	32.0	19.1	824.4	4.81	42.3
914 × 305 × 253	323	253.4	918.4	305.5	17.3	27.9	19.1	824.4	5.47	47.7
914 × 305 × 224	286	224.2	910.4	304.1	15.9	23.9	19.1	824.4	6.36	51.8
914 × 305 × 201	256	200.9	903.0	303.3	15.1	20.2	19.1	824.4	7.51	54.6
838 × 292 × 226	289	226.5	850.9	293.8	16.1	26.8	17.8	761.7	5.48	47.3
838 × 292 × 194	247	193.8	840.7	292.4	14.7	21.7	17.8	761.7	6.74	51.8
838 × 292 × 176	224	175.9	834.9	291.7	14.0	18.8	17.8	761.7	7.76	54.4
762 × 267 × 197	251	196.8	769.8	268.0	15.6	25.4	16.5	686.0	5.28	44.0
762 × 267 × 173	220	173.0	762.2	266.7	14.3	21.6	16.5	686.0	6.17	48.0
762 × 267 × 147	187	146.9	754.0	265.2	12.8	17.5	16.5	686.0	7.58	53.6
762 × 267 × 134	171	133.9	750.0	264.4	12.0	15.5	16.5	686.0	8.53	57.2
686 × 254 × 170	217	170.2	692.9	255.8	14.5	23.7	15.2	615.1	5.40	42.4
686 × 254 × 152	194	152.4	687.5	254.5	13.2	21.0	15.2	615.1	6.06	46.6
686 × 254 × 140	178	140.1	683.5	253.7	12.4	19.0	15.2	615.1	6.68	49.6
686 × 254 × 125	159	125.2	677.9	253.0	11.7	16.2	15.2	615.1	7.81	52.6
610 × 305 × 238	303	238.1	635.8	311.4	18.4	31.4	16.5	540.0	4.96	29.3
610 × 305 × 179	228	179.0	620.2	307.1	14.1	23.6	16.5	540.0	6.51	38.3
610 × 305 × 149	190	149.1	612.4	304.8	11.8	19.7	16.5	540.0	7.74	45.8
610 × 229 × 140	178	139.9	617.2	230.2	13.1	22.1	12.7	547.6	5.21	41.8
610 × 229 × 125	159	125.1	612.2	229.0	11.9	19.6	12.7	547.6	5.84	46.0
610 × 229 × 113	144	113.0	607.6	228.2	11.1	17.3	12.7	547.6	6.60	49.3
610 × 229 × 101	129	101.2	602.6	227.6	10.5	14.8	12.7	547.6	7.69	52.2
533 × 210 × 122	155	122.0	544.5	211.9	12.7	21.3	12.7	476.5	4.97	37.5
533 × 210 × 109	139	109.0	539.5	210.8	11.6	18.8	12.7	476.5	5.61	41.1
533 × 210 × 101	129	101.0	536.7	210.0	10.8	17.4	12.7	476.5	6.03	44.1
533 × 210 × 92	117	92.1	533.1	209.3	10.1	15.6	12.7	476.5	6.71	47.2
533 × 210 × 82	105	82.2	528.3	208.8	9.6	13.2	12.7	476.5	7.91	49.6

(*Source*: Structural sections to BS 4: Part 1 and BS 4848: Part 4 British Steel)

Table 11.21 (*Continued*)

(BS 5950)   (EC3)

Second moment of area (cm⁴)		Radius of gyration (cm)		Elastic modulus (cm³)		Plastic modulus (cm³)		Parameters and constants				Designation
								u	*x*	*H*	*J*	
X–X axis	*Y–Y axis*	*X–X axis*	*Y–Y axis*	*X–X axis*	*Y–Y axis*	*X–X axis*	*Y–Y axis*	*Buckling parameter*	*Torsional index*	*Warping constant (dm⁶)*	*Torsional constant (cm⁴)*	
1020400	26720	40.6	6.57	19700	1732	23180	2799	0.867	21.2	64.4	4276	1016 × 305 × 487
908900	23440	40.4	6.49	17720	1535	20740	2467	0.868	23.2	55.9	3166	1016 × 305 × 438
806600	20490	40.2	6.40	15880	1353	18520	2167	0.868	25.6	48.4	2314	1016 × 305 × 393
722100	18460	40.3	6.44	14330	1222	16570	1940	0.872	28.0	43.2	1706	1016 × 305 × 349
643200	16230	40.1	6.37	12860	1082	14830	1712	0.871	30.8	37.7	1253	1016 × 305 × 314
552900	14000	40.0	6.36	11170	934	12800	1469	0.872	35.1	32.2	826	1016 × 305 × 272
480300	11750	39.0	6.09	9799	784	11330	1244	0.861	40.1	26.8	575	1016 × 305 × 249
406900	9544	38.0	5.81	8387	636	9784	1019	0.849	46.0	21.5	384	1016 × 305 × 222
719600	45440	38.2	9.59	15630	2161	17607	3341	0.885	26.7	88.9	1734	914 × 419 × 388
625800	39160	37.8	9.46	13730	1871	15480	2890	0.883	30.1	75.8	1193	914 × 419 × 343
504200	15600	37.0	6.51	10880	1014	12570	1601	0.867	31.9	31.2	926	914 × 305 × 289
436300	13300	36.8	6.42	9501	871	10940	1371	0.866	36.2	26.4	626	914 × 305 × 253
376400	11240	36.3	6.27	8269	739	9535	1163	0.861	41.3	22.1	422	914 × 305 × 224
325300	9423	35.7	6.07	7204	621	8351	982	0.854	46.8	18.4	291	914 × 305 × 201
339700	11360	34.3	6.27	7985	773	9155	1212	0.870	35.0	19.3	514	838 × 292 × 226
279200	9066	33.6	6.06	6641	620	7640	974	0.862	41.6	15.2	306	838 × 292 × 194
246000	7799	33.1	5.90	5893	535	6808	842	0.856	46.5	13.0	221	838 × 292 × 176
240000	8175	30.9	5.71	6234	610	7176	959	0.869	33.2	11.3	404	762 × 267 × 197
205300	6850	30.5	5.58	5387	514	6198	807	0.864	38.1	9.39	267	762 × 267 × 173
168500	5455	30.0	5.40	4470	411	5156	647	0.858	45.2	7.40	159	762 × 267 × 147
150700	4788	29.7	5.30	4018	362	4644	570	0.854	49.8	6.46	119	762 × 267 × 134
170300	6630	28.0	5.53	4916	518	5631	811	0.872	31.8	7.42	308	686 × 254 × 170
150400	5784	27.8	5.46	4374	455	5000	710	0.871	35.5	6.42	220	686 × 254 × 152
136300	5183	27.6	5.39	3987	409	4558	638	0.868	38.7	5.72	169	686 × 254 × 140
118000	4383	27.2	5.24	3481	346	3994	542	0.862	43.9	4.80	116	686 × 254 × 125
209500	15840	26.3	7.23	6589	1017	7486	1574	0.886	21.3	14.5	875	610 × 305 × 238
153000	11410	25.9	7.07	4935	743	5547	1144	0.886	27.7	10.2	340	610 × 305 × 179
125900	9308	25.7	7.00	4111	611	4594	937	0.886	32.7	8.17	200	610 × 305 × 149
111800	4505	25.0	5.03	3622	391	4142	611	0.875	30.6	3.99	216	610 × 229 × 140
98610	3932	24.9	4.97	3221	343	3676	535	0.873	34.1	3.45	154	610 × 229 × 125
87320	3434	24.6	4.88	2874	301	3281	469	0.870	38.0	2.99	117	610 × 229 × 113
75780	2915	24.2	4.75	2515	256	2881	400	0.864	43.1	2.52	77.0	610 × 229 × 101
76040	3388	22.1	4.67	2793	320	3196	500	0.877	27.6	2.32	178	533 × 210 × 122
66820	2943	21.9	4.60	2477	279	2828	436	0.875	30.9	1.99	126	533 × 210 × 109
61520	2692	21.9	4.57	2292	256	2612	399	0.874	33.2	1.81	101	533 × 210 × 101
55230	2389	21.7	4.51	2072	228	2360	356	0.872	36.5	1.60	75.7	533 × 210 × 92
47540	2007	21.3	4.38	1800	192	2059	300	0.864	41.6	1.33	51.5	533 × 210 × 82

(*Source*: Structural sections to BS 4: Part 1 and BS 4848: Part 4 British Steel)

Table 11.21 (*Continued*)

Designation	Area of section (cm²)	Mass per metre (kg/m)	D Section depth	B Section width	t Web thickness	T Flange thickness	r Root radius	d Depth between fillets	b/T Flange	d/t Web
457 × 191 × 98	125	98.3	467.2	192.8	11.4	19.6	10.2	407.6	4.92	35.8
457 × 191 × 89	114	89.3	463.4	191.9	10.5	17.7	10.2	407.6	5.42	38.8
457 × 191 × 82	104	82.0	460.0	191.3	9.9	16.0	10.2	407.6	5.98	41.2
457 × 191 × 74	94.6	74.3	457.0	190.4	9.0	14.5	10.2	407.6	6.57	45.3
457 × 191 × 67	85.5	67.1	453.4	189.9	8.5	12.7	10.2	407.6	7.48	48.0
457 × 152 × 82	105	82.1	465.8	155.3	10.5	18.9	10.2	407.6	4.11	38.8
457 × 152 × 74	94.5	74.2	462.0	154.4	9.6	17.0	10.2	407.6	4.54	42.5
457 × 152 × 67	85.6	67.2	458.0	153.8	9.0	15.0	10.2	407.6	5.13	45.3
457 × 152 × 60	76.2	59.8	454.6	152.9	8.1	13.3	10.2	407.6	5.75	50.3
457 × 152 × 52	66.6	52.3	449.8	152.4	7.6	10.9	10.2	407.6	6.99	53.6
406 × 178 × 74	94.5	74.2	412.8	179.5	9.5	16.0	10.2	360.4	5.61	37.9
406 × 178 × 67	85.5	67.1	409.4	178.8	8.8	14.3	10.2	360.4	6.25	41.0
406 × 178 × 60	76.5	60.1	406.4	177.9	7.9	12.8	10.2	360.4	6.95	45.6
406 × 178 × 54	69.0	54.1	402.6	177.7	7.7	10.9	10.2	360.4	8.15	46.8
406 × 140 × 46	58.6	46.0	403.2	142.2	6.8	11.2	10.2	360.4	6.35	53.0
406 × 140 × 39	49.7	39.0	398.0	141.8	6.4	8.6	10.2	360.4	8.24	56.3
356 × 171 × 67	85.5	67.1	363.4	173.2	9.1	15.7	10.2	311.6	5.52	34.2
356 × 171 × 57	72.6	57.0	358.0	172.2	8.1	13.0	10.2	311.6	6.62	38.5
356 × 171 × 51	64.9	51.0	355.0	171.5	7.4	11.5	10.2	311.6	7.46	42.1
356 × 171 × 45	57.3	45.0	351.4	171.1	7.0	9.7	10.2	311.6	8.82	44.5
356 × 127 × 39	49.8	39.1	353.4	126.0	6.6	10.7	10.2	311.6	5.89	47.2
356 × 127 × 33	42.1	33.1	349.0	125.4	6.0	8.5	10.2	311.6	7.38	51.9
305 × 165 × 54	68.8	54.0	310.4	166.9	7.9	13.7	8.9	265.2	6.09	33.6
305 × 165 × 46	58.7	46.1	306.6	165.7	6.7	11.8	8.9	265.2	7.02	39.6
305 × 165 × 40	51.3	40.3	303.4	165.0	6.0	10.2	8.9	265.2	8.09	44.2
305 × 127 × 48	61.2	48.1	311.0	125.3	9.0	14.0	8.9	265.2	4.47	29.5
305 × 127 × 42	53.4	41.9	307.2	124.3	8.0	12.1	8.9	265.2	5.14	33.2
305 × 127 × 37	47.2	37.0	304.4	123.3	7.1	10.7	8.9	265.2	5.77	37.4
305 × 102 × 33	41.8	32.8	312.7	102.4	6.6	10.8	7.6	275.9	4.74	41.8
305 × 102 × 28	35.9	28.2	308.7	101.8	6.0	8.8	7.6	275.9	5.78	46.0
305 × 102 × 25	31.6	24.8	305.1	101.6	5.8	7.0	7.6	275.9	7.26	47.6
254 × 146 × 43	54.8	43.0	259.6	147.3	7.2	12.7	7.6	219.0	5.80	30.4
254 × 146 × 37	47.2	37.0	256.0	146.4	6.3	10.9	7.6	219.0	6.72	34.8
254 × 146 × 31	39.7	31.1	251.4	146.1	6.0	8.6	7.6	219.0	8.49	36.5
254 × 102 × 28	36.1	28.3	260.4	102.2	6.3	10.0	7.6	225.2	5.11	35.7
254 × 102 × 25	32.0	25.2	257.2	101.9	6.0	8.4	7.6	225.2	6.07	37.5
254 × 102 × 22	28.0	22.0	254.0	101.6	5.7	6.8	7.6	225.2	7.47	39.5
203 × 133 × 30	38.2	30.0	206.8	133.9	6.4	9.6	7.6	172.4	6.97	26.9
203 × 133 × 25	32.0	25.1	203.2	133.2	5.7	7.8	7.6	172.4	8.54	30.2
203 × 102 × 23	29.4	23.1	203.2	101.8	5.4	9.3	7.6	169.4	5.47	31.4
178 × 102 × 19	24.3	19.0	177.8	101.2	4.8	7.9	7.6	146.8	6.41	30.6
152 × 89 × 16	20.3	16.0	152.4	88.7	4.5	7.7	7.6	121.8	5.76	27.1
127 × 76 × 13	16.5	13.0	127.0	76.0	4.0	7.6	7.6	96.6	5.00	24.1

(*Source*: Structural sections to BS 4: Part 1 and BS 4848: Part 4 British Steel)

Table 11.21 (*Continued*)

BS 5950

(EC3)

Second moment of area (cm⁴)		Radius of gyration (cm)		Elastic modulus (cm³)		Plastic modulus (cm³)		Parameters and constants				Designation
								u	*x*	*H*	*J*	
X–X axis	Y–Y axis	X–X axis	Y–Y axis	X–X axis	Y–Y axis	X–X axis	Y–Y axis	Buckling parameter	Torsional index	Warping constant (dm⁶)	Torsional constant (cm⁴)	
45730	2347	19.1	4.33	1957	243	2232	379	0.881	25.7	1.18	121	$457 \times 191 \times 98$
41020	2089	19.0	4.29	1770	218	2014	338	0.880	28.3	1.04	90.7	$457 \times 191 \times 89$
37050	1871	18.8	4.23	1611	196	1831	304	0.877	30.9	0.922	69.2	$457 \times 191 \times 82$
33320	1671	18.8	4.20	1458	176	1653	272	0.877	33.9	0.818	51.8	$457 \times 191 \times 74$
29380	1452	18.5	4.12	1296	153	1471	237	0.872	37.9	0.705	37.1	$457 \times 191 \times 67$
36590	1185	18.7	3.37	1571	153	1811	240	0.873	27.4	0.591	89.2	$457 \times 152 \times 82$
32670	1047	18.6	3.33	1414	136	1627	213	0.873	30.1	0.518	65.9	$457 \times 152 \times 74$
28930	913	18.4	3.27	1263	119	1453	187	0.869	33.6	0.448	47.7	$457 \times 152 \times 67$
25500	795	18.3	3.23	1122	104	1287	163	0.868	37.5	0.387	33.8	$457 \times 152 \times 60$
21370	645	17.9	3.11	950	84.6	1096	133	0.859	43.9	0.311	21.4	$457 \times 152 \times 52$
27310	1545	17.0	4.04	1323	172	1501	267	0.882	27.6	0.608	62.8	$406 \times 178 \times 74$
24330	1365	16.9	3.99	1189	153	1346	237	0.880	30.5	0.533	46.1	$406 \times 178 \times 67$
21600	1203	16.8	3.97	1063	135	1199	209	0.880	33.8	0.466	33.3	$406 \times 178 \times 60$
18720	1021	16.5	3.85	930	115	1055	178	0.871	38.3	0.392	23.1	$406 \times 178 \times 54$
15690	538	16.4	3.03	778	75.7	888	118	0.871	38.9	0.207	19.0	$406 \times 140 \times 46$
12510	410	15.9	2.87	629	57.8	724	90.8	0.858	47.5	0.155	10.7	$406 \times 140 \times 39$
19460	1362	15.1	3.99	1071	157	1211	243	0.886	24.4	0.412	55.7	$356 \times 171 \times 67$
16040	1108	14.9	3.91	896	129	1010	199	0.882	28.8	0.330	33.4	$356 \times 171 \times 57$
14140	968	14.8	3.86	796	113	896	174	0.881	32.1	0.286	23.8	$356 \times 171 \times 51$
12070	811	14.5	3.76	687	94.8	775	147	0.874	36.8	0.237	15.8	$356 \times 171 \times 45$
10170	358	14.3	2.68	576	56.8	659	89.1	0.871	35.2	0.105	15.1	$356 \times 127 \times 39$
8249	280	14.0	2.58	473	44.7	543	70.3	0.863	42.2	0.0812	8.79	$356 \times 127 \times 33$
11700	1063	13.0	3.93	754	127	846	196	0.889	23.6	0.234	34.8	$305 \times 165 \times 54$
9899	896	13.0	3.90	646	108	720	166	0.891	27.1	0.195	22.2	$305 \times 165 \times 46$
8503	764	12.9	3.86	560	92.6	623	142	0.889	31.0	0.164	14.7	$305 \times 165 \times 40$
9575	461	12.5	2.74	616	73.6	711	116	0.873	23.3	0.102	31.8	$305 \times 127 \times 48$
8196	389	12.4	2.70	534	62.6	614	98.4	0.872	26.5	0.0846	21.1	$305 \times 127 \times 42$
7171	336	12.3	2.67	471	54.5	539	85.4	0.872	29.7	0.0725	14.8	$305 \times 127 \times 37$
6501	194	12.5	2.15	416	37.9	481	60.0	0.866	31.6	0.0442	12.2	$305 \times 102 \times 33$
5366	155	12.2	2.08	348	30.5	403	48.5	0.859	37.4	0.0349	7.40	$305 \times 102 \times 28$
4455	123	11.9	1.97	292	24.2	342	38.8	0.846	43.4	0.0273	4.77	$305 \times 102 \times 25$
6544	677	10.9	3.52	504	92.0	566	141	0.891	21.2	0.103	23.9	$254 \times 146 \times 43$
5537	571	10.8	3.48	433	78.0	483	119	0.890	24.3	0.0857	15.3	$254 \times 146 \times 37$
4413	448	10.5	3.36	351	61.3	393	94.1	0.880	29.6	0.0660	8.55	$254 \times 146 \times 31$
4005	179	10.5	2.22	308	34.9	353	54.8	0.874	27.5	0.0280	9.57	$254 \times 102 \times 28$
3415	149	10.3	2.11	266	29.2	306	46.0	0.866	31.5	0.0230	6.42	$254 \times 102 \times 25$
2841	119	10.1	2.06	224	23.5	259	37.3	0.856	36.4	0.0182	4.15	$254 \times 102 \times 22$
2896	385	8.71	3.17	280	57.5	314	88.2	0.881	21.5	0.0374	10.3	$203 \times 133 \times 30$
2340	308	8.56	3.10	230	46.2	258	70.9	0.877	25.6	0.0294	5.96	$203 \times 133 \times 25$
2105	164	8.46	2.36	207	32.2	234	49.8	0.888	22.5	0.0154	7.02	$203 \times 102 \times 23$
1356	137	7.48	2.37	153	27.0	171	41.6	0.888	22.6	0.00987	4.41	$178 \times 102 \times 19$
834	89.8	6.41	2.10	109	20.2	123	31.2	0.890	19.6	0.00470	3.56	$152 \times 89 \times 16$
473	55.7	5.35	1.84	74.6	14.7	84.2	22.6	0.895	16.3	0.00199	2.85	$127 \times 76 \times 13$

(*Source*: Structural sections to BS 4: Part 1 and BS 4848: Part 4 British Steel)

between the wall and the beam, as shown in Fig. 11.Q10.
(a) Calculate the safe inclusive floor load if the stress
in the timber has a maximum value of 7.0 N/mm^2.
(b) Choose a suitable section modulus for the main steel
beam if the stress is not to exceed 165 N/mm^2. Ignore
the weights of the joists and the beam.

Fig. 11.Q10

11 (a) Calculate the dimension x to the centroid of the
section shown in Fig. 11.Q11. (b) Determine I_{xx} and
the two values of Z_{xx} for the section. (c) What safe
inclusive uniformly distributed load can a beam of this
section carry on a span of 3.6 m if the tension stress must
not exceed 20 N/mm^2 and the compression stress
100 N/mm^2?

Fig. 11.Q11

12 How deep would a 150 mm wide timber beam need to
be to carry the same load as the beam investigated in
question 11 if the maximum flexural stress equals
8 N/mm^2?

13 Choose suitable section moduli and select appropriate
UBs for the conditions shown in Fig. 11.Q13(a) to (f).
$f = 165$ N/mm^2.

Fig. 11.Q13

14 A UB 620 mm deep has a section modulus (Z_{xx}) of
4.9×10^6 mm^3. The beam spans 10 m carrying an

inclusive uniform load of 100 kN and a central point load of 50 kN. (a) Calculate the maximum stress due to bending. (b) What is the intensity of flexural stress at a point 150 mm above the neutral axis and 3.0 m from l.h. reaction?

15 A steel tank 1.8 m × 1.5 m × 1.2 m weighs 15 kN empty and is supported, as shown in Fig. 11.Q15, by two steel beams weighing 1 kN each. Choose a suitable section for the steel beams if the tank may be filled with water weighing 10 kN/m^3. The permissible bending stress on the section is 165 N/mm^2.

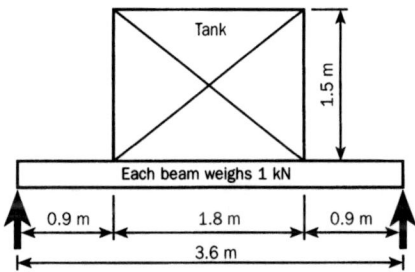

Fig. 11.Q15

16 Choose suitable timber joists and calculate sizes for UBs A and B for the floor shown in Fig. 11.Q16 if the inclusive floor loading is 8.4 kN/m^2.

Permissible timber stress = 7.2 N/mm^2

Permissible steel stress = 165 N/mm^2

Fig. 11.Q16

17 The symmetrically loaded beam shown in Fig. 11.Q17 carries three loads, and the internal span l has to be such that the negative bending moment at each support equals the positive bending moment at C. What is the span l? If each load W is 100 kN, choose a suitable UB (f = 165 N/mm^2).

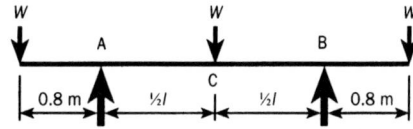

Fig. 11.Q17

18 A 610 × 305 UB149, 610 mm deep (I_{xx} = 1.25 × 10^9 mm^4) is simply supported on a span of l m. What will be the maximum permissible span if the stress in the beam under its own weight reaches 22 N/mm^2?

19 The plan of a floor of a steel-framed building is as shown in Fig. 11.Q19. Reinforced concrete slabs spanning as indicated ↔ are supported by steel beams AB. Each beam AB carries a stanchion at C, and the point load from each stanchion is 90 kN. The total inclusive loading will be 9 kN/m^2. Select a suitable beam AB for the floor, using a safe bending stress of 160 N/mm^2.

Fig. 11.Q19

20 A steel beam carries loads, as shown in Fig. 11.Q20. Calculate the position and amount of the maximum bending moment and draw the shear force and bending moment diagrams. Choose a suitable steel section for the beam, using a safe bending stress of 150 N/mm^2.

Fig. 11.Q20

21 A rectangular timber beam 300 mm deep and 250 mm wide, freely supported on a span of 6 m, carries a uniform load of 3 kN and a triangular load of 12 kN as shown in Fig. 11.Q21.

What is the greatest central point load that can be added to this beam if the maximum bending stress is 8 N/mm²?

Fig. 11.Q21

Answers to exercises

Chapter 5

1   110 N, 205 N

2   1.5 m

3   375 N, 225 N (upwards)

4   35 mm, 265 N

5   0.24 m

6   1.64 kN, 1.06 kN

7   4.23 kN, 1.53 kN (downwards)

8   $W = 22.5$ N, $A = 425.0$ N, $B = 237.5$ N

9   See Answers to Chapter 4

10   1.44 kN, 2.36 kN at 17.7° to the vertical

11   2.5 kN, 1.8 kN at 65.3° to the vertical

12   30.6 kN, 34.2 kN, 25.0 kN, 43.3 kN

13   6.0 kN, 5.34 kN downwards at 76.5° to the vertical

14   3.9 kN, 6.9 kN

15   (a) 0.41 m from hinge, 70 N, 176 N at 20° to the vertical; (b) 2.41 m from hinge, 4.12 kN, 6.10 kN at 42.5° to the vertical; (c) 2.27 m from hinge, 3.0 kN, 5.78 kN at 21.5° to the vertical

16   (a) 2.33 m from hinge, 3.5 kN, 5.7 kN at 38° to the vertical; (b) 1.8 m from the hinge, 30 kN, 39 kN at 40° to the vertical; (c) 3.17 m from the hinge, 15.8 kN, 21.8 kN at 46.5° to the vertical; (d) 3.0 m from the hinge, 10.0 kN, 22.4 kN at 27° to the vertical

17   15.0 kN, 9.92 kN at 41° to the vertical, 6.50 kN

18   300 mm, 45 000 N mm

19   (a) 50 kN, 70 kN; (b) 110 kN, 130 kN; (c) 120 kN, 10 kN; (d) 55 kN, 245 kN; (e) 70 kN, 150 kN

20   (a) 225 kN, 135 kN; (b) 199 kN, 249 kN; (c) 324 kN, 108 kN; (d) 172.8 kN, 115.2 kN; (e) 221.5 kN, 60.5 kN; (f) 242.8 kN, 107.2 kN; (g) 523.1 kN, 231.9 kN

21   $A = 40$ kN, $B = 50$ kN, $C = 40$ kN, $D = 10$ kN, $E = 26.7$ kN, $F = 13.3$ kN

22   14.07 kN

Chapter 8

1   $L = 91$ kN, $R = 59$ kN, $M_{max} = 58$ kN m 1.03 m from L

2   $L = 145$ kN, $R = 135$ kN, $M_{max} = 151.9$ kN m 1.75 m from L

3   $L = 100$ kN, $R = 60$ kN, $M_{max} = 83.3$ kN m 1.67 m from L

4   $L = 24$ kN, $R = 36$ kN, $M_{max} = 57.6$ kN m 2.8 m from L

5   $L = 31.5$ kN, $R = 73.5$ kN, $M_{max} = +16.5$ kN m 1.05 m from L and −15.0 kN m at R

6   $L = 140.4$ kN, $R = 114.6$ kN, $M_{max} = 219.1$ kN m 3.18 m from L

7   $L = 99.6$ kN, $R = 104.4$ kN, $M_{max} = +14.3$ kN m 1.79 m from L and −35.0 kN m at R

8   $L = R = 60$ kN, $M_{max} = 96$ kN m at centre of span

9   $L = 112.1$ kN, $R = 27.9$ kN, $M_{max} = +7.38$ kN m 0.87 m from L and −30.0 kN m at L

10   $L = 120$ kN, $R = 200$ kN, $M_{max} = +120$ kN m between 1 m and 5 m from L and −120 kN m at R

11 $L = 97.5$ kN, $R = 187.5$ kN, $M_{max} = +35.1$ kN m 0.25 m from L and -120.0 kN m at R

12 $L = 75$ kN, $R = 175$ kN, $M_{max} = +5$ kN m 1 m from L and -140 kN m at R

13 $L = 169$ kN, $R = 201$ kN, $M_{max} = 282.95$ kN m 2.04 m from L

14 $L = 230$ kN, $R = 140$ kN, $M_{max} = 512.88$ kN m 4.5 m from L

15 $M_{max} = +28.9$ kN m and -80.0 kN m

16 37.63 kN m

17 2.83 m ($\sqrt{8}$ m)

18 (a) $L = 150$ kN, $R = 145$ kN; (b) $+158.75$ kN m 4.5 m from L, -70 kN at L

19 (a) $L = 142$ kN, $R = 148$ kN; (b) 181.4 kN m 2.4 m from L

20 $R = 10$ kN, $M_{max} = -30$ kN m at support

21 Max. SF $= 146.7$ kN at R, $M_{max} = 136.67$ kN m 2.5 m from L

22 (a) $L = 215.5$ kN, $R = 235.5$ kN; (b) $M_{max} = 708.25$ kN m 5.5 m from L

23 (a) 15.0 kN m; (b) 245.0 kN m; (c) 357.5 kN m

24 400 kN m

25 (a) $R_L = 20$ kN, $R_R = 40$ kN; (b) $M_{max} = 46.20$ kN m; (c) $M_C = 31.11$ kN m

26 (a) $+20$ kN m; (b) -10 kN m; (c) $+5$ kN m

27 120 kN

28 6 m

29 60 kN

30 (a) $\frac{1}{2}Wl$; (b) $\frac{3}{8}Wl$

Chapter 9

1 444 mm east and 444 mm south of A

2 (a) 22.3 mm; (b) 55.9 mm; (c) 82.1 mm; (d) 104.2 mm

3 (a) $\bar{x} = 83$ mm, $\bar{y} = 325$ mm;
   (b) $\bar{x} = 134.7$ mm, $\bar{x} = 62.9$ mm;
   (c) $\bar{x} = 76.3$ mm, $\bar{y} = 49.6$ mm;
   (d) $\bar{x} = 83.8$ mm, $\bar{y} = 148.5$ mm;
   (e) $\bar{x} = 55.0$ mm, $\bar{y} = 41.7$ mm;

4 $I_{xx} = 381.24 \times 10^6$ mm^4, $I_{yy} = 47.50 \times 10^6$ mm^4

5 $I_{xx} = 247.30 \times 10^6$ mm^4, $I_{yy} = 126.25 \times 10^6$ mm^4

6 $a = 29.4$ mm, $I_{xx} = 4.20 \times 10^6$ mm^4, $I_{yy} = 9.54 \times 10^6$ mm^4

7 $a = 53.8$ mm, $I_{xx} = 11.6 \times 10^6$ mm^4, $I_{yy} = 2.15 \times 10^6$ mm^4

8 $a = 49.5$ mm, $b = 24.5$ mm, $I_{xx} = 6.56 \times 10^6$ mm^4, $I_{yy} = 2.37 \times 10^6$ mm^4

9 $a = 398$ mm, $I_{xx} = 998.79 \times 10^6$ mm^4, $I_{yy} = 76.00 \times 10^6$ mm^4

10 $a = 71$ mm

11 $I_{xx} = 12.13 \times 10^9$ mm^4, $I_{yy} = 3.19 \times 10^9$ mm^4

12 $x = 127.7$ mm, $I_{xx} = 199.34 \times 10^6$ mm^4

13 $x = 90.5$ mm, $I_{xx} = 117.51 \times 10^6$ mm^4

14 $x = 49.5$ mm, $I_{xx} = 6.56 \times 10^6$ mm^4

15 $I_{xx} = 37.83 \times 10^6$ mm^4, $I_{yy} = 9.02 \times 10^6$ mm^4

16 $I_{xx} = I_{yy} = 3.54 \times 10^6$ mm^4

17 $x = 37$ mm, $I_{xx} = 161.97 \times 10^6$ mm^4, $I_{yy} = 74.73 \times 10^6$ mm^4

18 $I_{xx} = 159.31 \times 10^6$ mm^4, $I_{yy} = 44.95 \times 10^6$ mm^4

19 24 mm

20 160 mm

21 24 mm

22 221 mm

23 $I_{xx} = 2.69 \times 10^9$ mm^4

Chapter 11

1 25 kN

2 258 mm

3 409 kN

4 169.5 kN

5 150 N/mm^2

6 96 kN

7 6.8 kN

8 8.8 kN

9   8.88 kN/mm^2

10   (a) 4.86 N/m^2; (b) $0.156 \times 10^6 \text{ mm}^3$

11   (a) 137 mm; (b) $I_{xx} = 280.9 \times 10^6 \text{ mm}^4$, $Z_{xxC} = 1.26 \times 10^6 \text{ mm}^3$, $Z_{xxT} = 2.05 \times 10^6 \text{ mm}^3$; (c) 25.3 kN/m

12   453 mm

13   (a) 305 × 165 UB40; (b) and (c) 305 × 102 UB83; (d) 610 × 229 UB101; (e) 457 × 191 UB82; (f) 254 × 146 UB37

14   (a) 51.0 N/mm^2; (b) 17.8 N/mm^2

15   152 × 89 UB16

16   Joists: 142 mm × 75 mm, 133 mm × 48 mm; A = 305 × 102 UB28, B = 254 × 102 UB25

17   l = 6.4 m, beam = 356 × 127 UB39

18   22 m

19   406 × 178 UB74

20   305 × 102 UB33

21   10.5 kN